White House Watch

The Ford Years

White House Watch
The Ford Years

BY

JOHN OSBORNE

Cartoons by RANAN LURIE

NEW REPUBLIC BOOKS
Washington, D.C.

Published in the United States of America in 1977
by New Republic Books
1220 Nineteenth St., N.W., Washington, D.C. 20036

This book consists in part of articles that appeared in
The New Republic between September 1974 and January
1977. The title is derived from the "White House
Watch," the standing head under which John Osborne
reported the Presidency for that magazine. Apart
from some changes of tense for present clarity, the
correction of typographical and similar errors, and the
addition of updating addenda at the end of a few
chapters, the originals have not been altered for this
publication. All articles are reprinted by permission of
the author.

Library of Congress Cataloging in Publication Data
Osborne, John, 1907-
    White House watch.

    "Consists in part of articles that appeared in the
New republic between September 1974 and January 1977."
    Includes index.
    1.   United States—Politics and government—1974-1977—
Collected works.   I.   Title.
E865.O8   973.925   77-5321
ISBN 0-915220-26-1

Trade distribution by Simon and Schuster
A Division of Gulf & Western Corporation
New York, New York 10020
Order No. 0-671-22961-3

Printed in the United States of America

For Trudie, John and Peggy

CONTENTS

Contents

Goodbye to Jerry

One of the few misfortunes of that fortunate man, Gerald R. Ford, is that it is difficult to think of anything more and better to say of his presidency than Jimmy Carter said in the first sentence of his inaugural address: "For myself and our nation, I want to thank my predecessor for all he has done to heal our land."

There is more to say and much of it is good. The purpose of this introductory essay is not to review and appraise the Ford performance. The purpose is to supplement the Ford story as it was known and told at the time with facts, viewpoints and insights that came my way after the pieces that are collected in this book were written or, in a few instances and for various reasons, were not reportable then. Nevertheless, and with no wish to give a flawed presidency a gloss that it and its central character do not deserve, a few summary observations are offered. In the main they are to Mr. Ford's credit.

Most of what Gerald Ford did "to heal our land" consisted of being himself or, it would be more accurate to say, being the self that he was perceived to be. The perceived Gerald Ford—honest, straight, frank, ordinary, a rather amusing and attractive bumbler in witnessed action and heard expression—differs

somewhat from the Gerald Ford who emerges from certain
elements of his record.

I remain troubled by his many assertions, some of them under
oath and one of them in answer to a question of mine at a press
conference, that he did what he says he did in 1972 to abort a
congressional investigation of the first indications of Watergate
scandal solely upon his initiative and at the request of fellow
Republicans in the House of Representatives, where he was the
Minority Leader. President Nixon's desire to thwart that
investigation was well known. He was taped saying that Gerald
Ford had to be gotten off his ass and put to thwarting it, and it
would have been natural and perfectly in order for the Minority
Leader to do what he could to accomplish what he must have
known his President wanted accomplished, with or without
explicit urgings or instructions from Nixon's lobbyists. A Special
Prosecutor's report in 1976 that he'd found no basis for charging
Mr. Ford with perjury must be respected, but one could wish that
in his accounts and denials Mr. Ford had at least fessed up to what
might be called atmospheric compliance with Richard Nixon's
wishes. Mr. Ford also has maintained that he undertook the
shoddiest enterprise on his record, his attempt to have Associate
Justice William O. Douglas impeached in 1970, entirely upon his
initiative, without prompting or prearranged assistance from
Attorney General John N. Mitchell. A former official who
worked on that seamy project with Mitchell tells me that Richard
Nixon had Mitchell set Gerald Ford after Justice Douglas.

As will be seen in some of the pieces that follow, I was less
disturbed by the suspicions and allegations than I was by
journalistic distortions and exaggerations, officially abetted, that
subjected Mr. Ford to damaging and unproved intimations of
scandalous conduct when he was seeking election to the office
that he held by appointment and succession. The point of
recalling all of that here is that after the fall of Richard Nixon our
national hunger for the honesty, goodness and straightness that
we perceived in Gerald Ford was such that there was very little
interest, in the media or elsewhere, in questioning the
perception. The post-Watergate appetite for scandalous implication and the related impatience with the old custom of requiring
proof before publication soon overcame the restraint that

prevailed for a little while after the resignation of President
Nixon and the accession of Gerald Ford on August 9, 1974. While
the mood of restraint lasted, the new President and all of us
benefited from it.

An official "Summary of Major Ford Accomplishments" fills 2
of 93 pages in a document entitled "The Ford Presidency: A
Portrait of the First Two Years." It was printed in August, 10
weeks or so before the 1976 election, at taxpayer expense,
although it was put together by a White House editorial staff that
had been assembled for campaign purposes. The list of "major
accomplishments" was pathetic when it appeared and became
more so before the election. "Key economic indicators" that were
said to be "moving strongly upward" in August turned
downward in the following weeks when their staying on the
uptrend was vital to Mr. Ford's chance of election. Of the 10
claims of positive accomplishment, only 3—that Mr. Ford had
arrested the downward trend of defense appropriations,
strengthened diplomatic and economic relationships between
the United States and its industrialized partners in western
Europe and Japan, and begun the restoration of national
confidence—could be factually attributed to anything that he and
his people had done. Yet there is, I believe, a different measure of
accomplishment that puts him and his administration in better
light than his campaign and postdefeat propaganda did. The
measure is what Jimmy Carter and the Carter administration
had to work with and on when they took office.

In foreign affairs there was not a single substantive problem
area in which Carter, Secretary of State Cyrus Vance and the
new President's assistant for national security affairs, Zbigniew
Brzezinski, could do more than follow or at best improve upon
the course and policies bequeathed to them by President Ford and
Henry Kissinger. President Carter's indicated intention was to
go after ratification and extension of the strategic arms
agreement-to-agree—and it was no more than that—reached at
Vladivostok in 1974 by Ford, Kissinger and Brezhnev with
substantially the same tactics and concessions that were adopted
and offered by Ford and Kissinger in 1975-76, rejected by the
Soviets and finally, under intragovernmental and political
pressures, temporarily set aside.

Essentially the same thing may be said of the ground laid by
Ford and Kissinger for Carter-Vance undertakings in the Middle
East and Southern Africa. No drastic departure from the
inherited policies in those areas was possible because the
inherited policies had recognized and responded to basic realities
that no administration may escape or ignore—including the
reality that Arab sensibilities must be accommodated along with
Israeli security interests if an Arab-Israeli peace is to be attained.
The Carter-Vance approach to resolution of the dispute with
Panama about control of and sovereignty over the Panama Canal
is a literal replay of the position defined by Nixon, Ford and
Kissinger in 1974 and rhetorically modified, though never
abandoned, by Ford under rightist pressure from Ronald Reagan
in 1976. The Carter-Vance reach for accommodation with
Communist Cuba seemed to be a bold advance beyond the
cautious Ford-Kissinger posture. It really wasn't all that much of
an advance. Carter first stated the same requirements for
accommodation—that Castro Cuba withdraw its troops from
Africa and cease its anti-U.S. and pro-Communist agitation in
the Western Hempisphere and elsewhere—which Ford and
Kissinger set forth before they let the whole endeavor lapse
during election year. Carter later modified these conditions
somewhat, but not much.

In the related defense area, Carter struggled in his first weeks
to reconcile his extravagant campaign promises of reduced
expenditure with his discovery that all that could be prudently
reduced in the near term were a minor few of Gerald Ford's
budgeted increases. Carter's policy and objective remained
identical with Ford's policy and objective: to sustain defense
appropriations at the levels, differing slightly, that each
considered necessary for United States security, and to fight off
congressional efforts to find more money for domestic expenditure by reducing defense expenditure.

The measure applies with less force to domestic policy and
accomplishment, but it has some domestic relevance. To what
extent, if any, Ford's policies of budgetary restraint combined
with mild fiscal stimulus kept the 1974-76 economic recession
from being worse and contributed to the recovery that began,
lagged and feebly resumed in calendar 1976 I am not equipped

and do not attempt to judge. It's worth noting, though, that Chairman Arthur Burns of the Federal Reserve Board argued from his familiar conservative stance that the Carter proposals for new stimuli were both unnecessary and dangerous because the prior Ford actions and nonactions were having a sufficient effect. President Carter found himself in principle though not in detail on the side of Gerald Ford, arguing with Congress that there could be such a thing as too much stimulus and warning that he, in the fashion of his predecessor, was prepared to veto anything that he considered to be excessive and inflationary.

Perhaps with undue compliment to Mr. Ford and unfairly to his successor, one other item that comes out positively for the Ford administration will be cited. President Ford made a great hullabaloo about deregulation and sent several proposals for it to Congress. They fared poorly, mostly because regulated business and industry just love federal regulation that protects them and detest only regulation that protects their competitors. An intensely regulated industry is the scheduled airlines industry. Mr. Ford, the Civil Aeronautics Board under a Ford-appointed chairman, John Robson, and Senators Edward Kennedy and Howard Cannon, among others, proposed forms of deregulation to open the industry to more and freer competition. All of the proposals died in the 94th Congress, Mr. Ford's last. One of President Jimmy Carter's first specific domestic policy statements was his announcement that he favored airline deregulation proposals pending in the 95th Congress. He evidently referred to a combined Kennedy-Cannon proposal. In all except detail he might as well have indorsed President Ford's proposal, so close in principle and free-market philosophy was it to the Kennedy-Cannon and CAB measures.

Leaving aside disputed appraisals of Mr. Ford's economic performance, his great domestic failure was in energy development and conservation and in environmental protection. The failure reflected the central defect of his administration and his central deficiency as a public person. He inspired hope, instilled confidence. But he did not and evidently could not inspire ideas, action, purpose. Two elements of his background probably explain much of the lack. He represented a conservative and *satisfied* Michigan district in Congress for 25 years. As an orthodox and conservative congressman, and especially after he became the Republican Minority Leader, both his duty and his forte were to further the ideas and positions of other people— particularly his President's—and to work out compromises of conflicting positions among his colleagues. It was not good training for assertive leadership.

Russell Train, first Nixon's and then Ford's administrator of the Environmental Protection Agency, said in the waning days of the administration that in his judgment President Ford was fundamentally bored by the environmental issue and never addressed himself to it in effective ways. Opposition such as Train's to the President's vetoes of two bills to control the strip-mining of coal seemed to puzzle and irritate him more than it interested him or gave him pause. He relied principally upon higher market prices for oil and natural gas to reduce the importation of oil and the consumption of fuel oil, gasoline and natural gas. Train and others urged him again and again to move from that negative and questionable position to a positive position, in which he would urge upon the public the certainty of continuing shortages and the absolute need to conserve and reduce the consumption of fossil fuels. He said the proper words in this vein, but never enthusiastically and never with effect. Ford's neglect of the issue and the fierce winter of 1976-77 gave Jimmy Carter his opportunity to exploit the positive line of conservation and permanent emergency that seemed to be beyond Gerald Ford's capacity and comprehension.

Now to the aforementioned facts, viewpoints and insights that may add something to knowledge and understanding of the Ford presidency. Much of what follows is derived from interviews and conversations, some on record and some off record at the time, that occurred during the last weeks of the administration with President Ford, Vice President Nelson Rockefeller, Secretary of State Henry Kissinger, Secretary of Defense Donald Rumsfeld, Secretary of Commerce Elliot Richardson, Secretary of the Treasury William Simon, campaign managers Howard Callaway and James Baker, and White House assistants Richard Cheney, Brent Scowcroft, John Marsh, Philip Buchen, Robert Hartmann, David Gergen, William Rhatican, John Hushen, Michael Raoul-Duval, Ron Nessen, William Greener, John Carlson and Lawrence Speakes. There were others. But these were the most helpful and forthcoming during the farewell research and indeed—President Ford excepted—over the preceding Ford years.

The history of Gerald Ford's abandonment of his statement at his vice presidential confirmation hearing in 1973 that "I have no intention of seeking public office in 1976" fascinates me for several reasons. It's a study in the pressures and the pull that the presidency exerts upon new Presidents. It's also a lesson in the fallibilities of memory and the consequent perils of undocumented oral history.

From the record of Mr. Ford's testimony before the Senate Rules Committee on November 23, 1973:

Mr. Ford: " . . . I first should reiterate a comment I made many times since October 12 [when he was nominated for the vice presidency]—that I had no intention of seeking any public office in 1976."

Senator Allen: " . . . You have . . . said that you do not intend to run for President or Vice President in 1976 . . . Do you think you might be subject to a draft?"

Mr. Ford: "Well, the answer is still 'no.' I have no intention to run, and I can foresee no circumstances where I would change my mind. I have no intention of seeking public office in 1976."

Vice President Rockefeller recalled in an interview that after his confirmation as Vice President in December 1974, reporters on Capitol Hill asked him whether he expected Mr. Ford to run for election in 1976. He said he answered: "Well, of course he's going to run." Rockefeller continued: "Somebody said then, 'Well, he said he wouldn't run.' So I called the President and I said to him, 'Look, you can't be effective as a President as a lame duck. Now whether you run or not in the end, that's another question, but it seems to me that you've got to give everybody reason to believe that you are considering it, at least."

It seemed to John Marsh, a former Virginia Republican congressman who was Mr. Ford's principal staff political adviser, that the new President was so preoccupied with being President that he didn't give serious thought for several months to whether he should run in 1976. In an interview with Mr. Ford on January 2—during his last flight as President aboard Air Force

One—I reminded him of his Senate testimony in 1973 and asked, "What led you to say that then?" His answer, quoted in full, throws a revealing light on his approach to the Presidency and his initial qualifications for it:

"Prior to that time, I had agreed with my wife that since I had not in five successive times been able to achieve the Speakership of the House, which would be the culmination of 28 years [actually 25 years], and I saw little prospect of getting enough Republicans in the 1974 elections, that I was going to just leave. I had made a contribution, done the best I could, but it seemed to me the time had come for me to step down. That was a commitment made, as far as my wife and I were concerned, before any nomination to the vice presidency.

"So what I was saying in that testimony was, it was a continuation of what I had previously decided and I, quite frankly, had never aspired to any executive responsibility. In fact, in 1968 nominee Nixon had asked me whether I wanted to be considered actively as a vice presidential possibility, and I said no, that the executive branch of the government really never was something I had contemplated. So that testimony was totally consistent with my previous commitment to myself and to my family and with my overall noninterest in the executive branch of the government."

Mr. Ford was asked when and why he changed his mind after he succeeded Richard Nixon. He answered:

"I can't recall the precise date, but it was quite obvious to me that if I was not to be considered just a lame-duck President for the next two, two and a half years, with all the handicaps that a lame-duck President has, that I had to revise my previous thinking. So somewhere in that span, from late September-October until the end of the year, my views changed, and they were based on (sic) that I could do a better job in the next two years if I were the potential candidate or an active candidate for the presidency."

When I told the President that his first press secretary, Jerrald terHorst, had indicated at a public briefing within two weeks of Mr. Ford's accession that he had changed his mind and probably would run in 1976, Mr. Ford answered: "Certainly my circumstances had changed very significantly. So mentally, I may have been reorienting my attitude. But I can't say that within two weeks or a month or six weeks there had been a deliberate, full change of attitude."

The White House briefing record shows that Vice President Rockefeller, President Ford and John Marsh misremembered. It was on the day of his nomination to be vice president, not on the day of his final confirmation, that Nelson Rockefeller told the President that he had to run or at least appear to intend to run and that Mr. Ford in effect recanted his 1973 testimony. From the briefing record of August 21, the thirteenth day of the Ford presidency:

Reporter: "Jerry, yesterday Governor Rockefeller said rather emphatically up on the Hill that President Ford would be the candidate in 1976. Is that correct?"

TerHorst: "I had a discussion with the President late yesterday and again this morning. And as you know, in the past President Ford has held the opinion that he would not run for the presidency in 1976. He is now of the opinion that he probably will run in 1976, assuming of course that he is nominated by the delegates at the Republican national convention."

Reporter: "What changed his mind?"

TerHorst: ". . . his position has changed, as we are all aware, and therefore he has changed."

Reporter: "Jerry, you used the word 'probably.' You still want to keep that in, do you?"

TerHorst: "Yes, I think I want to keep the word 'probably' in."

The reader may ask, why go through all this? There's an answer beyond the earlier reference to memory and oral history. It goes to Mr. Ford's confession that before Richard Nixon nominated him for the vice presidency "the executive branch of the government really never was something I had contemplated" and his further confession of "my overall noninterest in the executive branch of the government." Those remarks deserve a full context. Superior and effective Presidents have invariably wanted the job enough to fight for it, run for it, win it. Gerald Ford never wanted it at all until it was conferred upon him. Jimmy Carter's Vice President, Walter Mondale, didn't want the presidency badly enough to fight for nomination and election, either. He quit early in his candidacy for the 1976 nomination, saying it was just too much strain and trouble.

A minor addition to the story of the Nixon pardon told in the first chapter of this collection is best offered in a portion, abbreviated and edited for clarity but not distorted, of my January 2 interview with Mr. Ford. It includes references to Alexander Haig, Nixon's and Ford's White House staff chief; White House counsel Philip Buchen; Bob Woodward, one of the *Washington Post*'s Watergate team, and a *Post* story he wrote about the pardon in February 1976; Leonard Garment, a Nixon White House lawyer who stayed on with Mr. Ford for awhile; and Raymond K. Price, Jr., a former Nixon and Ford speech writer. The background is Mr. Ford's sworn testimony to a House subcommittee after he became President: "In summary, Mr. Chairman, I assure you that there never was at any time any agreement whatsoever concerning a pardon to Mr. Nixon if he were to resign and I were to become President . . . At no time after I became President on August 9, 1974, was the subject of a pardon for Richard Nixon raised by the former President or by anyone representing him. Also, no one on my staff brought up the subject until the day before my first press conference on August 28, 1974. At that time, I was advised that questions on the subject might be raised by media reporters at the press conference." Questions were raised. Mr. Ford said he possessed and reserved the right to pardon Nixon but intended to await further unfolding of the judicial process. He pardoned Nixon on September 8.

From the Ford interview:

Osborne: "Leonard Garment has told me that on August 27 [the day before the first press conference] he went to Haig that afternoon and told him that he had heard an argument, a strong argument, for pardoning Nixon. As a matter of fact, he heard it from me."

Ford (with a look and in a tone of unmistakable astonishment): "*From you?*"

Osborne: "From me, at lunch. I am not trying to drag myself into it, but that is a fact. And Garment went to Haig. Haig and he discussed it. Haig told him to go home and overnight draft a memorandum, to be addressed to Buchen with a copy to Haig,

setting forth what Len considered to be the salient reasons or
justifications for a pardon. Over that same night or the next
morning Ray Price—he has told me this is true—wrote a draft
handout statement announcing your intention to pardon Nixon.
Were you aware of any of that at the time?"

Ford: "To my best knowledge, I never saw one or the other of
those documents or memoranda—to my best knowledge."

Osborne: "And Haig didn't mention that Garment had come to
him with this thing?"

Ford: "My best recollection is negative. No. I was very careful in
that testimony [to the House subcommittee] to be as accurate as
possible. As I remember that testimony, I didn't mention it. And
the truth is, today, I have no recollection of seeing either a Price
or a Garment memorandum."

Osborne: "Bob Woodward reported in February of 1976 that
three of Haig's associates in the White House had said that you
assured him on August 28 that you were going to pardon Nixon.
Did you?"

Ford: "Not to my memory. As far as I can recollect, and I think it
is reflected in that testimony, Haig never got word from me nor
did he ever proposition it to me."

I believed in 1974 and believe now that Mr. Ford told the truth
and I am as glad now as I was then that he pardoned Richard
Nixon. He startled and disturbed me, however, when in an
interview with Barbara Walters of ABC he gave a reason for the
pardon—"the only reason," he said—that was new to me and
very different from the one he'd given to the House subcommittee. He'd said then, and on many other occasions, that he'd
acted "out of mercy" and in order "to change our national focus. I
wanted to do all I could to shift our attentions from the pursuit of
a fallen President to the pursuit of the urgent needs of a rising
nation" (a nation, he meant, rising from the Watergate mire). He
told Walters that he was overwhelmed by Nixon problems in
Congress and with the courts, and continued: "I was spending at
least 25 percent of my time listening to legal arguments about
what we should do with the Nixon papers, at a time when I
should have been working 100 percent of the time on the war in
Vietnam and the problems of the economy, and that is the only
reason that I really made the decision." When I told the President

that I'd read a transcript of the taped interview—it was to be broadcast that night—and had been surprised by the reason he gave in it for the pardon, he repeated the essence of what he'd said to Walters and concluded: "There were—there still are—some very significant, unresolved legal questions and I was listening to the pros and cons on almost a daily basis. It got to be very burdensome, time-wise and otherwise. So that was a factor." So it was "a factor," not "the only reason." I felt better.

In the parting interviews with the President and the Vice President, they discussed their relationship and some of the factors that led to Rockefeller's withdrawal first from consideration for the 1976 vice presidential nomination and later from overall direction of the President's Domestic Council. On the understanding that he would be quoted only after he and Ford left office, Rockefeller spoke of frictions, animosities and disillusionments that he had previously discussed on a cautious, background, not-for-attribution basis. The President commented for the record, also on the understanding that he would be quoted only after he left office.

One of the situations discussed was the antipathy between Rockefeller and Howard (Bo) Callaway, a Georgia millionaire, former congressman and Secretary of the Army who was the first chairman of Mr. Ford's campaign instrument, the President Ford Committee. Callaway's frequent, public insistence that the President could not hold the support of southern Republicans and therefore could not win the 1976 nomination if Rockefeller was his nominee for Vice President was the immediate though not the only reason for Rockefeller's withdrawal from consideration. Rockefeller held Donald Rumsfeld, chief of the White House staff and later Secretary of Defense, responsible for putting Callaway in the committee chairmanship and for putting him up to his sniping at the Vice President.

All of this was in mind when I drew Rockefeller into the following exchange on December 14, 1976.

Osborne: "You know, I once asked you to what extent if any you blamed Mr. Ford for that Callaway business. You said, *he allowed it to happen,* and I wrote that you felt that he had."

Rockefeller: "That is perfectly true. I said he allowed it to happen and I confirm what you said, because he didn't stop it. Now I don't say that he positively authorized it."

On October 28, 1975, Rockefeller handed Mr. Ford a letter asking that he not consider Rockefeller for the 1976 vice presidential nomination. Rockefeller announced the request at a press conference a few days later. In our December 1976 interview, this sequence was discussed as follows:

Osborne: "Did he try to discourage you, ask you to withdraw the letter, reconsider?"

Rockefeller: "No."

Osborne: "After your announcement, did he ever express any regrets to you?"

Rockefeller: "Well, considerably later, I said to him one day, just out of a whimsical thought, I said, 'You know Mr. President, I think I made a mistake.' He said, 'What's that?' I said, 'I should have said in that letter about Bo Callaway, when Bo Callaway delivers to you the southern delegations, *then* I'm off the ticket.' And he very graciously said, 'You didn't make the mistake. *We* made the mistake.'"

Mr. Ford discussed some of the foregoing in our January 2 interview, as follows.

Osborne: "Who thought up bringing Bo Callaway over to the President Ford Committee? Was it your notion, or did Rumsfeld suggest it?"

Ford: "We looked around and looked around and looked around. I can't recall who really came up with the idea. I spent a lot of time with Don, and Don came up with one idea after another, and his [Callaway's] name popped up, among others. The more we thought about it, the more appeal it seemed to have. But I can't recall who was the initiator."

Osborne: "I have written that Rockefeller holds you responsible for letting Callaway do to him what he thinks Callaway did to him, what he thinks Callaway and Rumsfeld did to him as a matter of fact: that is, driving him to the point of requesting you to withdraw his name from consideration for the vice presidency in 1976, and that you let it happen."

Ford: "There may be some credence to that. It in no way

undercuts my admiration and affection for Nelson Rockefeller. We were in a tight situation. In retrospect, I probably let it go further than I would if I were doing the same thing today. But I never told Bo Callaway to go out and make the statements. I can't believe Don Rumsfeld did either. But the statements were made and the momentum kind of let things get out of hand."

Osborne: "Is it true that Rockefeller gave you a letter requesting that he be withdrawn from consideration two or three days before he announced it and that he finally announced it because you never objected, you never asked him not to release the announcement?"

Ford: "I can't remember the precise details there."

Osborne: "Did you know it for awhile, that he was going to do it before he did it?"

Ford: "I may have. He gave it to me, but I can't remember the time sequence."

My reports showed some awareness of the animosities and frictions that seethed behind the seemingly placid Ford facade. But it was only in the twilight weeks, when Ford people loosened up and were more willing to talk than they had previously been, that I began to comprehend the depth and ferocity of the animosities. Donald Rumsfeld, whom I respected during his turn at the head of the White House staff and respect now, was the center and target of much of the distrust. Nelson Rockefeller was convinced that Rumsfeld deliberately frustrated his efforts to contribute to domestic policy formulation, engineered the pressures upon Rockefeller to withdraw from consideration for the 1976 vice presidential nomination, and beguiled Gerald Ford into firing Secretary of Defense James Schlesinger and CIA Director William Colby, replacing Schlesinger with Rumsfeld at Defense and Colby with George Bush at CIA, and depriving Secretary of State Henry Kissinger of his White House base and status as assistant for national security affairs on November 2 and 3, 1975. Of the persons named, only Rockefeller asserted on the record that Rumsfeld did all this in the interest of placing himself in line for the 1976 vice presidential nomination. Kissinger, Schlesinger and Secretary of the Treasury William Simon, who detested the White House staff under Rumsfeld and his successor, Richard Cheney, as thoroughly as Rockefeller did, shared the suspicions of Rumsfeld and found them believable. But they did not speak of them as accepted fact in the way that Rockefeller did. This welter of suspicion and hatred—the word hatred is justified—was discussed on and off the record with all of the principals named here and with President Ford during the final weeks of the administration. Some nuggets from the related interviews and conversations follow.

Osborne to Rumsfeld, December 23, 1976: "I've been collecting suspicions of Rumsfeld. Hell, you must be familiar with this. I guess the Number One suspicion of Rumsfeld is that he, for his own advantage, maneuvered the whole 1975 massacre—Schlesinger out of Defense, Colby out of CIA, and so forth."

Rumsfeld: "You've printed that stuff. I've seen that. It's just not true. The answer on the Schlesinger-Colby thing is that the President indicated what he wanted to do. I personally had felt that any strain he had with Jim [Schlesinger] was not Jim's fault and that he had his Cabinet set and he shouldn't make any change and argued against taking Jim out. When he later decided definitely he was going to do it, I indicated strongly that I thought it was a mistake to send Bush to CIA and Rumsfeld to Defense and as late as the day he did it I tried to get him to use people like Robert Ellsworth or William Clements or—who else was mentioned?—Elliot Richardson for Defense and CIA. I urged him very strongly not to do what he did. That's just a fact."

Osborne: "Well, one of the suspicions that I've picked up recently is that you recommended Bush for CIA, knowing full well that it would be the end of Bush's political career. I mean, the end of Bush for 1976."

Rumsfeld: "First of all, that is just a flat-out untruth. To the contrary, I argued against it. I told the President that if he was going to go to Bush [for CIA], he had to work it out so that Bush was not excluded from the vice presidential thing. I was shocked when I heard one day that the President had met with Bush and that Bush had asked him to take him out of consideration for Vice President and that the President had agreed to do it. It was completely contrary to what the President's intention had been when he named Bush."

Osborne: "I hear that you gave up the NATO ambassadorship and came back from Brussels with a firm understanding with Ford that he would name you to one of three major departments—State, Treasury or Defense."

Rumsfeld (wearily): "Well, not true. You just don't negotiate with a President like that. I didn't want to come back to Washington. The President asked me to come into the White House, I offered a lot of other suggestions of people who should do it, he insisted and decided that he wanted me to do it, and I ended up agreeing to do it."

Henry Kissinger remembered that he urged the President not to fire Schlesinger. Rockefeller remembered Kissinger saying that he had urged the President not to do it. Neither Kissinger nor Rockefeller recalled Rumsfeld resisting the discharge of Schlesinger or arguing against putting Bush at CIA. Rockefeller said that he thought Rumsfeld promoted Bush for CIA to eliminate him from consideration for the vice presidency. Elliot Richardson, who was called back from the U. S. ambassadorship in London to be Secretary of Commerce, remembered Rumsfeld taking part in some discussion to the effect that Richardson rather than Bush should take over CIA, in the belief that Richardson with his impeccable and varied background would be more likely than Bush to remain a viable prospect for the 1976 vice presidency. Some of these cross-currents of rumor, accusation and remembrance came up in my January 2 interview with Gerald Ford.

Osborne: "I have been told that three people—Rumsfeld, Kissinger and Rockefeller—argued against dismissing Schlesinger. Did they?"

Ford: "To a degree, to a degree. But I had made up my mind. I made it clear to everybody. I said, I have no apologies. I thought it [referring here to the whole packet of changes involving Schlesinger, Colby, Kissinger and Rumsfeld] was in the best interests of the administration. Each one of them raised questions about one part or another of this complex move. They all did it very objectively. I mean, it wasn't that they wanted something higher or they wanted to hurt somebody else."

Osborne: "I have also been told that Rumsfeld had to be

practically ordered—not by you personally, but by Dick Cheney and John Marsh—to take the Defense assignment. Is that your impression?"

Ford: "I don't know that."

Osborne: "I assume you know—I guess I am asking whether you do know—that some very responsible people in your administration suspect that Rumsfeld put you up to this whole thing."

Ford: "That is totally inaccurate and it is hundred percent a deviation from the truth. This was my—after an awful lot of thought, and without consultation because I knew what kind of arguments I would get—I sat down and put all these pieces together and Don Rumsfeld had no part whatsoever. Don Rumsfeld was as surprised as anybody when I unveiled this package to those [Rumsfeld and Kissinger, later John Marsh and Rockefeller] that I first spoke to about it."

Osborne: "Did Rockefeller tell you about his suspicion or conviction that Rumsfeld was leading you to make this whole series of mistakes?"

Ford: "I don't have any recollection of such comments. He may or may not have, but I have no recollection of that."

Osborne: "Was it suggested to you that you put Bush at Commerce and Richardson at CIA? That putting Bush at CIA would sink him politically for 1976, meaning the vice presidency? No such argument was put to you?"

Ford: "It may have been, but they weren't very forceful on it."

Osborne: "A story that goes around is that before Rumsfeld agreed to leave the NATO ambassadorship and come back to the White House, at your request, he had or thought he had your promise that after a few months getting the White House situation in order he would go to Treasury, State or Defense."

Ford: "There was no such commitment. There was no request and no commitment. Rummy came back, I think very unselfishly, from a job that he loved. We all knew that Al Haig [then White House staff chief] was going to have to move and because of my long, close relationship with Rumsfeld in the House, I thought that was an ideal spot for him to take over. But there was no request on his part and, obviously, no commitment on mine."

Long before the farewell interviews occurred, I had reason to believe that the President's decision to deprive Henry Kissinger of his White House role as assistant for national security affairs and have him concentrate on being Secretary of State surprised and disturbed Kissinger. I'd understood, however, that Kissinger didn't argue against the change and opposed only the decision to dismiss Schlesinger.

Osborne to the President: "I'm told that Kissinger did not argue with you against taking him out of the White House; that you just stated it as a fact, something you had decided, and he didn't argue."

Ford: "That is not quite accurate."

Osborne: "I'm also told that the reason you stated to him was that his dual role had become a political liability and you didn't want to live with it any more."

Ford: "No, that is not true. The reason was that we had come to the point where there had to be an overall reorganization."

Osborne: "This also concerns Kissinger and your relationship with him. During the two and a half years of your presidency, did you ever overrule Kissinger or go against his recommendations, his preferences of what he wanted to do, in any major, substantive matter of foreign policy?"

Ford: "There was never any time that there was an impasse we could not resolve, where I thought he was right and I was wrong, or vice versa. There was never any rupture, never a misunderstanding. Sure, there were differences. But there was never any major difference that wasn't resolved by a shift here or a change there."

Osborne: "I have a strong notion that that is just about what Kissinger would say in answer to that question."

Ford: "I think that is about what Henry would say."

Osborne: "I think you said publicly and you emphasized to me in the last talk we had that, if you were elected, you would certainly want Kissinger to remain as your Secretary of State, if he were willing to serve."

Ford: "If I were the elected President today, I would strongly urge him to stay on as Secretary of State."

Osborne: "By the time of the election, had you and he come to some understanding that he either would or would not stay on?"

Ford: "I don't think we had ever gotten into that detail. I think he knew that I would want him to stay on. I don't know what his attitude would have been. I do know this: that there are two, three or four things—the Middle East, southern Africa, SALT, and to some extent Panama, the Law of the Sea drafts—where I think Ford and Kissinger, working together, could have achieved very significant results. I absolutely believe that. I have the feeling that Henry felt the same way and, therefore, because those would have been very great accomplishments for the country, not just from our personal point of view, I think Henry might have stayed on just to achieve those results."

Osborne: "I'd bet you are right."

Ford: "We had prepositioned ourselves for those four or five very significant things. Because of his ability and other successes, and my relationships with people around the world, I am absolutely certain that within 6 to 12 months every one of those would have been solved."

Here the on-record discussion of Kissinger and the Ford-Kissinger relationship ended. Kissinger and I had discussed the same subjects in our last talk. If the Secretary of State had been talking for quotation, I think he would have said just about what Mr. Ford said in answer to each question, with some elaboration. His explanation of their rapport would have begun with the proposition that Presidents and their Secretaries of State must have a basic area of agreement on major issues, a shared fundamental philosophy, if their conduct of foreign policy is to be at all successful. Therefore the question of dominance by one or the other does not apply; given that necessary identity of fundamental belief, irreconcilable differences will never arise. So I was told over the Kissinger years, and I believe that this proposition applied to and governed Henry Kissinger's relationships with both Nixon and Ford.

The departing President's quoted conviction that he and Kissinger could have resolved the great and difficult problems of foreign policy that he mentioned does not adequately convey the intensity of his belief and of his disappointment—his grief, one is entitled to say—over being deprived of the opportunity to show what he could do as an elected President in foreign affairs. His frequent claims after the election that he recovered quickly from defeat and that printed and broadcast accounts to the contrary were false were themselves false, a form of inner defense. When we said goodbye on Air Force One, I was certain that Gerald Ford in defeat had suffered a wound that would never heal.

Two of the most interesting relationships and conflicts at the top of the Ford administration were those between Henry Kissinger and James Schlesinger, and between Ford and Schlesinger.

On the understanding that they would not be quoted, Kissinger and Schlesinger separately discussed their feelings toward each other several times. My resultant impression is summarized here on my own authority. In matters of policy there were differences, some of them serious, but there were no irreconcilable differences. The central conflict between them was a matter of pride, of style. Kissinger felt that Schlesinger wanted to get closer to the President and to wield more influence upon the President than he ever succeeded in doing. It seemed to Kissinger that Schlesinger sought to diminish Kissinger's standing and influence with the President in order to enhance his own standing and influence with the President. Yet I believed at the time of the 1975 "massacre" and still believe that Kissinger did indeed argue strongly against the dismissal of Schlesinger and did his best to convince the President that he was letting his own personal antipathy toward Schlesinger deprive him of a valuable Cabinet officer.

Schlesinger's attitude toward Kissinger was a good deal simpler. It seemed to Schlesinger that Kissinger could not tolerate a rival for the President's respect and attention in the field of foreign policy, in which a Secretary of Defense functions along with the Secretary of State. The result, in Schlesinger's view, was that Kissinger ceaselessly sought to deprive him, Schlesinger, of *all* standing and influence with the President. Schlesinger did not exactly blame Kissinger for the President's decision to dismiss him and replace him with Rumsfeld. But he did feel that Kissinger and Rumsfeld, acting separately for their own ends and not acting in concert, did much to create the climate in which the President decided to fire Schlesinger. If in nothing else, incidentally, Schlesinger was certainly correct in his assumption that Kissinger and Rumsfeld did not act in concert. Kissinger loathed Rumsfeld and thought his staff operation was unspeakably inefficient and harmful to the President. Rumsfeld

had great respect for Kissinger's abilities but felt that he was
capable of any trick or treachery to further his own ends. The
only comical aspect of a sad situation, at the time of and after the
1975 massacre, was Kissinger's conviction that Rumsfeld leaked
the story to *Newsweek* and Rumsfeld's conviction—or anyhow his
suggestion—that Kissinger or one of his people leaked it in order
to keep the President from changing his mind about firing
Schlesinger.

Ford's personal dislike of Schlesinger and his doubt that
Schlesinger understood Congress, a quality that Ford considered
essential for any Secretary of Defense, was first reported by me
in *The New Republic* in April 1974, on the basis of a talk with Vice
President Ford. That talk made it clear that he was already
thinking about what he'd do when and if he succeeded Richard
Nixon. My accounts of the 1975 massacre, which appear as
Chapters XXXVIII and XXXIX in this book, note the dislike and
the doubt as factors in the decision to dismiss Schlesinger. Mr.
Ford, however, added quite a bit to my knowledge and
understanding of that affair during the January 2 interview.

Osborne to Ford: "Looking back on it, what did you feel then, or in
retrospect what would you say now, was your chief reason for
firing Schlesinger?"

Ford: "Well, there was no single thing. It was a combination.
There were some personality differences. It was just one of those
nonsimpatico relationships. I admire Jim Schlesinger as an
intellectual person. I think he was totally patriotic. I think he
made a massive effort to run the department well. But there was
somehow a lack of personal relationship. I think you know me
well enough to know I like personal relationships. I am not
blaming him. There are certain people that you don't feel as
comfortable with as you would like to.

"Number two, there were some disappointments. Jim
Schlesinger had one approach to Congress to get a military
budget that the President had recommended. His approach was
to have a high degree of personal relationships with the power
centers in the House and Senate. In the old days, that worked. In
the aftermath of the Vietnam period, that power-center
relationship didn't produce results. Now you have to have a

broad-based understanding with well over a majority of the members. I still believe today, that is the way to get results."

Osborne: "Two of your assistants have an impression that Schlesinger, in addition to your feeling that he didn't know how to handle Congress, irritated the hell out of you by presuming to teach *you* how to handle Congress."

Ford: "Well, I wouldn't put it quite that way. But I thought there was a different and better way."

A final point is derived from unquotable portions of some of the farewell interviews. The reports in this collection, and my first reports on the Carter White House, reflected my impression that General Haig, Donald Rumsfeld and Richard Cheney, President Ford's successive White House staff chiefs, ran a generally orderly domestic shop, of course with some inefficiencies and rivalries persisting and some personnel difficulties and flaws unresolved because they involved favorites whom the President would not dismiss. It was known and reported, for instance, that Haig, Rumsfeld and Cheney in their turns detested and were detested by Robert Hartmann, Mr. Ford's friend and assistant of many years and head of his White House speech- and statement-writing operation. But I learned only in the last weeks of the administration that Rumsfeld and Cheney—Rumsfeld in particular—felt that Mr. Ford never let them run the White House and Executive Office establishment as they thought it should be run.

Mr. Ford began his presidency with much talk by him and Hartmann about the spokes-in-the-wheel analogy that Jimmy Carter and his people used at the start of the Carter presidency. Spokes-in-the-wheel symbolized the direct access that Ford and Carter wanted at their respective beginnings to grant a maximum number of senior assistants. Ford appeared to discard both the concept and the practice soon after Rumsfeld succeeded Alexander Haig at the White House. I was told near the end of the Ford time that Ford discarded it less in fact than in principle. In Rumsfeld's and later Cheney's view, he never let them exercise the authority that he gave them in principle to the extent and in the ways that they thought it should be exercised. Both Rumsfeld and Cheney were widely accused—by Jimmy Carter among others—of controlling access to the President much more thoroughly and tightly than any staff person should be allowed to do. They felt, and Rumsfeld felt with special intensity, that they were never allowed to exercise as much control as they should have exercised.

Rumsfeld blamed much of his difficulty with Rockefeller, and Rockefeller's dislike of him, upon what seemed to Rumsfeld to be the President's neglect or refusal to require adequate coordination between the Vice President's activities and statements and those of others in the President's service. It also seemed to Rumsfeld that Secretary of the Treasury William Simon was allowed to go off on his own tangents far too often and that both Rockefeller and Simon held him, Rumsfeld, responsible for the frustrations and misunderstandings that resulted. Cheney's similar feelings were said to be a good deal milder. But he often told his subordinates and associates that one of a staff chief's duties was to take the blame for other people's frustrations and disappointments. Cheney made it clear to some of Jimmy Carter's transition emissaries that he'd have run a much tighter shop than the one they found if President Ford had let him do things his, Cheney's, way. He and Rumsfeld believed that the President persisted to the end in allowing too many of his people direct and uncoordinated access to him and communication with him, and gave them too little authority to provide the missing coordination and direction. The consequence, they believed, and Rumsfeld believed with a passion bordering on ferocity, was a continuing condition of semi-chaos behind the orderly facade. The short of their opinion, as disclosed to me only when they were leaving office, was that good old Jerry was too damned good for his good.

I

The Pardon

Let the first of these reports on the Ford White House—what a dull ring the phrase has, incidentally—begin with a confession. I'm glad that President Ford pardoned former President Nixon. I hoped that Mr. Ford would do it before he did it and I'm sorry only that he did it in the worst possible way.

I hoped for, welcomed and still applaud the Nixon pardon for a reason that will seem to many and perhaps most readers of *The New Republic* to be empty, illogical and outrageous. It is a reason (or non-reason, some may say) that has nothing to do with the prerogatives of Presidents and respect for the presidency as such, although a tendency to respect Presidents and the presidency must have been apparent to readers of these reports in the Nixon time. I simply had and have a gut feeling that the prolonged spectacle of indictment, prosecution and trial of *this* former President, Richard Nixon, would have been bad for the country. It would be better, I thought and still think, to settle for the acknowledgment and plea of guilt that were implicit first in Mr. Nixon's resignation and then in his acceptance of the pardon. Some of the extreme demands that he explicitly acknowledge his guilt and the more strident denunciations of

Mr. Ford for not requiring Mr. Nixon to do so seem to me to have in them a quality of savagery that is close to sadism. What more should we require from the broken man who showed himself to the nation on television when he said good-bye to his staff on the morning of August 9? No more, I say. As for the complaint that the pardon jeopardized the prosecution and pending trial of H. R. Haldeman, John Mitchell, John Ehrlichman and three other Watergate defendants, and that it clouded the previous indictments, guilty pleas and convictions of numerous other Nixonites, I refer the screamers to Special Prosecutor Leon Jaworski. He knew without being told during the week before the pardon was announced that it was coming, and he did not object. On the contrary he let his staff's report that Mr. Nixon was under investigation in 11 areas of possible criminal involvement and his estimate that nine months to a year and possibly longer would have to elapse between indictment of Mr. Nixon and even the beginning of a trial be cited in support of the pardon.

So much for my opinion. Now to the little that I know and the much else that I heard but don't know to be true about the origins and aftermath of the Nixon pardon. It's a story that is notable for its gaps, anomalies and contradictions. It suggests that Mr. Ford and his people aren't telling a lot that needs to be told.

A fact that Mr. Ford at this writing has not confided to his closest and most senior associates is that he briefly but seriously considered announcing his intention to grant the pardon at his first press conference on August 28. Probably because he had not had time to have his own lawyers satisfy him that he had the power to pardon Mr. Nixon prior to the indictment or conviction, he postponed the decision and announcement. At the senior staff meeting at which the press conference was "game planned," with assistants trying anticipated questions out on the President and suggesting answers, one of the anticipated questions was whether he agreed with former Governor and Vice President-designate Nelson Rockefeller, who had just agreed with Senator Hugh Scott, that the departed Mr. Nixon had been "hung" and should not be "drawn and quartered" by indictment, prosecution and trial. The answer discussed at the preparatory meeting stopped with Mr. Ford saying merely that he agreed with Rockefeller and leaving the impression that he leaned toward leniency for the former President when and if it became necessary. The expected question proved to be the first question asked at his press conference and Mr. Ford began his answer as his assistants had understood he would. But in the rest of his first answer and in his answers to the second and third of four questions he got on the subject, he went on to say: "There have been no charges made, there has been no action by the courts, there has been no action by any jury. And until any legal process has been undertaken, I think it is unwise and untimely for me to make any commitment . . . Of course, I make no commitment one way or the other . . . I am not ruling it [a pardon] out. It is an option and a proper option for any president."

These answers were generally reported to mean that Mr. Ford had committed himself to await the indictment and possibly the conviction of Mr. Nixon before a pardon would be considered or granted. Did he mean to convey this impression and, if he did, what happened in the next 48 hours to cause him to indicate at a meeting with four senior associates that he was inclined to pardon Mr. Nixon as soon as possible? These remain essentially unanswered questions. They were poorly asked and feebly answered at his second press conference on September 17. Private inquiries got better answers than the September 17 performance did, but those answers as reflected here are far from satisfactory. One of the President's assistants understood him to say soon after the August 28 press conference that he hadn't meant to convey the reported impression. Another assistant understood him to indicate with regret that he had misunderstood the law of pardon and the extent of his power to pardon when he answered as he did. Nobody in his private counsels appears to have asked him explicitly whether he intended to convey the reported impression and, after he had decided to pardon Mr. Nixon immediately, whether he considered this a basic change of position. When Robert Hartmann, one of the few senior assistants that Mr. Ford brought with him into the presidency from the vice presidency, tried to warn him that an immediate pardon would surely be thought to be in total contradiction of his August 28 position, Mr. Ford showed a singular lack of interest. This suggested to me, though apparently not to Hartmann, that the President didn't think there was a substantial contradiction. At any rate the only development between the press conference on August 28 and a crucial meeting with four senior asistants on the morning of August 30 that is known to or acknowledged by some of these assistants is that the reaction to his statements at the press conference made Mr. Ford uneasy and caused him to call for two things. They were thorough research of the law of pardon and his power to pardon, and the best indication that could be obtained from Special Prosecutor Jaworski of the extent and imminence of Mr. Nixon's legal peril. In particular the President wanted to know how long the judicial process would take if it were allowed to proceed from indictment to trial.

The four assistants at the August 30 meeting were Hartmann; another counsellor, John Marsh, a former Virginia congressman and assistant to Ford during his brief vice presidency; the new President's staff counsel, Philip Buchen, a long-time friend and former law partner from Mr. Ford's hometown of Grand Rapids; and General Alexander Haig, the staff chief inherited from Mr. Nixon who was about to return to active army duty and take over the American and NATO military commands in Europe. They and one other, a young lawyer named Benton Becker who was a friend of Mr. Ford's and a temporary assistant to Buchen, were the only White House people who knew about the approach to an early pardon until it was disclosed to a very few others on Saturday, September 7. Haig didn't know before the preceding Thursday night and Hartmann learned on Friday the 6th that Mr. Ford had definitely decided to issue an immediate pardon. At the August 30 meeting he indicated his wish but not a firm decision to do so.

According to the assistants whose accounts are reflected here, including Philip Buchen and his statements at two on-record press conferences, four occurrences during the week following August 30 principally accounted for Mr. Ford's final decision to act as he did when he did on Sunday, September 8.

Buchen assured the President that he did have the power to pardon before indictment. Considering that President Nixon's lawyers had established this fact months before and had exhaustively discussed every implication of it, the asserted fact (I still find it hard to credit) that Mr. Ford didn't know this before and on August 30 indicates that the gulf between President Nixon's people and Vice President Ford's people before the resignation was even wider than it was known to be. The second major factor was Leon Jaworski's advice that nine months to a year and maybe longer would have to elapse after indictment and before trial could begin. The strong impression around Mr. Ford is that this estimate bothered him more than any other factor. The third element was the information, also from Jaworski, that no less than 11 areas of criminal misbehavior that could involve Mr. Nixon were under investigation. The fourth factor was the belated conclusion of an agreement between President Ford and former President Nixon, negotiated by Becker at San Clemente and signed by Mr. Nixon on Friday the 6th, committing the tapes and documents accumulated during the Nixon presidency to his custody in California under his and the federal government's joint control. Jaworski's staff and a congressional committee raised hell about this agreement later and Philip Buchen, acting for Mr. Ford, agreed to postpone transfer of the tapes and other materials to California. But the President was satisfied with it when it was signed. Although he had his spokesmen insist that a satisfactory agreement was not a condition to the pardon, Mr. Ford was equally insistent that he would not announce the pardon before an agreement was concluded. It appears, in short, that the agreement was a condition to the announcement but not to the pardon as such. The terms of the tapes agreements seem to have mattered much more to the President than the wording of Mr. Nixon's grudging admission of error but not of guilt did.

Benton Becker, the aforementioned lawyer and temporary assistant to Buchen, returned from San Clemente to Washington with the tapes agreement and reported to the President on Saturday, September 7. Haig, Hartmann, Marsh and Buchen were present when Becker reported to Mr. Ford. Accounts of that meeting are the most persuasive evidence known to me that Mr. Nixon's physical and mental health was not the decisive factor in Mr. Ford's calculations and decision to grant the pardon that it has been widely reported and believed to be and that he and his assistants say it wasn't. Mr. Ford spent far more time at the meeting on the tapes agreement and showed far more interest in it than he displayed in what Becker, who had conferred in person with Mr. Nixon, had to say about the former President's health. Becker said nothing about Mr. Nixon's spreading phlebitis and apparently didn't notice the enhanced swelling in the left leg that others have reported. Becker said that Mr. Nixon appeared to have aged and shrunken—*shrunken* was a frequent term. His shirt collar flapped around his neck. His jowls hung pathetically loose and flabby. His whole upper torso, hitherto massive for so slight a figure, appeared to have diminished. His attention span seemed to be short, he tended to leave remarks unfinished in mid-sentence, and he rambled. These last observations, which could have been taken to be indirect comments upon Mr. Nixon's mental state, did not particularly impress or interest Mr. Ford and the others present. Physical shrinkage apart, Mr. Nixon had been disjointed, rambling, prone to drift off into some far yonder for months before he resigned. Vice President Ford was talking about that in March 1974, to my knowledge.

After Becker finished his report he left the Oval office with Haig and Marsh. Hartmann and Buchen remained with the President. Mr. Ford leaned back in his chair, clasped his hands behind his head, and proceeded to tick off, for the benefit of Hartmann who would draft the pardon announcement, the reasons that should be stated for granting the pardon. Mr. Ford never once mentioned Mr. Nixon's health during this soliloquy. The reasons he mentioned were the reasons that Hartmann wrote into the delivered statement: mercy; an end to the passions and divisions that a trial would prolong; "Richard Nixon and his loved ones have suffered enough." When Hartmann gave his draft to the President on Sunday morning, Mr. Ford made two changes. Where Hartmann had written that the Nixon tragedy "could go on and on," the President wrote "on and on and on." He also inserted the subsequently famous reference to serious allegations and accusations "threatening

the former President's health as he tries to reshape his life."
These additions neither suprised not specially impressed
Hartmann and Mr. Ford didn't make any great thing of them.
What did impress Hartmann and Buchen during the final
preliminary session with the President on Saturday, after
Becker had reported and gone, was Mr. Ford's adamant
insistence that the pardon be announced immediately. He would
have done it that Saturday night if he hadn't been persuaded
with considerable difficulty that it would take time to complete
the necessary paper work and duplication, line up television,
and assemble the national press. He was urged to put the
announcement over into the following week. Mr. Ford said
Sunday at the absolute latest. He was asked why the rush? His
only answer was that somebody might ask him about it and he
didn't want to have to lie about it. Why not simply say, he hadn't
decided? "Because I *have* decided," the President answered. The
answer didn't satisfy the few assistants who heard it or learned
about it. They suspected that the President was holding
something back. A natural suspicion was that it had something
to do with concern for and about Mr. Nixon. If Mr. Ford was
holding something back and we knew what it was, we'd have
the solution of any mystery there may be about the Nixon
pardon.

Mr. Ford's press secretary and friend of 25 years, Jerry
terHorst, resigned in protest. A matter of principle, he said. He
is suspected at the White House of wanting out anyhow and of
using the pardon as a pretext. Mr. Ford believed it was indeed
an act of principle. "You just don't understand these evangelical
Michigan Dutchmen," he told an outraged loyalist.

September 28, 1974

———

Mr. Ford told a House subcommittee on October 17 that
General Haig, in the course of informing him on August 1 that
White House tapes about to be given to the House Judiciary
Committee so deeply and clearly implicated President Nixon in
the Watergate cover-up that he probably would have to resign,

mentioned a pardon for Mr. Nixon by his successor as one of the options being discussed by Nixon assistants. Mr. Ford also said: "I assure you that there never was at any time any agreement whatsoever concerning a pardon for Mr. Nixon if he were to resign and I were to become President." Longtime friends of Gerald Ford make sense to me when they argue that there didn't have to be an explicit agreement; nobody who knew Mr. Ford as well as they and Richard Nixon knew him could have doubted that the new President would at some point pardon the former President. Mr. Ford's account to the subcommittee of how he came to grant the pardon when he did coincided in all substantive respects with what I was told and wrote in the preceding piece a fortnight after the pardon was announced. The prediction that my approval of the pardon would outrage readers of *The New Republic* proved to be correct.

II

Settling In

In the seventh week of Gerald Ford's presidency his second press secretary and third spokesman—a deputy press secretary filled the gap between the first and second unfortunates who held the full title—thought it necessary to say to White House reporters: "It's a Ford White House now and it's not a Nixon White House."

This was begining to be true but it still was not entirely true when Ronald H. (Ron) Nessen, aged 40, a former UPI and NBC correspondent, said it at his first briefing in the White House press room on September 24. Four days, a weekend and a speaking trip to Detroit had intervened since Mr. Ford, obviously embarrassed, had introduced Nessen to the White House press corps as the successor to the President's first press secretary and friend of a quarter century, Jerry terHorst, who quit in protest against the Nixon pardon just before it was announced on September 8. In different words but in much the same way that terHorst had done, Nessen had gone through the ritual at his introduction on September 28 of saying that "I will never knowingly lie to the White House press corps" and "I will never knowingly mislead the White House press corps." "Lie" may be too strong a term for what all official spokesmen have to do at times. But Nessen presumably knew that he would be misleading the press by omission if not by explicit statement now and again.

Doubters are invited to compare the impression of a smooth and friendly transition that terHorst conveyed during his 30 days as press secretary with his account in the syndicated column that he began to write after he quit of "frictions" between Ford assistants and "the ongoing Nixon staff under General Alexander Haig." Reporters learned from terHorst in his column and after he resigned that Mr. Ford in early September was "spending an inordinate amount of time soothing his own loyalists and placating the sensitive feelings of Haig." There was nothing wrong, understand, with Press Secretary terHorst's withholding knowledge that terHorst the columnist was free to disclose and exploit. My point is simply that the numerous reporters and commentators, including some of the best in the business, who went practically ape over the "open" Ford White House that they thought terHorst bespoke and personified forgot that the controlling function of White House press secretaries and other official spokesmen is not to tell the truth. It is to put the best possible appearance upon what their principals do and say and, if necessary in the course of that endeavor, to conceal the truth. What my brethren in the White House press room were really celebrating, during the halcyon interlude that ended with the pardon of Richard Nixon, was the departure of Mr. Nixon and the quaint illusion that concealment and deception departed with him.

The occasion for Ron Nessen's statement that "it's a Ford White House now" was the announcement that Mr. Ford had chosen a successor to General Haig, the holdover chief of the White House staff who had been appointed commander of US military forces in Europe and had been accepted as the supreme commander of all NATO forces. The restoration of General Haig to active military duty with four-star rank and his assignment to the European commands is denounced elsewhere in this issue of *The New Republic* on the ground that some of the things he did for Richard Nixon and Henry Kissinger were

wrong. I hold that the good he did outweighs the bad. I hope
that he is allowed to return in peace and with honor to the
service from which Mr. Nixon recalled him on May 4, 1973, to
repair and run the White House system that had been eroded by
the evils of Watergate and shattered by the resignations of H. R.
Haldeman and John D. Ehrlichman.

My further interest here is not in the merits of the Haig
assignment but in how it came about when it did and in what it
tells about Mr. Ford and his administration. Haig's departure
and the choice of his successor tell us, first and above all, that
Mr. Ford is indeed settling into his presidency and, after a
judiciously slow start, is on the way to making it his White
House and "not a Nixon White House." It doesn't necessarily
follow, though, that the Ford White House will be as different
in method and in actual inward style from the Nixon White
House as the President, his spokesmen and the coterie of
assistants who think of themselves as peculiarly his men would
have the country believe.

One of Mr. Ford's criteria in choosing a successor to Haig was
that the new man have White House experience. The new man
who was chosen, NATO Ambassador and former Congressman
Donald Rumsfeld, had four years of Nixon White House
experience. After Mr. Nixon persuaded him to retire from
Congress and head up the Office of Economic Opportunity in
1969, Rumsfeld doubled and was paid as an assistant to the
President and spent approximately half his time in a West Wing
office at the White House. He later was a full-time counsellor to
the President and, when he was director of the Cost of Living
Council, he continued to regard himself and to be regarded at
the White House as a Nixon assistant. It was this experience,
rather than Don Rumsfeld's earlier association with and
support of Representative Ford in Republican factional battles
in Congress, that principally caused President Ford to insist that
Rumsfeld take a job that he'd recently been saying he'd never
take. Rumsfeld preferred either to retain his ambassadorship in
Brussels or to head a major federal department. He wanted an
assignment with a political future and White House staff
positions, however exalted, seldom offer that.

The formal announcement said that Rumsfeld was to be "an

Assistant to the President with Cabinet rank and with responsibility for the coordination of White House operations." It didn't say and Nessen, elaborating orally, refused to say that Rumsfeld was to be the President's chief of staff. The avoidance of the term was both deliberate and illusory. Why this is so brings us to why General Haig's reassignment and replacement were arranged a good deal sooner than President Ford had intended. The departure fitted in with Haig's desire to return to military duty and his feeling, fervently expressed, that failure to return him to it because of his "political" service would be unjust and wrong. But the initiative was Mr. Ford's.

As long ago as last March, when Vice President Ford was already thinking seriously and specifically about what he'd do when and if he became President, he foresaw that one of his difficulties was likely to be the relationship between Haig and Robert Hartmann, a former journalist who had worked for Representative and Minority Leader Ford in Congress and was the chief of his vice presidential staff. Ford had concluded, and thought Hartmann had agreed, that running the White House staff would be beyond him. The reality of submission to the quiet but rather imperious Haig proved to be more than Hartmann could stand, even though he was made a White House counsellor and accorded every sign of continued favor. Unlike the reclusive Mr. Nixon, President Ford dealt directly with Hartmann and other senior assistants. But Mr. Ford expected them to keep Haig informed of what they were doing and expected Haig to keep the President informed of how they were getting along with their assignments. The situation irritated some of the Ford people and was intolerable to Hartmann. Alone among the senior assistants, he refused to attend Haig's staff meetings. He planted news stories to the effect that Haig was obstructing the President's wishes in petty ways and was protecting the interests of such Nixon activists as Patrick Buchanan. Soon after Mr. Ford became President, he ordered his senior assistants to stop their bickering and get on with the job of remaking the presidency. The admonition did little good. Mr. Ford, well aware of where the potting at Haig was coming from, put up with it and finally decided that the general, whom he continued to esteem and value, had to go.

Ron Nessen, amplifying the announcement of Rumsfeld's appointment, said that "Don is going to have the coordinative and administrative functions that General Haig had" and that he would, among other duties, "control the President's time." In short the President understood that he had to have an effective chief of staff. Rumsfeld was expected to fill the need without the title.

The pressures affected Haig in unpleasant ways. Hitherto notable for his calm and utter confidence in himself and in the rightness of what he had done and was doing for his successive Presidents, Nixon and Ford, he grew defensive. In interviews both for quotation and off the record, he sought to disassociate himself from his sometime patron and benefactor, Richard Nixon. "I never was a Nixonite," he told Peter Lisagor of the *Chicago Daily News*. This and similar remarks didn't make pretty talk, coming from a soldier who during his first four years at the Nixon White House was promoted from colonel to four-star general and appointed vice chief of staff of the army and, in his final year of civilian service, was a fierce and willing advocate of the Nixon cause. It was time for Haig to go and, all else aside, going was a good thing for him. In a way that no other staff change would, his going symbolized the gradual transformation of the White House. But the Nixon connection remains. It is strong and visible and it will be the subject of another piece.

October 5, 1974

III

Ghosts

Within an hour after Vice President Gerald Ford became President Ford on August 9, he gathered some 20 of his predecessor's principal assistants in a conference room across from the Oval Office that had suddenly become his office and told them to relax. He said that he didn't want the automatic resignations that are customarily submitted to a new President. He said that he needed their help, he wanted them to stay with him "through the transition," and he wanted them to assure their subordinates that there were to be no abrupt changes and dismissals. There would be changes in due time, of course. But those who chose or were asked to leave the White House staff would have plenty of time to find other jobs and those who wished to work elsewhere in government would be helped to find jobs. Mr. Ford used a rather odd figure of speech to make his central point. Nobody, he said, was going to be thrown off the airplane without a parachute.

It was a kindly and generous gesture, in sharp and instantly noted contrast with Richard Nixon's cold and witless demand on the day after his reelection in 1972 for the resignations of most of his assistants. It also was in recognition of the obvious fact that the Nixon staff had to be kept pretty much intact for awhile if the business of the presidency was to be done. Some of the effects, however, were unintended and unfortunate for all concerned. Two months after Mr. Ford took over, many veterans of the Nixon time still didn't know whether they were expected to remain or quit. Many who knew that they were expected to leave didn't know when they had to be out. Very few had been given firm termination dates. A few assistants in the upper ranks had come to vague understandings with Gen. Alexander Haig, the staff chief who was replaced on September 30 by Donald Rumsfeld, that they'd have until dates ranging from October 15 to December 1 to find other jobs.

In the meantime the term "Nixon holdover" had become an epithet in the White House press room and in much of the media. Reporters and commentators reproached the President for not adopting and enforcing a policy of arbitrary dismissal that media union contracts generally forbid and a company management would be criticized for applying to its executives. Some of Mr. Ford's own people, under strict orders though they were to be considerate and patient, were getting impatient for a practical reason. They wanted to put their own choices into the budget slots still occupied by Nixon people and were beginning to let the Nixon people know it in ways varying from subtle to savage. Although I applaud Mr. Ford's policy of patience and deplore the vengeful attitude toward anything and anybody associated with Richard Nixon that accounts for much of the pressure upon the President to make a quick and total sweep, the Ford White House at times seems even to me to be populated with ghosts from the Nixon past.

Eight of the 13 assistants who attended the first senior staff meeting that Donald Rumsfeld, himself a former Nixon counsellor, presided over were Nixon appointees. No changes that can be attributed to Mr. Ford's advent have occurred on the staffs of two of the principal White House entities, the Domestic Council and the National Security Council. Kenneth Cole, executive director of the Domestic Council, says he's had enough of government after five years and intends to quit in early 1975. Tod Hullin and Joyanna Hruska, who were respectively confidential assistant and secretary to Cole's indicted predecessor, John Ehrlichman, remain on the council staff and are said to be doing good work. Lawrence Higby, a former assistant to the departed and indicted H. R. Haldeman, is at the Office of Management and Budget and hopes to stay. Rose Mary Woods, Mr. Nixon's $36,000-a-year executive assistant, and her $23,000 "staff assistant," Marjorie Acker, work on Nixon files in the former President's hideaway suite in the Executive Office Building.

One of the more interesting survivors is J. Fred Buzhardt, who was staff counsel to Mr. Nixon and briefly to Mr. Ford. Buzhardt and James St. Clair, the former President's chief Watergate lawyer, displeased President Ford by ruling rather arbitrarily that the tapes and documents accumulated by Mr. Nixon during his presidency are his personal property. A resultant and prevalent impression is that Buzhardt is an unwanted hanger-on at the Ford White House. Nothing could be farther from the truth. He remains, he hopes not very much longer, at the urgent request of his successor as counsel to the President, Philip Buchen. Buchen wants Buzhardt around for a fascinating reason. The written records of Mr. Nixon's Watergate maneuvers and defense are sequestered with other Nixon papers and are not available to the Ford staff. The chief and in some instances the only source of information that Buchen needs in dealing with the Watergate aftermath is Fred Buzhardt's memory of what went on. Michael Sterlacci, one of 15 lawyers who worked under St. Clair, is also helping Buchen and other Ford lawyers with Watergate problems. Sterlacci is among 22 government employees who were listed the other day as on detail to Mr. Nixon. Sterlacci was in San Clemente for a few days, working on legal problems connected with the transition, but at this writing is back at work for Buchen and the President. Jean Staub, another St. Clair lawyer, was retained until recently at the insistence of federal Judge John Sirica, who wanted a White House attorney available on demand to help him when he was screening subpoenaed Nixon tapes. She has joined a Washington law firm and Sterlacci is the only St. Clair attorney who remains on the Ford Staff.

Five assistants who were among the most aggressive in Mr. Nixon's defense and among the most bitterly hurt when he resigned provide a cross-view of what's happening. Bruce Herschensohn, who coordinated private support for Mr. Nixon, resigned four days after Mr. Ford became President and is executive director of a new conservative organization that professes to be dedicated to support of the presidency as an institution. Father John McLaughlin, a Jesuit priest who joined the Nixon staff as a speechwriter and wound up making speeches to conservative audiences in Mr. Nixon's behalf, resigned on October 2 after ignoring for many weeks repeated indications that his early departure from the Ford staff would be welcomed. Richard Moore, a lawyer and sometime broadcast executive who was a public relations adviser first to John Mitchell and then to Mr. Nixon, resigned on September 30 and probably will have departed when this is read. Patrick Buchanan, a conservative consultant to Mr. Nixon and an outspoken critic of what he considers to be the dangerously liberal and biased national media, hoped for awhile to stay in government and would have liked to be ambassador to the Union of South Africa. He's changed his mind or had it changed for him and in early October he was planning to quit and write a syndicated newspaper column.

The fifth example is Ken W. Clawson, who as Mr. Nixon's second and last director of communications managed the final propaganda campaign in his behalf. Clawson is one of the assistants who had or thought they had an understanding with Gen. Haig. It was that Clawson could count on remaining on the federal payroll until November 15 or December 1. Nobody pretended that he would do or would be expected to do any work for President Ford. Although he is not among the officials and employees listed on detail to Mr. Nixon, Clawson went to San Clemente in mid-September and was still there on October 1. He said in the previous week that "I'm simply doing for the Old Man what he's been asking me to do, which is just transition-type stuff." Mr. Nixon had entered a Long Beach hospital for treatment of his phlebitis. Clawson cited as an example of what he was doing a statement that he had drafted for Mr. Nixon, a statement thanking the thousands of people who had wired, written and telephoned their hopes for his recovery and their general good wishes. At this writing, no

trace of the statement has been noted in print or on the air.
Clawson, who was one of the best national reporters in
Washington when he let Charles Colson talk him into leaving
The Washington Post for the Nixon White House in early 1972, is
in the market for a job and hasn't been offered one that suits
him. It's no fun and no asset, being known as a loyal assistant to
and apologist for Richard Nixon.

October 12, 1974

———

I was writing this piece when Donald Rumsfeld, a friendly
acquaintance since he joined the Nixon staff in 1969, telephoned
and asked me what I thought most needed doing. All I could
think to say was that a lot of Nixon people needed to be told
where they stood with the new regime. Rumsfeld proceeded to
tell them or have them told, as he presumably would have done
anyway, with consequences that are noted in Chapter IV.

IV

Shakeout

White House happenings in the ninth and tenth weeks of Gerald Ford's presidency told something of how it was shaking out and shaping up.

When the President introduced General Alexander Haig's successor, Donald Rumsfeld, to the senior staff on September 30 and said that Rumsfeld was to be called and thought of as a coordinator rather than a chief of staff, Mr. Ford emphasized two other things. One of them was that he expected Rumsfeld to devise and administer an "orderly" decision process. The President bore down heavily on "orderly," implying a recognition that the presidential process since he took over from Richard Nixon on August 9 had been somewhat disorderly. The second thing he emphasized, with great force, was that he expected and wanted no leaks from his White House and looked to Rumsfeld to see that they did not occur. Just what Mr. Ford meant by "leaks" was not made clear. The sensible judgment among his hearers was that he meant advance, unauthorized reports of unannounced decisions that had been recommended to him or he was about to take. A plethora of such leaks, in advance of his economic speech to Congress, occurred forthwith and were followed by a series of errors and "clarifications" that reflected a bobbly staff process. My own experience, not necessarily typical, suggested that some of the President's assistants took him to mean that he wanted contact with the allegedly "open" Ford White House to be confined to his press spokesmen. Rumsfeld himself indicated as much in a brief appearance in the White House press room after his introductory session with the senior staff. He soon was the subject of a leak to the effect that Mr. Ford expected to replace Defense Secretary James R. Schlesinger with Rumsfeld in about six months. A supplementary rumor had it that Rumsfeld had told some reporters that he looked upon the White House assignment as a six-months job. Rumsfeld, who was about to leave for Brussels where he had to make his formal farewells as ambassador to the NATO Council, sent word to me that the six-months rumor was false. The extraordinarily weak denial that Press Secretary Ron Nessen accorded the Rumsfeld-for-Schlesinger story, followed by a spate of contradictory reports that the President was expecting and preparing to clean out the Nixon Cabinet after the November 5 elections, with no two accounts agreeing on whom he plans to keep and discard, reminded me of a conversation that Mr. Ford has acknowledged having with me last March 30 when he was still Vice President Ford. Then he was of a mind, among other matters, to fire Schlesinger and keep Labor Secretary Peter Brennan. The other day I read that he's firing Brennan and keeping Schlesinger. My policy is to await further word and action from Gerald Ford.

Rumsfeld moved fast to form his own temporary staff, lay the basis for a permanent central staff, and establish his primacy over the White House staff at large, including the very few chums and long-time associates whom Mr. Ford brought with him from the vice presidency into the presidency. Four lawyers and a political scientist who were associated with Rumsfeld after he quit Congress in early 1969 to become director of the Office of Economic Opportunity and to be simultaneously a White House assistant to President Nixon, comprise his temporary staff. The political scientist and, more recently, advisor to institutional investors, is Richard Cheney, Rumsfeld's executive assistant at OEO and now at the White

House. Three of the lawyers—John Robson, Don Lowitz and Don Murdoch—are friends and associates who have come aboard as temporary consultants and are fighting off suggestions from Rumsfeld that they take permanent staff jobs. The fourth lawyer, William Walker, is Rumsfeld's appointee to the powerful post of White House personnel chief, meaning chief recruiter both for the White House staff and for political spots in departments and agencies. One of the first assignments given Lowitz and Murdoch was to draft a code of ethical conduct for White House assistants, with provisions for monitoring and enforcing it in such a way as to prevent any more Watergates. The draft had been on Cheney's desk less than an hour when Cheney got telephone calls from journalists. They said a tipster outside the White House had a copy of the draft and was trying to sell it to them.

A lively question was whether and to what extent Robert Hartmann, a long-time and valued associate of the President and his principal speechwriter, would subordinate himself to Rumsfeld. Hartmann made no secret of his dislike of General Haig and of efforts, by means of news leaks and internal prods, to get Haig out. Along with other devices, Hartmann made a point of his refusal to attend Haig's senior staff conferences and of his instant access to the President without Haig's or anybody else's permission. Hartmann turned up at a few of Rumsfeld's morning staff meetings, so that nobody could say he refused to attend, and not often enough to acknowledge that he had to be there. Hartmann's appointments with the President suddenly began to be scheduled in advance through Rumsfeld, like those of other senior assistants. Hartmann's regular appointment, other events permitting, is at 9:15 am.

Initial organization and status apart, one of Rumsfeld's first moves was to resolve the problem posed by Nixon assistants and by Mr. Ford's overly vague and generous indication that they could stay until they had other jobs. Rumsfeld ruled that it was each division head's responsibility to indicate clearly who was to stay and who was to leave, and when. Where no division heads were available, Rumsfeld did it himself. He told Helen Smith and Lucy Winchester, respectively Mrs. Ford's press secretary and social secretary, that he wanted their resignations

effective November 1. They had understood that they were
welcome to stay until around January 1. Mrs. Winchester quit
immediately. Hurt but forbearing, Mrs. Smith agreed to stay
until November 1 to break in her successor, a TV newsperson
named Sheila Weidenfeld. Nancy Lammerding, a capable and
delightful veteran of the early Nixon press staff who lately had
been in the State Department's protocol office, succeeded Mrs.
Winchester. A typically injured and embittered victim of the
new precision was Ken Clawson, the Nixon regime's last
director of communications. He had understood from General
Haig that he might be detailed to Mr. Nixon until February 9 or,
failing that, retained until December 1. He was not detailed to
the former President and, while trying to negotiate a new job
from the strength of his White House position, was reminded
by Press Secretary Nessen that General Haig had gone. Nessen
told Clawson to submit his resignation effective as of
November 5. David Gergen, the competent and gentle chief of
the White House writing staff, and three of his writers were
told by his successor, Paul Theis, to be out by and as of
November 1. Raymond K. Price, Jr., Mr. Nixon's favorite writer,
was luckier than most. He has his own deal for a Nixon book
lined up and told the firers before they told him that he'd be out
and away in early November. The Rumsfeld, media and political
heat on Nixon holdovers caused Philip Buchen, the senior
among President Ford's three lawyers with the title of counsel,
to forgo his wish to keep former counsel J. Fred Buzhardt
around awhile for his knowledge of the Nixon tapes and the
Nixon time. Buzhardt left on October 5, well before he had
expected to.

Rumsfeld kept strictly out of a more important area of
Buchen's business. This was the attempt to renegotiate with
Mr. Nixon's chief Washington attorney, Herbert J. Miller, the
agreement on custody of the Nixon tapes and documents that
preceded President Ford's announcement of the Nixon pardon
on September 8. The negotiation was mainly between Special
Prosecutor Leon Jaworski, who had complained that the original
agreement gave Mr. Nixon too much control and the prosecutor
too little access to Watergate related tapes and documents in the
presidential files. Buchen delegated to Phillip Areeda, a

distinguished newcomer to the counsel staff from Harvard law school, and William Casselman II, the third counsel, the job of following the Miller-Jaworski negotiations. Before Jaworski resigned he, Miller and the Ford lawyers were close to a mutually satisfactory revision, leaving the tapes in White House custody and permitting shipment of most of the Nixon documents to California as originally intended. Congressional opposition to any surrender to Nixon's control of either tapes or documents wrecked the prospect. Miller was said at the White House to have argued, and Buchen to have agreed, that there would be no point in a new agreement that Congress seemed certain to abrogate. It was a serious matter. Mr. Ford, already committed to defend his unpopular pardon of Richard Nixon before a House subcommittee, faced the distinct possibility of having to accept or veto a bill that would require publication of the content of all the Nixon tapes. The President is said to believe that such a bill would constitute a gross violation of many people's privacy. He knows that he will be accused of protecting Mr. Nixon if he vetoes such a bill.

October 26, 1974

———

Mr. Ford reluctantly approved a law that, as interpreted by a federal court, retained the Nixon tapes and documents in federal custody while permitting Nixon access upon request to particular tapes and documents.

V

On the Stump

Late on the night of October 19, nearly 16 hours after he had left the White House for a day of campaigning for Republican candidates in the November elections that had him making six speeches at two airports, a newspaper plant, a nearby shopping mall, a party luncheon and a party dinner in South Carolina, North Carolina and Kentucky, President Ford strolled to the rear compartment of Air Force One and chatted with five "pool" reporters who were aboard for the flight back to Washington. This Saturday was the sixth day since October 7 that he had spent campaigning in nine states and three more trips to four more states were scheduled. A reporter asked the President why he risked his prestige in exercises that were mostly dreary and, assuming that the chances of most of his candidates proved to be as poor as they seemed to be, mostly futile. "If I don't do anything and we lose," Mr. Ford replied, "Republicans in the House would say I didn't even try. At least I tried and if the results are better than the polls say . . " His voice trailed off and he didn't finish the sentence. Counsellor Dean Burch, the staff assistant who managed the President's preelection efforts, had been saying for the record that Mr. Ford was going only to places where he thought Republicans had a chance to win Senate and House seats and state offices. Burch was talking for effect when he said this kind of thing. His actual view was that the President could fairly be said to be wasting his time if the only consideration was the number of votes he was winning for Republican candidates. What made the effort worthwhile, Burch was said to believe and Mr. Ford to agree, was that the President was showing that he cared about the election outcome and about his party in its season of trouble.

Regardless of what he might or might not be accomplishing for the Republican party, Gerald Ford on the stump revealed a good deal about himself. For instance he showed himself to be uncertain and defensive in ways and to a degree that the generally dim Republican prospects neither required nor explained. At the start of his preelection travel, notably in Detroit and Philadelphia, he omitted in his delivered speeches partisan praise of Republicans and criticism of Democrats that had been written into his prepared texts. It was as if he were imitating Richard Nixon's studied care in 1972 to disassociate himself from other Republican candidates and give as little offense as possible to the Democratic majorities in Congress. Later, particularly on his Southern trip, Mr. Ford grew positively savage in his attacks on the Democratic majorities. Thus in Greenville, SC:"We have a party controlling the Congress today that has controlled the national legislative process for 38 out of the last 42 years and for the past 20 straight years. It is a Congress, in my judgment, that is stacked against fiscal responsibility. And if they [the Democrats] increase their power instead of lose, if they multiply their strength, let me just make one observation: with a veto-proof Congress of the kind of membership they will get, tighten your seatbelts, folks. They will spend the dome of the Capitol right off Capitol Hill." From there, on this and other occasions, he went into his talk, rather odd for a former representative who still thinks and speaks of himself as a man of the Congress, about the evils of "legislative dictatorship" and the need for balance between congressional and executive power. Listening to this guff, I wondered at times whether he was going to beg his audiences not to give him Republican majorities. He didn't.

Gerald Ford the speaker seldom roused his audiences, even the clearly partisan devotees who had paid from $15 to $3,000 to meet him at receptions and eat with him at luncheons and dinners. Generally he seemed to stun and bemuse both these select groups and the miscellaneous crowds at airports and in auditoriums when he addressed them. But Gerald Ford the visiting President roused them when he went among them and within hand-shaking distance of them at airports, in halls, on streets. At the Indianapolis airport, he was separated from the crowd by a steel fence topped with three strands of barbed wire. Screaming, shouting, panting men and women and children on their parents' shoulders thrust their hands between the strands and Mr. Ford thrust his hands through the wire to them. No blood was seen to flow. At a shopping mall in Rock Hill, SC, a beefy fellow grabbed the President's right hand and held it while shouting, "Gimme the button! Gimme the button!" Obviously baffled and disturbed for a moment, Mr. Ford finally realized that the man wanted the large WIN ("Whip Inflation Now") button on the President's lapel. The President gave the man the button. Several sturdy youngsters grasped both of the President's hands and pulled him toward them. Richard Keiser, the chief of the traveling Secret Service detail, leaped to the President's side and pulled him away from the children before they pulled him off his feet. So it went, and it didn't mean a thing politically. To the end of his presidency, in the depths of ruin, Richard Nixon aroused the same frenzies in similar circumstances.

President Ford is likely to be remembered as Jerry the story killer. His principal composer of anecdotes and jokes is Robert Orben, a professional gagster who with his bald head and solemn mien resembles a monk in flight from a monastery. Some of the stories as delivered by the President during the week of October 14 were not worth killing. One of them follows exactly as Mr. Ford uttered it in Indianapolis: "As I was walking through the lobby [of the hall where he was speaking] a very friendly lady came up to me, shook my hand, and said, 'I know you from somewhere. But I just can't remember your name.' So in a friendly way I tried to help her out. I said, 'I am

Jerry Ford.' She said, 'No, but you are closer.' " One of the President's favorites had to do with a golden retriever puppy that his daughter Susan and a White House staff photographer, David Kennerly, recently presented to Mr. and Mrs. Ford. I refuse to go through this nigh interminable tale. Mr. Ford first related it in Philadelphia on October 9 and was still telling it in Kansas City and Sioux Falls on October 16. At Sioux Falls, Bob Orben was observed during the President's rendition. Orben's somber countenance was suffused with delight. His lips were moving. He was silently reciting the story, word for word, as Mr. Ford told it at least the fourth time. At every stop in South Carolina, the President rang (and wrung) the changes on the facts that Senator Strom Thurmond, who was accompanying him, married a young and second wife in 1968 when the senator was 66 years old and has sired a son and two daughters. Thus: "You know, the motto of the sovereign state of South Carolina is 'Prepared in Spirit and Resources.' One is election day; the other is Father's Day." At Rock Hill a girl who looked to be eight or 10 years old recited the pledge of allegiance and provided Mr. Ford with a supplement to his Thurmond story. Orben was not present. The addendum was Mr. Ford's very own and it went as follows: "I shook hands with her and thanked her. But you know what Strom Thurmond did? He kissed her."

At Greensboro, NC, near the end of a tiring day, the President seemed to be unusually strident and emphatic during his airport speech. He was especially so when he flung his arms wide and said in conclusion: "Really, I look in your eyes and I plead with you, I beg of you, not for yourselves, not for me, but for our country." At Louisville, the last stop, he appeared to be flushed, confused, unsure whether to address or handshake a small airport crowd. He did neither. Press Secretary Ron Nessen said the President used a two-hour interlude at a motel to nap and shower. That night he was brisk, assertive and repetitious during a speech that ran 28 minutes and seemed much longer. None of the accounts that I saw of the airborne chat mentioned at the start of this piece included the following passage in the pool report: "The President was in shirt-sleeves, holding a drink. He shook hands with the newsmen present and at the suggestion of one of the photographers placed the drink down on the table [out of sight] while he talked and was photographed."

November 2, 1974

———

So far as I know, the foregoing was the first published indication that President Ford sometimes drank a little more than was good for him. For a later reference, see Chapter XLIV.

VI

Ford Abroad

It was too bad that Gerald Ford and his associates couldn't put Richard Nixon behind them and out of mind when they visited Japan, South Korea and the Vladivostok area of Soviet Siberia during the new President's first venture overseas since he took the office last August. Maybe the comparative arithmetic of foreign travel set forth in fact sheets prepared for the horde of accompanying journalists—18 countries visited by Mr. Ford, 75 by Mr. Nixon—bugged them a little. But the main reasons for the note of mingled envy, recrimination and braggadocio that marred an otherwise moderately successful trip were all too plain. Disassociation from the sick and disgraced former President was deemed to be desirable and essential. Along with others who had owed a great deal to Richard Nixon, Mr. Ford was seeking it before he went abroad. And President Ford, tainted by past identification with his predecessor and diminished in public esteem by the pardon he had granted to Mr. Nixon, needed something more than a moderate success on this trip. He needed a triumph. Before he left the Soviet Union for home and after he got back to Washington, he showed that he was not above letting his people claim a triumph for him at the expense of the man who had put him in line for the presidency by appointing him to the vice presidency after it was vacated by that confessed and unpardoned felon, Spiro T. Agnew.

The claimed triumph was the agreement to negotiate a new, 10-year agreement on strategic arms limitation that the President and General Secretary Leonid Brezhnev concluded at their meeting near Vladivostok. Some aspects and oddities of the agreement to attempt agreement—and it was just that, no more—are discussed later in this report. The point made here is the way in which good, decent, modest, forbearing Gerald Ford had let certain of his associates and spokesmen denigrate his predecessor and, in the process, distort the record of strategic arms negotiation that preceded his first meeting and negotia- tion with Brezhnev. Secretary of State Henry Kissinger initiated the operation at the expense of his former President for the benefit of his new President. Messrs. Ford and Brezhnev were still in Vladivostok when Kissinger recalled defects of Mr. Nixon in negotiation with Brezhnev that he, the Secretary of State, had not previously been heard to mention. Kissinger said to my informant (not to me and, so far as I know, not to other reporters) that President Nixon never looked Brezhnev and other Soviet negotiators in the eye. He seemed to them to be at once shifty and arbitrary, inflexible, prone to enter negotiation with excessively rigid and structured sets of ideas that he was unwilling or reluctant to modify and that, in consequence, hindered rather than furthered effective negotiation. This was strange and ugly stuff, coming indirectly but authoritatively from an official who before, between and after the Nixon- Brezhnev summit meetings in 1972 and 1973 praised Mr. Nixon's grasp of the problems under negotiation, his skill at seeking and finding sensible compromise, and, in particular, his excellent relationship and usefully high standing with Leonid Brezhnev. True enough, Kissinger had been saying recently and said publicly during the Ford trip that Mr. Nixon's last meeting with Brezhnev in Moscow and the Crimea in July 1974 was a failure. But that, he also said, was because "in July, for a variety of reasons, things were not ripe for an agreement." After the first of Mr. Ford's encounters with Brezhnev in Vladivostok,

Kissinger discovered in his new master qualities of flexibility and rapport with the Soviet leader that were suddenly held to have been lacking in Richard Nixon.

Aboard a special train transporting President Ford and his party from Vladivostok to a remote Soviet airbase, after the agreement to attempt futher agreement was announced, Press Secretary Ron Nessen said: "It was something that Nixon couldn't do in three years, but Ford did it in three months. I don't know what it was—they hit it off." Aboard Air Force One, flying home to Washington with the President, Nessen showed no more awareness than he had on the train that the Vladivostok agreement, whatever it eventually amounts to, is the culmination of years of prior effort and incorporates important elements of the 1972 Nixon-Brezhnev agreements. Instead he actually raised the paeanical ante, saying: "Richard Nixon could not achieve this in five years. President Ford achieved it in three months." Still speaking of Messrs. Ford and Brezhnev, Nessen also said: "They have a similar sense of humor and that's why they got along better than Nixon and Brezhnev got along." This arrant nonsense had an interesting effect upon the White House press corps. It aroused the first expressions of sympathy for Mr. Nixon and of outrage on his (and history's) behalf that I'd heard from that company for many months. At the White House, the day after Mr. Ford returned, Nessen was asked whether the President knew about the remarks and how he reacted to them. Nessen said the remarks had been discussed with the President and "he wasn't critical."

Mr. Ford's stay in Japan was notable principally for its shortage of notable achievement and event. Here again, though in an oblique and more kindly way, the remembrance of Richard Nixon was pervasive. The principal purpose and accomplishment of the visit to Japan, in fact, were to assuage the hurts and angers that resulted from Mr. Nixon's and Henry Kissinger's failure to inform the Japanese government in advance of the US approach in 1971 toward accommodation with Communist China and from a similar failure to forewarn the Japanese government of US economic moves that gravely affected the Japanese economy. Mr. Nixon was gone but Kissinger was still

blamed, and he bespoke a good deal of inner comfort and relief
on his own part when he said in Tokyo that "perhaps the most
important result of the visit—beyond any of the specifics that
were discussed—has been the frankness, cordiality and
completeness of our exchanges." Kissinger also perceived a
parallel with the Nixon past that did not permit public mention.
Everyone knew by the time Mr. Ford arrived that Prime
Minister Kakuei Tanaka, caught up in revelations of the
personal wealth that he had accumulated during his political
career, would have to resign within days after the President
departed. It seemed to Kissinger that Tanaka had worked all his
adult life for the eminence that he was about to lose, just as
Richard Nixon had, and that in this sense both men were the
central actors and victims of similar tragedies. Kissinger had
thought of and coached Mr. Ford in a way around the
embarrassment that the imminent fall of a disgraced Prime
Minister who was also the President's host (along with the
Emperor) would normally cause. It was an argument to the
effect that Japanese Prime Ministers, unlike US Presidents,
weren't really bosses of anything but were merely the
temporarily ascendant members of a likeminded community of
politicians—transient chairmen of the board, Kissinger put it,
whose rise and fall made no serious difference. This theory bore
little relation to the jugular realities of Japanese politics. But it
appeared to comfort the President and his entourage and made
it easier for journalists to concentrate upon such matters as Mr.
Ford's appearance on a ceremonial occasion in ludicrously short
morning trousers.

The universally accepted impression was that Mr. Ford
visited Seoul, the capital of South Korea, because it was close to
Japan and avoiding it would have been a grievous insult to an
ally. Before he began his trip, the President was known to labor
under a related and somewhat confused notion that the detour
to Seoul became unavoidable when a Korean resident of Japan
tried to kill President Park Chung Hee and accidentally killed
Mrs. Park. Just what this had to do with Mr. Ford's itinerary I
never understood; I simply report that he thought it had a good
deal to do with the decision to visit Seoul. One gathers that
Secretary Kissinger either originated or shared this thought.

According to the official account, Presidents Park and Ford concentrated in their discussions upon what Park called "this bond of friendship, confirmed in blood" during the Korean and Vietnamese wars and upon Mr. Ford's declared intention to continue a high level of American military supply to South Korea along with the continuing and unreduced presence of American troops. The visiting reporters tended to concentrate upon President Park's notorious policy and practice of domestic repression and upon whether President Ford had any thought of making the mitigation or abandonment of this policy a condition of further American aid. Secretary Kissinger delegated to Assistant Secretary of State Philip Habib, a former ambassador to South Korea, the task of saying no more on the matter at a press conference in Seoul than that "the subject came up as part of a general discussion between the two Presidents" and that "our fundamental concern and attention has been devoted to the problems of peace and security in the peninsula." My impression, derived from other things Habib said, is that Mr. Ford actually warned President Park that the next Congress, with its increased majority of Democrats, is unlikely to sustain a high level of military and economic aid to South Korea unless the current repression and harassment of dissidents is substantially modified. But Kissinger had forbidden Habib to say so, presumably in consideration of President Park's sensitivities, and the burden of reports from Mr. Ford's official party was that he really didn't give a damn about what happened to President Park's critics and opponents.

The essence of the strategic arms agreement to seek further agreement announced at Vladivostok, Mr. Ford's last foreign stop, was that US and Soviet negotiators would try between now and a summit conference in the US in mid-1975 to figure out ways for each of the two countries to limit itself to an equal number of strategic nuclear delivery vehicles, principally meaning missiles and bombers, and also to an equal and smaller number of missiles equipped with multiple nuclear warheads. A joint statement said, and Kissinger repeated, that the equal numbers to be aimed at in both categories were agreed upon at Vladivostok. Kissinger also said that President Ford and General Secretary Brezhnev agreed to withhold the numbers from publication until Mr. Ford had time to impart them to congressional leaders in Washington. The prior and subsequent shenanigans having to do with these numbers and with the overall Vladivostok discussions and agreement, rather than the arguable merits and demerits of the provisional nuclear agreement as such, occupy the remainder of this report.

Reporters on the President's homebound plane were told that the actual reason for delaying publication of the vital numbers—knowledge that intelligent judgment of the announced objectives requires—was that Mr. Ford wanted to have the presumably agreed totals in hand in a formal, signed Soviet document before he committed himself to them. The evening after he returned and before he met congressional leaders, White House reporters were told first that he would not and then that he would divulge the agreed numbers to the leaders and ask them to keep the figures secret for a few days. Senator Henry Jackson, a powerful critic of the administration's previous nuclear and strategic policy, was probably in the ball park when he guessed that the agreed overall total was around 2300 (*The New York Times* said below 2500). The determining factors, unknown at this writing, were the mix of missiles and bombers that each government intended to establish within the agreed totals and the size and power—"the throw-weight"—of each country's missiles.

Kissinger said last October, after a meeting in Moscow, that the prospects for a long-term agreement seemed to be good. Then he drew back in caution and was still cautious when he talked to reporters while the President's plane was landing at a Soviet airbase some 80 miles from Vladivostok. The most to be expected, he said then, was some further reduction of the differences between the two governments. The Soviet journalists and other propagandists who awaited the President's press party at a hostel on the outskirts of Vladivostok differed with and resented this estimate of prospects when it was conveyed to them. They said much greater things were to be expected and would be realized if the President and Kissinger responded adequately to unspecified Soviet offers. Before the following dawn Kissinger was a changed statesman: he was busting out with optimism, discernibly having to struggle to restrain himself from predicting a major breakthrough. Within hours on that same morning, the Soviet informants were also changed—the other way. They said things were grim: the Americans had arrived with nothing in hand but obstructive objections to Soviet proposals. At around 1 pm, a Moscow journalist who is highly esteemed as a source by some of the American press party's most distinguished ornaments said he had it straight from the conference center that the arms discussion had ended in hopeless impasse.

It didn't, of course. In the late afternoon, just before the President left for home, Kissinger said the joint statement "marks the breakthrough with the SALT negotiations that we have sought to achieve in recent years and produces a very strong possibility of agreement, to be signed in 1975." His exuberant manner more than his words led some reporters to elide "strong possibility" and jump to "agreement." I didn't and don't.

December 7, 1974

———

For the agreed numbers, see the next chapter.

VII

Arming Up

Here is the gist of the Ford administration's case—its very best case—for the agreement to negotiate a new agreement on the limitation of strategic nuclear arms that President Ford and General Secretary Brezhnev reached at Vladivostok. It is a case that deserves to be presented without the intrusion of hostile expertise and that is the purpose of this report. Secretary of State Henry Kissinger tried to make the case at two press conferences in Vladivostok. Mr. Ford also tried, in expectably and understandably oversimplified fashion, at a press conference in Washington on December 2 and Secretary Kissinger will probably have tried again at another press conference before this is read. But mass and open press conferences and briefings, infested as they are nowadays with reporters who mistake them for public crucifixions, are seldom occasions for the quiet and considered presentation of complex arguments. The State Department provided such an occasion in Washington on December 3, with the requirement that attending reporters attribute what they heard to "State Department sources." I trust that I will be forgiven for noting that the performance enhanced my respect for Henry Kissinger and my gratitude to President Ford for keeping Kissinger in the dual role that Richard Nixon created for him. Henry Kissinger continues to be both assistant to the President for national security affairs and Secretary of State and all of us are lucky that he does.

The President at his press conference, having received written affirmation of the figures from Moscow, said that he and Brezhnev had agreed in principle at Vladivostok to limit the overall total of nuclear warhead carriers that each country may maintain to 2400 and the total of missiles that each country may top with multiple warheads to 1320. Mr. Ford acknowledged that all that he and Brezhnev had agreed upon at Vladivostok was "the general framework for a new agreement that will last through 1985." The hope is that the "new agreement" can be negotiated and made ready for signature before Brezhnev visits the US next May or June for the fifth US-Soviet summit conference since 1972. Both the President and the "State Department sources" tended to minimize the difficulties that remain to be negotiated out and, when they got into the swing of their argument, to speak as if a binding new agreement had

11-26-74

LURIE'S OPINION

been concluded and already existed. The fact that it has not
been concluded and may never exist should be kept in mind as
the following summary of the case for what was projected at
Vladivostok and remains to be negotiated is read.

Although the aforementioned ceilings of 2400 and 1320 are
the gut of the tentative agreement, several other aspects of it
were disclosed only after the President returned to Washington
from Vladivostok and Kissinger returned from a side trip to
Peking. Some of these newly disclosed factors strengthen the
case for the projected agreement. It has been agreed in
principle, for instance, that the number of each country's
landbased missile silos "will remain constant"—neither the US
nor the Soviet Union can build any more silos if and after a final
agreement is completed. Existing silos may be enlarged no more
than 15 percent. This part of the intended agreement
constitutes an advantage for the US, for interesting reasons,
and bears importantly upon the merits and demerits of the
potentially agreed ceiling of 1320 on the total of multiple war-
headed (MIRVed) missiles to be allowed each country. The US
silos for its landbased Minuteman missiles were designed to
take considerably larger missiles than the ones now in them.
The bigger and more powerful the missile, the more separately
targeted warheads can be mounted on it. The US has not
decided to build bigger missiles and may never do so, but it can
do so without enlarging its silos if it so chooses. The Soviet
Union's silos exactly fit the missiles now in them. The present
silos have to be enlarged in order to accommodate the Soviet
Union's series of three new monsters—SS 17s, 18s and 19s—
that it has MIRVed or is MIRVing experimentally and intends
to deploy. Enlarging land silos is a visible activity, readily
detectable by US surveillance satellites, and the US intends to
rely chiefly upon this capability to make sure that the Soviet
Union stays within the limit of 1320 MIRVed missiles.

Submarine-launched missiles are harder to track. Mobile,
land-launched missiles will introduce another source of
uncertainty when and if the Soviet Union resorts to them, as it
will be free to do under the intended agreement. The governing
US calculation is that neither factor will be critical. Soviet
officialdom was told by Kissinger at a preliminary meeting in

Moscow in late October and Brezhnev was reminded at
Vladivostok that the US intends to assume that *all* Soviet
missiles of any type that have been tested with multiple
warheads will be MIRVed. Three new Soviet missiles of two
types have been tested with multiple warheads so far and it's
impossible to test them without detection. This assumption and
this intention to count *all* such missiles against the agreed
MIRV total are the core of the US checking system. Brezhnev
has not accepted this as the basis for assuring compliance and
some Soviet military and civilian factions are known to oppose
accepting it. If it is not accepted by Soviet negotiators in the
coming phase, the whole projected agreement falls apart and
there would be very little chance of finding a new basis for
agreement. But this doesn't worry Messrs. Ford and Kissinger
very much. They assume that Brezhnev, knowing as he does
what the US intention is, would not have gone as far as he has
toward a binding agreement if he planned to reject a compliance
system that should, for him, have the attraction of eliminating a
need for on-site inspection.

The major argument against the projected agreement that
Senator Henry Jackson and other critics are already making
derives from the unquestioned fact that the Soviet Union
presently has *no* MIRVed missiles deployed. This agreement, if
concluded, would sanction a Soviet build-up from zero to 1320
MIRVed missiles with several thousand warheads on them.
What's the good and sense of that? The good and sense of it,
according to the US argument, is that this aspect of the
proposed agreement does not really give away to the Soviet
Union what it appears to give away. For the past 18 months or
so, the CIA and other US intelligence agencies have been
providing the National Security Council with low, median and
high estimates of Soviet missile capacity and intentions. The
lowest estimate of the number of missiles that the Soviet Union
intended to MIRV was well above the tentatively agreed 1320.
The median and, judging from the past record, probably more
accurate estimate exceeded the 1320 by many hundred missiles
and several thousand warheads. If this is true, as Senator
Jackson will soon be told at subcommittee hearings he intends
to hold on the matter, the projected agreement does in fact "put

a cap on the stategic arms race" and bind the Soviet Union to a lower level of nuclear armament than it could and would attain without the agreement.

A related argument against the Vladivostok prospect is that the US should be negotiating a reduction from present levels of strategic armament and expenditure rather than limited increases to higher levels. The counter-argument comes down to the bald assertion that the Soviet Union simply and certainly is not prepared to negotiate reduction from present levels. It would be bound by the projected agreement, along with the US, to begin negotiation of some reduction from the agreed levels no later than 1980-81. That is held to be a gain of sorts, however tenuous.

One of the disclosures made in the course of justifying the proposed agreement fascinates me for a special reason. It is that until recently the Soviet Union asked that Communist China's nuclear potential be taken into account, along with our Europe-based bombers and French and British nuclear forces, in calculating any agreed overall total of nuclear carriers. All of these demands have been dropped. At Kiev in 1972, after the first Nixon-Brezhnev summit, I enraged Henry Kissinger with a query about a report I'd heard. It concerned Soviet-Chinese military tensions and was so explosive that I cannot further describe it. Kissinger, trembling with rage, said that whoever had told me the story was a lying son-of-a-bitch and that I was a son-of-a-bitch for even mentioning such a report to him. Some day, maybe, I'll learn whether the story was true and, if it was, tell it.

December 14, 1974

New factors including the "Badger," or "Backfire," a Soviet bomber with disputed range, and our "cruise" missiles complicated the negotiations and delayed agreement. Brezhnev didn't visit the US in 1975 or 1976, and late in that year President-elect Carter reserved the right to review the premises of the Vladivostok agreement to seek agreement. I still didn't know in late 1976 whether that Soviet-Chinese story was true.

VIII

Making Ford's Mark

During a period when President Ford was making the most for himself of his arms discussions with Leonid Brezhnev at Vladivostok and conferring or preparing to confer with West German Chancellor Helmut Schmidt, Israeli Foreign Minister Yigal Allon and French President Valery Giscard d'Estaing, Mr. Ford also was approving the final details of a White House staff reorganization, agonizing over how far to go in replacing the Cabinet that he inherited from Richard Nixon, thinking about how to use Nelson Rockefeller in the vice presidency without being overwhelmed, and working out with advisers and assistants some substitutes for manifestly inadequate economic and energy programs. It was a fantastically busy time at the White House, a time when the President was observed in varied forms and degrees of stress. It therefore was a good time for a reporter to seek impressions of how Gerald Ford appeared to associates at the end of the first four months of his unprecedented and accidental presidency.

A frequently remarked impression is that Mr. Ford was more strongly struck after he returned from Vladivostok, Seoul and Tokyo than he had previously been with the spoken and printed criticism, in Congress and in the media, of the leadership he has provided since he replaced Richard Nixon on August 9. The new President is said to be more puzzled than troubled by the criticism, and at the same time determined to alleviate and disprove the criticism. He is said to be determined above all to place the mark of Gerald Ford upon the Ford administration without succumbing to the advice and temptation to sacrifice, at the risk of lifelong harm, good men who served his discredited predecessor and the country well.

His puzzlement goes to a feeling, one that says much about Mr. Ford, that under the most difficult circumstances he offered Congress, the media, the public a leadership that has not been fairly recognized and followed. New Presidents normally have nearly three months between election and inauguration for planning their presidencies. Mr. Ford had a few days at the most, a few hours at the least, depending upon whether you believe his account or that of others (departed White House staff chief Alexander Haig in particular) of the specific notice he had that Richard Nixon was about to resign. In terms of expectation and secret preparation he had more time than most new Presidents have. But it's fair enough to claim, as his people do, that in terms of hard notice he really had no transition time at all. It is from this perception that Mr. Ford's sense of injury is said to rise. He feels that he has tried every known form of leadership and that none has worked. He left it to Congress to act, and Congress didn't. He offered it an anti-inflation program on October 8, and Congress ignored it. He revived and supported President Nixon's energy supply and conservation proposals and added some, none very impressive, of his own, and they were largely neglected.So what is he to do?—the presumably reflective complaint among his assistants runs. He is damned if he does and damned if he doesn't. That has never been a persuasive line, at the White House or anywhere else, but the inquirer hears a lot of it at the Ford White House. One hears more of it, in fact, than I heard in five and one-half years at the Nixon White House. A survivor of the Nixon time at the White House, a fellow who has lived with (though not in) Congress for many years, said in comment upon the tendency among both Republicans and Democrats in Congress to blame

Mr. Ford for a failure of leadership without offering any of its own, "the best thing that Congress does is nothing." He meant that Congress as an institution, and particularly the next House of Representatives with its host of first-term members, is inherently unequipped to provide the leadership and the programs that Mr. Ford is taxed with not providing. The merits of Mr. Ford's performance to date apart, and it seems to me to have been pretty feeble, the quoted White House assistant had a point that is all too likely to be proved sound in 1975.

One of the most interesting facets of the President's behavior after he returned from his visits to Tokyo, Seoul and Vladivostok was his effort to show himself independent of Secretary of State Henry Kissinger without disassociating himself from Kissinger or undercutting Kissinger. It was a difficult act, rather like a dog on two legs sniffing at its trainer, but Mr. Ford brought it off with considerable grace. In an interview with *Newsweek* after he returned from Vladivostok, Mr. Ford in his account of the arms negotiations with Brezhnev seldom mentioned Kissinger and suggested that the negotiations were in a deadlock at a point (the midnight of the first evening's talks) when Kissinger indicated in Vladivostok that they were close to sensational success. Kissinger was in Peking finding out what if anything was left of the US-Chinese accommodation built upon his personal standings with sick Chou En-lai and aging Mao Tse-tung, when Mr. Ford briefed the joint Republican-Democratic congressional leadership upon the Vladivostok negotiations. Several of Mr. Ford's assistants were pathetically proud of the skill with which they thought he did it without the company or assistance of Henry Kissinger. One of the attending assistants remembered that Mr. Ford turned once to Lieutenant General Brent Scowcroft, the President's deputy assistant for national security affairs, to check a point and Scowcroft answered, "That's right, sir." If General Scowcroft said it was right, it was right.

The Ford White House relationship with Nelson Rockefeller in the weeks and days preceding his prolonged interrogation and confirmation may have been very different from the personal Ford-Rockefeller relationship. About the latter, I know nothing. The White House relationship with Rockefeller and his staff was in effect nonexistent. Hugh Morrow and James Cannon, the Rockefeller assistants who were principally available to Mr. Ford's staff coordinator, Donald Rumsfeld, and his assistants said that Mr. Rockefeller had forbidden them to discuss with anyone at the White House anything connected with his functions and the staff structure that he intended to install when and if he became the nation's second appointed Vice President. Rumsfeld and his assistants had to devise a theoretical structure derived from one authorized originally for Vice President Agnew and adapted, with considerable pain and friction, to the requirements of Vice President Ford when he succeeded Agnew. The start of the estrangement between Mr. Ford's chief assistant in the vice presidency and one of his chief assistants in the presidency, Robert Hartmann, and Mr. Nixon's second and last staff chief, General Alexander Haig, lay in the argument between them over what staff level Vice President Ford should be allowed. The outcome of that hassle—in essence that Vice President Ford could have about 10 more professional assistants than Agnew was allowed *if* Mr. Ford was willing to do without substantial secretarial and other supporting help— provides the basis of the staff projected for Vice President Rockefeller. Because of his refusal to indicate any staff nominees before he is confirmed, his people will come aboard as consultants and be put as fast as possible through the security and other checks that must be completed before they attain the status of salaried federal employees. So far as I could determine in mid-December, the inescapable question of whether Rockefeller will be allowed to supplement his federally paid staff with a personally paid staff had not been raised or discussed at the White House. The assumption at a high staff level was that he would not be allowed to do it or want to do it in view of his difficulties with personal beneficence at his confirmation hearings.

Mr. Ford and Donald Rumsfeld, sweating out the Rockefeller problems, more or less simultaneously worked out a series of senior staff and Cabinet changes. The primary object of the staff exercise is to put the President in a position to say that no Nixon assistants remain in responsible positions at the White House as of January 1. That is a mildly absurd claim, the chief

Nixon holdovers at the White House being Messrs. Ford and Rumsfeld, not to mention Rumsfeld's chief assistant, Richard Cheney; his personally chosen White House and government-wide personnel man, William Walker, and others too numerous to list here. They are capable people, no reflection intended, apart from a profound weariness, on my part, with the media and congressional preoccupation with "Nixon holdovers" and the fallacy that they are inherently disqualified. My information as of December 10 is that Mr. Ford has decided to replace two members of his Cabinet and is resisting the arguments of Donald Rumsfeld, Robert Hartmann and John Marsh among others on his senior staff, that he ought to replace several more department heads in order to put the Ford stamp on the Ford administration.

Here you have to distinguish between Cabinet members and assistants with Cabinet status. Roy Ash, director of the Office of Management and Budget, has Cabinet status by grace of the President and is to be replaced. I'm authoritatively advised to believe reports that James T. Lynn, a Nixon holdover who was Secretary of Commerce and lately has been Secretary of Housing and Urban Development, will replace Ash. I believe these things when they happen. Kenneth Cole, who succeeded John Ehrlichman as director of the Domestic Council, is resigning at his own initiative. His deputy and another Nixon holdover, James Cavanaugh, deserves to succeed him and it's widely assumed at the White House at this writing that he will. He won't and that is too bad. My impression is that the Domestic Council directorship is being reserved for somebody chosen by Nelson Rockefeller, the council and its staff being among the very few areas of government where a Vice President may reasonably be expected to do much of use beyond presiding over the Senate and continuing to breathe with constructive regularity.

Rumsfeld is about to announce the areas of responsibility that he and the President have assigned to nine members of the senior staff, along with assurance that it's all in the interest of orderly presidential processes and a damn sight better than what went on when Rumsfeld was an assistant to Richard Nixon. What interests me more is the essense of the

explanation offered as to why Mr. Ford is so reluctant to clean
out the Nixon Cabinet. An amalgam of several opinions heard
at the White House is that President Ford is instinctively and
fundamentally opposed to abrupt and cruel change. In time, yes,
which is to say well before the 1976 presidential campaign. Mr.
Ford is a professional politician and compromiser, accustomed in
those capacities to making do with what he has. What he has
and Mr. Nixon left him isn't too bad in most instances. He
intends to follow his better or anyhow his true nature, which is
to go slow and easy with Cabinet changes. So I'm told, and how
wrong I could be!

December 21, 1974

———

I was right.

IX

Ruffles and Shuffles

President Ford's staff chief and coordinator, former congressman and Nixon assistant and NATO Ambassador Donald Rumsfeld, said after he returned to the White House in October that his first task would be to make sure that "the organizational arrangements" there were such that Mr. Ford "finds then useful and is comfortable with them." Rumsfeld's organizational rearrangements won't in themselves be very meaningful to most people. But the changes tell something about the kind of presidency that Gerald Ford wants to conduct and for that reason a few of them are worth reporting and explaining in some detail.

The President discouraged others from calling Rumsfeld "chief of staff" when he took the job, the thought being that the term was too reminiscent of the bad old Nixon days when H. R. Haldeman and General Alexander Haig were known by it and had all the power that it implied. Rumsfeld no longer quibbles at it, knowing full well that he is in fact the chief of staff and that any President in these times has to have one. He oversees—he prefers to say, coordinates—the entire White House operation. He and his nearest assistant, Richard Cheney, supervise the

President's schedule and, without exercising the absolute control over it that Mr. Nixon required his administrators to maintain, pretty well determine who sees Mr. Ford.

Like Haldeman and Haig before him, Rumsfeld concerns himself very closely with the personnel process both at the White House and throughout the federal government. A recent and little noted change in the name of the sizable office that manages the hiring and firing of senior personnel symbolizes Rumsfeld's interest and the range of his authority over it. Under Fred Malek and his first successors, it was the White House Personnel Office. Under William Walker, a lawyer who worked for Rumsfeld at the Office of Economic Opportunity and the Cost of Living Council and later was general counsel of the Federal Energy Office, it's the *Presidential* Personnel Office. The office always was concerned with the 1240 executive level and noncareer, upper-grade positions that are filled by presidential appointment in the government at large, not merely at the White House, and the new name indicates its sweep and power.

Walker emphasizes the fact that he's a lawyer, not a professional personnel specialist, and the word put out to his staff of some 35 people, including about 20 professional assistants, is that President Ford wants appointees with substantive abilities and substantive interest in issues rather than the management-consultant types that are alleged (with some exaggeration) to have been favored in the Nixon period. At the moment two of Walker's assistants are assigned full time to interviewing defeated Republican candidates for Congress and finding out whether they want federal jobs and, if so, what if anything they are qualified to do. Rumsfeld took the blame, though it really belonged fundamentally to Mr. Ford and immediately to Walker, for an appointment snafu that caused important changes in the recruiting system. This was the President's personal firing of John C. Sawhill as director of the new Federal Energy Administration and the hasty appointment of Andrew Gibson, a former assistant secretary of Commerce and president of an oil tanker company, to replace Sawhill. The remarkably generous severance arrangement that Gibson got from his oil company became known to the President and

Rumsfeld only after the appointment was announced, though one of Walker's assistants was said to have known about it and paid it no heed. The appointment was canceled, Rumsfeld insisted that all subsequent prospects for appointment be subjected to complete field and other background checks before their hiring was confirmed and announced, and the whole process has been greatly slowed in consequence. The affair was especially embarrassing to Mr. Ford because of a change in the senior recruitment process that he had instituted. President Nixon let Haldeman and then Haig "sign off"—that is, finally approve—all but the highest and most critical appointments. Rumsfeld reviews prospective selections at least twice. But Mr. Ford "signs off" on all of the final choices and discusses them, however briefly, with Walker and Rumsfeld.

One of several counsellors with Cabinet status, former Congressman John Marsh of Virginia, has oversight responsibilities in the revised Rumsfeld setup that suggest that he may be in line for Rumsfeld's job when and if the ambitious gentleman, a politician from Illinois who is known to yearn for a return to elective office, moves on to something more promising that a White House slot. Marsh, a stolid and respected man who is thought by some of his senior associates to be among the ablest Ford assistants, has been assigned supervisory responsibility for the preparation of legislation and for lobbying it through Congress. He also oversees an operation called Public Liaison, run immediately by assistant-to-the-President William Baroody and charged with educating influential segments of society—labor, management, farmers, educators, "women" (you name it)—in the policies and purposes of the Ford administration. It's an adaptation, polished and presumably cleaned up, of the Nixon operation invented by Charles Colson. Marsh's assignments also include communication, what little there is of it, with former President Nixon and his diminishing staff in San Clemente; preparatory liaison with Vice President-designate Nelson Rockefeller; and oversight of the national Bicentennial Commission and its activities, a celebratory exercise that Marsh helped initiate when he was in Congress.

Two long-time friends of the President from his home city of

Grand Rapids are confirmed in senior staff responsibilities. William Seidman, a certified public accountant and lawyer and sometime Federal Reserve bank chairman in Detroit who doesn't claim to be a professional economist but does assert for himself a basic competence in practical economics, continues to be *the* assistant for economic affairs. Philip Buchen, Mr. Ford's first law partner and a leader of the Michigan bar, is reaffirmed in his position as the senior of three counsels to the President. The junior and youngest of the three is William Casselman II, formerly general counsel to Vice President Ford. The most distinguished of the trio, Phillip Areeda, will soon be leaving the White House and presumably returning to the Harvard law faculty unless he gets an appointment that he considers to be in keeping with his professional stature.

The senior staff relationship that interests journalists more than any other is that between Rumsfeld and counsellor Robert Hartmann. The best to be said for it is that it's considerably less cold than the relationship between Hartmann and General Haig was. Hartmann, a former reporter and for many years chief assistant to Congressman and Vice President Ford, planted some nasty gossip against Haig, notably in the Evans-Novak newspaper column. Items glorifying Hartmann and obviously aimed at Rumsfeld continue to appear occasionally in Evans-Novak, generally to the effect that the President is letting Rumsfeld isolate him from old friends including Hartmann. The word from Hartmann's vicinity is that other friends are planting recent items. Hartmann is said to long for the old days when he spent hours jawing with Gerald Ford and to recognize that it has to be different now. He cannot enjoy seeing on the President's private schedule, which is prepared under Rumsfeld's supervison, an item that usually reads: "9 a.m.—Hartmann—15 minutes." In the revised or Rumsfeld dispensation, Hartmann is allotted overall responsibility for the drafting of presidential speeches and statements—something he is extremely good at—and for political relationships other than those with Congress.

Much could be said in this piece and will be said in a later one about the President's image operation. The Baroody-Marsh "public liaison" function previously mentioned is part of it. The rest of it is immediately under Press Secretary Ron Nessen, who has taken his lumps and seems at the moment to be settling into what appeared at first to be a job that was beyond him. One central point must suffice here. Don't believe that stuff you read in some places about good ol' plain-shoe Jerry Ford who doesn't care about his image. He cares a lot and his image machine is at least as elaborate as Richard Nixon's was.

December 28, 1974

X

Ford on Balance

At this writing, 143 days after Richard Nixon said farewell to power and Gerald Ford at the door of a helicopter on the south lawn of the White House and Mr. Ford took his oath as the first President of the United States who had not been elected either to that office or to the vice presidency, a reporter finds that there is at once saddeningly little to say and more than some commentators are saying for the Ford presidency to date.

The judicious time for adding up the score is probably not now but a little later, after Vice President Nelson Rockefeller has had a chance to begin contributing whatever his job and his President allow him to contribute to the administration and after Mr. Ford has delivered or failed to deliver on the big talk of vigorous action and leadership that has preceded his first State of the Union message to Congress. But there is certainly a point in summarizing a White House observer's impressions of President Ford in his introductory period.

This observer's personal impressions are based upon one luncheon with the President, in the company of three White House assistants and four other journalists; the little that was seen of Mr. Ford at a White House dinner for visiting German

Chancellor Helmut Schmidt; and the press conferences and other open occasions, at home and abroad, that the American and world publics see on television. To these immediate impressions, of course, must be added the cumulative and second-hand impression that a reporter gets from dealing with the White House staff. It is from that staff and from the statements and actions of the President, most of the latter fashioned for him by his staff and modified by him to varying and generally unknown extents, that a reporter's overall impression of the presidency as distinct from the President is obtained.

My total impression, stated with a second and last reminder that it is offered ahead of Mr. Ford's trial in his State of the Union message and in awareness that it's a very common impression, is that Gerald Ford is an awfully nice man who isn't up to the presidency. Why President Nixon chose him to succeed Spiro T. Agnew in the dying days of the Nixon presidency has never been adequately explained, by Mr. Nixon or anyone else. The obvious explanation, believable until a better one is offered, is that Mr. Nixon knew in late 1973 that he shouldn't risk and couldn't win any serious fights with Congress and that Mr. Ford, a pliant and respected and sensationally undistinguished congressman from Michigan for 25 years, was unlikely to have trouble being confirmed and unlikely to make any additional trouble for the President who had nominated him after he was confirmed. Both assumptions, whether or not they were the governing assumptions, proved to be correct.

Here I pause for a reflection upon the act and nature of journalistic judgment. The perpetrator of the foregoing paragraph—I, Osborne—wrote during the presidential campaign of 1968 that Richard Nixon was a repellent character who just might have the makings of a more than adequate President. I also wrote at the end of Mr. Nixon's first year in office that he'd been a better President than I'd thought him capable of being and got myself thanked by various people at the Nixon White House, Mr. Nixon not included. Now here I am, writing that Gerald Ford is an awfully nice man who isn't up to the presidency. There is nothing more to say in this essentially irrelevant connection except that I believed what I wrote about Mr. Nixon in 1968 and early 1970 and am understating, on the polite side, what I believe at the end of 1974 about Mr. Ford's capacity to be President.

Before getting to what little there is to offer here about Mr. Ford's substantive performance, a couple of observations about him as a person may be in order. He's a stubborn cuss. To my limited knowledge he has shown his stubborness more often in mainly personal decisions than he has in those decisions of public policy that are partly his and partly those of a clutch of advisers who may or may not become known as contributors to the decisions in question. Three examples follow. In the spring of 1974, when Vice President Ford knew but wasn't saying for quotation that he might become President at any time, he took a personal scunner on Secretary of Defense James R. Schlesinger, principally because of what he thought to be Schlesinger's inability to understand and deal with Congress. Schlesinger probably would have been out within weeks if Mr. Ford had succeeded President Nixon then. Before Mr. Ford became President, but well after the springtime of his dislike, he decided for himself that he was wrong about Schlesinger and now you couldn't get Schlesinger out of there with dynamite. The second example is Mr. Ford's reaction to advice that he was getting, from within and outside government, that he was about to make a terrible mistake in visiting Japan, South Korea and the Soviet Union last November when things were beginning to go to pot at home. He said *"I'm going"* in a tone that implied without saying "to hell with *you*." He did go and, in my opinion, it's a good thing he did. The third example, reflected in a nationally distributed newspaper column on December 30, is the view that he should have at least consulted with opposed White House advisers before he took a skiing vacation in Colorado. He likes to ski, he did it in Colorado when he was Vice President, and was determined to do so again despite a feeling that he ought to mind the store in Washington. I respect him for having the guts to do what he wanted to do, at no discernible cost to the nation except the cost of flying him, courier planes and some 15 economy and energy advisers out to confer with him.

The hard measure of President Ford's leadership and

substantive accomplishments in 1974 is the response to his economic address to Congress on October 8. That's the one in which he said he proposed 31 concrete steps to halt inflation— "our number one enemy"—and lick the energy crisis brought on mainly by the foreign oil producers' increases in oil costs and temporary oil embargo. Leaving aside whether there really were 31 concrete proposals (they're hard to find in that number), the interesting fact is that at Mr. Ford's own White House there is a tendency to overstate the disaster that the speech proved to be. The White House cliché is that there was no response at all from Congress and none worth mentioning from the public. Well, there was some. Two steel companies, US Steel and Bethlehem, and the Ford Motor Co. reduced previously announced price increases in response to urgings begun in the October 8 speech. Mr. Ford clearly indicated in that speech that energy needs such as the demand for strip-mined coal would come before his concern for the environmental harm of strip-mining and nobody should have been surprised when he vetoed a bill that would have curbed though by no means prohibited strip mining and related environmental crimes. To general astonishment, and in demonstration that Gerald Ford can surprise his derogators, he also vetoed a bill that would have eventually required the transport of 20 percent of imported petroleum in high-cost US tankers. It had been widely assumed and reported that the President had swapped a promise to sign the outrageous oil cargo preference bill for support of the trade reform bill that Richard Nixon originated and Mr. Ford got through Congress in diluted but constructive form.

The controversial part of the trade bill was its conditioned grant of equal trade status and limited credit to the Soviet Union. Mr. Ford and Secretary Henry Kissinger did extremely well, it seemed to me, in getting this bill through the mill despite the obstructions of Senator Henry Jackson, who persisted (with some success but not as much as he claimed) in forcing Kissinger to extract vague concessions from the Soviet government on Jewish emigration. At the close of 1974 Jackson was locked with the President and Kissinger in a fight over the merits and demerits of the Vladivostok agreement to try to agree on further strategic arms limitation. My New Year's wish is that Messrs. Jackson, Ford, Kissinger and numerous critics and supporters of the Vladivostok formula stop speaking of it as a finished agreement. It isn't. When and if it is, in anything near its present form, it will do Mr. Ford a degree of credit that I started off denying him.

January 4, 1975

———

For a somewhat heightened opinion of President Ford, see Chapter XVI.

XI

Rocky at Work

According to former congressman, Defense Secretary and White House counsellor Melvin Laird, a momentarily retired politician who does not minimize his prescience and his part in great affairs, he told Gerald Ford in August of 1973, when Mr. Ford was still a Michigan congressman and leader of the Republican minority in the House of Representatives, that he was likely to be the next Vice President and President of the United States and that, if and when he succeeded both Spiro T. Agnew and Richard Nixon in their offices, he should nominate Nelson Rockefeller to be the nation's second unelected Vice President. Whether or not Laird foresaw events as accurately as he says he did, and I'm inclined to believe he did, his story adds to the evidence that Mr. Ford started thinking about what he'd do in the presidency long before he replaced Mr. Nixon last August 9 and that, all along, his one and only choice for the vice presidency was Nelson Rockefeller. It turned out that way, anyhow. Rockefeller took his oath as the 41st Vice President on December 19 and, after a vacation at a Rockefeller-owned resort in the Caribbean, reported for work on Saturday,

January 4. This is a report on what and how he's been doing since then and what his performance to date tells about him.

The most interesting thing the initial performance tells is that Rockefeller, one of the world's richest men and a four-term governor of New York and a perennial seeker of the presidency, suffers from a nervous uncertainty that seems to be common to Vice Presidents. He shows it in the way that his immediate predecessors, Agnew and Gerald Ford, showed it. Agnew, a former county official and governor of Maryland, surrounded himself with assistants from Maryland. Vice President Ford relied mainly upon assistants who came with him from Congress. In the presidency he has brought in two senior assistants from his hometown, Grand Rapids, and two others who served with him in Congress. Vice President Rockefeller's

10-11-74

LURIE'S OPINION

"MY SALARY IS LOUSY... THANK GOODNESS FOR THE TIPS!"

senior staff consists entirely, without a single exception, of people who worked for him in the governorship and on his handsomely paid private staff. This is understandable. There is nothing wrong with it. But even when it's not been taken to the extreme that Rockefeller takes it, reliance to such a degree upon familiars suggested to me during the Agnew and Ford tenures and still suggests a fundamental nonconfidence and fear of unknown quantities and factors.

Rockefeller's staff structure was prepared for him at the White House before he was finally confirmed after months of inquiry, mostly silly and destructive, into his acknowledged habit of sharing his immense wealth, in outright gifts and cancelled loans, with favored employees and associates. The prolonged uproar in Congress and in the media rubbed the Vice President and his people raw and importantly affected the way in which he organized himself for the vice presidency. There were, for instance, two conscious and specific decisions *not* to supplement his federally paid staff with a privately paid staff and *not* to supplement federal salaries with his money. President Ford himself shared in some of this discussion. The specific question discussed between Rockefeller and the President was whether the Commission on Critical Choices for Americans, a think tank set up by Nelson Rockefeller and his brother Laurance and initally financed with gifts of one million dollars from each of them, should retain its substantial staff and continue its studies of just about every conceivable social and economic problem facing the country. Mr. Ford, who as House minority leader became an *ex officio* member of the commission and is still a member, and Rockefeller agreed that it is a valuable instrument and should continue its work. Whether it does depends mainly upon whether individuals and foundations deliver on pledges amounting to about $1.5 million in addition to the Rockefeller brothers' two million dollars. There is a tacit understanding that Rockefeller may continue to consult with members of the commission's staff and with such dependents as William J. Ronan, a former New York state and city official who is a salaried adviser to the Rockefeller family and has testified that he received $665,000 in gifts and cancelled loans from Nelson Rockefeller between 1962 and 1974. Peter Wallison, a

33-year-old New York lawyer who was counsel to the commission and is the Vice President's chief counsel, holds that Rockefeller may properly contribute more money to the commission if he chooses. After the burning Rockefeller got during his confirmation hearings, others on his staff expect him to be very cautious about that and also about consulting with private advisers and dependents upon matters of vice presidential business.

How Rockefeller came to be appointed chairman of the executive commission set up to explore reports in *The New York Times* that the CIA during and before the Nixon presidency engaged in illegal domestic surveillance illuminates his standing with President Ford and the problems that all Vice Presidents have to live with. Rockefeller said after he was appointed that he was not consulted about the choice of the commission's other members, all of whom are solidly entrenched establishment types, and that appears to be true. It was, according to both White House and Rockefeller staff accounts, a choice made in desperation and in circumstances that hardly flatter the Vice President. It's said at the White House that federal Judge Henry Friendly of New York first agreed and then declined to serve as a member (not as chairman) because of possible conflict with his judicial responsibilities. Erwin Griswold, a former US solicitor general and dean of the Harvard law school, tentatively accepted the chairmanship and then suggested that the President and his assistants had better consider whether the possibility that he might have to testify in cases involving an ITT antitrust settlement disqualified him. Mr. Ford decided that this prospect ruled Griswold out as chairman but not as a member of the commission. Late on Saturday, January 4, the President asked the Vice President to take the chairmanship and Rockefeller agreed. He expected his and the other members' appointments to be announced the following Monday or Tuesday. They were announced on Sunday, while Rockefeller was week-ending in New York. More interesting to me than all this are two corollary assertions at the White House. One is that the rumor that Rockefeller's friend and former employee, Secretary of State Henry Kissinger, maneuvered Rockefeller into the chairmanship in order to protect Kissinger from embarrassing exposure is sheer bunk, which I'm disposed to think it is. The other assertion (or admission) is that the President and his advisers gave no thought whatever to the possibility of maintaining that the law in fact permits the CIA to engage in some forms of domestic surveillance and simply challenging the *Times* to prove its charges of "massive" illegality. Mr. Ford and his advisers ran like hounded rabbits and required Rockefeller to join them.

Democratic Senator Walter Mondale of Minnesota, Republican Senator James Pearson of Kansas and 40 colleagues in both parties confronted Vice President Rockefeller, in his capacity as president of the Senate, with what could be the only substantive issue he will have a chance to decide or influence. At the opening of the 94th Congress on January 14, they proposed to change the rule that requires a two-thirds vote to shut off filibusters and make it three-fifths of the Senate membership (60 instead of 66). Rockefeller may have to decide that the proposal is or is not in order and that a simple majority of the Senate may or may not change the rules at the opening of a new Congress. Mr. Ford, who likes to be thought of as "a man of the Congress," officially took the position that he has no position on the issue and left the whole thing to Rockefeller. The key question was whether he'd have the courage to order a vote without debate and thus keep conservative opponents of the charge from filibustering it to death as they did in 1971.

During his first week on the job Vice President Rockefeller was put on the Senate payroll (at $62,500 a year plus $10,000 for expenses), paid 20 cents per mile for his flight (in one of his private planes) from Tarrytown, NY, to Washington, and briefed in exhaustive detail by a Senate clerk named William Ridgeley upon the emoluments that go with being an employee of the Senate. Rockefeller terminated a prolonged exposition of the insurance and other options open to him by saying with a grin, "Okay, okay, I'll take the best."

January 25, 1975

XII

More about Rocky

Here is a second report on how Vice President Nelson A. Rockefeller and his chief assistants are settling into their jobs and fitting into the Ford administration.

The President is said to be pleased. His staff chief and coordinator, Donald Rumsfeld, said of Rockefeller the other day: "He is doing everything absolutely right. Recognizing the historical difficulties in the relationship between Presidents and Vice Presidents, I'm satisfied that this President and this Vice President are going to make it work." Senator Mike Mansfield, the Democratic majority leader, took note January 17 of the extraordinary sight of a Vice President actually doing the only thing the Constitution authorizes him to do, which is to preside over the Senate, and doing it not merely once in a while but four days in a row. "That is a record, at least since 1967," Mansfield said. Rockefeller caused some confusion and violated a Senate tradition by leaving the presiding officer's chair vacant for a moment on the first day of the new Congress. But he did well in general and showed a fine sense of decorum when, after listening through a long afternoon to arguments for and against reducing the vote required to close debate and shut off filibusters, he thanked the leading proponents and opponents of the change for educating him in so complex a subject without giving them the slightest inkling of how he intended to rule when the matter came before him on any one of several procedural points that could determine the outcome.

It wasn't all roses. For Vice Presidents, it never is. It had been officially said, for instance, that he as the President's second choice for chairman of the commission investigating charges of domestic misbehavior by the CIA would be allowed to pick its executive director. "The Vice President will recommend someone and the President will appoint him," Press Secretary Ron Nessen had said. As has happened all too often, Nessen didn't know what he was talking about. The President picked David W. Belin, a Des Moines lawyer whom Mr. Ford came to know and respect when he was on the staff and Congressman Ford was a member of the Warren commission that investigated the assassination of President Kennedy. It was said for the Vice President, with a trace of embarrassment, that he was sufficiently acquainted with Belin to be able to say that he approved the choice and that one of several lawyers suggested by Rockefeller might have been appointed if they had been available for immediate duty.

Another staff appointment, still to be decided and made when this was written, went to the fundamentals of the relationship between the President and the Vice President. It was the appointment of a successor to Kenneth Cole, executive director of the Domestic Council and a Nixon veteran who expects to leave in February. Ron Nessen, ticking off several assignments that the President had given on December 21, said that Mr. Ford had asked Rockefeller "to be Vice Chairman of the Domestic Council, with a strong emphasis on working with the White House to find a new executive director to replace Ken Cole." This statement fell considerably short of saying that the Vice President would pick the director, but some of the Vice President's assistants assumed that he would. A logical choice appeared to be Richard Dunham, who was New York State's budget director under Governor Rockefeller and his defeated successor, Governor Malcolm Wilson, and joined Vice President Rockefeller's staff as his assistant for domestic affairs. Cole, it happens, is Mr. Ford's assistant for domestic affairs as well as executive director of the Domestic Council. James Cannon, a sometime political reporter and editor who has been a Rockefeller assistant since 1969, was also a prospect for the Domestic Council job. Within the President's senior staff, however, some serious questions and discussion developed. By law and in necessary fact, the Domestic Council is the President's policy instrument. Its executive director is the President's appointee and servitor, and in the nature of things that official's first allegiance should—some would say, must—be to the President. Without suggesting any disloyalty to Mr. Ford, it has to be said that the first allegiance of Dunham and Cannon is to Nelson Rockefeller. So went the talk and concern around Mr. Ford, along with acute awareness that appointment of a Rockefeller man to the council directorship would constitute and reflect a revolutionary change in the traditional relationship between Presidents and Vice Presidents. Vice President Rockefeller's predecessors, Spiro Agnew and Gerald Ford, were promised large roles in the Domestic Council and powerful representation on its staff. They didn't get either the roles or the representation. They never hoped to get the directorship.

The senior and probably most interesting person on the Vice President's staff is the designated chief of that staff, Ann Whitman. I have to say "probably" most interesting because she refuses to talk with reporters, including me. Mrs. Whitman—she uses and welcomes the "Mrs."—was the late Dwight D. Eisenhower's confidential secretary before, when and after he was President. She went to work for Rockefeller in 1962. She is divorced. She is the only Rockefeller assistant who gets the top salary allowed federal staff employees—$42,500. President Ford is allowed 14 assistants at that level. It's said of Mrs. Whitman that she really is the chief of staff, meaning that the Vice President's other assistants jump when she says jump. They are said to know from experience that her orders are always Nelson Rockefeller's orders and never hers alone. She and James Cannon attend Donald Rumsfeld's 8 am meetings of the President's senior staff, a group that is at the top of the White House totem pole. Mrs. Whitman and Cannon are said to find the Rumsfeld meetings useful for expectable reasons, such as that the atmosphere at them is open, frank, brisk, informative. Attending them has another use which is very real but goes unspoken. The presence of Mrs. Whitman and Cannon keeps the President's people from indulging, at least at those meetings, in the cracks and quips at the Vice President and the inherent deficiencies of the office that have helped to denigrate it and embitter the relationship in past regimes.

Three Rockefeller assistants, Cannon, Dunham and the press secretary, Hugh Morrow, get $41,000 a year. Harry Albright, New York state's former Superintendent of Banks, is also paid at that rate but is aboard for only three months, helping the Vice President organize and staff his operation. Staffing it is fairly simple, given the Vice President's previously noted affinity for assistants who worked for him in the governorship and on his private staff. For the latter, notably including Mrs. Whitman, Cannon and Morrow, working for Vice President Rockefeller is costly. Morrow has said that his $41,000 represents a salary cut of 40 percent. Joseph Persico, Rockefeller's chief speech writer since 1966 (excluding 1968, when author Emmet John Hughes briefly and disastrously superseded Persico) gets at $40,000 about what he did on the state payroll and a lot less than he got after Rockefeller resigned the governorship. At around $37,000, Roger W. Hooker, Jr., chief of the Vice President's congressional staff, gets about what he did when he worked for Governor Rockefeller in New York and Washington. A rare exception to the generalization that Rockefeller seems comfortable only with assistants who have worked for him in the past is Frank Pagnotta, a retired army officer and civil bureaucrat who was Vice President Ford's and is Vice President Rockefeller's assistant for administration. A second exception is John Mulliken, a *Time* correspondent who was hired as Hugh Morrow's deputy and suddenly found himself in Rockefeller's immediate service when Morrow became ill.

What matters, of course, is whether the Vice President and his principal people are good enough for their jobs and for the higher jobs to which they may be called at any time. There is no doubt among them that they are. James Cannon bespeaks the confidence and sanctimony that pervade the Rockefeller scene when he says: "You do have this feeling that working for Nelson Rockefeller puts you in an enterprise that is larger than yourself. But it's not a cult. People who work for Nelson Rockefeller feel that they are dedicated to what he is dedicated to, which is the good of the country." Rockefeller is still "the Governor" to his assistants. Cannon, referring to a past event, said rather wistfully that it occurred "when the Governor was Governor."

February 1, 1975

XIII

Containing Poverty

What's left of the war on poverty that John F. Kennedy originated, Lyndon Johnson canonized and Richard Nixon debased figures so modestly that it's hard to find in President Ford's mountainous budget for fiscal 1976. It could hardly be otherwise, given the philosophy that the President set forth in his budget message. He said that "the tremendous growth in our domestic assistance programs in recent years" will, if not limited to "sustainable levels" over the next 20 years, bring about "insupportably heavy" taxation of individuals and businesses. With exceptions that will arouse clamorous objection from glandular liberals and the enlarged Democratic majorities in the new Congress, the actual numbers in the budget generally support the assertion of Roy Ash, the departing director of the Office of Management and Budget, that "no program—almost no program—is being cut in absolute amounts that bear upon the poorer people of the country. It is merely a containment of the level of increase in these programs." The rub, of course, is that containing the level of increase subjects the beneficiaries of the affected programs to penalties of inflation that are more severe than those inflicted upon society as a whole.

Here we concentrate upon two programs and an institution that over the years have come to symbolize the federal effort to eliminate or at least alleviate poverty in the United States. The programs are the federally financed and locally operated endeavors that go under the rubric of Community Action and federally funded legal services for poor people. The institution is what until January 4 was the Office of Economic Opportunity and is now the Community Services Administration. Their budget stories are interesting and their treatment at the Ford White House tells a great deal about that establishment and its head, the President. Outwardly, the Ford White House is open, bland and orderly. Inwardly, the legal services story in particular shows it to be secretive, tumultuous and rather disorderly.

In the flush of his 1972 reelection, President Nixon set out in early 1973 to abolish OEO and its biggest and most costly program, Community Action. He tried to do this in two ways. He provided no money for either OEO or community action in his fiscal 1974 budget and he installed Howard Phillips, a Republican troglodyte from Boston, at the head of OEO with orders to dismantle it and its chain of some 900 local community action agencies by June 30. Phillips went about both tasks with sadistic relish. A federal judge found that what he was doing was illegal and that the effort to evade the law requiring OEO directors to be nominated and confirmed by the Senate, by continuing Phillips in office as an unnominated acting director, was also illegal.

A series of subsequent events shook the Nixon White House and provided lessons that were not lost on the Ford White House. Congress refused to abolish OEO and provided funds—$348 million in calendar 1973, $308 million in 1974—to keep it and its principal programs going at least two more years. Alvin Arnett, Phillips' successor and supposed disciple, astounded his associates and enraged Mr. Nixon and some of his staff by proving himself to be a vigorous advocate of both OEO and community action. One of the last acts of the dying Nixon presidency was to fire Arnett in July 1974. But his work had

been done, with lasting effect. He had stumped the land, warning state and local officials that the community action programs in their areas would die if the Nixon administration had its way. Many of these worthies suddenly realized that *their* agencies, however rambunctious and annoying they had been in the early years, had tended to settle down and become buffers between the discontented poor and regular officialdom. The community action bureaucracy—and the Nixon people were quite right in saying there was one, all too often overpaid and underbrained—hired lobbyists to press its cause in Washington. One of the lobbyists was Gerald Ford's friend and former congressional colleague, William C. Cramer of Florida, whose Washington law firm was paid $25,000 a month.

The lobbying, a lot of genuine conviction, and a strong sense in Congress that the federal government has a duty and must have a central instrument to combat poverty paid off on May 29, 1974, with a vote in the House of Representatives that astonished the most hopeful advocates of federal antipoverty action. The House voted 331 to 53 to retain and fund the community action programs. On its face the vote was against OEO as such, but it really wasn't. The proposal voted upon would have abolished OEO and transferred community action to the Department of Health, Education, and Welfare. The saving, subsurface fact was that the size of the majority and the accompanying requirement that community action be administered by an autonomous replacement within HEW indicated a powerful, bipartisan commitment to the principle that OEO represented.

Al Arnett's successor as OEO director, a Colorado Chicano lawyer named Bert A. Gallegos, is rated by some of his best friends in Congress to be nothing better and nothing worse than a pallid, competent caretaker. Even so, he speaks out for an independent antipoverty agency and, without discernible harassment from the Ford White House, is quietly lobbying against the President's declared intention to abolish OEO and transfer its successor, the Community Services Administration, to HEW. The same forces that brought about the 1974 vote compelled the Ford administration to accept a compromise that the President didn't like in December. It renamed OEO the Community Services Administration and left CSA in charge of two principal programs, community action and community economic development. In its compromise provisions, the act permits the President to submit to Congress a reorganization plan that would transfer CSA and community action to HEW and community economic development to the Commerce Department. Normally a presidential reorganization plan dies if it is rejected by a simple majority in either House or Senate. Only a majority vote of both House and Senate can reject the CSA reorganization, the President may veto the rejecting resolution, and a two-thirds vote would then be required in both houses to kill the reorganization and save CSA as an independent agency. The reorganization plan is being drafted. Antipoverty advocates are fairly confident that they can muster simple majorities in both chambers but far from sure that they could muster a two-thirds vote (or four-fifths if a current attempt to change the rules succeeds) in the Senate. As for funding, various figures in the new budget can be read to indicate an increase of about $60 million in recommended 1976 appropriations for CSA. Actually because of technicalities in OEO-CSA funding, the real recommendation remains at around the $308 million provided in fiscal '75.

The legal services story goes back to the early years of the Nixon presidency, and to Richard Nixon's then ascendant and now disgraced and convicted assistant, John Ehrlichman. By 1970, after five years in existence, OEO's Office of Legal Services and the local agencies that it financed and loosely supervised had frightened and offended many state and local officials and bureaucracies. The service had done this by obtaining court rulings that exposed and corrected abuses and deprivations of rights that had generally been taken for granted by all except the poor and disadvantaged people who suffered from them. The result was enormous pressure upon the Johnson and Nixon administrations to terminate or at least curb a federally supported service that, in the most aggravating instances, attacked public policies and entities with public employees—the Legal Services attorneys—and public money. The leading foe of federally supported legal service for the poor was Governor Ronald Reagan of California, a conservative Republican rival whose favor and support the President deemed vital. There were others, among them Congresswoman Edith Green of Oregon, who like most of the critics professed to be for legal services in principle and only against the excesses that occasionally marred a generally good performance.

In dealing with what for them was a serious political problem, Messrs. Nixon and Ehrlichman decided upon an approach that could have been worse and, everything considered, did them credit. Their solution was not an attempt to abolish Legal Services, but instead to get it and the burden of complaints that it generated off the President's back. This they proposed to do by removing the function from OEO, which was a part of the Executive Office of the President, and placing it in an independent and theoretically nonpolitical Legal Services Corporation. Congress limited the President's freedom and power to choose the directors who would set up the corporation to such an extent that he vetoed the first Legal Services Corporation Act. In 1973, when a renewed proposal from the President reached the floor of the House, Mrs. Green attached to it a set of amendments that were so restrictive that they would have gutted the function and the corporation. Gerald Ford, the Republican minority leader, voted for the Green amendment and for the final bill. The Senate refused to accept that bill and a compromise, trading the minimal restrictions that conservative critics of the whole concept insisted upon for the freedom of selection that the President demanded, was signed by Mr. Nixon, in one of his last presidential actions, on July 25, 1974. When he signed the bill he told one of his staff counselors, Dean Burch, that he knew his doing so would "piss off the conservatives" and that it therefore would be politically necessary to include a goodly number of nonenthusiasts among the 11 members of the corporation board of directors to be nominated by the President, subject to Senate confirmation.

Although several hundred names had been suggested for nomination to the corporation board before the bill was passed and signed, the process of serious consideration and selection had barely begun when Mr. Nixon resigned and Gerald Ford replaced him on August 9. There then ensued three and a half months of frantic, mostly hidden activity, controversy and confusion within the Ford establishment. Two circumstances dominated the process and imposed the little order there was in it. The first circumstance was President Ford's view and insistence, identical with his predecessor's, that the initial board be "balanced"—a favorite word of the President's in this connection—between advocates of effective legal services and conservative advocates of a narrowly restricted service. The second circumstance was that Dean Burch, a conservative attorney from Arizona and a friend and ally of Senator Barry Goldwater, was commissioned by President Ford as he had been by President Nixon to oversee and, when necessary, control the selection process. "It was a Burch operation," another assistant who was intimately involved in it said afterward. The accompanying confusion of competing lists and controversy between the proponents of various lists was such that it seemed to some others involved that it was not really anybody's operation. But the assistant who was just quoted was right: it was Dean Burch's and Gerald Ford's operation.

The operation had some odd and revealing aspects. A Ford assistant who might have been expected to be deeply involved and was among the least involved was Philip Buchen, the President's hometown friend, first law partner and senior counsel at the White House. Buchen was not exactly excluded from the process; he had and claimed no particular expertise or experience in publicly provided legal assistance and appears to have wanted as little as possible to do with the selection process. The second of the President's three staff lawyers with the title of White House Counsel, Phillip Areeda, wanted and was denied a major role in the process. He briefly reviewed an interim list of prospective nominees and was appalled by some of the people on it. He had just begun to revise it when he either perceived that the effort was hopeless or was abruptly detached from the operation—both explanations are given at the White House with approximately equal authority. The President's staff chief, Donald Rumsfeld, a former OEO director who in the first Nixon years had much to do with legal services and fired one of the OEO Legal Services directors for what Rumsfeld considered to be insubordination and excessive zeal, was said on the best possible authority to have bowed out of the process and to have turned the whole thing over to Areeda. This simply was not true. Next to Dean Burch, the assistant who was most involved was William Walker, Rumsfeld's appointee as head of the Presidential Personnel Office.

The most revealing and least noticed aspect of the entire business was what happened—or didn't happen—to John Cummiskey, a Grand Rapids attorney and specialist in labor law who is a friend of Buchen's and considers himself to be "a friend and a very strong supporter" of the President. Cummiskey happens to be the only known friend of Gerald Ford who is experienced in and strongly advocates effective legal aid for the poor. He participated in legal aid service in Grand Rapids, the President's hometown, long before federally funded legal assistance was thought of. He headed the American Bar Association's Committee on Legal Aid and Indigent Defendants from 1961 to 1966 and, as a member of the ABA's board of governors from 1968 to 1971, was among the many ABA leaders who vigorously supported an effective federal program. He urged President Nixon to sign the 1974 bill and to appoint directors who genuinely believe in publicly supported legal services. He has not been invited to express his views directly to President Ford and has not done so. He has told his friend Philip Buchen of his desire to be a member of the new Legal Services Corporation board. Cummiskey was not on the list of prospective nominees announced on December 19 and at this writing has had no indication that he will be on the revised list which—as will shortly be explained—is being prepared. According to a White House assistant who was closely involved in putting together the December list, Cummiskey's name was on a preliminary list for a while last September and October and was stricken from it on orders from "surprisingly high authority." I conclude but have not been told that the President had his friend Cummiskey's name removed from the list.

Three people on the December list of intended nominees utterly outraged legal services advocates and activists. They were Denison Kitchel, an Arizona attorney and friend of Burch and Senator Goldwater, who was the President's choice for chairman of the new board; William L. Knecht of California, who was proposed for the board by Governor Reagan and had spearheaded Reagan's fight to eviscerate legal services in California; and Edith Green, who retired from Congress at the end of its last session. These choices were "balanced," as Mr. Ford would say, by several prospects who were thoroughly acceptable to true believers in federal legal services. Among the applauded choices were William T. Coleman, Jr., a respected and black Philadelphia attorney; Dean Abraham Goldstein of the Yale Law School; and Revius O. Ortique, Jr., a black attorney in New Orleans who is president of the National Legal Aid and Defender Association, the principal organized advocate of strong legal services. But the balance was not enough to satisfy legal services supporters who in other matters are as conservative as the President is. One such is William T. Gossett of Detroit, a past president of the ABA and attorney for the Ford Motor Company. Gossett declared his emphatic objections to the December list in a recent conversation with Philip Buchen and in letters to Buchen and the President.

The outcome of the December announcement was closer to farce than tragedy. Denison Kitchel, aged 66, was told—he really was, I'm assured—by his ear doctor that he was too deaf to serve and thereupon asked the President to withdraw his name. Dean Goldstein withdrew because (he says) he's starting a sabbatical year this spring and won't be around during the corporation's formative period. The President nominated William Coleman to be Secretary of Transportation, thereby disqualifying him for service on the board. Benito Moliero Lopez, Jr., a partner in the eminent New York law firm of Dewey, Ballantine, Bushby, Palmer and Wood, who was the last man put on the list and got there principally because Senator Jacob Javits insisted on a New Yorker being on it, withdrew for reasons that nobody at the White House seems to be wholly clear about. Omer W. Franklin, Jr., general counsel to the Georgia State Bar, withdrew ostensibly because his employers required his full-time presence and actually (according to Atlanta supporters of Legal Services) because leaders of the Georgia Bar doubted his fitness for the board. They had long preferred and urged the nomination of Mrs. Betty Knehr, an Atlanta lawyer who has made a career in state-supported legal aid. Edith Green has developed recent doubts that she'd have the time to serve and has written the President to that effect. At the White House on January 27, however, he told a group of civil rights leaders that he was determined to nominate Mrs. Green. At this writing the President's assistants, chiefly Rumsfeld and William Walker, are trying to assemble a revised list that will appear to be less shoddy than the December one but will still be "balanced" in the President's way.

The 1976 Ford budget allows Legal Services, whether still in the Community Services Administration or in the new corporation, the same $71.5 million that it's had since 1973. Congress authorized $90 million for the present fiscal year and

$100 million for fiscal year 1976. According to Legal Services officials, the recommended $71.5 million is bound to result in slow strangulation. One gets an impression that this would not acutely pain the President.

February 15, 1975

———

For improvement in the Legal Services nominees, see Chapter XV.

XIV

Nixon Then and Now

A new book and news accounts from San Clemente depict Richard Nixon as he appeared to one of his White House writers before Watergate destroyed his presidency and as he is in exile and nearly total seclusion six months after his resignation. The book is William Safire's *Before the Fall* (Doubleday; $12.50). The occasion for the San Clemente reports is that the official period of transition from the presidency to pensioned retirement has ended and that, with its end, federal support drops at least until June 30, 1975, to a level that in its paucity and stringency should satisfy the most virulent Nixon haters.

A composite of the San Clemente accounts runs as follows. Mr. Nixon is lonely, ill, frustrated, rambly and disjointed in much of his thoughts and talk. His phlebitis persists, so crippling his left leg that he risks falling if he tries to walk more than a few yards. He is deep in debt—for his oceanside estate; to the IRS for unpaid taxes; to his lawyers—and a publisher's advance for his intended book or books probably won't do much more than meet the expenses of research and writing assistance. A congressional statute and court and White House rulings that make him the first former President to be denied ownership and custody of the presidential papers and (alas for him) the presidential tapes accumulated during his tenure hamper his book project, embitter him and add to his conviction that he is being treated with unprecedented shabbiness.

At the end of the transition on February 9, his federally paid staff fell from about 12 to four: Rose Mary Woods, his long-time confidential secretary, at $36,000 a year, and three other secretaries whose salaries range from $15,059 to $18,061 a year. Prorated over the nearly five months between February 9 and the end of this fiscal year on June 30, the four salaries just about eat up the $45,000 allowed him for staff support and other expenses during that period. His pension of $55,000 for 11 months from last August 9 takes the rest of the $100,000 appropriated for his direct support. The General Services Administration assigns and pays an electrician and two laborers to care for office space on the Coast Guard base adjoining his San Clemente estate. Marjorie Acker, Miss Woods' secretary-assistant, who got $23,500 a year before she went off the federal payroll, is staying on as an "unpaid consultant." Dianne Sawyer, sometime assistant to sometime press secretary Ronald Ziegler, is staying a while as a volunteer. Frank Gannon, a researcher-writer who got a federal salary of $35,300 at the White House, goes on Mr. Nixon's private payroll. Ziegler is leaving. Two army Signal Corps telephone lines and a direct line from the White House switchboard in Washington to the San Clemente offices have been terminated. Things may look up at the start of the next fiscal year, but not much when the support is weighed against the expectations of a former President. The Ford administration recommends in its 1976 budget that Mr. Nixon be paid the pension of $60,000 per year provided by law and allowed the full $96,000 authorized for staff salaries. About $107,000 is recommended for other forms of support (including $55,000 for "rent, communications and utilities" that really goes to GSA rather than to Mr. Nixon for use and maintenance of the San Clemente office space). If Congress is as vengeful as it was when it appropriated $200,000 for the transition and first post-transition periods, it will provide something less than the recommended total of $263,000 for Nixon support in fiscal 1976.

There of course is an immense difference between the sodden gloom reported to prevail at San Clemente and the atmosphere described by William Safire in his "inside view of the pre-Watergate White House." But the difference is far from total. Safire, a former public relations man who was one of three chief speech writers at the White House until March 21, 1973, when he prudently quit to write a column for *The New York Times*, asserts here and there in the prodigious 693 pages of *Before the Fall* that Richard Nixon was in the presidential years a chap of unappreciated humor, gentleness and pleasantry in his best moments. One of Safire's White House jobs, in fact, was to feed lightsome tidbits from the seemingly grim Nixon establishment to receptive reporters and columnists. He finds remarkably few such moments to recount and document in the book. One reason was that Mr. Nixon and his chief of staff, H. R. Haldeman, between them smothered whatever tendency to pleasantry there was. Safire once suggested that somebody "with a light touch"—he had himself in mind—attend private presidential meetings and record examples of Richard Nixon being human. Haldeman grabbed and ruined the notion, organizing teams of "anecdotists" for assignment to the meetings. The result, according to Safire, was that a good idea was "crunched into a superorganized pulp." Haldeman is quoted saying of his role and of the President, "He doesn't want to organize, he wants to *be* organized." Safire says of Haldeman: "His job as chief of staff also included chief of public relations, keeper of the myth, expert on how to influence public opinion. He understood public relations to be the use of techniques to badger, bully, bribe, entice and persuade people to your 'side' . . . The President agreed . . . But the hard sell was not 'PR' . . . As a professional PR man, Haldeman was merely a good ad man." Safire has good to say of Haldeman, particularly that he was Mr. Nixon's "guardian of open options, making certain that the President never received only one view on an issue." A surprising judgment is that John Ehrlichman, arrogant and narrow to the last in the general view, "matured and developed" into "a man of balance and compassion, the 'closet liberal' on many matters."

Safire was one of 13 officials whose home telephones were

tapped, along with those of four journalists, in 1969-70, with the authority of the President and (in Safire's and most other cases) upon the orders of Henry Kissinger and his assistant, Colonel (later General) Alexander Haig. Safire acknowledges that the experience "colors what I write about Kissinger." He says that Kissinger and Haig lied to him when they first denied any knowledge that he'd been tapped and implies that they perjured themselves in their disclaimers under oath before congressional committees. One of Safire's best lines— unfortunately for the overall quality of his mammoth book, he is not very good at characterizing people—occurs in a reference to Kissinger's "ability to project childlike anguish at the reaction of others to actions he had recommended with cold precision."

The eavesdropping was in Safire's view a part and symptom of the malaise that led to Watergate. This malaise, according to Safire, was rooted in the President's hatred of the press. His conviction that "the press is the enemy," the consequent fear of leaks and the desire to prevent and punish leaks brought on the 1969-1970 wiretaps, the attempt to steal Daniel Ellsberg's psychiatric records from his psychiatrist, and finally the Watergate burglary and bugging. Safire thought throughout his White House service that the President "was at bottom realistic about the adversary relationship" between him and the media. "I was wrong about that," Safire writes. He continues: "When Nixon said, 'the press is the enemy,' he was saying exactly what he meant: 'The press is the *enemy*' to be hated and beaten, and in that vein of vengeance . . . lay Nixon's greatest personal and political weakness and the cause of his downfall." In a typical display of ambivalence, a quality that this reporter is in no position to deplore, Safire also writes: ". . . But judging Nixon only by his close-to-irrational animus to the press, or judging him only by the [White House tape] transcripts, is . . . misleading. There is more to this many-faceted man than his worst side. The press that Nixon hated has often over- looked the sympathetic and even noble side of this President, for good reason—because it was faced with the most mean- spirited and ignoble side."

Safire refuses to discuss a telephone conversation that he had with Mr. Nixon in December, on the last day that changes in the text were possible, except to say that he picked up a few pieces of information. A paraphrased passage and a direct quotation near the end of the book read as if they came from this conversation or perhaps from previous talks with Mr. Nixon. The passage: "Why did Nixon permit the tapings of himself in the first place? Because he was convinced left-leaning historians would try to deny him his place in history; because he wanted to write memoirs better than Churchill's; and because he was sure he would have the same total control of his tapes as Kennedy and Johnson had of theirs. [A snide line, presumably reflecting Richard Nixon's snidery; Kennedy and Johnson did not tape on anywhere near the Nixon scale.] Why didn't he destroy them when Alex Butterfield revealed their existence to the Ervin committee? Because Nixon thought that such an act would make him look guilty, because he did not realize how bad the tapes' transcripts would appear in cold print, and because he was certain the wall of presidential privacy could not be breached . . . To this day, Nixon cannot understand why he was pilloried for acts that he considers no different than those condoned by his predecessors . . . And the actual decision that brought him down—to use the CIA to block the FBI investigation of the Watergate break-in—was, he still feels, a legitimate act to prevent disclosure of related national security surveillances."

The quotation: "There may be some understanding and perspective some day," he told a friend as the year of his resignation drew to a close, "but it will take a long, long time. I'm a fatalist."

William Safire's judgment of his patron, friend and leader: "In time, the grisly deception will be seen in the light of great achievements, but those who invested their lives in the causes he shared will never forget that Nixon failed, not while daring greatly, but while lying meanly."

February 22, 1975

———

The government support authorized by law for ex-Presidents

and voted by Congress, his publisher's provision of a small staff
to research and help write a book due for publication in 1977,
and deals for serialization and television interviews enabled Mr.
Nixon to fare better than seemed likely in early 1975. Of the
people named above, only Dianne Sawyer and Frank Gannon
were with him in late 1976. Dianne left in 1977.

XV

Ford's Image Machine

This report deals with two of 19 specific actions that President Ford took and announced during the week of February 10 and with the elaborate public relations apparatus—his image machine—that exists to put the best possible appearance upon everything he does.

One of the actions discussed here, the revision of a list of prospective nominees to the board of a new Legal Services Corporation that is supposed to begin providing federally financed legal asistance to poor people some time in 1975, was so quickly and rightly praised in hitherto critical quarters that it didn't need the ministrations of Mr. Ford's publicists. The other action, an unprecedented gift of power and position to Vice President Nelson Rockefeller, was so baffling in its nature and implications that the President's spokesmen didn't try to explain it. Press Secretary Ronald Nessen, the President's principal image machinist, was excluded months ago from the discussions that preceded the event and privately confessed utter ignorance of how it came about.

The praise accorded the replacement of five of the 11 original choices for the legal services board was in part an expression of relief, a reflection of the suspicion among advocates of effective legal aid for the poor that the Ford administration is fundamentally hostile to such federal programs. Three of the tentative choices announced last December 19—conservative attorneys Denison Kitchel of Arizona and William Knecht of California, and former Congresswoman Edith Green of Oregon—appeared to confirm this view. Although Knecht and Mrs. Green remain on the revised list, the five "preliminary selections" announced February 14 were considered to assure a board majority that would be friendly or at least not downright opposed to adequate legal services. Two critics of the December list, President James D. Fellers of the American Bar Association and Executive Director James Flug of the National Legal Aid and Defender Association, welcomed the changes. Fellers said that the replacements "are excellent choices" with "the kind of positive approach to legal services which is so necessary if the program is to be all we hope for it." The potential nominee who is principally responsible for the plaudits is Mr. Ford's new choice for chairman of the corporation board, Dean Roger C. Cramton of the Cornell University law school. Cramton, aged 45, is remembered in Washington as a tough-minded assistant attorney general who got himself fired by Richard Nixon in early 1973 for refusing to say that Mr. Nixon's impoundment of nine billion dollars in funds appropriated to clean up waterways was legal. The US Supreme Court unanimously held on February 18, as Cramton had asserted in 1972, that the impoundment was illegal; Cramton made his low opinion of some of the people on the December list known to the President's personnel director, William Walker, and through him to Mr. Ford's staff chief, Donald Rumsfeld. They responded by challenging Cramton to accept a nomination and the chairmanship and he rather unhappily assented. The most interesting of the other additions is Robert J. Kutak, an Omaha attorney who blends practical liberalism with ideological conservatism. He is a former assistant and still a friend of conservative Senator Roman Hruska and, in his liberal guise, chairman of the ABA's Committee on Individual Rights and Responsibilities.

The possibility that President Ford might appoint a

Rockefeller man executive director of the Domestic Council and assistant to the President for domestic affairs was reported in *The New Republic*'s February 1 issue. Despite misgivings and opposition among the President's senior staff to so substantial a delegation of presidential power to the Vice President, Mr. Ford announced his decision to do this and more on February 13. James Cannon, a former journalist who hitherto has been more concerned with Rockefeller politics than with Rockefeller policies and programs, was appointed council director and assistant to the President. Richard Dunham, another Rockefeller assistant, was appointed deputy director. Mr. Ford simultaneously issued a somewhat flowery restatement of the council's mission. The council itself, composed of domestic department and agency heads, hasn't met since December of 1971 and has never amounted to much. It's the council staff of 30 people, including 15 functional assistants, that matters. Along with some Rockefeller-type rhetoric about "assessing national needs and identifying alternative ways of meeting them," the Ford statement adds one thing of substance to what the council staff has been doing. Rockefeller as the council vice chairman and what will soon be his staff are given a specific role in the Office of Management and Budget's reviews of proposed legislation and in the extremely important policy aspects of budget-making. Rather uneasily and without great conviction, some of the President's people point out that James Cannon is to be assistant *to the President* and that Press Secretary Nessen wasn't talking idly when he emphasized in his announcement that "the President considers the Domestic Council [sic] an integral part of the White House staff." Just in case Cannon was in any doubt on the point, he was gently told to move himself out of Rockefeller country in the Old Executive Office Building and across the street into the West Wing of the White House, where Mr. Ford's senior assistants have their offices. Whatever Mr. Ford hopes to gain from the business, and what he can expect to gain apart from Nelson Rockefeller's gratitude is a mystery to me. He incurred a serious loss in the person of Phillip Areeda, since last September the second in rank among three attorneys with the title of White House Counsel. Areeda, a Harvard law professor and specialist in antitrust law, was one of the very few people at the Ford White House who had some claim to distinction before coming there. His intention to quit unless he got a suitable assignment was reported here several weeks ago. Areeda thought he was promised the Domestic Council directorship and resigned when he learned that he wouldn't get it. My impression, unsupported by any concrete evidence or statement, is that his basic reason for leaving was more subtle and more significant than the mere denial of a job he wanted. I suspect that Phillip Areeda suffered the frustrations of a first-rate talent who found himself submerged among and subordinated to associates whom he considered second-raters.

The most cogent point to be made about Press Secretary Ronald Nessen, the mechanic in charge of the biggest part of the Ford image machine, is made in conversation by Nessen himself. He says: "I think you ought to separate my personality out from what we do here. Okay, I have a temper and I've lost it a couple of times. And so what? I don't think that should completely obscure our accomplishments." Separating and setting aside Ron Nessen's personality is a pleasure. Suffice it to say that in his public performance he is good natured most of the time, temperish and petty a little of the time, and positively cloying some of the time. His calculated displays of good humor take the form of what Nessen calls "my allegedly terrible one-line jokes." He is sensitive about any personal reference, whether it's intended to be favorable or unfavorable, and he is especially sensitive to cracks about his cracks. A recent example: "Happy Valentine Day. It even gets the press secretary out here [to the briefing room podium] on time." Nessen is obsessed with the escapist notion that his principal problem is neither himself nor his President but the poisoned press room atmosphere that he found in the wake of Watergate and Ronald Ziegler. He furthers this idea when he says that his jokes "are not meant to be a night-club act. They are meant to relax the place. It's a delicate effort to change the mood of the place." The mood has changed, for the better. But the White House press room should never be a really happy place and, fortunately for all concerned, neither Nessen nor any other press secretary can make it so. There is a fundamental, unavoidable conflict between press secretaries and the press and Nessen frets about it more than he should.

President Ford said of Nessen in Nessen's presence the other day, "I think he's doing a helluva good job." Nessen groaned in mock dismay, "Oh, God, there goes my credibility." On the whole, though many in the press room would disagree, the facts support the President's judgment. Nine press conferences in six months, a dozen or so individual interviews, and many more background conversations, quickie chats with reporters and editors, and group sessions with television, radio and printed media news executives constitute, as Nessen says, a record of presidential access that Richard Nixon neither wanted nor tried to match. The question is what of substance comes out of it all, and the answer is very little.

Nessen's establishment, including peripheral staffs and activities that were under President Nixon's directors of communication, has been reduced in personnel from 58 to 45. It includes two deputy Press secretaries, six assistant press secretaries, two television advisers and five photographers. One of the deputy secretaries, Gerald Warren, four of the six assistant secretaries, and three of the five photographers are survivors from the Nixon time. Mrs. Ford's press secretary, Sheila Weidenfeld; her assistant, Patti Matson; and their office secretary, Nancy Cherdon, operate independently of Nessen but accept without exactly welcoming occasional guidance from him. Gerald Warren, two assistant press secretaries and three other assistants at "professional" levels have three principal functions. They are seeing to it that department and agency officials and press spokesmen understand and accurately reflect administration policy as it is stated and amended by the President and Nessen; correcting and countering what Warren considers to be errors of fact or judgment in printed and broadcast comment; and providing print and broadcast journalists outside of Washington with the nearest possible equivalent of the information, propaganda and official briefings that journalists in Washington get. Preparing the President's daily news summary, a Nixon service retained by Mr. Ford, may have been put in Warren's bailiwick when this is read.

Warren works closely with William Baroody, Jr., another Nixon survivor who glories in the title of "assistant for public liaison." Saying so causes shudders at the White House, but the fact is that Baroody has taken over, consolidated and more or less cleaned up the group contact function that Charles Colson developed and corrupted. Baroody and his staff of 30, including some 15 "professionals," organize White House seminars in Washington and around the country and try to maintain friendly communications with leadership types among blacks, hispanics, labor unions, women's groups, educators and any other categories that can be conveniently packaged. The Baroody operation demonstrates among other things that thousands of Americans are glad to travel at their own or their organizations' expense to Washington and to regional centers in order to hear administration spokesmen, occasionally including the President, expound and defend administration policy. Baroody would argue that he isn't a cog in the President's image machine. "What I'm doing," he says, "is not public relations, though there's a lot of that in what I do. Probably the fundamental is *process*—a process where the private sector is given access to government equal to that of the press and Congress."

Because of what it tells about Gerald Ford, the part of the Nessen function that interests me most is the White House photographic operation. Its director and the President's personal photographer, 27-year-old David Hume Kennerly, acknowledges with discernible pain that his shop is a part of the Nessen shop, structurally speaking. That's as far as he will go, in words and in practice. "I don't work for Nessen," Kennerly says. "I work for the President—period." Kennerly is a former *Time* photographer who won a Pulitzer prize in 1972 for pictures taken in Vietnam and India and covered Vice President Ford for *Time*. He was the first staffer hired by Mr. Ford when he became President last August. The President and the Ford family are extremely fond of Kennerly—as fond of him as he is of himself if that be possible. Although Kennerly exaggerates the differences, his access to President Ford is much more complete than the access of his predecessor, Ollie Atkins, was to President Nixon. "Ollie was summoned to take pictures,"

Kennerly says. "I'm never summoned. I'm always there. I'm probably the only guy who can walk into that office without being asked. I go in and out." He says that either he or, on rare occasions, another staff photographer has recorded literally every meeting that President Ford has had and that he stays throughout most of them. Ollie Atkins snapped a few pictures and then left. According to Kennerly, the President asked him beforehand to leave only two meetings after taking one or two pictures for the record, "and they were when he was telling a couple of guys they didn't have jobs any more." Both Kennerly and Nessen say that Mr. Ford shows absolutely no interest in the photographs taken of him, never calls for prints and never suggests that a certain picture be hung on White House walls. Nixon showed some interest; Lyndon Johnson was an avid viewer and critic of his staff photographs. Gerald Ford's alleged indifference is interesting precisely because he lets so many pictures be taken by so many photographers. Kennerly has arranged unprecedented access to Mr. Ford by other photographers. Fred Ward, a Washington free-lance, had nearly total access to the President and the inner offices of the White House for two months. The result, a picture book with text by Hugh Sidey, *Time's* White House columnist, will be published by Harper & Row in May. Kennerly says that at least 20 other magazine and newspaper photographers have had generous and unusual access to the President, though none in this or any other presidency has had the equal of Fred Ward's free and prolonged run. Photographers aiming at book and magazine publication are especially welcomed and get the best treatment. It's something to remember, as I've previously noted, when you come upon accounts of good old, plain old Jerry Ford, running around in baggy suits with dog-biscuit crumbs in his pockets and not caring a whit about his image.

March 1, 1975

XVI

Pressing Congress

If the perceptions and judgments that prevailed at the White House in early March of 1975 prove to be correct, and they probably will, the period between then and the turn of last November-December will be remembered as the time when it ceased to be possible for a reporter to write in fairness, as I did in late December, that "Gerald Ford is an awfully nice man who is not up to the presidency." In that period, with the formulation of his economic and energy programs and his handling of them in a doubting, fractious and heavily Democratic Congress, and his general handling of himself as a person and a President, Mr. Ford convinced an impressive variety of politicians, officials, journalists and concerned citizens that he is indeed "up to the presidency." Evidence that this is so is also evidence that Gerald Ford in this time at least began to surmount the enormous handicap inherent in the fact the he was the first Vice President and is the first President who entered the two offices by appointment and without a national constituency.

Senator Mike Mansfield of Montana, the Democratic majority leader, put in *The Congressional Record* of February 27, with unusually prominent display on the first page of the Senate section of that day's issue, a Wall Street Journal columnist's lyrical testament that "Maybe a lot of us are being too rough on Jerry Ford . . . Mr. Ford is not only a lot smarter than his critics suggest, but he's also an unusually honest and straightforward man, of considerable personal and professional integrity." Although Mr. Ford should "be judged primarily on policies and performance," the columnist continued, "it would be wrong and unfair if his more personal contributions to the American presidency were slighted or ignored." Two respected Washington correspondents, Lou Cannon of *The Washington Post* and Martin Schram of the Long Island, NY, *Newsday*, stayed in Florida after Mr. Ford went there for one of his rounds of regional seminars and press conferences (along, in that instance, with an afternoon's play in a crassly commercial golf tournament). After interviewing people who had met and heard the President, Cannon and Schram reported that they found heightened respect for him and moderately increased support for his programs. At his Florida press conference the President was asked in successive questions whether he'd recommend a change in the 25th Amendment to the Constitution, under which he was appointed to the vice presidency and succeeded to the presidency, and whether "you feel any handicap for not having won a presidential election?" They were touchy questions and they could have elicited a display of the nervousness that Mr. Ford in fact feels on both scores at times. Instead the questions induced a display of total confidence. The President's response to the first question was, "I guess I could say it worked pretty well this time," and to the second, "The answer is no." Image manufacture of the kind discussed in a previous report was involved here, but the effect was valid.

Before the President's economic and energy programs were announced in a televised speech on January 13 and his State of the Union speech to Congress on January 15, he and some of his associates, official and unofficial, went through two months of grueling preparation and debate. The resultant programs were so complicated, especially on the energy side, that they are poorly understood to this day. It is enough to say here that the energy proposal rested essentially on two devices: reducing the consumption of imported petroleum and other scarce fuels by increasing their prices rather than by arbitrary quota and allocation; and returning to the consuming public and industry in tax rebates, tax reductions and direct grants the many billions of dollars (30 to 46, depending on how it's figured) that the President's tariff and tax measures would annually suck out of the economy. A combination of rebates to individuals from tax payments on calendar 1974 incomes and of increased investment credits to business, including agriculture, would reinject about $16 billion into the ailing economy during 1975. This anti-recession proposal was simpler and easier to understand than the energy program, a fact that caused some uneasiness within the Ford councils and led to insistence by staff chief Donald Rumsfeld, among others, that the controversy between Congress and the administration over the energy proposals not be allowed to obscure (as it did for awhile) the President's concern that an immediate tax reduction and rebate of some sort be quickly enacted.

In the period of formulation before January 13-15, Mr. Ford was warned by some of his advisers (among them Bryce Harlow, a corporate and presidential lobbyist who's been in and out of Republican White Houses since the Eisenhower administration) that the future of his presidency, in this mini-term by succession and in a full elective term if he goes for it next year, would turn upon whether he let the new Congress, not only Democratic but infused with a dismaying number of feisty freshman representatives, run over him and his programs. If he allowed this to happen, Mr. Ford was told and no doubt was quite capable of concluding for himself, he'd be finished, a doormat, a sad-sack President until he was displaced on January 20, 1977.

He prepared himself against this eventuality in two ways. First, he and his people wrote into his State of the Union address and the televised speech that preceded it, and into formal legislative proposals, escape language designed to sanctify every likely and conceivable compromise that he might be called upon to make. Thus what was widely interpreted to be faltering and weakness when he excepted New England and Florida from the impact of higher imported fuel costs, and farmers from higher costs of fertilizers derived from petroleum, had actually been foreseen and provided in the fine print of his proposals. Second and more importantly, he set out in the initial speeches, in every subsequent public statement on the subject, and in the daily pronouncements of his spokesmen, to prod and goad congressional Democrats with the assertion, first and accurately, that he had a program and they didn't, and when they finally began to come up with bits and pieces of alternative programs, that he still had the only comprehensive and coherent one. He, as a 25-year veteran of the House, must have known that in getting a tax relief bill (not his, but a variant that was acceptably close to his proposal) through the House committee stage and bringing Senate and House Democrats close to agreement on an energy alternative, the legislators were acting with better than average speed. Yet, as late as February 26 in Florida, he moaned that "I am really perplexed" by the failure to produce a finished tax bill and to convene Senate and House committee hearings on energy proposals. It was all calculated. It was marred, at the White House end, by a few bobbles such as baffling but relatively minor differences between Press Secretary Ron Nessen's and the President's evaluations of a House Ways and Means Committee energy proposal as "a basis for compromise." On the whole, however, it was a skillful performance. In a burst of smartly figured compromise on March 4, the President vetoed a House-Senate bill that would have deferred for 90 days his authority to impose additional tariffs on imported oil and postponed two stages of the previously ordered increase for 60 days.

Whatever the consequences, and they are in doubt at this writing, two elements of the Ford performance and its impact should be kept in mind. First, his strictures upon Congress were expressed civilly and within bounds that should prevent lasting scars. Seventy of 75 first-term House Democrats breakfasted with the President at the White House on March 4 and emerged as if bewitched, praising his courtesy and his asserted wish to cooperate with them rather than fight them. Second, the Democrats as a group were going beyond what the President wanted to do in the way of tax reduction and federal spending for economic stimulation. But, in the energy area where lasting impact upon the economy and the society is likely to be had, they in early March were inclining toward rather than away from his fundamental policy of minimizing arbitrary federal controls and relying instead upon market and price mechanisms to get and keep energy consumption within practicable bounds. The President and his programs appeared to be in better shape than many Washington observers, this writer included, thought a month ago that they could be.

March 15, 1975

———

Sad to say, "the President and his programs" appeared to me to be in a damn sight better shape then they actually were when I perpetrated the concluding sentence of this report.

XVII

Ford and Rocky

This report on how the President and his assistants dealt with a couple of their problems in late February and early March continues an effort to convey some notion of how the Ford presidency is developing in its eighth month.

The assistant principally considered here, Vice President Nelson Rockefeller, presumably won't mind being identified in that way. He professes to regard himself and to want others to regard him as nothing more and nothing less than a loyal assistant to President Ford. On a plane flying back to Washington from Detroit the other night, and at a press conference the next day in New York, reporters irritated him with questions assuming that he still hopes to be President and has thoughts of standing for the Republican nomination next year or in 1980. Understandably enough, since he's 66, the reference to 1980 particularly annoyed him. He brought hundreds of letters and telegrams from outraged moralists upon himself by saying on the plane, into a network microphone, that "I don't think anyone gives a good God damn, if you'll forgive me, about 1980 politics." All he was doing and wanted to do, he said, was "help the President" solve "the problems we face today."

One of the President's other assistants took the Vice President literally, in a rather wry fashion, in the course of discussing Mr. Ford's unprecedented grant of full authority over the Domestic Council staff to Rockefeller. Two of the Vice President's chief assistants, James Cannon and Richard Dunham, have been appointed respectively executive director and deputy director of the council staff and Cannon has also been appointed assistant to the President for domestic affairs. When the Ford assistant was asked whether the President looks upon Cannon as an assistant to him or to the Vice President, the President's man answered in effect: "What difference does it make? The President regards *the Vice President* as his assistant for domestic affairs. Jim Cannon and Nelson Rockefeller are assistants to Gerald Ford and that's that."

Cannon, Dunham and James Cavanaugh, who was deputy director of the council staff in the last Nixon years and shares both the title and an office suite with Dunham, have tentatively divided their duties among themselves in an interesting way. Cannon has assumed overall direction of the council staff, clears papers on domestic policy before they go to the President through White House staff chief Donald Rumsfeld, and attends Rumsfeld's senior staff meeting at 8 o'clock each weekday morning. Cannon also spends a good deal of time with the Vice President. They were together much of the morning of March 11, for instance, before Rockefeller joined the President at a conference on economic and energy matters and then rode up to Capitol Hill in a White House Cadillac to lunch with Republican senators and preside over the Senate for awhile. Cavanaugh concentrates upon legislative and other domestic problems of current concern to the President and presides over the council staff's daily meeting at 7:30 am. Richard Dunham, who was New York state budget director during Rockefeller's last years as governor, attends a meeting of the President's economic advisers at 8:30 each morning and, in his council work, is perfecting plans to devote more of its time and energies to the long-range problems that Rockefeller loves to ponder and discuss. Two other members of the Rockefeller staff, Richard

Parsons and Arthur Quern, have been transferred to the Domestic Council staff and the White House payroll. The four slots on the Vice President's staff that have been vacated by Cannon, Dunham, Parsons and Quern are very welcome. Thanks in part to Donald Rumsfeld's insistence upon cutting the White House establishment, including the Vice President's smallish part of it, by an overall average of 10 percent, the Rockefeller managers haven't found the money to pay for transcripts of his speeches, news conferences and other statements. In that respect, a point of major concern only to the press, the richest Vice President in history provides the poorest service in memory.

The aforementioned Richard Parsons figured importantly in an episode that was of great concern to Mr. Ford and that the Vice President recalls and recounts with immense pleasure. This was the Senate debate, lasting many weeks and concluded on March 7, over whether and how to change the rule that since 1917 has required the approval of two-thirds of the senators present and voting to end a filibuster. In his capacity as President of the Senate—his and all Vice Presidents' only constitutional duty, apart from waiting for Presidents to quit or die—Rockefeller presided at crucial stages of the debate and with his rulings on parliamentary questions greatly influenced the outcome. Without getting into the burdensome details of a very complex subject, an exercise that Rockefeller will engage in as long as a listener will put up with him and it, the situation may be briefly described as follows. A group of more or less "liberal" senators—notably Mondale of Minnesota, Pearson of Kansas, Cranston of California, Javits of New York—undertook to reduce the requirement from two-thirds to three-fifths of senators present and voting. Senate conservatives of both parties, led by the technically Democratic Senator James Allen of Alabama, rallied against the effort to change what they rightly regard as a fundamental protection of minority rights in a body that, unlike the House, has been designed since the founding of the nation to restrict the power of simple minorities and enable numerical minorities, on occasion a minority of one, to delay and obstruct and even to prevent actions that a majority may favor. Filibusters, of course meaning prolonged talk to keep issues from coming to a vote, are by no means the exclusive property of conservatives. Liberals use them, too. But the right to filibuster is dearer to conservatives than to liberals and, for reasons that go back to and precede the Goldwater nomination and campaign of 1964, Nelson Rockefeller is personally and peculiarly hated by rock-hard conservative Republicans. Tradition and prejudice thus combined to embitter this year's debate over changing the cloture rule and the reaction to Rockefeller's role in it.

Richard Parsons is 28 years old, black, and in Rockefeller's opinion an extraordinarily brilliant lawyer. He was on Governor Rockefeller's legal staff in New York, accompanied Vice President Rockefeller to Washington, and served as Rockefeller's personal parliamentarian before and throughout the cloture debate. The Senate's official parliamentarian, Murray Zweven, also coached the Vice President. But it's Parsons who stars in Rockefeller's account. The Vice President displays with pride an elaborate chart that Parsons drew up in advance, marking every stage of two different routes that a cloture debate might take, one involving a series of decisions by majority vote and the other an equivalent set of decisions by two-thirds vote. Rockefeller also displays a stack of statements that he and Parsons prepared in advance, for every conceivable eventuality. Apart from his natural interest in the matter as a conservative member of Congress for 25 years, Mr. Ford had a profound interest in holding the support of conservative senators, Republican and Democratic, on such upcoming legislative issues as his veto of a bill that would have limited his authority to increase tariffs on imported oil. Both his inclination and his immediate interest therefore were to preserve the two-thirds rule. Rockefeller's inclination was to favor the proposed modification whenever he could, subject to his basic conviction that the Senate itself should determine the central questions. His rulings consistently infuriated opponents of the change. Senators Allen, Barry Goldwater, Jesse Helms of North Carolina and Russell Long of Louisiana denounced him. Senator John Tower of Texas visited President Ford on February 27 and told him he was going to lose vital Republican support if he didn't curb the Vice President. Recalling Tower's action later, Rockefeller growled, "I don't take kindly to blackmail."

Rockefeller's and the President's accounts of Mr. Ford's role agree in substance but differ in nuance. At a press conference on March 6, Mr. Ford said it would have been "inappropriate" for him to interfere with the Vice President's "constitutional responsibility" by telling him how to rule "and therefore I did not." Rockefeller said to me: "I went to the President in January and told him this was coming up and it was hot. I asked him if there was an administration policy on it. I told him that he had two choices. He could say there was an administration policy and then I of course would follow it. Or he could say that it was my constitutional responsibility and that he should stay out of it." Mr. Ford probably would have stayed out of it anyhow, but Rockefeller clearly weighted his inquiry in that direction. When he was asked whether the President indicated any regret or annoyance because some of his supporters were angered, Rockefeller answered, "No, never—*never!* The President is a gutsy guy, a real gutsy guy."

On March 7 the Senate changed the requirement from two-thirds of senators present and voting to three-fifths of all 100 senators. Hereafter, 60 senators may end a filibuster. It thus will be a little easier to do than it's been since 1917.

March 22, 1975

XVIII

Ford and Crisis

Here is an account of how the President and some of his assistants conducted themselves in late March and early April, a time of severe crisis at home and abroad and a time, too, of test and reexamination of both domestic and foreign policy.

For Mr. Ford and his closest assistants, it was a time of paradox in their personal relationships and in their views of each other. He seemed to some of his assistants to be ever surer of himself, ever firmer in his decisions, less and less inhibited by his previously acute awareness that he is the nation's first appointed and unelected President. He seemed, in short, to the people around him to be "more presidential" with every passing day. Secretary of State Henry Kissinger, whose policies and performance confronted the President with some of his most difficult problems and choices, marveled to other officials and to reporters at Mr. Ford's serenity, his calm acceptance of trouble and his cool search for remedies. Yet at this same time and among these same people there was more dispute about what the President should do, more doubt of his judgment and more questioning of his choices and decisions than there had been since he succeeded Richard Nixon.

The differences around the President ranged from the momentous to the trivial. All of them were indicative of the way in which he and his presidency were developing. His decision to sign rather than veto the messy tax reduction bill that Congress presented to him in late March was preceded by a sharp division among his counsellors that was widely reported and readily confirmed by his spokesmen. Chairman Arthur Burns of the Federal Reserve Board and Treasury Secretary William Simon urged him to veto the bill. Chairman Alan Greenspan of the Council of Economic Advisers and the President's long-time friend and staff economics counsellor, L. William Seidman, urged him to sign it. The interesting thing was that the outcome represented the President's first decision to do something of importance that he believed to be wrong. His behavior during his first weeks in the presidency indicated that he entered the office in the hope that at long last, after 25 years of bargaining and equivocation in the House of Representatives, he would have the power and the freedom to do in large matters only what he believed to be right. His pardon of Richard Nixon was the first sign of his determination to behave in that fashion. His early vetoes, made with very little consideration of whether they would or wouldn't be sustained, brought upon him much admonition from the Republican floor leaders, Senator Hugh Scott and Representative John Rhodes, to the effect that he had to heed political and congressional reality more than he was initially inclined to do. His signing of the tax bill completed his retreat from the arbitrary standard of rightness that he had set for himself. He was prepared to accept, as he said, the net revenue reduction of $23 billion rather than the $16 billion he had recommended. But his distaste for the extraneous amendments added to the reduction itself and for the threats of truly monstrous deficits that the total bill enhanced was so strongly expressed, to congressional leaders and to his assistants, that several of his own people thought 24 hours before he announced his decision to sign that he was going to veto and insist that Congress enact an early, uncluttered substitute of the kind he had originally proposed.

His resolution of other differences suggested that "more presidential" could be interpreted to mean "more stubborn."

Several of his assistants, for instance, believed and told him that he was making a mistake in dashing off to Palm Springs, California for an Easter weekend and a following week of vacation in millionaire style, at the home of a millionaire friend, right after signing the tax cut bill, while South Vietnam and Cambodia were crumbling under military attack, and just after his and Henry Kissinger's Middle East policy had fallen apart. By the Friday noon before his departure from Washington, his determination to go anyway had been so clearly and crisply indicated that the only question remaining was when he should go. Press Secretary Ronald Nessen suggested in the last of several memos on the subject that Mr. Ford at least let a decent interval elapse between signing the unsatisfactory tax bill and flying to California. The President brushed the suggestion aside and left when he'd intended to. Mr. Ford saw some acrid cartoons and commentaries, contrasting his play in the desert sun with his professions of sympathy for the human suffering and horror being portrayed in television reports from Vietnam. His associates gathered that he was sorry critics felt that way but he really didn't give a damn. Nessen never mentioned in his public briefings in Washington, though he did mention privately to a few reporters, a fact that if publicized could have taken some of the edge off the criticism. The minimized fact was that this was the Ford family's ninth Easter in Palm Springs. The place is a habit with Gerald Ford, a habit he wasn't about to break. The reason for obscuring the fact could have been that from the millionaire friend's house where he stayed this time he could look down on the lush, synthetic oasis of the Walter Annenberg estate, where President Nixon arranged for him to stay last year. Reminders of Gerald Ford's prior identity with Richard Nixon are not in fashion at the Ford White House. Assurances that the President wasn't sponging were in fashion. He paid $100 a day to the friend who owned the Palm Springs house and vacated it for the Fords. A three-bedroom suite at the Tennis Club Hotel, one of many luxury hostelries in the vicinity, would have cost $165 a day.

There were small signs of a certain defensiveness in contrast with the show and, in my view, the fact of growing presidential posture and firmness. There were several side trips to San

Francisco, San Diego and Las Vegas for speeches, a press conference, a conference of community leaders, and the like. Two of them were to the Elk Hills naval oil reserve, which is soon to be opened to commercial exploitation in the name of energy independence, and to a cluster of natural geysers north of San Francisco. Murmurs that the Elk Hills visit was nothing but a show for media purposes caused Nessen to say that reporters who thought so were welcome to pass up a subsequent visit to the geysers, where a modest amount of geothermal power is derived. The President was going, Nessen said, with or without reporters and cameramen. All of them went, in rain and misery and to no great purpose. Another side trip was from Palm Springs to the San Francisco international airport, where Mr. Ford greeted 325 Vietnamese orphans who arrived on a privately chartered Boeing 747. A few reporters were privileged to stand for an hour in a driving rain in order to watch the President lug two orphans down the plane ramp and into an army bus. The laudable purpose was to dramatize the President's and the country's sympathy for the victims of the Vietnam tragedy. In the Ford entourage after the trip, there was an uneasy feeling that it had been a mistake. Some of the organizers of the event had made it clear that they regarded the President's presence as an unnecessary complication in an already complicated situation. Besides, it was poorly timed for national television notice. What I as one of the few reporters present got out of it was colossally unimportant proof that Mr. Ford had the same look of benign concern when he carried the orphans down the ramp that he displayed when he gazed upon 3500 broadcasters and wives whom he addressed in Las Vegas on his way back to Washington.

Foreign affairs, or rather the progressive collapse of the United States position in Cambodia and South Vietnam, dominated the news during the Palm Springs week despite Mr. Ford's efforts to keep at least a portion of public attention focused upon the threat—very dire and very real, in my opinion—of more and truly disastrous inflation if the fiscal 1976 deficit is not held reasonably near the $60 billion that the President is prepared to tolerate. In what follows it is assumed that readers have had their fill of the rhetoric in speeches and at press conferences with which the President and Henry Kissinger have announced and reiterated their refusal to "furl the flag" and have asserted their belief that the world is in as great and widespread a need of United States leadership as it's ever been since World War II. The purpose here is briefly to summarize reasons for suspecting that a much broader recognition of change both in the world and in the United States stance toward the world is in process at the peak of American policy than is evident in the rhetoric, and that a change in the relationship that Henry Kissinger has enjoyed with two Presidents, Nixon and Ford, is also in process.

My chief reason for suspecting a greater change in the American stance than the rhetoric indicates is that the rhetoric is so worn, so extreme and so irrelevant to manifest public and congressional attitudes that it would have to be adjudged downright irrational if it were not in fact intended to provide a sort of protective preparation and cover for the very shrinkage of United States responsibility and influence that the President has been saying he will not permit or encourage. A secondary reason is knowledge that within the Ford establishment there is a belief, embryonic at this point but growing, that the President in his own interest and in the interest of creating public belief that there is a *Ford* policy must somehow disassociate himself from policies that are indelibly identified with Henry Kissinger and Richard Nixon. In Palm Springs my attention was authoritatively called to a passage in a *Chicago Tribune* interview with Mr. Ford last February 9. When the President was asked, "Did you ever think what would happen to our foreign policy if something should happen to Dr. Kissinger?," Mr. Ford was seen by two people who were present to tense up and answer with unusual emphasis. He said in part: "I think first we are lucky to have a man of that outstanding capability available during this very critical period. I don't know just how the decisions were made before I became President, but I can tell you that the final decisions in these cases today are made by me. I get recommendations or I get options from him or from the National Security Council, so that although he is extremely valuable and I think most important, it doesn't mean that he makes the decisions."

Mr. Ford asked Kissinger to stay and Kissinger promised on March 24 to stay through the present term. But that was only a phase of a continuing process of change. In Palm Springs and then in Washington, on the probably specious claim that he'd been "misinformed" by an NSC assistant, Nessen opened an attack on the Kissinger system of keeping the White House press staff informed on foreign policy matters that no press secretary would have dared to attempt a few months ago. At a party in Palm Springs, Mr. Ford was overheard saying to Nessen something like: "I've taken care of that. How often do I have to tell you, *he* is not the President. *I* am the President." An official who was privy to the conversation said later that it concerned Henry Kissinger and a matter other than the aforementioned staff flap.

April 19, 1975

———

For more on the Ford-Kissinger relationship, see the next chapter.

XIX

Kissinger and Ford

The Sunday night before President Ford returned to Washington from Palm Springs, with a stopover at Las Vegas to address the National Association of Broadcasters, the White House staff and Secretary of State Henry Kissinger's assistants understood that Kissinger would bypass Las Vegas and fly straight back to Washington. He didn't. When a line of White House and association officials preceded the President to the speaker's table in Las Vegas, there was Henry, bowing and smiling with evident pleasure and looking as if he were not at all surprised by the standing ovation that he received from the audience. The ovation gave Mr. Ford cause to open an otherwise dreary speech, one that was acknowledged later in Washington to have been "a throwaway," with the following tribute: "Let me personally express my appreciation for the very warm welcome and reception that you have given to our great Secretary of State, a person of unbelievable wisdom and, I think, the finest background and knowledge in the field of foreign policy of anybody in my lifetime and, of course, his indefatigable dedication."

This effusion occurred at a time of gathering crisis in the

world—in Vietnam and Cambodia; in the Middle East, where Kissinger had recently failed to bring about the accommodation between Israel and Egypt, as a step toward overall Israeli and Arab accommodation, that he had thought to be within his grasp; and in capitals from the Far East to Europe, where the collapse of American hopes and policy and the ruin of American friends in Indochina were leading governments and leaders to reevaluate the worth of United States promises and leadership. The tribute also occurred just after the President had asked his Secretary of State to remain in office and just before Mr. Ford delivered to Congress the most important and the most carefully prepared statement on foreign policy that he has undertaken since he assumed the presidency. In the preparation of that statement, a call for renewed assistance in Vietnam and for sustained world leadership, Kissinger demonstrated his continued ascendance over all other presidential advisers, domestic and foreign, and both by this means and in private conversation suggested that he really needed no reassurance of his high standing with the President.

But he did. That was what the Las Vegas tribute was all about. The facts that he should have needed it and that the President should have known that he needed it at this time of crumbling and crisis and reassessment constitute a remarkable but not unprecedented chapter in the Kissinger story as it has unfolded since Richard Nixon persuaded him to leave Harvard and Nelson Rockefeller and join the Nixon administration in 1969. H.R. Haldeman, President Nixon's staff chief, told in a CBS television interview how Kissinger threatened to quit soon after he became the President's assistant for national security affairs, in the mistaken notion that Mr. Nixon was about to repudiate his view of Vietnam policy, and how later he "many times" put about the idea that he might leave. The best known of these occasions surfaced on January 16, 1971, when Mr. Nixon in a famous letter thanked Kissinger for resigning from the Harvard faculty in order to stay at the White House and wrote: "Frankly, I cannot imagine what the government would be like without you."

Like Mr. Nixon before him Mr. Ford was recently called upon to imagine what government would be like without Kissinger. I came very near writing last January that Kissinger intended to quit next summer or fall, given the sequence of successes that he expected in the Middle East, in the conclusion of the nuclear arms control negotiations that followed the President's visit to Vladivostok, and, finally, a trip to Communist China during which Kissinger would introduce President Ford as he had introduced President Nixon in 1972. As has so often happened in matters concerning Henry Kissinger, I'd have been right in January and wrong in April. Kissinger intended in January precisely what I was told he did and the President soon came to know that he did. There was specific discussion at the White House of whether Kissinger would be an asset or a liability in the 1976 presidential campaign, assuming (as I do, short of certainty) that Mr. Ford stands for election.

All of this changed when the crumbling began. When the at least temporary failure in the Middle East was obvious, and soon after the calculation of Kissinger, the President, and everyone else officially concerned that North Vietnam would withhold a decisive offensive in South Vietnam until 1976 proved to be disastrously in error, anyone who knows Kissinger at all well should have assumed that his own wishes and plans, the President's aside, would change. They did. Henry Kissinger is no man to quit when quitting would appear to be running from failure. It also turned out—one may guess, to Kissinger's immense relief—that the President concluded that he couldn't do without his Secretary of State, who continued to double under Mr. Ford as he had under Mr. Nixon since 1972 as the assistant for national security affairs and chief of the National Security Council staff. On March 24, as has been widely reported, Mr. Ford asked Kissinger to stay. The president told Kissinger that he simply couldn't leave him, Gerald Ford, with all this stuff and trouble on his hands. Kissinger agreed to stay. Press Secretary Ron Nessen said in confirming the reports that Kissinger had been asked and had agreed to stay "through the present term, at least." It wasn't quite that way. The Ford-Kissinger discussion was only in terms of staying on the job, not in terms of staying through the present term or any other specific period, and Kissinger is known to be determined not to stay into another Ford or other presidential term after 1976.

Kissinger is also known, however, to assume and to assume that the President assumes that he is expected to remain through the present term. This may seem to be distinction without difference, but it isn't. All that either man is actually obligated to is that Kissinger not quit now or soon.

Press Secretary Nessen played an odd part in a related and accompanying sequence that is both odd and distressing. It's the sort of thing that couldn't and wouldn't occur in a White House as well ordered as the one administered for Mr. Ford by his staff chief, Donald Rumsfeld, is supposed to be.

It must be understood that tensions have existed between presidential staffs and NSC staffs since the NSC was created in 1947. They existed under Nixon and they exist under Ford, partly for reasons that have to do only incidentally with personalities. One reason is and always has been that NSC staff members consider themselves creatures apart from the ordinary run of White House hacks. Press Secretary Ronald Ziegler's and now Press Secretary Nessen's discontent with the system of communication between the NSC and press staffs centered upon the assignment of a junior NSC assistant—one of the first was David Young, later caught up in the "plumbers" horror— to keep the press secretary and his staff filled in on foreign policy matters. Ziegler wasn't and Nessen isn't denied access to higher-ups, Kissinger included, and Nessen in the past has boasted of his ready access to both Kissinger and Lieut. Gen. Brent Scowcroft, the President's deputy assistant for national security affairs. But the resentment was there and the access was thriftily used.

At Palm Springs on April 1, a mix of factors—staff tensions, slow news, the insatiable hunger of the competitive wire services for "hard" story leads, and a glaring indiscretion by Nessen—erupted at and after a routine Nessen press briefing into a situation that should have but didn't end as a minor staff flare-up. Near the briefing's end Nessen remarked offhandedly that the President that morning had mentioned among other factors in the Vietnam situation "that there have been, and are, ongoing diplomatic efforts to have a negotiated settlement. . . ." The wire services, Reuters in particular, leaped upon this tidbit and its thin amplification in the same briefing. Kissinger in

Washington was said to have ejaculated, "Bullshit!," when he read the Reuters bulletin. He telephoned Scowcroft at the White House and growled, "Does Ron Nessen know something that I don't know?" Scowcroft telephoned Nessen in Palm Springs and asked what the hell was going on. Nessen said that after the President mentioned "ongoing efforts" he, Nessen, telephoned Margaret Vanderhye, the latest NSC assistant assigned to press staff liaison, and asked her what the President was talking about. He understood from her that there were new initiatives. She said later, and Scowcroft believed, that Nessen misunderstood her. But Donald Rumsfeld, Scowcroft and Kissinger, reached in turn by Nessen and exposed by him to his towering rage, approved a formal, written statement by Nessen that "I was misinformed on this subject today by a member of the National Security Council staff and as a result you were given some inaccurate information." Rumsfeld seems to have believed that Nessen really was misinformed. Scowcroft and Kissinger gathered at worst that Vanderhye had been less than clear. Nobody in responsibility seems to have told Nessen that his dropping of such information on such a basis at a routine briefing was utterly idiotic, in any case.

It should have ended there, with some discomfort for Margaret Vanderhye and nothing worse. But it didn't. Nessen's subsequent harping on the incident, to me and other reporters, led to a spate of printed and broadcast reports that Kissinger was in disfavor with such Ford assistants as Rumsfeld, Robert Hartmann, John Marsh, and that some assistants had recommended to the President that he disassociate himself from Kissinger and Kissinger-Ford policy at least to the extent of getting himself another assistant for national security affairs. I collected a swatch of denials from people who didn't want their denials attributed to them. Let it be said for Nessen, he never went as far in conversation with me as some of the reports indicated somebody at the White House had gone with other reporters. One of the more ridiculous consequences was a meeting at which Rumsfeld assembled Nessen, Hartmann and Marsh. They swore to each other that they were not the sources of the stories. I understand that Mr. Ford said flatly that nobody had recommended that he displace Kissinger in his staff capacity.

On Friday afternoon, April 11, Nessen fired assistant press secretary Louis M. Thompson, Jr., a former army press officer who, in my limited experience with him, had been discreet and helpful since he joined the Nessen staff last October. Nessen said privately and on the public record that his only reason for letting Lou Thompson go was that the need for his services had ended. Nessen wrote Henry Kissinger that he had identified the source of the anti-Kissinger stories and had solved the problem by firing the source. Three times in conversation with Nessen, I said I had been told this and invited him to say whether it was true. Three times he said: "I do not discuss my communications with Henry Kissinger." I had to conclude that it was true and that a brutal injustice had been done to a good and loyal White House assistant.

April 26, 1975

———

It developed that Kissinger was not then or ever as determined as I thought he was "not to stay into another Ford or other Presidential term after 1976."

XX

In the Beginning

This is a story from another time and another presidency. It is about the beginning of serious US interest and involvement in the Indochina that the Ford administration is sadly abandoning. The record that the story summarizes may be usefully resurrected and reviewed by officials and presumed experts at the Ford White House and the Kissinger State Department. Like most other Americans, many of them have forgotten it or were never familiar with the evidence in it that the US involvement, however botched it was in execution and however tragic it was in the final consequence, was not at the beginning the work and caprice of fools or maniacs. The involvement arose from concepts of the American role in the Pacific and the world that were imbedded in the accepted wisdom of the time and in essence were not very different from the concepts that Gerald Ford and Henry Kissinger urge upon us today.

The time was the late 1930s and early 1940s. The presidency was Franklin D. Roosevelt's. The first American presence in Vietnam dates back a century before then, to 1833, in the persons of a special envoy named Edmund Roberts and the navy sailormen who reluctantly transported him there at the order of

President Andrew Jackson. Roberts failed to establish a trading relationship with the Vietnamese, as many Americans after him were to fail in less benign endeavors. Serious and substantial American concern with Indochina as a place in Asia that could affect the interests and security of the United States began during the prelude to American entry into World War II. It was initially linked to concern with the American place and stake in pre-Communist China. It soon exceeded the concern with China, however, and became a concern with Indochina itself and particularly with the part of Indochina that we know as South Vietnam.

The concern had nothing to do with the people, governments and welfare of Indochina. Although composed of five entities subject to varying degrees of French control, the whole of Indochina was regarded as a French possession. It had been so since 1893, when the Kingdom of Laos joined Cambodia and three parts of what the enlightened minority of natives called Vietnam—the original French colony of Cochin-China in the south, and the protectorates of Annam at the center and Tonkin in the north—in subservience to France. The colonial advance of France through these lands and of Britain through upper Burma to the borders of China disturbed the US only insofar as it touched the contest between European powers, and between them and the United States, for economic and political advantage in China. European possession elsewhere in Asia was a welcomed fact. In the 1930s and early 1940s, the imperial system came to be sanctioned in the declared American policy of "respect for the *status quo*, except as changes may be and are brought about through orderly process with due regard for the rights and interests of all concerned." It was a worldwide policy, a formula of opposition to change everywhere through the use of military force. But it identified the interests of the United States in the Far East with the imperial *status quo* and particularly, as the State Department was soon saying, with "the maintenance of the *status quo* in Indochina."

Japan's invasions of Chinese Manchuria in 1931 and of China proper in 1937 had a minimal impact upon the United States. President Herbert Hoover's refusal to entertain the slightest thought of going to war for Manchuria reduced Secretary of

State Henry L. Stimson to diplomatic pulings. So long as Japan confined its second round of aggression to China, President Roosevelt and Secretary of State Cordell Hull confined the American reaction to similar protests, with similar noneffect. It was only when Japan, at first with threats and then with action, reached beyond China to Indochina, that the United States began to perceive in the Japanese aggression a possible and, at the end, a sure cause of war.

The protectorate of Tonkin, approximating today's North Vietnam, bordered upon the Chinese provinces of Yunnan and Kwangsi and, through the port of Haiphong, provided the most useful route of supply from the outer world that remained open to China after Japan sealed off its ports of Shanghai and Canton. Annam and Cochin-China, "southern Indochina" in the parlance of 1938-41 and later South Vietnam, were of a different and greater order of importance to the United States. They were considered to command the way to the American Philippines, to British Malaya and Singapore, and to the Dutch East Indies, not to mention Thailand, Hongkong, Burma and even India if Japan's expansionist ambition stretched that far. Although these apprehensions were very real, they elided the fact that the perceived peril arose more from the identity and purpose of the occupier than from geography. Southern Indochina, left to France, troubled only the inhabitants who wished to be free of France. Japan in the event made little use of the south as a staging area for the forces that attacked the Philippines, Malaya and Singapore, and the East Indies. But Japan undertook the attacks and struck Pearl Harbor only after it occupied southern Indochina. The act of occupation proved to be what Roosevelt and Hull took it to be, a signal that Japan's ambition confronted the United States with the choice of war or of consent without war.

In and after 1938 the drumming references to Indochina in messages to the State Department from the Far East and from Europe became ever more frequent and ever more insistent. When the French ambassador in Washington, Count Saint-Quentin, pleaded in the late 1930s that open and formal collaboration against Japan was "imperative because of the vulnerability of French Indochina to Japanese attack," Undersecretary of State Sumner Welles replied as American spokesmen replied to such entreaties throughout the decade from the Japanese invasion of Manchuria to the day of Pearl Harbor. Welles said that the US government "was taking and would take an independent course, depending upon the fundamental interests of the United States." Until the summer of 1941, the "independent course" in the Far East consisted largely of deploring events and urging France to make it as difficult as possible for Japan to overrun Indochina. In this France did extraordinarily well, before and after it surrendered to Hitler Germany and Marshal Philippe Petain established his truncated government at Vichy.

American officials in Washington could never quite follow and never quite believe the bewildering story in diplomatic dispatches of obstruction, deception and procrastination that France practiced against the Japanese. Aware that they were being lied to and hoodwinked, the Japanese were not much more exasperated than the baffled Americans in Washington were. In September of 1939 the State Department instructed Ambassador William C. Bullitt in Paris to get from the French government an explicit statement of just what military and other supplies could be transshipped to China. Bullitt advised the department not to be silly; US shipments through Indochina would not be detained "provided they are labelled on the principle that a rose by any other name would smell as sweet." He added that he would spell out the obvious if the department was so dense as to require it. "The situation is clear," the chastened department replied. "No further explanation is necessary."

A Japanese army spokesman, advising the British embassy in Tokyo to pay no attention to US attempts to negotiate the mounting differences with Japan, said in June of 1940 that "there is nothing now to stop Japan from seizing French Indochina, the Netherlands East Indies, or Hongkong or all of them." It was true: Secretary Hull could do no more than beg the British and French to "devise parleys and protract the situation" while the United States muddled through its slow awakening to perils that its people, Congress and press did not want to recognize. France had just surrendered in Europe,

Britain stood alone in defense of its home island, and Japan saw that its time to move had come.

It moved first against Indochina, in two stages. On August 4, 1940 it demanded of the new Petain government in Vichy recognition of Japan's "special interest" and "privileged position" in Indochina, with the right to occupy the port of Haiphong, suppress the supply of China through the port and Tonkin, and generally establish a Japanese military presence in Tonkin. On July 12, 1941 Japan demanded Vichy's assent to the military occupation of southern Indochina. In both instances the feeble Vichy government and the isolated, thinly armed colonial administration at Hanoi resisted the initial demands, "protracted the situation" with skill and stubbornness, considerably reduced the formal concessions, and finally capitulated. Although it occurred in two phases it was a continuous process of pressure and retreat in which the United States played a part.

The American role amounted to a deliberate, cruel and in the circumstances justified play upon the profound sense of humiliation from which the defeated French already suffered. Washington told Vichy again and again that concession to the Japanese would abet the debasement of France and further diminish its low standing with the US and the world. The harried Vichy officials taunted the Americans with the contrast between their preachments and their government's refusal to enforce its principles with armed action or even with joint diplomatic action. Secretary Hull, professing alarm at reports of substantial French concessions to the Japanese, ordered the small American mission in Vichy to say that the concessions "would create an unfavorable impression in this country." H. Freeman Matthews, the career officer in charge of the mission (Admiral William D. Leahy had not yet been appointed ambassador) replied in evident sympathy with his French friends that they were trying to "obtain the best possible bargain." The State Department continued to complain about "the measure of assent" to Japanese demands and ordered Matthews to emphasize that "our interest is the maintenance of the *status quo* in Indochina." A bargain in principle, less onerous than might have been expected, was struck on August 30. But the messy business dragged on until September 23, when the Japanese attacked a border fort at Langson in Tonkin and 800 French and native soldiers died in its defense. After an agreement was signed, leaving French sovereignty and the colonial administration nominally intact, the Japanese insisted upon coming as conquerors. They bombed Haiphong, occupied airfields by force, and rapidly made Tonkin their military fief.

At this stage the US made no use of the only two sanctions open to it, short of military action. They were restriction of US trade with Japan and suspension of the Japanese-American discussions that proceeded in Tokyo and Washington. Whether successive Japanese governments seriously hoped to compose the differences or continued the diplomatic discussions only as a cover for war preparations, the Japanese seemed to value the negotiations and to fear their suspension. Anxious to deter Japan, the US government was deterred by its own fear that substantial sanctions would incite expanded Japanese aggression.

It was in this agonizing context of countervailing interests, fears and weaknesses that the American government deplored without materially resisting or penalizing the Japanese move into northern Indochina. The record indicates that the Japanese presence there would have been tolerated indefinitely, as the Communist presence would be tolerated afterward, if the presence had been confined to Tonkin. This was not to be. Signs that the Japanese were looking southward appeared before 1940 was out. Between December of 1940 and July of 1941, Japanese spokesmen in Tokyo, Europe and Washington spread the word, often in cloudy ambiguities, that Britain was plotting with Gaullist Frenchmen in Indochina and possibly with the Dutch to mount an assault upon Japan from southern Indochina. The implication was that any Japanese advance from northern to southern Indochina would be in self-defense and also in a righteous endeavor to prevent the spread of the European war to the Far East. The Americans at whom this fantasy was aimed did not believe it as such. But they took it to be a portent of things to come.

The foreseen events occurred with paralyzing speed in July: on the 12th, in temporary secrecy, a Japanese ultimatum demanding military access to southern Indochina; on the 21st, preliminary agreement; and on the 29th formal cession to Japan of eight airfields, naval facilities at Camranh and Saigon, and the right to introduce unlimited numbers of troops. Again Washington ordered its Vichy mission, now headed by Admiral Leahy, to press for delay and emphasize the shame of surrender. Again Vichy bargained down the initial concessions and retained sovereignty. Again the French relieved their humiliation with galling references to American inaction. Leahy reported that when he told Petain that Japan would now be in a position to attack the American Philippines from southern Indochina, "he admitted that but said that France is helpless and that he himself 'is not a free agent.'" Quelling any qualms that it may have felt about the American posture, the department told Leahy in October that it was "not impressed with the vigor of French resistance."

Washington was hardly entitled to sneer at the French. The US government was in no shape politically or militarily to do much if anything more than it did in the months of peace remaining to it between the events of July and the sweeping away of all doubts and hesitancy at Pearl Harbor. Only the fact of war reconciled the American people to war. But the Japanese move into southern Indochina forced US officialdom to face the prospect of war as nothing previously had done. In the words of a State Department memorandum written six months after Pearl Harbor, the seizure of southern Indochina "constituted an overt act menacing the security of the United States . . . It created a situation in which the risk of war became so great that the United States and other countries concerned were confronted no longer with the question of avoiding such risk but from then on with the problem of preventing a complete undermining of their security."

The seizure of the south recurred again and again in the last US-Japanese exchanges as the intolerable act and symbol of Japanese aggression. President Roosevelt refused to meet the Japanese premier, Prince Konoye, in a final search for peace at the summit because Japan would not attest its good intentions by withdrawing from southern Indochina. The last American act in the prelude to war, Roosevelt's famous and futile message of December 6, 1941, to Emperor Hirohito, dealt almost entirely with the Japanese presence in the south. The message concluded with the statement that "a withdrawal of the Japanese forces from Indochina would result in the assurance of peace throughout the whole of the South Pacific area."

Pearl Harbor had been attacked and Japanese forces were attacking or approaching the Philippines, Thailand, Malaya and Singapore, Hongkong and the East Indies when the message reached Tokyo. It was never answered.

May 10, 1975

———

This piece was the sort of flight from current considerations that journalists seldom manage. It also was a useful reminder that tragic national miscalculations and failures can grow from legitimate roots. The article was derived from research for a book in favor of our Vietnam involvement that President Johnson persuaded a major publisher to arrange in early 1966. I was then an advocate of the involvement, and the publisher commissioned me to do the book. Two months in Vietnam convinced me that I and my country were terribly in the wrong and I abandoned the project. It was never revived.

XXI

Footnotes

Here are notes—really footnotes, considering the relative unimportance of the subjects—about some of the things that went on in Gerald Ford's and Henry Kissinger's foreign affairs bailiwick while Cambodia and South Vietnam were falling to the Communists and the United States position and policy in Southeast Asia were falling into ruins.

Senator Henry Jackson, a Democrat who hopes to be elected President in 1976 and evidently figures that one way to fulfill that ambition is to keep himself identified as a knowing and courageous critic of administration foreign policy, raised an enormous and essentially pointless flap by telling the Senate on April 8 that he'd been "reliably informed that there exist between the governments of the United States and South Vietnam secret agreements which envision fateful American decisions, yet whose very existence has never been acknowledged." It soon became evident that Jackson was referring to private communications, written and oral, between President Nixon and President Thieu of South Vietnam in late 1972 and early 1973, when Nixon, Kissinger and their occasional emissary, General Alexander Haig, were telling Thieu that he would either have to accept the peace terms being negotiated with the North Vietnamese or be abandoned by the US.

The peace accord signed in January 1973 embodied these terms, with some modifications, and Thieu rightly perceived that it left him and his country in dire peril while enabling the US to remove the last of its combat forces from South Vietnam and recover its POWs from Hanoi. The fact that the January agreement would have to be enforced if it was to mean anything at all, and that only the United States would or could enforce it, was obvious then and later. President Nixon said in his (and Kissinger's) 1973 foreign policy report, issued May 3, that the North Vietnamese would "risk revived confrontation with us" if they violated the January agreement by resuming the military offensive in South Vietnam and that "we have told Hanoi, publicly and privately, that we will not tolerate violations of the agreement." It had to be and was assumed at the time that Thieu had been told the same in terms that gave him at least some assurance of renewed US protection if it became necessary. The assumption that this was so and that Richard Nixon was capable of renewing US military intervention, plus the fact that he was still bombing in Cambodia, caused Congress on August 3, 1973, to forbid any further US military activity after August 15 in, over, or off the shores of Cambodia, Laos, North and South Vietnam. On the previous June 29, at the crux of the House debate on this prohibition, Republican minority leader Gerald Ford told his colleagues that President Nixon had "assured me personally" in a telephone conversation that he would accept this prohibition and would not veto it as he had vetoed a similar restriction in May. On August 17, two days after the prohibition took effect, Defense Secretary James R. Schlesinger said at a press conference that "the American commitment has been to give South Vietnam the opportunity to withstand aggression. I believe that that commitment in a general way still persists and if Hanoi were to make the mistake of outright aggression against South Vietnam, I think that the President would request support from Congress and from the American public." This was cloudy. But the implied and intended meaning was support for renewed military intervention.

President Ford had these and similar statements in mind when he said on April 16, replying to Jackson and to demands that the Nixon-Thieu correspondence be given to congressional committees: "I have personally reviewed the correspondence . . . and I can assure you that there was nothing in any of those communications that was different from what was stated as our public policy." A previous complaint by the President that Congress had made it impossible for the administration to fulfill "solemn commitments" led Henry Kissinger to say at a press conference on April 5 that "he was not talking of a legal commitment. He was talking of a moral commitment . . . We did not give them [the South Vietnamese] any definite promises except to indicate that, obviously, having signed the Paris agreement, we would have an interest in its enforcement . . . it was never put in the form of a legal commitment and it is not that we are violating a legal commitment." The President, Kissinger and Press Secretary Ron Nessen were still talking in this way when a Vietnamese assistant to Thieu, who by then was deposed and in exile on Taiwan, turned up in Washington on April 30 and distributed photocopies of letters that Richard Nixon wrote to Thieu on November 14, 1972 and January 5, 1973. Nixon to Thieu on November 14: "You have my absolute assurance that if Hanoi fails to abide by the terms of this agreement it is my intention to take swift and sure retaliatory action." And on January 5: ". . . you have my assurance of continued assistance in the post-settlement period and that we will respond with full force should the settlement be violated by North Vietnam." Although the President stretched the facts when he said that nothing in these assurances "was different from what was stated as our public policy," he was right in his insistence that the assurances were consistent with stated policy. What interests me more than the patent obfuscation practiced by the President and Kissinger is the fact that never once during the debate over the August 1973 prohibition did President Nixon have his lobbyists and congressional defenders argue that the restriction made it legally impossible for him to carry out a specific commitment. Melvin Laird, who managed the affair for Mr. Nixon and persuaded Congress to allow the President 45 more days than he would otherwise have had to bomb Cambodia, says that the then President never told him that Thieu had been given "absolute assurance."

A somewhat similar battle of semantics revived the notion in some quarters that President Ford and Henry Kissinger are playing games with each other. It's a false and foolish notion and the purpose here is not to further and preserve it. With that said, however, it must also be said that Kissinger unwittingly perpetuates it with his habit of groaning in semi-private to such journalists as Hugh Sidey of *Time* and James Reston of *The New York Times* about his growing and serious difficulties with Congress and his readiness to leave office when and if it appears to him and the President that his usefulness has ended. He is extremely sensitive to any suggestion that he wants office for its own sake and that he somehow invites presidential invitations of the sort that he has received from both Richard Nixon and Gerald Ford to remain in the government. A report in this space that the President had not actually and specifically asked Kissinger to remain for the whole of the present term preceded Mr. Ford's statement in a CBS television interview that "I have asked him to stay and he is committed to stay through the end of this administration, January 20, 1977." It turned out that I'd been deliberately misinformed, in the belief that Kissinger ought not to commit the President to keeping him around through the entire remainder of the term. In this administration, no less than in the Nixon administration, a reporter has got to restrain any tendency that he may suffer from to put unqualified confidence in unquotable sources.

Now back to the aforementioned semantical hubbub. It began with a single sentence in a speech, mainly aimed at persuading the nation to focus on future goals rather than past agonies, that Mr. Ford delivered on April 23 to an impressively friendly and receptive student audience at Tulane University in New Orleans. The sentence was: "Today, America can regain the sense of pride that existed before Vietnam, but it cannot be achieved by refighting a war that is finished as far as America is concerned." Reporters instantly asked, had Kissinger been consulted about and did he approve this flat statement, first of its kind, that this country's part in the Vietnam war "is finished"? During the return flight to Washington the President answered with an abrupt "no" when he was asked whether Kissinger had played a part in preparing the speech. This seemed to encourage the effort of certain Ford assistants, notably Press Secretary Nessen and Robert Hartmann, the chief speech writer and staff politician, to get across the message that Gerald Ford is able to formulate and express his foreign policy without always relying upon Henry Kissinger.

The questioned sentence and the entire speech were in fact pure Kissinger, in spirit though not in direct composition. Thus Kissinger at a press conference on April 5 and with identical language in a speech on April 17: "The Vietnam debate has now run its course. The time has come for restraint and compassion." That's what the President intended to say and didn't say so well at Tulane. The "war is finished" line was cooked up during final drafting on the President's plane, enroute to New Orleans, and was not cleared with Kissinger or his assistants on the National Security Council staff. Kissinger's attitude afterward was, so what? On the afternoon of the speech he kept getting rumors from New Orleans that the President was going to say something in the speech that hadn't been cleared with Kissinger and his people. Kissinger had Lieut. Gen. Brent Scowcroft, his staff deputy at the White House, check out the rumors with Ford assistants in New Orleans. They assured Scowcroft, and Scowcroft assured Kissinger, that there would be nothing in the speech that would surprise or disturb Kissinger. That proved to be true.

May 17, 1975

XXII

Moynihan and Scali

Two minor mysteries of the Nixon administration are why Daniel Patrick Moynihan twice dallied with the thought of being US ambassador to the United Nations and why President Nixon gave that job to John A. Scali in December 1972. Now President Ford has asked Pat Moynihan to replace Ambassador Scali at the UN and the resultant hassle provides one of those stories that don't really matter very much but tell a lot about how life can be at the upper levels of government.

Moynihan was one of the stars of the first years of the Nixon presidency, the years that promised so much and proved to be prelude to the Watergate tragedy. He was a Democrat, a certified liberal, a specialist in urban affairs who was also the holder of a doctorate in international relations, a presidential assistant and counsellor who brought a touch of wit and elegance to a rather drab administration. In November of 1970, after nearly two years at the White House, he was ready to quit, partly because the maximum leave normally granted to tenured Harvard professors was running out and partly because, without foreseeing Watergate, he perceived a hardening of attitudes and a narrowing of the circle around the President—in preparation, he then supposed, for the 1972 reelection campaign. Mr. Nixon suddenly offered him the UN ambassadorship and Moynihan jumped at it.

Why he should have wanted the post was a mystery at the time and still is, the UN ambassadorship being by custom, circumstance and law no job for a person of Pat Moynihan's vigor and independence. The 1945 law that authorized and still governs US participation in the United Nations says that the senior ambassador and the four other "representatives" who serve with him "shall, *at all times,* act in accordance with the instructions of the President, transmitted by the Secretary of State." That's true of all ambassadorships, of course, but the UN ambassadorship is the only one that is specifically and particularly restricted by law. With less than his usual good sense, Moynihan brushed that consideration aside at the time and is again brushing it aside. An embarrassing accident saved him from the thralldom of the UN post in 1970. A Harvard colleague heard about the prospective appointment and blabbed to a Boston newspaper before incumbent Ambassador Charles Yost, a respected career diplomat, had been told that he was to be replaced. Rather than be party to such a rudeness, Moynihan asked Mr. Nixon to nominate someone else. Former Congressman George Bush, now chief of the US mission in Peking, got the place. Moynihan returned to Harvard, served as a part-time member of the American delegation to the UN General Assembly in 1971, and in December 1972 was offered his choice of two ambassadorships—to the UN and to India. He chose India and put in two unhappy and frustrating years there. He had just returned once more to Harvard and had joined the faculty of the university's school of government when President Ford offered him the UN ambassadorship. Moynihan requested and, against all rule and precedent, was granted a third two-year leave from Harvard. An additional and hitherto unreported reason for wondering why he'd take the job—he insists that he didn't seek or want it—is the fact, known to him, that he was Mr. Ford's second choice. The President first offered the post to one of his cronies and unofficial advisers, former Governor William Scranton of Pennsylvania, and Scranton declined it.

John Scali is a sometime wire service and broadcast reporter, war correspondent and specialist in diplomatic news who became a staff consultant to President Nixon in April 1971. The theory was that he'd backstop Henry Kissinger in briefing journalists, usually on a background basis, on matters having to do with foreign policy. Scali soon came to detest Kissinger and Kissinger held Scali in utter contempt. Nobody has satisfactorily explained to this day why President Nixon chose Scali in December 1972 to be the chief US ambassador to the UN and why Kissinger tolerated the appointment. The choice astonished Scali and everyone who knew him. He had been a first-rate journalist, he was better versed in foreign affairs than most political appointees to ambassadorships. But for reasons having partly to do with his rather acerbic personality and free-wheeling life-style, John Scali just wasn't anybody's model of a top-level ambassador. A Nixon assistant who was asked what he thought of appointing Scali recalls that he replied: "Mr. President, I understand that the US ambassador to the UN is provided with a splendid apartment in the Waldorf Towers. I also understand that the ambassador has a big, black, chauffeured limousine. I predict that when John Scali gets out of that limousine and takes the elevator up to that apartment, he will enjoy it and do it in style. He will be a credit to the United States." Scali did and was. He proceeded to do a far better job than most people who knew him expected him to do. Even Henry Kissinger, who wouldn't ask anyone who knows the two of them to believe that Scali is among his favorite human beings, says for quotation that "John Scali has been one of our more effective UN ambassadors." Scali considers, and people at the State Department generally share the opinion, that he attained the peak of his performance on December 6, 1974, with a speech in which he warned the General Assembly majority of small and "third world" nations that many of their recent votes and decisions had "deeply disturbed" the American people and Congress and that as a result US support for the United Nations "is eroding." Scali thought he was riding high when the President summoned him to Washington on April 15, thanked him for doing a good job, and told him that he was being replaced.

Scali concluded and remains bitterly convinced that Henry Kissinger had finally done him in. He is equally convinced, and confides to friends with equal bitterness, that Moynihan wanted the job, maneuvered to get it and, in a reversal of the 1970 news leak, tipped *Newsweek* to the fact that he'd been offered the appointment. A widely acclaimed essay by Moynihan in the March issue of *Commentary*, taking somewhat the same line on American problems with and attitudes toward the UN that Scali had taken in his December 6 speech, without crediting Scali with being there first, compounded Scali's hurt and anger. Stories of Scali's reaction inevitably got back to Moynihan and, so the latter's friends understood, made him wonder whether he really should take the job. If the doubts were genuine, it was strange that they had not been conveyed to Ford assistants as late as May 14.

Much inquiry into the background of Scali's displacement and the choice of Moynihan suggests that Scali is wrong on every count, including his suspicion that Moynihan leaked the story in order to speed up the actual nomination. It appears that Moynihan talked about the offer in Cambridge and Boston just as he had in 1970 and that somebody reported the talk to *Newsweek.* The key to the decision to replace Scali is that the UN ambassadorship has cabinet status. Mr. Ford's determination to transform the Nixon cabinet into a Ford cabinet firmed up last October and it was then that he instructed his personnel staff to begin looking around for a new UN ambassador. After the President offered the post to William Scranton and Scranton said no thanks, Kissinger remarked rather casually during a discussion with Mr. Ford that Pat Moynihan might be available. Many weeks later, after the *Commentary* article had focused much attention upon Moynihan, the President offered him the post. Moynihan demurred, fretted, told some of his closest friends that there were personal and family reasons why he probably shouldn't take the job, and finally said he would take it. When he was asked on the record the other day why he had accepted it, he answered: "Because the President asked me to, that's all. I was asked, and that's the only operable explanation."

You can't know Pat Moynihan without knowing that he does have a profound sense of duty to his country and of obligation to Presidents. He displayed it during his time with Richard Nixon and it is thoroughly believable that he felt and succumbed to it when President Ford invoked it.

May 24, 1975

———

Moynihan's subsequent grandstanding in the ambassadorship, his staged and recanted threat to quit after a few months, and his later resignation fooled many people, including my associates on *The New Republic,* into thinking Ford and Kissinger wanted and maneuvered him out. The performance convinced me, then and still an admirer of Pat Moynihan, that he was setting himself up to run for the US Senate seat that he won in 1976.

XXIII

Rocky Digs In

Vice President Rockefeller presided on May 20 at two closed meetings of the presidential commission investigating allegations of CIA misdoing and, between the morning and afternoon sessions, addressed an economic forum on the woes and needs of minority unemployed that was sponsored by the Congressional Black Caucus. Rockefeller asserted recognition of "the need to achieve as full employment of our nation's people as possible" and proper horror at the estimates of extremely high rates of unemployment among blacks in general and black teenagers (40 percent) in particular. He was headed for the door when Congressman Charles B. Rangel of New York shouted that he supposed that the Vice President's words meant that he fully supported the Black Caucus demand for all the federal money it might take to accomplish truly full minority employment. Rockefeller had meant nothing of the kind and his deputy press secretary, John Mulliken, gently hastened the Vice President's departure before he could pause and get himself into a characteristic and pointless argument with Rangel. At the CIA commission's meetings, among its last, Rockefeller and the other members in attendance went over every sentence of a voluminous staff draft—"lawyer's language," Rockefeller called it with obvious distaste—and debated, point by point, the essential conclusions to be stated in simpler form by the Vice President's long-time spokesman and writer, Hugh Morrow, in a report scheduled to be issued on or around June 6. It had been a tiring day and Rockefeller was visibly tired when, at the end of it, he chatted with a reporter. The Vice President was friendly, alert, responsive, but his evident weariness was a reminder that he will be 67 years old next July 8 and 68 when the Republican national convention nominates candidates for President and Vice President in 1976.

Five months after he took his oath as the nation's second appointed Vice President and the first to serve under a President who had been the first appointed Vice President, Nelson Rockefeller tells associates at the White House that he hopes he has just about got through the initial period of adjustment to a new role, with the traditional emphasis upon ceremonial rather than substantive activities and the frustrations that commonly afflict Vice Presidents. For reasons to be cited shortly Rockefeller believes that he is or soon will be in a position to make substantive contributions to the national and presidential policy process, chiefly on the domestic side but also in the foreign policy area. He has pretty well completed the reorganization and expansion of his own staff. With the assent and encouragement of President Ford, he has also completed an unprecedented takeover of the Domestic Council staff that, along with the much larger staff and directorate of the Office of Management and Budget, collects and collates for the President the attitudes and views of the huge domestic bureaucracy. Rockefeller, in short, has dug in for what's left of his and Gerald Ford's present terms and for whatever the President and fate may hold for him in and after 1976.

The Vice President's "downtown staff," the one that works for him in the Old Executive Office Building next door to the White House and is distinct from the staff that serves him on Capital Hill in his capacity as president of the Senate, has grown from around 15 to 23 professional assistants and a total of 70 including drivers, secretaries and the like. The most recent recruit is Alexander ("Cousin Sam") Aldrich, who was a New

York state official during part of Rockefeller's long governorship and will be the Vice President's staff specialist in urban affairs. He's called "Cousin Sam" because he is one of Nelson Aldrich Rockefeller's Aldrich cousins and Sam, for no discernible reaon, is his nickname. Two senior and more prestigious acquisitions are former Governor Raymond P. Shafer of Pennsylvania and John G. Veneman of San Francisco, who was Undersecretary of Health, Education, and Welfare from 1969 to 1973.

Shafer and Veneman are history's first "counsellors to the Vice President." Shafer is to specialize in intergovernmental relations, meaning federal dealings and communications with state, municipal and county officials and governments, with emphasis on possible solutions of the problems inherent in these relationships rather than upon nuts-and-bolts matters. In theory, a theory that had better work if hopeless confusion is not to arise, the nuts-and-bolts of the relationships will continue to be handled by James Falk, the Domestic Council official who is assigned to the same area. Because of Veneman's long tour as No. 2 man at HEW and Secretary Caspar Weinberger's intention to quit this summer or early fall, there naturally has been speculation that Veneman may get the HEW secretaryship. He's receptive but this inquirer is told at the White House not to expect it. Veneman's specialty with Rockefeller is to be an in-depth study of "federal human service programs," including everything from social security to unemployment benefits, food stamps, health insurance. Here again there are the makings of conflict and overlap with the reorganized Domestic Council functions of oversight and coordination in the same areas. Subject to actual experience, one must accept the argument that such difficulties and complications will be resolved or avoided by friendly coordination and by virtue of the knowledge of all concerned that they are working for both the Vice President and the President. Above all, the corrective fact is supposed to be that the Vice President considers himself, his intermittent Senate duties apart, nothing more and nothing less than a staff assistant to the President.

The grave doubts, in and outside the White House, that

preceded and followed the President's agreement to make James Cannon, one of the many long-time associates on Rockefeller's gubernatorial and private staffs who came with him to the vice presidency, executive director of the influential Domestic Council staff, and Richard Dunham, another Rockefeller man, one of two deputy directors, have dissolved and vanished in remarkably short order. Cannon, a sometime journalist who in past years had been more of a lobbyist and a political arranger for Rockefeller than a substantive adviser, predicted before he was appointed executive director that if he got the place his approach and emphasis would be more upon the politics of the operation than upon the substance of programs. According to him and to White House officials who work with him, the opposite has happened. There is said to be more emphasis upon substance and less upon the mechanics of the federal operation than there was under either John Ehrlichman or his successor, Kenneth Cole. Not that the mechanics is neglected: the second deputy director, James Cavanaugh, a veteran of the Ehrlichman and Cole regimes, is responsible for oversight of current domestic operations and problems. The oversight is less rigid and inclusive than it was in the Ehrlichman days, but it's still there. Cannon takes that part of his responsibilities very seriously and, in concert with Richard Parsons and Arthur Quern, two other Rockefeller veterans who have been assigned to important slots on the Domestic Council staff, does what he can to make certain that no department or agency official does anything that would harm the President or be contrary to the President's wishes.

The council staff structure has been changed from five to nine principal policy and functional areas, based more upon the nature of issues than upon departmental and agency patterns. Dunham, the senior deputy director, concentrates upon study of existing practices and policies and upon recommendations for change where change is indicated. "Review groups" staffed by departmental and agency officials and managed by Domestic Council assistants are to conduct these studies and formulate recommendations. In one instance, social programs in the HEW-human service area, John Veneman is to oversee the Domestic Council overseers of the studies. Veneman, Dunham and other officials refuse to bother about the conflict and confusion seemingly built into this arrangement. Rockefeller certainly doesn't bother. It's this looming emphasis upon in-depth, long-range study and recommendation that principally explains and justifies his hope that he soon will be participating importantly and effectively in the policy process.

The Vice President and this reporter got into his present and prospective roles to some extent during the aforementioned conversation on May 20. Rockefeller's political prospect was the first subject. Last March 27, in a press conference aboard the plane bringing him home from the funeral for murdered King Faisal of Saudi Arabia, Rockefeller explicitly disputed Ford statements that had seemed and were intended to dispel any doubt that the President considers himself committed to keep Vice President Rockefeller on the Republican ticket with him next year. In a remark that was widely unreported because of preoccupation with the beginnings of collapse in South Vietnam, Rockefeller said: "I feel very strongly that the President ought to wait until he gets close to elections and then he ought to see who will best serve him and then he makes the decision and I don't want to be in any way in a position where he feels that he's lost his freedom of movement." When he was asked whether he'd ever said this directly to the President, Rockefeller answered: "I told him just the other day what I've been saying publicly, that I don't think he ought to commit himself." When asked what the President's reactions was, Rockefeller answered: "What he's said publicly was his reaction. I appreciate his generous remarks. But I feel he needs the freedom. Neither of us has been elected and"—staring grimly at the reporter—"that's a *very* significant factor. He's gonna run and he should keep the freedom to act as he thinks necessary when the time comes." When told that the emphasis with which he had said, *he's gonna run*, indicated no doubt whatever about that, Rockefeller said: "I said that the first day I was on the Hill [as Vice President]: I can't imagine a man accepting appointment to the vice presidency and succeeding to the presidency in these circumstances and then immediately turning himself into a lame duck."

Here Rockefeller went into a mild lecture to the press upon what he considered its neglect of "a good story"—namely, the growth of Gerald Ford in the presidency. Rockefeller on President Ford: "His confidence, his strength, his determination is growing all the time. One of the most interesting stories anyone could do would be about how much this man has changed in the five months I've been observing him. It's been a very interesting evolution to a decision maker from however you describe a congressman's role."

Rockefeller was asked what part he took in deciding how to handle US problems in the wake of South Vietnam's fall and what to do about the seizure of the *Mayaguez.* Rockefeller ducked a direct answer, picking up the reporter's reference to the fact that he'd attended all NSC meetings on these matters, and said with evident pleasure: "I attend *all* the meetings. The President has been very generous in inviting me to all the meetings. If I have anything to say that I think would be useful to him, I say it. But I recognize fully that it's his responsibility and the Secretary of State's responsibility."

The reporter shifted to domestic policy and said he understood that the Vice President was both free and articulate in expressing differences, when there were any, with the President during their weekly discussions of domestic subjects. Rockefeller said this was so and continued: "He's an extraordinary man. He doesn't want people who parrot his points of view, then he makes his own judgments. So my role in those discussions would be to express a position but not to press a position." Had he taken a position for or against vetoing the coal stripmining bill? No, Rockefeller said, because a staff position paper had set forth every conceivable point of view and there was nothing for him to add. But, he went on, there was a good example of his intervention in domestic discussions that he could talk about. It was the recent visit of Governor Hugh Carey of New York and Mayor Abe Beame of New York City to plead with President Ford for $1.5 billion in federal emergency loans to save the city from bankruptcy. Rockefeller, who had repeatedly expressed his scorn for what he considered to be the mismanagement and gimmickry that had got the city in its current shape, attended the meeting with the President and recalled his part as follows: "I commented, I intervened when I thought that information being presented to the President was incorrect. The Governor implied that federal help was their last resort, their last court of appeal. He didn't use those words, but that was the meaning. I said, 'Mr. President, you ought to know that the state of New York has the capacity to do exactly what the governor is asking you to do.'" Here Rockefeller went into technicalities that the reporter didn't understand. The essence of it was that the state in fact had the authority to loan the city the money it needed, on short term notes. Rockefeller said he also observed that if the city's credit was as good as Mayor Beame said it was, the city government could borrow emergency money from five to six billion dollars it had accumulated in pension funds. With wry and obvious satisfaction, Rockefeller said in conclusion: "My intervention was not exactly welcomed [by the Governor and Mayor]. But that's a good example. I do speak up, but I always wait until I know whether a point that ought to be made has been made or will be made."

The last question that the reporter had time for had to do with the Vice President's friend, protegé and employee in years past, Henry Kissinger, and the pressures and attacks that he is suddenly under. How did the Vice President feel about it all? In view of his and Kisssinger's past association, the reply was surprisingly detached and cool. Chuckling and grinning, Rockefeller said: "The wonderment is that it didn't happen before. He [Kissinger] has led a charmed life. Now he's joined the rest of us. And I must say, he's taken it like a real pro. I've been just delighted with the way he's rolled with the punches." As if realizing that he might have been expected to be a bit warmer than he seemed to be, the Vice President then said: "I've always had, as I'm sure you know, the most tremendous admiration for him, as well as affection. If you want to do what is right in this world, especially in a democracy, you're bound to have people criticize you and disagree with you. The test of leadership is the ability to take it."

May 31, 1975

———

As we shall see, Rockefeller's satisfaction and his hopes of effective participation in the making and execution of policy were not to last out 1975.

XXIV

Mayaguez Questions

Between 6 and 7 am of Monday, May 12, the tendency among the few officials at the White House and the Departments of State and Defense who had seen or been told about a message that had been received in the dawn hours from the US Embassy in Jakarta was to suspect that it reported a hoax. The message was that fragmentary radio signals purporting to be from the American cargo ship *Mayaguez*, on the way from Hongkong to the Thai port of Sattahip, reported that it had been boarded on the high seas and seized by armed Cambodians at about 2 am, Washington time. Assistant Secretary Joseph Laitin, the Defense Department's chief spokesman, was shown a copy of the embassy message when he arrived at his Pentagon office at 7 o'clock. He assumed but didn't bother to check that Secretary James R. Schlesinger reached his office and saw a copy at about the same time. Laitin recommended in a memo to Schlesinger that nothing be said or done about the reported seizure until it was verified. Schlesinger, Secretary of State Henry Kissinger and President Ford had not been awakened by overnight duty officers, as they would have been if so serious a report had been wholly believed when it was received.

Lieut. Gen. Brent Scowcroft, the deputy assistant for national security affairs, told Mr. Ford about the message at 7:40 am, during the intelligence briefing that Scowcroft routinely gives the President each morning. Kissinger learned of it a little later, at the senior NSC staff meeting that he convenes at 8 am at the White House when he is in Washington. By then or shortly afterward, a US reconnaissance plane, presumably from Thailand, had sighted the *Mayaguez* and verified that it was indeed in enemy possession, apparently proceeding toward the Cambodian port of Kompong Som, about 60 miles from where it had been seized. Kissinger thereupon set in train the arrangements for the first of a series of NSC meetings with the President. Reporters knew nothing about the seizure and Press Secretary Ronald Nessen didn't mention it during his regular White House briefing session, which on this day ran from 11:30 am to 12:30 pm and was devoted in part to a heated argument between Nessen and some of the journalists over whether the Ford White House is really as "open" as it's claimed to be. It's not. The word from NSC quarters was that in this instance Nessen was not deliberately withholding information. It appears that neither Scowcroft, Kissinger, nor the President told Nessen about the seizure until just before 1:50 pm, when he called an unusual second briefing and read a statement: "We have been informed that a Cambodian naval vessel has seized an American merchant ship on the high seas and forced it to the port of Kompong Som. The President has met with the NSC. He considers this seizure an act of piracy. He has instructed the State Department to demand the immediate release of the ship. Failure to do so would have the most serious consequences."

This statement contained the first two of a succession of flaws, petty and major, that marred the subsequent American performance and continued for quite a while after the President announced the recovery of the ship and its crew of 38 at 12:27 am, on Thursday, May 15, Washington time. The *Mayaguez* had not been "forced . . . to the port of Kompong Som"; it was moored off Koh Tang (Tang Island), a small, rocky and wooded islet about 30 miles from where it had been seized and also about 30 miles from Kompong Som. The seizure was not "an act of piracy," though the President doubtless thought of it in that fashion. Piracy is a private act; this was the act of the newly

Communized government of Cambodia. This said, let the following also be said. In my opinion the President in ordering the use of armed force and personnel to recover the ship and crew acted properly, legally, courageously, and as necessity required. The flaws were mostly inevitable in so confused a situation. The questions that were raised by reporters who covered the affair and queried officials at the White House, the Defense Department and the State Department were for the most part proper questions. But the manner and tone rather than the thrust of some of the questions and of some of the comment by journalistic thumb-suckers who were nowhere near the scenes of action and decision were in my opinion a disgrace to journalism and to the journalists concerned. All too often at the White House, and from what I heard and read of the press proceedings at the Defense and State departments, I got the impression that some of the reporters would have been happy if the *Mayaguez* affair had proved to be an unmitigated disaster rather than a flawed success for the United States. Watergate, the recent and now total collapse of American policy and position in Indochina, and the repercussions in the rest of Southeast Asia and throughout the world, including the Middle East, have created a deep and seemingly insatiable media appetite for disaster and official victims. Journalists and politicians, whatever their ideology, don't have to be jingoists and "yahoos"—as Anthony Lewis of *The New York Times* called people who applauded Mr. Ford's handling of the *Mayaguez* affair—in order to perceive some good and gain in it.

One of the flaws was indeed disturbing, avoidable, and to be deplored. Henry Kissinger (in his guise as the quotable "senior official aboard" the plane that took him and a small press contingent to Vienna on May 18, in advance of Mr. Ford's first presidential visit to Europe) confirmed reports that B-52 bombers had been alerted, loaded with bombs, and ordered onto runways at Guam, with crews standing by for retaliatory raids on Cambodia. The conveyed impression, believable but not verified to my satisfaction at this writing, is that Kissinger and the President favored and would have ordered the raids if the carrier *Coral Sea,* along with the marines who were choppered onto Koh Tang and who boarded the *Mayaguez* from a US destroyer, had not arrived in the area in time to prevent the removal of the ship to the Cambodian mainland. To his immense credit James Schlesinger argued strongly against the use of B-52s in any circumstances, partly because of predictable domestic and world reaction and partly because heavy bombing would almost certainly have worsened rather than bettered the lot of the *Mayaguez* crewmen. The claque of White House assistants who continue to use every available occasion to further the notion that the President is deliberately downgrading Henry Kissinger and anyone else, in this instance Schlesinger, who may compete with Mr. Ford for media credit in foreign policy matters, put about the fabrication that the President insisted upon a higher level and greater variety of force than Schlesinger thought necessary. I'm told and believe that, once the B-52 issue was resolved, Schlesinger approved the force that was used in the bombing of Koh Tang, an airfield and an oil refinery near Kompong Som, and at least three Cambodian gunboats, and in the attempts to interdict naval and fishing vessels that could have been—and in one instance were—used to remove the captured crewmen to the mainland.

A legitimate question of law and the President's adherence to or violation of it was also raised. Anthony Lewis and Raoul Berger, a Harvard law professor who for years has construed any President's constitutional authority at the absolute minimum, were among those who said that Mr. Ford had violated both the law and constitutional limitations and that the majority of congressmen, Republican and Democratic, who applauded him blindly and supinely ignored the legal realities. This is fundamentally a political question, one that a journalist is entitled to judge. My opinion is that Mr. Ford skillfully and adequately complied with the War Powers Act of 1973, a statute that President Nixon vainly vetoed in the belief that it would paralyze all Presidents. The narrower August 1973 prohibition of the further use of US military force in, over and off the shores of Indochina presents a different problem. A review of the debate that preceded passage of that limitation demonstrates that Congress never intended it to forbid the sort of restricted police action that Mr. Ford took in the *Mayaguez* affair. B-52 retaliation might have been a gross violation, but that did not occur. Related arguments that the *Mayaguez* may indeed have been in Cambodia's territorial waters and therefore subject to seizure are nonsense. Even if a claim of territoriality within 12 miles of tiny offshore rocks is accepted, there is no evidence whatever that the *Mayaguez* was not exercising the internationally recognized right of innocent passage.

Finally, there is a question whether the administration purposely withheld, delayed and falsified casualty figures in order to sustain as long as possible the general glow that followed the recovery of the ship and crew. Communications that were so good that a pilot who was about to strafe a Cambodian boat could be ordered by radio to abstain in time to save the vessel and its occupants make it hard to understand why it took nine days to bring the announced total from one dead, a few others missing and between 70 and 80 wounded up to five and finally 15 dead and down to 50 wounded. The exclusion from the acknowledged total of 19 air force policemen and four chopper crewmen who were killed in a crash in Thailand, during a preliminary concentration of some 100 air police who were not used in the actual operation, is inexcusable. Nevertheless I buy the administration claim that no intentional deception was involved.

June 7, 1975

———

For afterthoughts on *Mayaguez*, see Chapter XXVII. President Ford told Nessen about the seizure at around 9 am. Nessen withheld the information from the press and from his own staff until his second briefing at 1:50 pm.

XXV

Gunning for Henry

During President Ford's absence in Europe, from May 28 to June 4, several of the senior assistants who stayed in Washington were more accessible and had more time than usual for talk about attitudes and concerns at and near the peak of White House power. The account that follows is mostly derived from these conversations, in part from interviews that preceded the President's journey, and in smaller part from reported events and statements on the trip.

A major topic of the conversations was the relationship between the President and Henry Kissinger. Let it be said at once that I brought the subject up; the assistants didn't. The Ford-Kissinger story is largely a media creation. It persists in print and in broadcasts mainly because journalists and commentators continue to be fascinated and to assume that their readers and listeners are fascinated with the supposition that Gerald Ford is taking charge of foreign policy in ways and to an extent that he didn't even attempt when he succeeded to the presidency and that Richard Nixon never attempted, either. A related supposition is that in the process Mr. Ford is deliberately and necessarily changing and diminishing Secretary

Kissinger's role. It was noted in this space in April that the President had begun the previous February to say in interviews, with great emphasis, that *he* was determining and conducting US foreign policy. Mr. Ford was quoted saying of Henry Kissinger that "although he is extremely valuable and I think most important, it doesn't mean that he makes the decisions." There really hasn't been much more to say on the matter since then, but the reports keep turning up and here I am back at the subject.

On the morning of the President's departure for Europe, *The New York Times* front-paged a long account to the effect that Mr. Ford was looking beyond Kissinger to other advisers. Godfrey Sperling, the respected chief of *The Christian Science Monitor's* Washington bureau, reported from Brussels that the President "is beginning to put his own unique, 'instinctive' stamp" on US foreign policy and that "for Henry Kissinger there is simply no option but to step aside a bit." Aldo Beckman of *The Chicago Tribune,* one of the sharpest reporters on the White House beat, wrote in Brussels that White House staff chief Donald Rumsfeld and Press Secretary Ron Nessen were trying and failing to keep Kissinger out of the public spotlight during the European trip. Aboard the President's plane on the flight from Washington to Brussels, Rumsfeld with an uncharacteristically silly stunt encouraged a suspicion that he's been behind a lot of the effort to derogate Kissinger. When he talked to pool reporters on the plane, Rumsfeld insisted upon being identified only as "a senior American official very familiar with NATO who was traveling with the President." Rumsfeld was US ambassador to NATO from early 1973 until President Ford recalled him to the White House last fall, a fact that irritated reporters promptly noted in quoting the "senior American official." Kissinger, who had preceded the President to Europe, dotes on being identified as "the senior American official" aboard *his* plane, and Rumsfeld's plaint to reporters on the President's plane that questions about a diminished role for the Secretary of State were "mischievous" had a somewhat hollow ring.

The fact that gives the subject some continuing legitimacy, however empty much of the discussion of it may be, is that any reporter who wants support for the suggestion that the President is subtly downgrading Kissinger can find it in respectable White House quarters. Without seeking that kind of support—I remain convinced that the supposition is hogwash—inquiries at the White House during the President's absence developed quite a lot of information about senior staff attitudes toward Henry Kissinger and the Kissinger-Ford relationship.

There is in truth a substantial, fairly widespread belief among some of the President's closest assistants that Mr. Ford *ought* to diminish his reliance upon and identification with Henry Kissinger. Where reports based upon private information to this effect go wrong is in jumping to the conclusion that the President is doing what some of his people think he should do. He just isn't. At the NATO summit sessions in Brussels, for instance, and in press conferences there and elsewhere explaining the Ford purpose and performance, Kissinger figured as prominently as he ever has.

Most of the staff feeling that the President should reduce Kissinger's role and end what some of the assistants consider to be Kissinger's "monopoly" is connected with two circumstances. Alone among the President's staff advisers, Henry Kissinger has a solid, regularly scheduled hour with Mr. Ford every weekday morning when the two are in Washington. Over the course of a typical Washington day, Rumsfeld spends more time with the President than Kissinger does. But neither Rumsfeld nor any other assistant has that sacred, unbroken hour with Mr. Ford. Although this makes for plain jealousy, a more substantial objection is heard. It is that too many snap decisions are made during these private talks, without proper "staffing out" and sufficiently broad discussion. The other target of complaint is Kissinger's unprecedented dual function as both Secretary of State and the President's assistant for national security affairs. With subtle encouragement from Kissinger, Richard Nixon invented the duality in 1972 as a way to make the secretaryship acceptable to Kissinger. Both men understood that Secretary Kissinger would never tolerate an assistant for national security affairs who would try to dominate him as he had dominated Secretary of State William P. Rogers. One might suppose that President Ford settled the question of continuing the dual assignment when he said in a television interview on April 21 that Henry Kissinger is a "unique" individual who "can very successfully handle" both jobs and will continue to handle them. An assistant who is much involved in such matters said the other day that to his knowledge nobody on the staff has actually dared to recommend to Mr. Ford that the functions be divided. That's hard to believe, considering that one of the assistants who holds most firmly that the functions should be divided is Philip Buchen, the President's chief counsel, first law partner and hometown friend. Buchen is also among those who feel strongly about that morning hour. But that particular complaint is muted nowadays, compared to the amount of private discussion accorded it when Mr. Ford first succeeded President Nixon. It's the dual job of Secretary of State and staff assistant that remains in active discussion and objection very near to Mr. Ford if not in his presence.

An illustration of how wishful White House talk can get translated into alleged fact is to be found in the previously mentioned *New York Times* piece. Grave note was taken of the fact, disclosed in White House staff photographs, that Rumsfeld and Counsellors John Marsh and Robert Hartmann attended a National Security Council meeting called to consider the *Mayaguez* seizure by the Cambodian navy and what to do about it. The presence of Marsh, Hartmann and Rumsfeld was said to prove that the President is broadening the number and variety of advisers to whom he turns in foreign policy discussions, with the implication that here was one more sign of diminished reliance upon Henry Kissinger. An anonymous White House assistant was quoted to this effect. The quoted assistant couldn't have known much about the NSC and the *Mayaguez* discussions. Rumsfeld frequently attends NSC meetings and, on those and other occasions, advises the President on foreign policy. There's nothing new about that. Philip Buchen, who wasn't mentioned by the *Times*, attended the *Mayaguez* meetings because what the law and the Constitution did and didn't permit the President to do was a live question. John Marsh, whose many responsibilities include oversight of White House dealings with Congress, was present because the matter of how and when to inform congressional leaders of what the President decided to do was an important aspect of the problem. Hartmann was there because of the political implications. His and the others' presence at the *Mayaguez* meetings was not intended to establish a precedent and signaled no change whatever in Henry Kissinger's preeminent standing with the President.

June 14, 1975.

———

Kissinger's loss of his dual status was nearer than I suspected when the above report was written. Rumsfeld did not insist upon being identified as I say he did; the pool reporters aboard the President's plane embarrassed him by doing it.

XXVI

CIA Screw-Up

The Ford administration emerged in better shape than it deserved from the fantastic screw-up that preceded the release of the Rockefeller commission's report on "CIA activities within the United States." *The New York Times,* gloating over what it took to be confirmation of "the basic elements" in a *Times* story that appeared last December 22 and precipitated the Rockefeller inquiry and wider congressional investigations, editorially judged the commission report to be "a trenchant, factual and plain-spoken document" instead of "the whitewash that many critics had predicted." The hitherto skeptical *Washington Post* said the report "appears at first reading to be a full and reliable account." Unlike the *Times,* which denounced the President's decision to keep the commission's incomplete study of allegations that the CIA had plotted to assassinate some foreign leaders secret for awhile, the *Post* concluded that Mr. Ford's wish to leave to congressional committees headed by Democrats inquiries and findings that seem bound to reflect upon Presidents Eisenhower, Kennedy and Johnson "is reasonable." A report that finds the CIA guilty of frequent and gross abuses of its limited authority to operate within the United States certainly should not be scorned and dismissed as a whitewash. The commission's overall judgment that "the great majority of the CIA's domestic activities comply with its statutory authority" seems to me to be supported by the evidence set forth or summarized in the report. Beyond those observations, my subject is the previously mentioned screw-up.

The beginnings go back to President Ford himself and to a view of the Rockefeller inquiry's proper scope and limitations that he expressed in deepest secrecy to a group of *New York Times* executives on January 16, just 12 days after he established the commission and formally limited its inquiry "to activities conducted within the United States by the Central Intelligence Agency." According to an account published in the *Times* after the Rockefeller report was released, the President's view was that "if the commission should wander into the foreign field, it would stumble upon all kinds of activities, including assassinations . . . There was nothing to be gained by opening the Pandora's box of assassinations. It would only lead to futile recriminations. Well-meaning people in the past had ordered activities that seemed right and proper at the time, but might seem wrong and improper in the light of new circumstances. The new generation should not pass judgment on the old. Those were the themes of President Ford's concern in January, after he had read the charges against the CIA [in the *Times*] and had a briefing on them from William E. Colby, director of Central Intelligence, a briefing that included some information on assassinations."

It may be argued that the origins of the screw-up, using the term to connote a colossal and continuing misunderstanding and underestimate of the problems raised for the administration by the *Times* and other allegations of CIA misbehavior, go back and beyond that occasion to December 22, when reporter Seymour Hersh's charge that the CIA had conducted a "massive, illegal domestic intelligence operation" appeared in the *Times* and President Ford flew from Washington to Vail, Colorado, for a winter vacation. Ford assistants in Vail differed over whether the Hersh report posed a serious problem. Staff chief Donald Rumsfeld was among those who had to be convinced that it did. The arguments, presumably reflecting the

President's uncertainty, continued after Mr. Ford received an initial report from Director Colby. The doubts and differences in themselves are not to be sneered at and I'm in no position to sneer: I thought for a long while that Seymour Hersh had gone overboard and taken the *Times* with him. The relevant point is that the arguments around the President reflected a confusion, a capacity for inconsistency that became both acute and manifest in March when Mr. Ford, in contradiction of the view that he had emphatically expressed in January, either authorized or ordered that Rockefeller commission to investigate developing, published charges of CIA plotting to assassinate Fidel Castro and Dominican Republic dictator Rafael Trujillo, among others.

The Rockefeller report said that the President "concurred" in the commission's decision to look into these allegations. Roderick Hills, a White House attorney, said four times at a White House briefing, in slightly varying words, that "the President asked the Rockefeller commission to examine the allegations." The account obtained privately from Ford and Rockefeller assistants tends to support the commission version. It also throws considerable light on the relationships between the President and the Vice President and between the White House and Rockefeller staffs, including the commission staff. The impression at the White House is that David Belin, a Des Moines lawyer who was the commission's executive director and worked with Mr. Ford as an attorney when the Warren Commission investigated the Kennedy assassination, originally persuaded the CIA commission's chairman, Vice President Rockefeller, that the current assassination charges should be investigated, and made that aspect of the inquiry his personal chore. Throughout the commission's inquiry, from January 4 to the end of its deliberations in late May, Messrs. Ford and Rockefeller met at least once a week for a private talk when they were in Washington. It's assumed that the Vice President kept the President posted on the commission's secret proceedings and progress during these talks. But did he? Hugh Morrow, the Vice President's chief spokesman, knows of only one occasion when commission business was discussed. This was in March, when according to Morrow the Vice President told the President that it looked as if the commission was going to have to get into the assassination allegations and the President reluctantly agreed.

Before the commission was formed and Rockefeller was asked to be its chairman, the President and his staff chief, Donald Rumsfeld, made two decisions that had much to do with the subsequent screw-up. The first decision was that the White House staff should have as little as possible to do with the commission and its staff, lest the notion already abroad that the commission was merely a creature of the President and the administration be encouraged. The second decision was that the White House counsel's office, headed by Philip Buchen, rather than the National Security Council staff should handle what liaison there had to be with the commission. Because the 1947 National Security Act makes the CIA subject to NSC supervision, members of the NSC staff were bound to be interested parties in any investigation of the CIA. A result of these decisions was that to all effects there was no White House liaison with the commission and its staff until the commission began its inquiry into the allegations of CIA assassination plots. Even then the primary White House interest was not in the commission's conduct and progress. It was in getting and

6-12-75

by Ranan Lurie

passing along commission materials and information to the special investigating committee headed by Senator Frank Church.

Three White House lawyers—Buchen, Roderick Hills and James Wilderotter—did this work. Hills did most of it. His relations with Belin, the commission's staff director, and with the Church committee and its staff got pretty rough at times. Hills felt that Belin was unduly slow in realizing that he and his small staff could not possibly complete the assassinations inquiry in time to meet Vice President Rockefeller's deadline of June 6, and even slower in conveying this and other essential information to Hills and, through him and Buchen, to the President. Near the end Belin demanded and got some material from NSC files and complained that he hadn't been given all he needed. When the Rockefeller report was released, Hills and Wilderotter were still combing through NSC files back to 1959, in the Eisenhower administration, both to satisfy Belin and to assemble the same material for the Church committee. In late May the committee staff strained Hills' patience with a demand for the complete files and transcripts of the Rockefeller hearings before the commission report had been completed and submitted to the President. Before tempers cooled, there was talk of making the committee subpoena the material.

Hills insists, and Rockefeller people agree, that it was always intended to treat assassination as a matter separate from the commission's general inquiry and to report any findings about it separately. What was not intended until the very last was that the main commission report say nothing whatever about assassination except that evidence concerning the allegations was being submitted separately to the President. Hills and his White House colleagues feel that they were informed of this decision very late in the game. Hills said publicly that the White House staff learned of it only two weeks before the commission report was completed; privately, a few days before it was completed. Hills, Donald Rumsfeld and others involved at the White House acknowledge that they were extremely slow in comprehending the certain effect of the Rockefeller commission's failure to make the decision known as soon as it was reached. At Hills' fierce insistence, and after a hassle over language with the Vice President and his people, the commission announced the decision to skip assassination on Thursday night, June 5, hours before the report was submitted to the President the next day.

The cynicism generated by this mess was compounded by confusion, believable only because it occurred, over release of the report. As early as May 20, to my knowledge, Rockefeller was saying it was to be made available to the media on June 6, when it was to be delivered to the President, for publication on Sunday the 8th. He was still saying this on Monday, June 2, and Wednesday, June 4, without mentioning the decision to omit any findings about assassination and leaving an impression that in this and other respects the CIA had been found guilty only of marginal offenses. Here again Hills, Rumsfeld and others on the Ford staff acknowledge that they awoke with incredible slowness to the certain impact. The issue of when to release the report was put seriously to the President only on Friday morning, less than two hours before he received it. An assistant who was present recalls that Mr. Ford said, not in anger but with unusual emphasis: "I think I ought to have a chance to read it first." At his regular briefing afterward, Press Secretary Ron Nessen left an impression that the report might not be released at all. It was released, of course, after the President read it over the weekend and defended it at a press conference on Monday evening. It was easier to defend than the foul-ups that all but turned the release of a creditable report into a disaster.

The abrupt move of Rumsfeld, Hills and other Ford assistants into the situation after the President returned from Europe on June 4 created an impression that Mr. Ford's people had decided it was time to put down Rockefeller and show his people who was boss. Hugh Morrow, the Vice President's spokesman, was moved to say: "I don't feel put down and I'm certain that Nelson Rockefeller doesn't feel put down. If anybody at the White House thinks anybody around here needs to be reminded of who is boss—we *know* who's boss."

June 21, 1975

XXVII

Afterthoughts

Here are some points and thoughts in the aftermath of a piece about the *Mayaguez* affair and in the wake of the Rockefeller Commission report on CIA behavior.

My conclusion that President Ford "acted properly, legally, courageously and as necessity required" in using military force to recover the *Mayaguez* and its crew from the Cambodian Communists aroused a response that in volume and ferocity hasn't been equaled since readers discovered in the early Nixon years that I was capable of granting Richard Nixon occasional benefit of doubt. Some of the *Mayaguez* letters persuade me that I overstated my position: I'd omit "courageously" if I were writing the piece now. Questions that should have been raised were not. Generally, however, the reader reaction suggests the existence and prevalence of attitudes that are more interesting than the merits and defects of my view.

It was evident, for instance, that news reports of the seizure and recovery put far more emphasis upon the questionable aspects of the affair than one would have supposed from reading the newspapers commonly read in Washington. It was even more evident that readers and listeners, at least the kind who seem to read *The New Republic*, were more inclined to believe negative reports than they were to believe the more favorable reports and the administration claims. This seems to me to have been fair and healthy enough, except for one consideration. It's bad, I think, when propositions and assumptions that are open to reasonable doubt are taken to be established fact when they reflect upon the administration and are rejected as flat falsities or lies when they support an administration view or action. An instance is the legitimate question whether the *Mayaguez* was on the high seas when it was seized some 60 miles off the Cambodian mainland. The US government held that it was in international waters. The ship was certainly in a regularly used sea lane. It was also about eight miles from a small islet that Cambodia claims. The previous Cambodian government had declared that sea spaces within 12 miles of its shores, whether mainland or island, were its territorial waters. The US has always rejected 12-mile and more expansive claims, holding that its claim of territorial sovereignty up to no more than three miles from its shorelines is traditional, practical and proper.

That brings us to my statement that there was "no evidence whatever that the *Mayaguez* was not exercising the internationally recognized right of innocent passage." Nothing in the piece infuriated readers more. Upon further inquiry it turns out to have been a factual oversimplification. The US in the *Mayaguez* affair never claimed "the right of innocent passage;" it relied entirely upon the claim that the *Mayaguez* was seized in international waters. Innocent passage applies only in territorial waters and it's a qualified right. A government is entitled to establish that the passage of a foreign ship through its territorial waters is in fact "innocent" and it may do this by stopping and searching a ship. The US view seems reasonable to me and to lawyers whom I have consulted. It is that the Cambodians went beyond the recognized right to stop and search when they seized the *Mayaguez*, directed it to a Cambodian anchorage, and removed the crew.

Another facet of the reader reaction fascinated me. I'd never realized that the working press in Washington, especially as it's represented by some of our more aggressive questioners, has so many friends around the country. In the Nixon years the TV networks were deluged with complaints when viewers saw reporters at presidential press conferences glaring, jabbing and shouting at Richard Nixon. Something seems to have happened since then and I don't know what it is. My remark that the behavior of some of the reporters at White House, State and Defense briefings on the *Mayaguez* episode indicated that they "would have been happy if the *Mayaguez* affair had proved to be an unmitigated disaster rather than a flawed success for the United States" enraged readers. Who authorized this jerk, they asked in effect, to pass judgment on his peers? It's a good question and it raises another question. Could it be that some of the angered readers "would have been happy if the *Mayaguez* affair had proved to be an unmitigated disaster?" I suspect so.

The following afterpoints and thoughts about the Rockefeller-CIA report have to do with the event itself rather than with my account of the boggles that accompanied the report's release. It became evident during the 10 days that followed publication of the Rockefeller report that President Ford and his people were extraordinarily nervous about the continuing rumors and assertions, usually unattributed to the sources, that the late President John F. Kennedy and his brother, Attorney General Robert Kennedy, were going to be tainted as evidence bearing upon allegations that the CIA plotted the assassination of Fidel Castro, among others, during their tenures comes out. Mr. Ford at his press conference on June 9, explaining his decision to withhold the commission's evidence about assassination from publication and pass it along to congressional committees and the Justice Department for further inquiry and evaluation, increased the suspicion that material affecting past Presidents is involved. He said: " . . . under no circumstances do I want to sit in 1975 passing judgment on decisions made by honorable people under unusual circumstances . . . That's why I caution the House and Senate committees to use utmost prudence in how they handle the material I'm giving them . . . I am not passing judgment on whether they [past Presidents] were right or wrong. I simply am saying that for us, 15 or 20 years later, to put ourselves in the position of people who had the responsibility in the highest echelons of our government—we shouldn't be Monday morning quarterbacks, if I could invent a cliché." Vice President Rockefeller on a TV panel show was actually more cautious and restrained in the implications of some of the answers forced upon him than the President was. But Rockefeller was damned for pointing at the Kennedys, and White House reporters asked whether the President was displeased with him for that reason. The given answer was, no. On the face of it, the President had no right to be displeased and I'm told that he had no grounds to be. I'm also told to be very cautious indeed about absolving the Kennedys or falling in with the attempts of former Kennedy associates, notably Adam Walinsky and Frank Mankiewicz, to suggest that Ford apologists are deliberately smearing John and Robert Kennedy in order to get at Senator Edward Kennedy.

Within a week after publication of the Rockefeller report, Mr. Ford had a definite change of mind about how to handle the assassination phase of the commission inquiry. He concluded that his responsibilities as President required him to do something more than simply pass relevant information to Senator Frank Church's select investigating committee, an equivalent House committee if it ever got going, and the Justice Department. It may be, though I don't know it to be a fact, that he was simply bugged by the suggestions in print, on the air and in questions put to him and his spokesmen that he was "passing the buck." Press Secretary Ron Nessen read an impassioned and muddled sermon to the White House press corps on the evils of "a continuing series of leaks of partial information and . . . a lack of respect for handling this kind of thing in a careful way. The President really wants to reiterate his feeling that it needs to be handled with utmost prudence." Two days afterward the President still had not decided how he was going to handle whatever facts there were behind the continuing rumors of past discussion of and participation in plans for assassination "in the highest echelons of our government."

A victim of the *New York Times* allegations that led to the Rockefeller inquiry was James Angleton, former CIA chief of counterintelligence, who was driven from his job and close to mental and physical collapse by the *Times'* assertion that he directed much of the illegal domestic surveillance known within the agency as Operation CHAOS. I'd think better of the *Times* and its reporter, Seymour Hersh, if they'd given adequate corrective prominence to the following passage on page 145 of the Rockefeller report: "The Counterintelligence chief was technically responsible . . . for Operation CHAOS . . . . But the available evidence indicates that the Chief of Counterintelligence had little connection with the actual operations of CHAOS."

June 28, 1975

XXVIII

Bowing to OPEC

The last serious and thorough interagency federal study of this country's foreign oil problem was initiated in March 1974, six months before Gerald Ford succeeded Richard Nixon in the presidency. The basic conclusion of the study that the only escape for the US from the grip of the foreign oil cartel known as OPEC is through the reduced use of imported oil and the development of alternative energy sources was identical with the one that was reached and announced by President Nixon on November 7, 1973. In essence the sanitized version of the 1974 study published in November and the energy program submitted to Congress by President Ford in January, 1975, justified and elaborated upon the policy approach that Mr. Nixon had adopted without benefit of the study. Even the title of the published study and the symbolic phrase that Ford officials and spokesmen continue to use—"Project Independence"—was borrowed from Richard Nixon and it is as deceptive now as it was when it was first proclaimed. True independence from imported oil was not intended in 1973 and is not intended now. The most that President Nixon actually hoped for and the most that President Ford hopes for is reduced vulnerability to the price and related pressures that foreign oil producers, particularly Iran and the Arab producers in the Middle East, can bring to bear upon the United States so long as this country depends to the extent it does upon their oil.

The core assumption of the adopted policy and of the view underlying it is that the United States has no practical and predictably effective way to prevent further increases in the price of OPEC oil, much less to induce or compel rollbacks in the present inflated price, and won't have for at least two more years. The argument presented in *The New Republic* of July 5 and 12, to the effect that the US does have means of "calling OPEC's bluff" by using American economic power against the OPEC governments, is considered to be foolishly and dangerously mistaken by the officials who expound and are trying to implement Ford energy policy. In the words of one such official: "Most of that stuff is nonsense. It won't work. What it comes down to is that we need their oil. The be all and end all of our industrial development is their oil—OPEC oil. It's all very well to say we're strong and we're tough and we ought to act like it, but one would have thought that we got out of that notion in Vietnam. We are strong, we are tough and all that, but when it comes to doing things that are intended to get these countries to reverse policies that they consider to be in their interests, getting tough with them just isn't going to work so well."

Because of the respect that the backgrounds and demonstrated expertise of some of these officials demand, I would find their argument more persuasive than the counterargument offered in this journal's July 5 & 12 issue were it not for a fact that emerges from several weeks of inquiry at the White House, the Federal Energy Administration and Treasury, State and Defense Departments. The fact is that since the fall of 1974 there has been no formal and serious questioning, no fresh interagency and White House review of the assumptions that underlie the conviction just quoted that "most of that stuff is nonsense." More specifically and, to me, more disturbingly, there has been in recent months no organized, interagency search for and examination of non-military sanctions that might deter further OPEC price increases and perhaps encourage rollbacks in present prices.

7-25-75

LURIE'S OPINION

VETO

US. ENERGY PLANS

HIGHER OIL PRICES

LURIE

HIGHER OIL PRICES

HATCHING

The proffered excuse is that every conceivable sanction of this kind was discussed, considered and rejected during the aforementioned 1974 study and during the less intensive review that preceded the Nixon proclamation of Project Independence in 1973. The inquirer is also told in carefully veiled terms that possible military sanctions, up to and including the seizure by American forces of key oil fields in the Persian Gulf area, were discussed and considered with equal thoroughness, and rejected with equal finality, in 1973 and 1974. A classified summary of these discussions and of the factors cited for and against military retaliation at the time of the 1973-74 Arab oil embargo was included in the 1974 "Project Independence" report and deleted from the published version. The proffered excuse is not good enough. It is astonishing, it is disturbing, that President Ford has neither called for nor been offered a fresh and serious examination of the proposition that the US is as helpless in dealing with the OPEC price squeeze as Nixon-Ford policy assumes it to be.

This is not to say that there are not individual dissenters within the Ford bureaucracy. There are dissenters, advocates of a bolder and more positive policy in lieu of the prevailing and fundamentally passive policy. Some of them are in high positions. The public utterances of Treasury Secretary William Simon suggest that he'd take a much harder line than the administration is taking, particularly against the Arab producers who dominate OPEC. (An overlooked fact is that there are *two* foreign oil cartels, the Organization of *Arab* Producing and Exporting Countries and the larger, Arab and non-Arab Organization of Producing and Exporting Countries. It's OPEC that raised the price and threatens to raise it again, but it was OAPEC that embargoed the US and other industrialized consumers in 1973-74.) Yet Simon, like others whose views are reflected in what follows, vigorously supports the adopted policy in public. Treasury's representatives, for example, press for adoption of such Ford-Kissinger devices as the proposed "minimum safeguard" floor under imported oil prices at the Paris meetings of the consuming nations' principal instrument of cooperation, the International Energy Agency. Secretary Kissinger's idea that such a guaranteed minimum would keep the OPEC countries from undercutting domestic producers and hence wrecking any incentive for developing new oil and other energy sources seems ludicrous to me. But, with some important modifications, it's enthusiastically endorsed and furthered by people, including William Simon's people at Treasury, who ought to know what they are doing. Behind this show of intragovernment unity, however, there are nuances and differences that seem never to come to the President's attention.

There is a view that Mr. Ford should be much more aggressive and forthright than he is supposed in the bureaucracy to be when he deals, directly and through others, with such OPEC moguls as the Shah of Iran and Prince Fahd of Saudi Arabia. A measure of the prevailing passivity is the assertion, heard in quite authoritative quarters at the Treasury and Defense Departments, that President Ford never so much as mentioned the oil price issue during his recent talks with the Shah at the White House. A White House informant with access to the secret records of those conversations said the other day that the subject was raised and discussed. Whether the

162 WHITE HOUSE WATCH

President stated his public view that future OPEC price increases in rumored ranges of one dollar to four dollars per barrel would be "totally unacceptable" was not disclosed. Two possibly indicative facts were that it was said at the White House that the President didn't really mean what "totally unacceptable" might be taken to mean when he used the phrase at a press conference, and that immediately after his last meeting with Mr. Ford the Shah told reporters that a ruinous 35 percent increase in the current OPEC price would be justified and might be imposed in September.

A related opinion, clearly not shared by the President and seemingly not even conveyed to him in recent months, is that firm presidential statements to responsible OPEC leaders that any further price increase is indeed "totally unacceptable" to the United States should be followed with quiet, gradual denial to the principal OPEC gougers, notably Iran and Saudi Arabia, of the American weaponry, technology, training and other goods and services that they want and gladly pay high prices for. The official counter to this argument, a counter that Henry Kissinger has recently made to officials who present it to him, is that the OPEC governments would turn to such other suppliers as Britain, France and Germany and, in the last extremity, to the Soviet Union. A middle-level advocate of economic deterrence of this kind shrugs and says "so what?" when Kissinger and others argue that other suppliers would simply displace the US. Iran and Saudi Arabia obviously prefer what the US has to offer over what other countries have to offer and—so the argument goes—they'd think twice before dealing themselves out of the American market for things they need. Whether sanctions of this sort would actually have the desired effect is, however, a genuinely open question. An indication that they might not is the noneffect of a hard-nosed policy that William Simon has applied in an area where he is more or less free to do what he pleases. Excepting only projects that have been in the works for a long time, with guarantees of US financing, he has required the Export-Import Bank, over which the Treasury has policy control, to deny new loans and underwriting to OPEC governments and to prospective American suppliers of those governments. With considerable though not entire success, he has advocated a similar policy of denial at the World Bank and such regional institutions as the Inter-American and Asian Development Banks. This approach pleases fellow toughies in the government, but it has had no discernible impact upon OPEC price policies. All of the private dissents rest upon two convictions. One of them, voiced in administration propaganda but none the less valid for that reason, is that nothing the US can do will be effective unless Congress enacts a sound domestic energy program. The other conviction, never openly voiced, is that if the US gets tough at all it must be prepared to get tough militarily when and if the Arab producers react to the point of what Kissinger calls "strangulation."

Perhaps the most interesting argument heard at working levels in concerned departments and agencies is that the US will never put itself in a position to overcome OPEC dominance until it views the problem seriously enough to bring into risk the many and complex political and national security factors and relationships that are involved. For instance: is the potentially disastrous erosion of industrial economies, not to mention the impact of arbitrarily high and fixed oil prices upon the economies of developing countries, so grave that political and security relationships with such countries as Iran and Saudi Arabia must take second place? The prevailing official view is that the consequences of present and prospective foreign oil prices are not that serious. The dissenting view is that they are and that the US has got to accept the view that they are truly ruinous, not only to industrialized consuming countries but, in the foreseeable end, to the producing countries as well.

A knowledgeable official friend who is much involved summed up the problem: "It's a controversial area and a new area and there's no way one can look at it with a great degree of certainty and say that one thing is right or wrong. We're groping around, sort of searching for solutions. This Project Independence may not be the perfect one or even the best one. Who knows? I don't. You don't."

July 19, 1975

XXIX

Ford's First Year

At a press conference in Chicago on July 12, Gerald Ford was asked what he considers to be his "biggest personal accomplishments and failings as President" now that he is approaching the end of his first year in the office and is a declared candidate for nomination and election in 1976. His answer indicated some interesting priorities and capsuled the arguments that he will be using to persuade the Republican national convention to nominate him and the voters to elect him next year.

Mr. Ford's first emphasis was upon himself and what he thinks he has done for the presidency. As he put it, saying "we" but meaning "I": ". . . we have restored public confidence in the White House and in the executive branch of the government." His other points, in the order he stated them: the annual rate of inflation has been halved from between 12 and 14 percent to "roughly six percent"; unemployment stays up but it's going to decline and (he implied) the recession is ending; his energy program, now in revision and still to be enacted, should make the country "energy self-sufficient and less vulnerable to foreign oil imports"; and, last in this statement but certainly not least in the claims to come, "considerable progress" in foreign affairs as well as in domestic policy and performance. Here, without attempting detailed review of the record, are a few judgments of that record and of the President's claims.

The general perception of Gerald Ford near the end of his year is demonstrably close to his perception of himself. Recent and successive polls give him growing leads over all other prospective candidates for the presidency in both parties and particularly over the Democrat who has been presumed to be that party's strongest figure, Senator Edward Kennedy. Reporters and columnists who have talked to Mr. Ford lately, individually and in small groups, come away with impressions of "a confident President," sure of himself in ways and to an extent he didn't seem to be during his first months in the office. My impression, based only upon his public appearances in recent months along with a good deal of talk with some of his associates, pretty well coincides with a view expressed the other day by Bryce Harlow, a Washington lobbyist who worked for Presidents Eisenhower and Nixon at the White House and is one of President Ford's cronies and unofficial advisers. "That office," Harlow said, "either flattens the man in it or makes him stand tall. It hasn't flattened Jerry Ford." In an odd way the suggestion that the presidency has changed Gerald Ford for the better offends some of his associates. After Vice President Rockefeller was quoted here as saying the media ought to pay more attention than had been paid to President Ford's remarkable growth during the months that Rockefeller had been his Vice President, a senior Ford assistant and long-time friend grumped that this was nonsense. It wasn't that the President had changed, counselor Robert Hartmann said, he was the same old Ford. It was simply that Rockefeller had come to know him and see him close-up for the first time.

The press in mid-July was more preoccupied with what seemed to be evidence that the President was deliberately disassociating himself from his Vice President than it was with Mr. Ford's alleged personality growth. Howard (Bo) Callaway, the President's preconvention campaign chairman, said in so many words that he was seeking delegates for Mr. Ford, not for Nelson Rockefeller, and excluding Rockefeller from the Ford campaign because to do otherwise would alienate Republican conservatives who detest the Vice President. The President, who's been saying for months that he wants and expects the

Vice President to be on the 1976 ticket, spoke in Chicago of "the Vice President seeking his delegates and I seeking mine." It was an inept remark, not because it indicated a real schism between the President and the Vice President (there isn't any) but because Rockefeller had just said in Atlanta that he wasn't running for anything. Mr. Ford in fact was at last doing what Rockefeller had been advising him to do since February, which was to follow custom and avoid commitment to a candidate for the vice presidency until the candidate for the presidency is nominated.

The President is correct in his claim that the inflation rate has been halved since he took office. His accompanying admission that it's down partly as a result of sustained high rates of unemployment is rare in national politics. "As you bring down inflation," he said on June 25, "we may have to suffer for a short period of time higher unemployment than we like." The policy that the remark reflected is repugnant, but the admission is courageous and therefore admirable. In my judgment several of Mr. Ford's attitudes are far from admirable. During a recent trip to Ohio, a trip acknowledged to be political in purpose, he spoke repeatedly and rather defensively of his dual obligation "to preserve what is best in our environment" and simultaneously to "pursue the objective of maximum jobs and continued economic progress." This rationale as the President applies it keeps bringing him down against environmental protections and on the side of business management and profits at the expense of social needs. His two vetoes of strong bills to control strip mining and his recommendation that Congress repeal the current requirement that the automobile industry substantially strengthen emission standards are examples. His most recent pitch for what he calls "regulatory reform" suggests a repellent willingness to place millions of Americans at the mercy of market forces that have never been and are not now the agents of benevolence that the President implies and seemingly believes them to be. Mr. Ford's reference on July 3 to "the mistaken, stupid idea that regulation protects people" is appalling in its indiscriminate sweep and its misreading of history and our society. Some regulation is mistaken and excessive, no doubt, but I suspect that the biggest flaw and deception in the whole Ford approach lies hidden in his vague

generalities about "regulatory reform." Two of his recent
remarks on the subject are straight lifts from Richard Nixon, a
fact that in itself does not invalidate the points but does put Mr.
Ford's continuing effort to disassociate himself and his
administration from his predecessor and the Nixon administration in perspective. The remarks were: "And don't forget that a
government big enough to give you everything you want is a
government big enough to take from you everything you have";
and: "Declaring our independence from too much government
does not mean sounding a retreat from the legitimate
responsibilities which government must and ought to assume."

Gerald Ford as manager—and Presidents are rightly expected
either to be or find good managers—leaves a lot to be desired.
His reconstituted cabinet is an improvement over the one he
inherited. But his immediate establishment, the White House
Office staff and the larger Executive Office operation more or
less supervised by staff chief Donald Rumsfeld, is looser,
sloppier, occasionally less competent than Rumsfeld's initial
declaration of intent to assure an "orderly decision process" for
the President led this observer to expect. An interesting
explanation of why these defects could exist was offered after a
recent example—a silly and avoidable brush between Press
Secretary Ron Nessen and Secretary of State Henry
Kissinger—was reported here in somewhat acidulous detail.
The explanation was that Rumsfeld's declared dedication to
orderly process had been misread. He hadn't meant that the
operation was to be orderly in the totally controlled sense that
H.R. Haldeman and then Gen. Alexander Haig meant and
required. President Ford demanded much wider access to his
senior assistants than Richard Nixon had wanted or tolerated.
In keeping with this attitude Rumsfeld deliberately held a looser
rein and, though he wouldn't put it exactly this way, permitted
a freedom to make mistakes that would have been considered
subversive in the Nixon White House. It's been an exercised
freedom, God and presumably Gerald Ford know. Witness the
recent foul ups of the Solzhenitsyn affair, release of the
Rockefeller CIA report, and the President's revised proposal to
decontrol domestic oil prices.

July 29, 1975

XXX

Ford in Europe

Before turning to the serious side of the President's trip to Bonn, Warsaw, Helsinki, Bucharest and Belgrade—and serious and useful work was officially said to have been done, news reports and considerable evidence to the contrary notwithstanding— some of the lighter aspects of Gerald Ford's second trek through Europe in three months will be noted.

The only sloppy honor guard observed during the trip was West Germany's. The loose gray jackets, wrinkled trousers and dusty boots worn by the Federal Republic's soldiers, and the correspondingly casual dress of its sailors and airmen, seemed to comprise a deliberate caricature of the jack-booted, goose-stepping Prussians of bygone times. The smartest honor guard with the harshest, loudest goose-step was Communist Poland's, followed in order of snap and dash by Communist Romania's and Yugoslavia's. Fifteen motorcycle police in white helmets, white jackets, white trousers and black boots escorted President and Mrs. Ford in Bonn. Germans call these officers "white mice." Heads of state get 15 of them, prime ministers seven, foreign ministers five and other cabinet-rank officials three. These statistics came to reporters' attention on the President's first morning in Bonn when the 15 motorcyclists roared into the courtyard under his and Mrs. Ford's bedroom window just after Mr. Ford had complained that noise in the courtyard was keeping him and his wife awake.

At every stop the President thanked his hosts for their welcomes to him, "my wife Betty and our son Jack." Jack Ford, aged 23, and 13-year-old David Kissinger, the Secretary of State's son by his first marriage, were all over the place. Unlike his father, David Kissinger is handsome. He is also prematurely sage of visage, startlingly adult at first look. He and Jack inspected factories, visited a famous university in Cracow, Poland, and on their formal sorties were accompanied by "pools" of reporters and cameramen, just like their parents were. During an early morning hunt on the estate of the owner of the castle where the Fords stayed in Germany, Jack killed the extraordinary total of four boar. His host, a baron, said he usually killed no more than one or two in a whole hunting season. Jack, somewhat embarrassed, said he suspected the baron's beaters had made things unusually easy for him. Jack Ford, who recently earned a university degree in forestry, told reporters that he'd like to join the US Forest Service but can't because it would smack of nepotism. So he's going to spend the next year or so campaigning for his father's nomination and election.

Two of the President's foreign opposites, First Secretary Leonid Brezhnev of the USSR and President Tito of Yugoslavia, were observed by reporters with special closeness, Brezhnev because of his rumored illness and Tito because he seems to be astoundingly trim and vigorous at the age of 83. Brezhnev's entourage denied that anything is wrong with him. The slow and rather halting delivery of his address to the European security conference in Helsinki, and his abbreviated attendance on at least one public occasion suggested that it may be true that he's suffering from severe dental trouble at best and cancer of the mouth at worst. On the one occasion when I saw him close-up, awaiting Mr. Ford at the Soviet embassy in Helsinki, he made a show of striding up and down the driveway at the entrance and, when the President arrived, joshing and throwing out his right fist and generally professing to be in fine fettle. During the wait he joked with his interpreter, Victor Sukhodrev, and with

Foreign Minister Andrei Gromyko. Brezhnev in these exchanges had what I took to be a look of sardonic amusement, a look that persisted when he was joined by President Ford. Tito with his jet-black hair, his firm voice in speeches and toasts, and his brisk stride at the Belgrade airport and elsewhere, appeared to be in excellent physical shape, except for one observed circumstance. During an appearance with President Ford, billed as a joint report to the press on the visit to Belgrade, Tito never once lifted his head from the back of the sofa where he and his guest were seated while they delivered their respective statements.

On a long and pointless journey by train from Bucharest into the Romanian countryside, a good example of the insanely crowded schedule that the President let his hosts and staff impose upon him throughout the trip, Henry Kissinger accompanied Mr. Ford on a tour of magnificent Peles Castle, once a home of Romanian kings. The President asked to be shown "the king's bedroom" and, in that rococo chamber, said to Kissinger, "Henry, the royal bedroom." A Romanian official remarked that Kissinger appeared to be all for monarchy. "Only for myself," Kissinger retorted.

Fresh insight into the current mood of Secretary Kissinger, still as always since 1969 the most interesting member of the Republican administration, was acquired along the way. His mood in essence is a contradictory blend of confidence and something close to despair—"my paranoia," he calls the latter in his joking fashion. As recently as early 1975, he was saying that he'd serve through the present term if the President continued to want him to, but not a day after the close of the term in 1977. Now, to the distress of some of his closest and most devoted associates, he does not exclude the possibility of remaining in office if Mr. Ford is elected next year and asks him to stay. Kissinger is under the impression that the President has already invited him to stay. The associates find this change distressing because it indicates to them that Kissinger has succumbed to a vice that in others he regards with the utmost contempt: namely, a yen for status and power for their own sake, along with a conviction that he is indispensable. I give him better than that, believing that he really means it when he says that the continued easing of tensions in the world and the furtherance of détente with the Soviet Union constitute an opportunity, a mission, that no man is entitled to forgo or desert if he is offered the chance and has the ability to promote those great purposes.

Kissinger has seen all the evidence concerning his connection with wiretapping, CIA activities and other questioned practices that has been gathered from White House, NSC, CIA, State Department, Defense Department, FBI and other files and provided to the special investigating committee headed by Sen. Frank Church. Kissinger is convinced that nothing in these documents is sufficiently damning to ruin him. And yet, he recognizes the possibility that in the current climate of suspicion and tendency to assume guilt a hostile senator or House investigator may make enough of some of the evidence to seriously impair his effectiveness or even—the thought occurs to him—persuade the President that his Secretary of State must go. Kissinger perceives no sign of the latter consequence and, in his happier moments, is certain that it will never happen.

Along with the confidence there is a defensiveness. Kissinger consciously tries nowadays to restrain his inclination to call in journalists and correct references to him and his policies that seem to him to be unjust or inaccurate. On this trip a senior member of his personal retinue, State Department Counselor Helmut Sonnenfeldt, did it for him. Sonnenfeldt rebuked reporters for stories adding up Kissinger's drolleries into an account that seemed to make light of the whole journey; suggesting that the "Act of Helsinki" that Mr. Ford and 34 other statesmen signed at the close of the European security conference was little more than a mess of empty rhetoric; and, contrarily and to the great fury of Sonnenfeldt, holding that the President's signing of the same document signified Republican ratification and acceptance of the surrenders of principle and advantage allegedly made by Franklin Roosevelt to Josef Stalin at Yalta in 1945.

Kissinger suspects that Defense Secretary James R. Schlesinger was the source of a recent report that Kissinger advocated and Schlesinger opposed the use of B-52 bombers to compel the Cambodian Communists to release the seized freighter *Mayaguez*. The story heard in Kissinger's vicinity is that it never came to advocating or opposing the actual use of the bombers; he did argue for placing B-52s in readiness, in case President Ford ordered retaliatory action before the carrier *Coral Sea* got close enough to Cambodia for operations against the captors of the *Mayaguez*. Kissinger does not, however, regard Schlesinger as a critic or rival who acts and talks against him in a malicious way. Kissinger reserves that distinction for senior White House assistants whom he does not name but are known to include Counselor Robert Hartmann and Press Secretary Ron Nessen. "Bullshit!" Nessen exclaimed in Helsinki when he was told that he was rumored to be the source of a UPI report that some Ford assistants were complaining that Kissinger is "not a team player." Kissinger finds it difficult to believe that one of the White House sharpshooters is staff chief Donald Rumsfeld, who professes profound admiration and friendship for the Secretary of State. Kissinger also finds it hard to believe that some of the high-level sharpshooting could be occurring without Rumsfeld's knowledge.

An example of Kissinger's role on the European trip and the cloudy rumors that obscured the role was provided by the President's visit to Auschwitz, the Nazi concentration camp in Poland where at least four million Jews and non-Jews were worked, starved, beaten, tortured, gassed and shot to death. Former Chancellor Willy Brandt of West Germany, Prime Minister Harold Wilson of Great Britain and President Giscard d'Estaing of France had visited the camp, now a national Polish memorial to Nazi bestiality, and had spent up to two hours touring its abandoned brick dormitories, the ruins of its gas chambers and crematories, and the museum where mounds of human hair and gold teeth taken from murdered victims are among the preserved reminders of horror. President Ford's original schedule called for him to pass a total of 12 minutes at the camp site, three minutes at the brooding bronze monument that marks it, and not a second in actual inspection of the camp. American embassy officials in Warsaw and members of the White House advance party understood that Kissinger, a Jew who was born in Germany and knew that six of his relatives had died at Auschwitz, opposed a visit to the camp and, once a visit was decided upon, insisted upon the shortest possible stay there. In the event, the President spent 20 minutes at Auschwitz,

including seven minutes at the monument and in a very brief
look into one of the dormitories. When the President's Polish
guide and Communist First Secretary Edward Gierek, Mr. Ford's
senior host in Poland, urged him to take the few additional
minutes necessary for a pause at a dormitory, reporters saw Mr.
Ford look toward Kissinger. Kissinger nodded assent and the
President walked to a dormitory door and stared inside. Later
that day, during the flight from nearby Cracow to Helsinki, Press
Secretary Nessen told Kissinger of the rumors that he had first
opposed and then minimized the visit to Auschwitz. Kissinger
said that was ridiculous. Why on earth would he oppose it? What
possible policy considerations could there be for opposing it? All
that he had opposed and prevented, he told Nessen, was a visit to
the museum. He had maintained, he said, that it would be
unfitting for a President of the United States to spend an hour or
more looking at the hair, the teeth, the flogging benches, the
instruments of torture, the documents of Nazis and victims that
make up the exhibits. As for the incredible American and Polish
snafus that accompanied the decisions first to bar most of the
Ford press party from visiting the camp and then to let the entire
party go there, Kissinger said he had nothing to do with that
phase of the affair.

American officials in Warsaw confessed that the President and
Gierek had very little substantive business to transact, the major
matters pending between Poland and the US having been
wrapped up when Gierek got a lavish welcome in Washington
last year. Enroute from Helsinki to Bucharest, it was evident
aboard Air Force One that the President hadn't bothered to study
the schedule prepared for him in Romania. The time spent in
patently empty ceremony in Bonn and Belgrade suggested that
little if any more of substance was attempted or accomplished
there. Bonn aside—a presidential visit to the capital of a
committed friend is always in order—why had Mr. Ford and
Kissinger decided to visit the three capitals of Communist
Poland, Romania and Yugoslavia? The answer was obvious and,
in my opinion, very sound: of the Communist countries in
Eastern Europe, those three had dared to show the strongest
desire for maximum attainable independence from the Soviet
Union. Tito had declared his government's operative in-

dependence in 1948; President Ceausescu of Romania had in later years been almost as open and outspoken in his insistence upon the same independence; and Edward Gierek, the most cautious of the three party and national leaders, was steadily edging toward a similar position. Kissinger had no difficulty in reconciling encouragment of this trend with his labors for accommodation with the Soviet Union. Maximum pressures from the USSR's European family and borders, he reasoned, made for maximum Soviet readiness to offer the concessions necessary for effective US-Soviet détente.

From the official American standpoint, that is what the European security conference and the President's signature of the concluding Act of Helsinki are principally about. The non-binding commitments to human rights are important, but they are not central to the American interest in and subscription to the Act of Helsinki. The central American interest is in the acceptance by the Soviet Union, in the person and with the signature of Leonid Brezhnev, of such language as the statement that: "The participating states will respect each other's sovereign equality and individuality as well as all the rights inherent in and encompassed by its sovereignty, including in particular the right of every state to juridical equality, to territorial integrity, and to freedom and political independence." Such language can be far more significant than accompanying references to "the in-violability of frontiers" and the qualifying statement that frontiers are subject to change only by peaceful means and agreement. Kissinger was prepared to say, if he had been asked at his press conferences in Europe (he wasn't asked), that Soviet acceptance of the quoted language amounted at least in principle to repeal and invalidation of the infamous "Brezhnev doctrine," first enunciated in 1968 after the Soviet occupation of Czechoslovakia. The doctrine held that the Soviet government has the right to intervene militarily in any "Socialist" country where the Soviet version of "socialism" is threatened. As President Ford kept saying in an effort to placate suspicious American critics, both conservative and liberal, nothing in the Act of Helsinki requires the Soviet Union, the US, or any others of the 35 participants to do or not do anything. But it seems to me, as it does to Kissinger, that the concession in principle

Ford in Europe   175

inherent in the cited language makes nonsense of the complaints that at Helsinki the US surrendered Eastern Europe to the Soviet Union. What do these blithering conservative and liberal idiots want—resumption of cold-war confrontation?

August 16-23, 1975

———

Why Ford and Kissinger continued after Helsinki to endure without effective rebuttal the charges that they'd sold Eastern Europe out to the Soviets at Helsinki, and to neglect the counter-argument that they had maneuvered the Soviets into a substantial retreat from the Brezhnev doctrine of domination of the satellites, still puzzled me in late 1976. Perhaps the confusion of mind indicated by the President's disastrous assertion in the third campaign television "debate" that "there is no Soviet domination of Eastern Europe" had something to do with it.

XXXI

Ford from Afar

Between August 10 and 25, when the President vacationed at Vail, Colorado, and visited six other places for speeches, seminars and local interviews, this reporter stayed in Washington and took a holiday, too—from television and radio as well as from other forms of work—and neither saw nor heard Gerald Ford. Texts and transcripts of his speeches and question-answer sessions were obtained at the White House, but they added little or nothing of substance to what he was reported to have said. No White House assistants were asked to amplify and explain what he said. The result was a fortnight's unaccustomed impression of the President from afar, derived from approximately what any other lazy citizen would have known about what Mr. Ford was doing and saying during this period.

The texts did highlight one characteristic that had been previously noticed but never paid much heed. Mr. Ford distrusts the simple and unadorned declarative sentence. His participation in the preparation of his speeches varies from none to a lot, depending upon the importance he attaches to the occasion and the subject. Once the drafts have been prepared, however, he departs from them only to add a cosmetic emphasis that is unconvincing. In one of the more important speeches of the tour, the one to the American Legion at Minneapolis in which he warned both the Soviet government and congressional critics of his arms control policy that failure to achieve and consummate a satisfactory SALT II agreement will result in a two to three billion dollar annual increase in US arms expenditures, the statement in the advance text that "I commend the American Legion" became "I strongly commend." "I am glad" became "I am very, very happy." "All Americans are proud" became "all Americans are terribly proud." Typically, "I hope" came out "I honestly and sincerely hope." Mr. Ford's greatest asset as a candidate for nomination and election in 1976 is his reputation for being honest and sincere about everything in contrast with his predecessor's reputation. Mr. Ford's reputation is more likely to survive if he omits the cosmetics.

The effects of the appointed President's formal declaration of candidacy in July became ever more apparent in August. Snipey questions at White House briefings about who was paying for his trips, including the trips that supplemented the Vail excursion, crept into print. The official explanation that the taxpayers were paying only for strictly presidential journeys required difficult distinctions between Mr. Ford's role as President, as leader of his party, and as candidate, and between the portions of his travels that were undertaken in each of the roles. His needs and sensitivities as a candidate clearly accounted for some of the defensive references to his continuing quest for accommodation ("détente") with the Soviet Union and to the criticism from the political right and left that in this endeavor, and particularly in his signing of the European security declaration in Helsinki, he was selling out American principles. "Freedom must come first," the President said repeatedly in differing words, trying to placate the critics. He also concealed a deserved rebuke to some of the critics in his statement that: "It is easy to be a cold warrior in peace time, but it would be irresponsible for a President to engage in confrontation when consultation would advance the cause of peace."

The requirements of the candidate—no imposition, of course, upon a politician who had been in public office for 26 years— became most evident when the President had to deal with the impact of some remarks that Mrs. Ford had made in a magazine interview given months ago and published while he was in Vail, and in a later television interview. As columnist George Will pointed out, Betty Ford deliberately manufactured a chance to say in the magazine interview (before a cancerous breast was removed) that she invited her husband to sleep with her "as often as possible." She remarked in the television interview that she wouldn't be surprised if the Ford's 18-year-old daughter Susan confided that she was having an affair. Mrs. Ford also implied that in times past the Fords had assumed that one or another of their four children had dabbled with marijuana. A few Republican politicians complained, and Mr. Ford's own informants evidently told him, that the remarks about Susan and marijuana had outraged a significant number of prospective voters. The uproar, a mild one from where I sat, impelled the candidate and President to say in Milwaukee: "Let me . . . put this in proper perspective . . . What Betty was really trying to say was because of the closeness of our family and the understanding between children and parents, we are deeply concerned by the moral standards by which the family has been raised . . . So, I am real proud of what Betty tried to say and I regret there might have been some misunderstanding of what she did say." There was no misunderstanding. It's too bad that the President felt that he had to apologize for his wife's candor and indicate in the process that she didn't know how to say what she meant to say.

John R. Coyne, Jr., a former White House speech writer who worked for two Presidents (Nixon and Ford) and two Vice Presidents (Agnew and Ford), observed in *The New York Times* that the experience had taught him that "it is nearly impossible to arrive at conclusions about the reality of the political man beneath the surface of his rhetoric" and that this was specially true of Gerald Ford. It was obviously true of Mr. Ford in the period particularly cited by Coyne, the 1974 congressional campaign, when "he never knew what to say next and neither did the four of us who did the bulk of the writing for him." But some of the President's delivered remarks during the Vail period make me doubt that it's always true of Gerald Ford. One may be sure that the President meant and believed every word of it when at a

LURIE'S OPINION

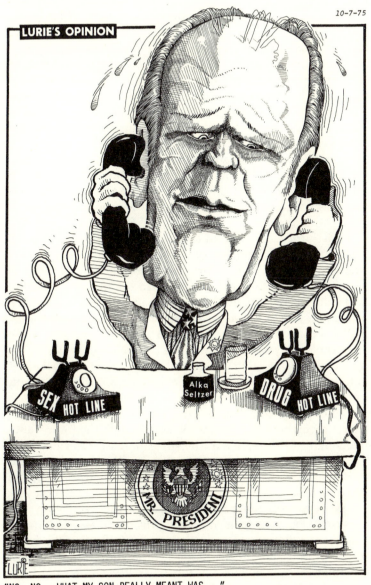

SEX HOT LINE

Alka Seltzer

DRUG HOT LINE

MR. PRESIDENT

"NO, NO - WHAT MY SON REALLY MEANT WAS..."

"BELIEVE ME, BETTY DOES SUPPORT MARRIAGE!"

symposium in Vail he defined the dubious basis of his energy policy: "Painful as they are, higher prices do promote conservation, and higher prices do promote increased efficiency in the use of petroleum products." He dramatized and completed the current rejection of a premise that until lately underlay one of the major elements of orthodox American wisdom when he said: "Cheap energy encourages waste and preserves inefficient energy technology. When the price of energy reflects its true value to society, as determined by the market place, there will be an incentive to stop squandering it . . ." He has tried to master the complexities of the energy problem. But he was reflecting the true Gerald Ford when he said in answer to a question about balancing economic against environmental needs that the way to do it is to get FEA Administrator Frank Zarb and EPA Administrator Russell Train together and let them work it out.

The President's definition of himself in a Milwaukee television interview (quoted here from the transcript) as "a practical conservative with a middle-of-the-road orientation" was standard political hackery, but his performance generally seemed to bear it out. Practical conservatism, for instance, required him to qualify a blanket reference in July to "the mistaken, stupid idea that regulation protects people." In the course of restating and broadening his declared determination to "take the shackles off American businessmen" by eliminating or reducing enormous areas of federal regulation, he grudgingly acknowledged in a Chicago speech that "some—and let me qualify it by saying some—regulations are necessary and appropriate; for instance, involving health, safety and the environment." His audience of hardware manufacturers made it clear by the ups and downs of their applause, as other audiences with their own special interests have when the President is on his deregulation kick, that they oppose all regulation except the regulation that protects them and their markets. Mr. Ford asserted in the Chicago speech, more clearly and emphatically than he has in others on the same theme, that he proposed to compensate for deregulation by stepping up anti-trust law enforcement and dealing by other means "with areas that anti-trust laws do not touch, these other regulated and legal monopolies and the government sanctioned cartels." A mid-level official who has helped the President formulate this policy and the expression of it was asked after Mr. Ford returned from Vail whether the President fully understood the extent of the challenge to powerful and protected segments of the American economy that he professed to be proclaiming. The official said he thought the President understood it but wasn't sure he did.

September 6, 1975

XXXII

In the Press Room

The agreement of Israel and Egypt to begin to agree on a secured border zone in the Sinai had a worthy though incidental and unnoticed effect in Washington. It provided the occasion for a couple of hours of good humor in the White House press room, a place where the recent norm has been sour and unproductive conflict between Press Secretary Ron Nessen and the 30 to 40 reporters who regularly attend his briefings.

The good humor prevailed partly because the occasion for it arose on the Labor Day holiday, partly because Nessen wasn't there, and partly because the President placed himself for promotional purposes in a ludicrous situation that had nothing to do with the importance and merits of the Israeli-Egyptian agreement. Nessen was with the Ford family at Camp David, the presidential retreat in the Maryland mountains near Washington. Word that the Israeli cabinet had approved the agreement had hardly arrived at Camp David when it was decided that televising the President in successive telephone conversations with Henry Kissinger and Prime Minister Yitzhak Rabin in Jerusalem and with President Anwar Sadat in Alexandria would be a splendid thing to do. A CBS camera crew, pooling for all the networks, was summoned from Washington and made it only in time to photograph the President in his attempt at conversation with Sadat. The White House press office and press room, closed for the holiday, were opened. Washington news offices and reporters, many of whom were at home, were alerted by telephone. Most of the few press staff members and the 20 or so reporters who turned up, male and female, were in slacks, sweaters, windbreakers, tennis or sports shoes. They were in a mood to be amused and they were when the recorded conversations were transmitted to the press room from Camp David. Nessen bet Bill Roberts of his staff a dollar that the media would find a way to make fun of the event. Nessen won.

For openers, the President on the telephone to Jerusalem called Henry Kissinger "Ron" and continued: "I have to tell you and later when I talk to the Prime Minister and the President [tell them] that Walker is recording this conversation." 'Walker' is the staff code name for the White House Communications Agency, an army facility that provides and protects special presidential communications channels. Mr. Ford didn't tell Messrs. Rabin and Sadat that they were being recorded. The President later mentioned, as if it were something he had nothing to do with, a statement that had been drafted and was issued in his name at the White House before he got on the telephone. The statement reflected the Ford staff's incessant effort to establish the President's primacy over Kissinger in foreign affairs. It had Mr. Ford saying near the beginning: "I have consistently worked for this outcome. I am deeply gratified . . ." Secretary Kissinger and his "tireless efforts" were mentioned and commended in the last sentence. After telling Kissinger that he was being recorded "for historical purposes" and being told by Kissinger that "I have no objections," Mr. Ford evened matters by speaking as follows: "Well, let me say, Henry, very very deep, very deeply, how very grateful I am for the tremendous effort you have made in this last round of negotiations. I know how long and hard and devotedly you have spent many, many hours not only with me but with Prime Minister Rabin and President Sadat. I think this is a great achievement, the most historic, certainly, of this decade and perhaps in this century. . . ." Kissinger is aware of the staff manuevers and is also aware that Mr. Ford values the appearance of primacy almost as much as his staff does. The Secretary of State presumably had all this in mind when he replied in part: "I appreciate this very much, Mr. President, and of course we have spent more time on the Middle East, you and I, than on almost any other problem." After further discussion of what the President called "one of the great achievements for the world," Kissinger said near the close of the conversation: "Well Mr. President, we have worked together on this and your strong support and your leadership in your talks [in Salzburg and Washington] with Sadat and Rabin made this possible."

This Alphonse-and-Gaston act and the chummy conversation with Prime Minister Rabin that followed mildly amused the reporters. The third conversation, mostly between the President and a dim voice that seemed to belong to either an Egyptian telephone operator or a Sadat assistant and was heard to say only "hello" at intervals between Mr. Ford's dogged efforts to thank Sadat "for your statesmanship" and "the leadership that you've given," reduced the press room audience, including the White House employees, to unkind but justified laughter. Two of the remarks that were clearly Sadat's were "I hope you are well" and "I hope . . . the momentum of this course continues." Mr. Ford seized with plaintive joy upon the second remark, saying three times in slightly different words that "I assure you, Mr. President, we're going to keep the momentum going." All good or anyhow refreshing things must end and this one mercifully did with Mr. Ford's rather strained "the best to you, sir. And Henry will be there shortly. Okay—bye, bye."

Things in the press room were back to normal the next day with reporters snarling at Nessen and Nessen poorly prepared for the day's briefing. Any meaningful amplification of the published texts would—he said—have to await Kissinger's return. In the course of doing his best to field questions about who would protect the proposed team of American technicians in the surveillance zones, Nessen seemed to be either unaware or lacking the wit to say that the UN Emergency Force stationed between Israeli and Egyptian areas would have that responsibility. In trying to answer a series of questions put to him by one of the press group's leading snarlers, based on the illusion that the

US is promising "to pay for Israel's oil for years and years to come," Nessen seemed not to know that the US promises only to assure Israel of a steady oil supply, not necessarily or explicitly to pay for the oil.

Here a point should be made that is seldom made in Nessen's behalf. He and his senior deputy, William Greener, usually meet before the briefings with staff chief Donald Rumsfeld, deputy chief Richard Cheney, and Counsellor John Marsh. Then Nessen, Rumsfeld, Marsh, chief lobbyist Max Friedersdorf, sometimes Cheney, and Counsellor Robert Hartmann meet with the President. Nessen and his assistants do a lot of other checking. But it is principally at these meetings that Nessen is informed, coached, and given the line to take on important and anticipated subjects. Kissinger's and the Kissinger NSC staff's grudging cooperation with Nessen, a circumstance that arises in part from Nessen's known antipathy for Kissinger, contributes to the press secretary's appearance of uncertainty in dealing with foreign affairs. It therefore is inaccurate and unfair to charge Nessen with sole or, in some instances, main responsibility for his displays of ignorance and-or ineptitude. He reflects an ineptitude and deficiency of comprehension that are characteristic of the Ford White House. A cliché in pieces on this subject is that no press secretary can be successful and effective in the post-Watergate period. This observer has come to doubt that any press secretary can be successful and effective at the Ford White House.

The White House press corps has its own deficiencies. One of them is a pervasive and humorless self-righteousness. It is typified by the almost total lack of any indication in questions on a currently favored subject—who pays for the President's travels in this political season—that service to the press is an important item in these controversial costs. Four members of the White House press and transportation staffs are on the West Coast at this writing, preparing for the Ford press party on an overnight trip to Seattle and Sacramento. Recently and secretly, Nessen broached an idea that he probably will put into practice. The purpose is to reduce the travel costs that the President's personal campaign committee will have to pay, and that will be chargeable against the new pre-nomination expenditure limit of $10 million, once Mr. Ford admits that he is campaigning for the 1976 nomination. The idea is to let 20 to 28 instead of the usual seven or eight journalists ride on Air Force One and charge their employers the equivalent of first-class fares. Hubert Humphrey and George McGovern met most of their plane costs that way in 1968 and 1972. Presidents never have.

September 13, 1975

———

Mr. Ford thought he was talking to Nessen when he seemed to call Kissinger "Ron." The code name for the communications agency is "WACA" and sounds like "Walker," which I should have known. The foregoing attempt to place the blame for some of what seemed to be Nessen's deficiencies where it actually belonged was not appreciated by Nessen or anyone else at the White House.

XXXIII

Shooting at Ford

Back in August, well before Lynette Fromme aimed a .45 caliber pistol at the President in Sacramento and the woman who calls herself Sara Jane Moore fired a .38 revolver at him in San Francisco, some of Mr. Ford's senior assistants looked over the schedule that he had approved for the next four weeks, with one to four-day trips out of Washington every weekend and a midweek, 12-stop campaign dash through New Hampshire in behalf of a Republican candidate for the Senate, and told him that he just couldn't do it. The assistants' concern was not for the President's safety. It was rather that he was about to over-strain himself and a White House staff that was being gradually reduced, invite a suspicion that he was neglecting work that he ought to be doing in Washington, and—this last more implied than stated—to defeat his purposes by making it distressingly clear that he really didn't have enough to say that was worth saying so many times in so many places. A participant in discussions in which these points were put to the President recalls the argument and the response as follows: "Some of us got after him as soon as we saw it all laid out and said, look, you've got something scheduled every weekend and you just can't do that

and he said in effect, the hell I can't. He was damned if he was
going to cancel any of the commitments that he's already made.
But he sort of sheepishly, ruefully is probably the right word,
agreed that maybe he'd better not add any more."

Others who discussed the subject with the President
understood that he'd agreed and committed himself to a good
deal more. They understood that he'd promised to cut back
substantially on presidential travel in October and November,
and they professed to be ready to argue hard and seriously with
him and with the two assistants principally responsible for
preparing his schedules, staff chief Donald Rumsfeld and Jerry
Jones, a Nixon holdover (like Rumsfeld) who had recently been
staff secretary and lately had been put in overall charge of
scheduling by Rumsfeld, if the originally modest October travel
plans were significantly increased. These advocates of reduced
travel and exposure to the hinterland public had better start
arguing. On September 24, two days after the President was
fired upon in San Francisco, plans for eight trips from
Washington by the end of October, including two that could be
accomplished within an afternoon and evening and six requiring
a day or more away from the capital, were far enough along in
preliminary commitment to have been submitted to Mr. Ford for
his approval. They could and at this writing were expected at the
White House to take him to Illinois, Nebraska, West Virginia,
New Jersey, North Carolina, Tennessee, Michigan, Kansas,
Florida, Georgia and Alabama and finally back to California,
where within 17 September days he had twice been close to
assassination.

"We've got a lot of amateur security experts around right
now," an assistant to the President who is also a close and long-
time friend remarked, referring to the professional libertarians
in the White House press corps who at the daily news briefings
indicated by their questions that they were suddenly for
requiring the Secret Service and local police to lock up everybody
who might be suspected of designs upon his safety and life.
Having no pretensions to that kind of expertise, I stick to what
the President and his spokesmen, Press Secretary Ron Nessen
and staff chief Rumsfeld, have said on the subject and matters
related to it since Lynette Fromme thrust a .45 Colt within a few

feet of Mr. Ford's face in Sacramento on September 5. The comments amount to an interesting study in the attitudes and personality of Gerald Ford and in the collective attitudes and personality of his White House establishment.

At Sacramento, less than three hours after (in his words) he had seen "a hand coming up behind several others in the front row and obviously there was a gun in that hand," the President said to reporters and TV cameras: "This incident under no circumstances will preclude me from contacting the American people as I travel from one state to another and from one community to another. In my judgment, it is vitally important for a President to see the American people, and I am going to continue to have that personal contact and relationship with the American people." Listening to him in the hotel lobby where he spoke, I thought he was pale and his voice was shaky, although later on the tube he looked and sounded firm. Remarks prepared for delivery at a White House seminar in St. Louis had him saying: "Only by going around the country to meetings like this, by meeting people face to face and listening to what they have to say, can you really learn what people feel and what they think. Doing this is an important part of my job. I have no intention of abdicating that responsibility. I have no intention of allowing the government of the people to be held hostage at the point of a gun." Mr. Ford offended newspaper and electronic reporters who in early accounts had emphasized the last sentence of the foregoing passage when he omitted the entire statement from his delivered remarks—because, he said, he wanted to get away from the prepared script and allow more time for questions at the seminar. He actually omitted it, I am told at the White House, because at that time (Sept. 12) he did not want to capitalize upon the Sacramento incident.

At a press conference in his White House office on September 16, the President said to a reporter who expressed doubt that he learned anything from his prized contacts with people in crowds: "You'd be very much amazed at how often people in the course of shaking hands or greeting them, they will make specific recommendations or comments. It is rather amazing and very encouraging." It's amazing, all right. As a dedicated trudger after Mr. Ford when he in journalism's term "makes the crowd," I have yet to hear anybody say anything to him more informative than "You're doing great, Mr. President." On Air Force One, flying home to Washington after the President was shot at in San Francisco, Donald Rumsfeld said: "I think that political leadership in our country represents people and they have to deal with people and there's no question but that this President and Presidents in years to come will be traveling and meeting people in various ways. It's inevitable. It's part of our system." Five minutes before the midnight of his arrival at the White House from San Francisco, the President said: ". . . I don't think any person as President or any person in any other major political office ought to cower in the face of a limited number of people, out of 214 million Americans, who want to take the law into their own hands. The American people . . . want a dialogue between them and their President and other public officials . . . Under no circumstances will I, and I hope no others, capitulate to those that want to undercut what's all good in America."

During repeated, prolonged and futile efforts in the White House press room to get Ron Nessen to modify the line thus set by the President, one of the few productive questions asked was whether Mr. Ford's public assertions of refusal to "capitulate" might incite rather than deter the kind of people who in California had threatened to shoot and had shot at the President. Nessen, reading from notes that he had prepared after discussing the San Francisco episode and its implications with Mr. Ford, answered: "The President feels that his travel and his demeanor and the things he's said publicly, to him at least do not represent any kinds of actions or remarks that could be considered as flaunting himself or his office in front of people who might belong to this tiny minority, nor does he feel that anything he's said or done represents in any way a dare or an egging on of these individuals." Presumably without intending to do so, Vice President Rockefeller said something that could be taken as a commentary upon the Ford-Nessen posture. The Vice President said: "Let's stop talking about it. Let's stop putting it on front pages and on television. Psychiatrists say every time there is any publicity, it is stimulating to the unstable." Rockefeller then proceeded to say essentially what the President had been saying, in these words: "Let's not give up what we've got for a miniscule of society. This is the big deal of the moment. Let's not panic. Let's keep an open society."

Ranking assistants who discuss the problem of public appearance and contact with the President say that he truly and deeply believes what he says about the necessity of any President's access to the public. After the shooting in San Francisco, the first reaction of one such assistant was a fear that it might drive the President to retract the concessions that he had reluctantly made to security after the threat in Sacramento, rather than appear to be "capitulating." The pattern of Mr. Ford's behavior on the road since Sacramento suggests that he will display more caution and allow more caution to be exercised in his behalf in the near future. With a few exceptions on the trip that ended with the unforgettable *crack* of Sara Moore's .38 in San Francisco, the President confined his crowd contacts to airports. For one day only, on the New Hampshire trip, he wore a discernible and obviously uncomfortable protective vest. He ventured no public walks, even for short distances, of the kind he was taking when Lynette Fromme's hand with the gun in it rose before him. My opinion is that he should restrict his presence and his walks to the White House grounds for awhile, maybe until January 20, 1977.

October 4, 1975

———

The caution waned and Mr. Ford soon returned to the crowds.

XXXIV

Ford and Deregulation

President Ford pleased the dozen or so White House assistants and other officials who are working to put some substance in his regulatory reform program by laying off the subject for awhile. Apart from passing references in a few interviews and minor speeches, he last plugged the theme on August 25, when he told a convention of hardware manufacturers in Chicago that his objective is to "take the shackles off American businessmen" and "get the federal government as far out of your business, out of your lives, out of your pocketbooks and out of your hair as I possibly can." This sort of rhetoric horrifies the people who are doing the serious work of deregulation because it overstates the possibilities, distorts the objectives, obscures the fact that there's hardly an American business person who doesn't cherish some of the shackles, and makes Mr. Ford out to be more naive and more indifferent to the general welfare than officials who discuss the program with him find and believe him to be.

There is plenty of skepticism. Ralph Nader has said the Ford deregulation line is a fraud. I have written that the Ford rhetoric could conceal the biggest fraud and deception in the whole Ford posture. Yet the most interesting aspect of the deregulation debate turns out upon examination to be the breadth of agreement that American society and particularly the business and industrial elements in it are over-regulated. Nader and Mr. Ford are together in their premise that federal regulation originally intended to suppress monopoly and promote competition actually suppresses competition and protects installed interests and entities. Peter H. Schuck, director of the Washington office of Consumers Union, sets forth in *Harper's* the same indictments of the regulatory system and the same arguments for relaxing its grip upon central elements of our economy and society that one hears at the Ford White House. After considerable inquiry there and in affected agencies and departments, the doubt remaining with me is whether the President adequately comprehends the extent of the challenge that he is posing or pretending to pose to powerful interests, notably labor and corporate interests, and whether, if he does comprehend it, he really intends to sustain and press the challenge. The sum of the available evidence, always keeping in mind Mr. Ford's fundamental and avowed conservative bias, is that he comprehends the nature and gravity of the challenge and intends to sustain it. Roderick Hills, a White House lawyer who has been coordinating the reform effort, accompanied the President on his latest trip to the West Coast. During conversational interludes aboard Air Force One, Hills discussed with Mr. Ford pending proposals to relax rate controls and open up competition in the airline and trucking industries, and the opposition that would surely be encountered from managements, unions, congressmen and federal regulatory agencies. Hills told White House associates that the President took it all in and said, *go ahead.* Paul MacAvoy, a member of the President's Council of Economic Advisers and a free-market economist who understands that markets can't be entirely free in modern societies, has spent many hours talking over the problems of regulation and the powerful resistance to meaningful change with the President and is convinced that Mr. Ford understands what he's getting into. After representing a conservative Michigan constituency in Congress for 25 years, MacAvoy asks, how could the President not understand?

The deregulatory measures proposed and the few

deregulatory actions taken since the President got on this kick a year ago must convince any reasonable observer that it's not all rhetoric and pretense. The proposals of the White House and inter-agency committee variously called a task force and a review group have aroused bitter controversy behind the generally smooth facade of the Ford administration. Two Ford appointees, Attorney General Edward Levi and Chairman John Robson of the Civil Aeronautics Board, argued for weeks over whether the Department of Justice should take from the CAB its authority to sanction airline agreements and mergers that otherwise would be subject to antitrust prosecution. Upon the advice of MacAvoy, Hills and another Ford appointee, Secretary of Transportation William T. Coleman, Jr., the President sided with Robson. The result is that airline legislation to be announced at the White House and sent to Congress will retain the CAB's primary authority but give Justice enhanced rights of review and intervention in CAB decisions. Other provisions, mostly opposed by the industry and viewed rather warily by the CAB, would if adopted by Congress give interstate airlines a delayed and restricted but nonetheless revolutionary right to revise their fares up or down within prescribed limits without CAB permission, gradually open interstate air routes to the competition of new entrants, and generally introduce a degree of price and service competition that the CAB now forbids and the certificated lines fear. Robson is regarded at the White House as one of the few cooperative and friendly chairmen of regulatory agencies. He has instituted a CAB study aimed at experimental approaches to freer entry and more freedom than the industry now has to vary rates and services without CAB approval. At his instance, however, the five-member board unanimously refused to participate in framing the White House proposals, or to comment upon them, and said it will withhold its view for Congress. Another friendly chairman and a vociferous advocate of extensive deregulation is Lewis Engman of the Federal Trade Commission, a Nixon appointee who has justified this writer's assertion at the time of his nomination that a member of the Nixon White House staff wasn't necessarily being sent to the FTC to sabotage its regulatory work. A revealing index to the difficulties of actually reducing regulation and to the need in a complex society for a lot of it is provided by current FTC statistics. With all of Engman's calling for deregulation and weighing of the demonstrable benefits against the costs of regulation, his commission issued 226 complaints and 147 orders in fiscal 1973; 227 complaints and 202 orders in fiscal 1975.

The model for deregulation of transportation, a field selected for initial effort because its problems are known and the restriction of competition in it is beyond dispute, is the Railroad Revitalization Act that the President submitted to Congress last May 19. Its opponents include large segments of the protected and widely bankrupt railroad industry and that industry's protective regulator, the Interstate Commerce Commission. The ICC is regarded at the White House as the second worst of the 10 federal regulatory agencies in terms of both competence and philosophy. The worst agency is considered to be the Federal Maritime Commission, whose area of control is being approached very slowly and carefully by the White House deregulators because of the power of the marine unions. In the aspects of chief interest here, the rail act would greatly restrict the ICC's power to disapprove freight rate reductions; give the railroads authority to raise or lower rates without ICC approval within limits varying from seven to 15 percent over three years; and remove many of the exemptions from antitrust prosecution that protect the industry's cooperative rate-setting "bureaus." Despite massive opposition, the administration approach has had surprising support in Congress—with one exception. The proposal to guarantee railway loans up to two billion dollars has run into demands that the amount be doubled or even quadrupled, to levels that the President would probably veto even if he got approval of his regulatory reforms.

The administration's third transportation proposal, for the interstate trucking industry, follows the principles of the rail legislation. Interstate trucking is one of the most closely protected industries. White House deregulators are convinced, for instance, that the ICC keeps rail rates artificially high and is slow and reluctant to approve innovations in rail freight methods and equipment in order to discourage effective rail competition with the truckers. New entry into interstate trucking is restricted almost to the point of prohibition. There are complex route rules, certificates specifying what goods licensed lines can and cannot carry between what points, and such prohibitions as the one forbidding "private carriers"—that is, producers and processors who deliver their own products to distant markets—to haul anything for revenue on the return trips. The proposed legislation would open up new entry to some extent, give carriers limited freedom to vary their rates, and permit private carriers to haul goods related to their products—chicken soup, for instance, derived from delivered chickens, or canned orange juice derived from delivered oranges—back to their home depots. It's a fairly modest package, it's been months in preparation and is months behind schedule for submission to Congress. But it raised unshirted hell when, at the President's order, its major elements were described to President Frank Fitzsimmons of the Teamsters' union and five companions who were invited to a White House meeting on September 30. The federal conferees—among them Vice President Rockefeller, Hills, MacAvoy, and Calvin Collier and Stanley Morris of the Office of Management and Budget—were cursed, shouted at, waved at. "It was hairy," one of the federal participants said. Only Fitzsimmons and the union's Washington lobbyist, Don Rogers, kept their cool. The union hasn't formally opposed the proposal, but the show of fervent love for the status quo was ominous.

The Ford deregulators have also run into trouble with Secretary of Agriculture Earl Butz. Two of the White House target areas are the department's system of meat and poultry inspection and its marketing orders systems. Two federal laws, one for meat and one for poultry, require individual, specific, on-spot inspection of every cow, pig, chicken, rabbit, etc. that is slaughtered and processed for interstate shipment. Federal grant restrictions encourage, practically require, the states to operate similarly detailed inspection systems. Some 9000 inspectors are employed in the federal system. Mr. Ford's deregulators propose to substitute random checking, with high quality standards and severe penalties for violations. Butz is doubtful but has instituted a departmental study of the proposal. Where he balks is at a proposal to modify or abolish the department's system of milk marketing orders, also mandated by law. When a group of producers in a local area, a state or a region demand it, the department must initiate a complicated sequence of proposals, hearings and referenda that eventually lead to minimum prices that milk wholesalers or other handlers must pay milk producers. Butz has told the deregulators, who regard this as a prime example of arbitrary price fixing, that they will touch his milk marketing orders only over his body. MacAvoy has told Butz that the deregulators are ready to march right over his body, if necessary. They will be marching without Roderick Hills, the chief deregulator, who is leaving the White House staff to become chairman of one of the busiest and toughest regulatory agencies, the Securities and Exchange Commission. MacAvoy, who is Hills' logical successor at the head of the review group, prefers that the assignment go to a Ford assistant, a lawyer like Hills, who is not identified with such White House factions as the Domestic Council or MacAvoy's own Council of Economic Advisers.

October 11, 1975

XXXV

Three to Go

Three of the President's assistants are leaving him and taking other government jobs. Their experience at the White House and the circumstances of their departures tell quite a lot about how Mr. Ford uses his staff and how his staff serves him.

Stanley S. Scott, aged 42, was Richard Nixon's second in-house black and has served Gerald Ford in that capacity, with the title of special assistant, since Mr. Ford became President. Scott is to be assistant administrator of the Agency for International Development, overseeing US economic aid to the countries of black Africa. His predecessor in that job, Samuel C. Adams, Jr., was one of the first black career officers in the US Foreign Service and retired September 27 after 25 years in government. Scott's predecessor at the White House, Robert Brown, quit and was succeeded by Scott on February 5, 1973, during the mad turnover of White House and other presidential appointees with which Richard Nixon celebrated his reelection in 1972. About all that Stan Scott and Bob Brown had in common was that both of them were black Republicans. Brown came from a poor North Carolina family and worked his way up to moderate affluence in the public relations business to which he returned when he left the White

House. Scott comes from a wealthy family of Southern newspaper publishers. He worked for the family's *Atlanta Daily World,* ran its *Memphis World,* and was a NAACP public relations man and a broadcast reporter before he joined the White House staff in June 1971 as an assistant to communications director Herbert Klein.

Watergate was just beginning to close in upon President Nixon when Scott became his special assistant and the two were never close, officially or personally. Mr. Nixon, ever the recluse, wasn't very close to Bob Brown, either, but they were accustomed to each other and got along pretty well. Scott did what he could for the President in the way of maintaining the relatively little rapport with black communities, black politicians and black leaders that Brown had been able to establish. Scott came into his own and began to feel that he was really valued at the White House after Gerald Ford succeeded to the presidency. They hit it off from the day that Mr. Ford took office as the first appointed Vice President. Only one of the 17 black members of the House of Representatives who were then in office, Scott's friend Andrew Young of Atlanta, had voted to confirm Gerald Ford's nomination to the vice presidency. "This President needed help and knew it," Scott recalls, and the first quarter in which Scott proceeded to provide the needed help was the Congressional Black Caucus. It had taken Richard Nixon more than a year to get around to a requested meeting with the Black Caucus. Scott arranged an early meeting between President Ford and the caucus and the relationship, though hardly warm, continues to be better than it was in the Nixon time. According to Scott, President Ford had more encounters with black groups and individuals during his first 14 months than President Nixon had in five years.

Yet there were some odd and revealing differences between the experience of Brown and Scott under President Nixon and Scott's experience under President Ford. Brown or somebody from his staff frequently attended Nixon Cabinet meetings and Scott did so after he succeeded Brown. Scott has never attended or been invited to a Ford Cabinet meeting. Scott was on Capitol Hill calling on senators who will be voting for or against his nomination as assistant AID administrator, when the President held his latest Cabinet meeting on October 8. As assistant to Herbert Klein and later to President Nixon, Scott never had any trouble getting to that President's two staff chiefs, H.R. Haldeman and Gen. Alexander Haig, when he needed to. He's just about given up trying to get in touch, by telephone or in person, with Mr. Ford's chief of staff, Donald Rumsfeld. Good and close though his personal and working relationship with Mr. Ford has been, Scott has found the going rough when he has to deal with the Ford staff in general. Scott is known to share the opinion of the White House assistant who says of Don Rumsfeld, unfairly in my judgment: "He's another Bob Haldeman, only he smiles."

Roderick M. Hills, aged 44, is leaving the White House staff to be chairman of the Securities and Exchange Commission after six months as the junior of two attorneys who hold the title of Counsel to the President. The senior Counsel is Mr. Ford's first law partner and friend of many years from Grand Rapids, Philip Buchen. Buchen's first deputy, Phillip Areeda of the Harvard Law School, lasted an even shorter time at the White House than Hills did. Areeda left in part because he didn't get the job he wanted, which was executive director of the Domestic Council, a post that went instead to Vice President Rockefeller's assistant and protegé, James Cannon. Hills is leaving because the President and a lot of other people, including Secretary of the Treasury William Simon, Chairman Alan Greenspan of the Council of Economic Advisers, and numerous brokers and others in the investment business would rather have him in the SEC chairmanship than the principal competitor for that position, SEC member A.A. Sommer, Jr., a Democrat who was strongly recommended to the President by the outgoing chairman, Ray Garrett, Jr.

Both Garrett, a Republican, and Sommer took office the same day—August 6, 1973. A story accepted as true in the investment world but not confirmed at the White House is that Garrett, a Chicago lawyer and former member of the SEC staff, had an understanding with President Nixon that Sommer would be appointed chairman midway in his and Garrett's terms. Sommer is a Cleveland attorney with an extensive background in the investment business that Hills cannot claim, though Hills has represented clients in complicated SEC proceedings. Sommer's advent to the chairmanship was feared and opposed, and prevented by the President, for two reasons, one general and one specific. Sommer is known as a shaker-upper, an advocate of change in a world that detests change. Specifically, he is assumed to favor either abolition or drastic modification of the New York Stock Exchange's precious Rule 394, which used to make it virtually impossible and still makes it difficult for member brokers to buy or sell NYSE listed securities on any other exchange. The conventional Wall Street view is that the New York exchange would collapse without Rule 394 or a reasonable facsimile of it. Hills said in effect at the Senate hearing on his nomination that he has an open mind on the issue, which comes to hearing before the SEC on October 14. He plans to attend the hearings on 394 as an observer and to move into the chairmanship on November 1.

In his six months at the White House, Hills established himself as a star performer in that rather drably staffed institution. He was best known to the public and to Washington reporters, a few of whom he trusted and assisted to an extent that is far from common at the allegedly open Ford White House, as the staff attorney mainly responsible for handling the President's difficult problems with the Senate and House select committees investigating US intelligence agencies. Frederick A.O. Schwarz, Jr., chief counsel to the Senate committee, is among many people who consider that Hills did a good and honorable job for the President with that committee and its staff. Hills is the first to acknowledge that he didn't do so well with Rep. Otis Pike's House committee and blames himself for failing to awake as soon as he should have to the problems it posed. A less noted but more burdensome role was his assignment to coordinate the President's program of regulatory reform.

It's practically illegal to mention Rod Hills in print without noting that his wife, like him a former Los Angeles attorney, is the Secretary of Housing and Urban Development. Sen. William Proxmire, who presided at the committee hearing on Hills' nomination, pounced upon this fact in a particularly nasty variation of his niggling objection to providing senior federal officials with chauffeured automobiles. Proxmire made Hills promise to ride to work at the SEC in his wife's limousine or else drive his own car. A more pertinent fact is that Carla Hills had a good deal to do with Hills' willingness to leave the White House. He is among the many who think it quite likely that she will be the first woman appointed to the US Supreme Court, when and if President Ford has a vacancy to fill. Roderick Hills doesn't want to be on the President's staff, and therefore subject to suspicion that he influenced the appointment, when and if it occurs.

Soon after Richard Dunham, aged 45, was transferred from Vice President Rockefeller's staff to the White House staff as one of two deputy directors of the Domestic Council, a ranking assistant to the President said to him: "We understand that your loyalty is to the Vice President." Dunham snapped in reply: "Now just a minute! I'm not the Vice President's man any more; I'm the President's man." Like his immediate superior and former associate on the Rockefeller staffs in New York State and then in Washington, James Cannon, Dunham since March has in a sense been both the President's man and the Vice President's man. He probably would say of that dual loyalty what Cannon said about his relationship with Rockefeller after he, Cannon, was appointed assistant to the President for domestic affairs and director of the Domestic Council: "He is there when I need him and I am here when he needs me."

Dunham, a deputy director and director of the budget in New York State when Rockefeller was governor, has had overall responsibility for policy formulation on the Domestic Council staff. The second deputy, James Cavanaugh, a Nixon veteran, has handled day-to-day council operations. Now Dunham is to be chairman of the Federal Power Commission. A businessman (computer data processing) before he joined the Rockefeller administration in New York, he is the first non-lawyer in many years to be FPC chairman and also the first chairman in a long while who has had no particular experience with or in utilities. The short explanation of why he is going to FPC, and why Roderick Hills is going to SEC, was stated by the President when he said recently that if these and other regulatory commissions don't cooperate in chopping back federal regulation, "we'll change the commissions." The remark borders upon improper invasion of independent regulatory agencies by the executive, but Mr. Ford has got away with it so far. Dunham says that neither the President, Donald Rumsfeld, presidential personnel director Douglas Bennett, nor anyone else at the White House asked him before he was nominated about his views of FPC regulations and, most especially, whether he agrees with Mr. Ford's emphatically expressed determination to abolish federal control of the rates charged for natural gas in interstate commerce. Dunham assumes that the President knew that he does agree.

A natural assumption is that Rockefeller recommended Dunham for the FPC and that the appointment constitutes an extension of Rockefeller influence. According to Dunham, the Vice President met him in an Executive Office Building hall a week or so after Dunham was offered the job and said, "I hear you've been offered a place on some regulatory commission." Dunham told him it was the FPC.

October 18, 1975

XXXVI

Hard Times

President Ford was having a hard time convincing anyone except his own officials, and some of them seemed to be in doubt, that such major initiatives as his proposals to commit $100 billion to the development of new energy sources over the next decade and to couple a $28 billion cut in federal taxes with a reduction of the same amount in projected federal spending were for real. The suspicion that these and other proposals and positions were political gimmicks, designed to secure his nomination and election next year to the office that he now holds by appointment, thoroughly galled him. One of the signs that it did appeared on October 14 when he turned up in person at a White House briefing at which Secretary of the Treasury William Simon, Chairman Alan Greenspan of the Council of Economic Advisers, and budget director James Lynn had expected to instruct 18 invited columnists in the merits of the tax and spending cut. Simon, Greenspan and Lynn performed as intended, but only after the President had dominated the occasion for 30 minutes.

His first purpose, Mr. Ford said at the start, was to "put to rest" the notion that his tax and spending proposal was "something that came out of thin air at the last minute." He said the truth was that "the whole thought really began sometime early this year and has been worked on over a period of several months in some detail." The serious question was whether the tax cut, taking effect many months before the spending cut could begin to apply, would have the inflationary result of enormously increasing an already enormous federal deficit. President Ford dealt with the question mainly by referring it to Messrs. Simon and Greenspan, who thereupon entertained the audience with the argument, a truly remarkable one for two famed hard-core fiscal conservatives, that a huge and suddenly enlarged deficit didn't have to be inflationary at all and in this instance could actually be counter-inflationary by raising the prospect of a balanced budget within three years. Before Simon and Greenspan got into that line of talk, however, the columnists kept Mr. Ford on the defensive with a series of questions that culminated with the following barb: "The question is whether it is true, as alleged in *The Wall Street Journal*, that you decided it (the tax and spending proposal) in a golf course conversation with Mel Laird." The President's equivocal answer—"There is no validity to that latter part, that it was decided on the golf course, no truth whatsoever"—left the impression that Mr. Ford's crony and unofficial adviser, former congressman and defense secretary Melvin R. Laird, may indeed have had a part in concocting the

proposal. Subsequent inquiries as to whether he did or didn't produced an account that is offered herewith in the belief that it at least approximates the truth.

The final decision to link a tax cut of $28 billion in calendar 1976 with a demand that Congress commit itself to hold federal spending $28 billion below what it might otherwise be in fiscal 1977, a period that begins in 1976 for the first time on October 1 instead of July 1, was taken at a White House meeting on Sunday morning, October 5. Laird wasn't present but he'd known what was up for quite a while and he and the President discussed the decison during a golf game at the Burning Tree country club that Sunday afternoon. Laird had some doubts, chiefly going to the size of the proposed tax cut and more importantly to Mr. Ford's inclination, followed in due course, to label it "a permanent tax cut." Laird foresees that the next President, whether he be Gerald Ford or somebody else, may be recommending tax increases rather than reductions and argues that this President should guard against that possibility. In the main, though, he encouraged the President to go ahead with the combined tax and spending proposal and predicted a congressional reaction that was the reverse of what occurred.

Laird thought, and told the President to expect, that the Democratic majority and its leaders in Congress would jump at and accept the President's proposal and figures in the typically devious calculation—typical for Melvin Laird, that is—that Mr. Ford would actually be putting himself rather than the congressional Democrats on the spot. The Democrats, Laird reasoned, could resolve to hold 1977 outlay to the demanded $395 billion—$25 billion more than it's expected to be in the present fiscal year but $28 billion below what it could be at present spending levels in the next fiscal year—without actually binding themselves to do it. They wouldn't be binding themselves because it's legally impossible to do so, a fact known equally well to them and to President Ford. Laird further reasoned that the Democrats would await Mr. Ford's fiscal 1977 budget, which he has to submit in January 1976, and do battle with him over the nature and categories of the spending cuts that he would have bound himself to propose, while taking all the credit they could for enacting the 1976 tax cut. In any event the Democrats denounced the twin proposals as a campaign phoney and knotted themselves in attempts to come up with counter-proposals.

Although the understanding was that the October 14 briefing would be confined to the tax-spending proposal, a reporter managed to drag Vice President Nelson Rockefeller and his seeming difference with the President over federal policy toward near-bankrupt New York City into discussion. The New York City matter was raised with the following question: "Are you and Mr. Rockefeller now taking different positions on the possible need for some federal assistance to New York City?" Mr. Ford, looking pained, answered that "I would say it [the difference] is minimal," and then fled from the question with a renewal of his familiar plaint that Mayor Abe Beame was still far short of the measures necessary to start the city's budget toward balance and so restore its credit with banks and in the bond markets. If and when New York, City and State, authorities between them accomplished that, Mr. Ford had been arguing and the Vice President until recently had agreed, there would be no need for federal grants, loans or guarantees to save the city from imminent default and the nation from that event's possibly disastrous impact. Now the Vice President was saying that a default would be "a catastrophe" and that, even when and after the state and city had begun to end the long era of piling loan upon loan to meet current expenses, Congress would have to provide some sort of federal "bridge" to see the city through to solvency over the next three years. The President's claim and the Vice President's feeble agreement that the public difference was "minimal" when in fact it was large and fundamental precipitated much printed and broadcast speculation that Gerald Ford was dumping Nelson Rockefeller.

The interesting story is how the Vice President came to change his view and why and when he told the President that he had changed. Nelson Rockefeller's brother David, board chairman of the Chase Manhattan Bank, visited Mr. Ford at the White House and pleaded with him for federal intervention on September 23. The easy supposition is that this either signalled or caused the

Vice President's shift. Known events don't support the supposition. On September 25, in an interview with the editors of *US
News & World Report*, the Vice President made one of his strongest
and harshest statements that "I don't think the Federal
government can stand back of a history of over-spending and
over-commitment with a blank check operation and still preserve
the solvency of our nation." On September 26, the Vice President
held at his New York home in Pocantico Hills the annual
"Governor's Lunch" for New York Republicans that he
instituted when he was governor. Sixty-two county Republican
chairmen attended. When Rockefeller asked them what they
thought the federal government should do about New York City,
the majority said they personally didn't give a damn what
happened to that detested metropolis. Politically, however, they
thought that some show of federal compassion for the city and its
people was necessary and would be wise. At his regular weekly
meeting with the President on October 2, the Vice President
relayed the chairmen's view and said he was going to adopt and
publicly express it. Mr. Ford immediately told Simon, Greenspan,
Lynn, Chairman Arthur Burns of the Federal Reserve Board, and
other fiscal advisers that Rockefeller was about to jump the ship.
Most of the advisers urged the President to stick to his past and
deeply felt view that nothing but steadfast federal refusal to
promise help would force New York, city and state, to do what
was necessary to restore solvency and confidence. Mr. Ford did
so, with ever increasing vehemence. At a press conference in
Portland on October 3, the Vice President suggested for the first
time that only Congress could authorize federal help and might
have to do it. From that rather tepid position he moved steadily
and by stages to the view he expressed in a speech in New York
City on October 11: "Time is of the essence and the resolution of
this immediate New York City situation is crucial. After the state
. . . and . . . city have acted to restore fiscal integrity it will be the
true test of the responsiveness of our congressional system as to
whether the Congress can act in time to avoid catastrophe."
Simon and several other presidential advisers professed to be
astounded and outraged. They were outraged, all right, but they
weren't astounded. They'd known since October 2 that it was

going to happen. Ford and Rockefeller people agree that the President took it calmly and remained on good terms with his Vice President.

November 1, 1975

————

So it seemed. Later, I suspected that this business made it easier for Howard Callaway, Donald Rumsfeld, and others to persuade the President that Rockefeller's withdrawal from the 1976 vice presidential list would be good for Mr. Ford. It turned out to be very bad for Mr. Ford, as will be seen.

XXXVII

Report on Rocky

This account of how Nelson Rockefeller views himself, his job, his prospects and his relationship with President Ford at the end of his 11th month in the vice presidency is derived from his public statements, from talks with Rockefeller people, and from impressions gathered during a political trip with him on October 23 and 24 to Indianapolis, Decatur, Illinois and Milwaukee.

My report in April 1974 that Vice President Gerald Ford was already thinking in explicit detail about what he'd do when and if he succeeded Richard Nixon raised a storm from commentators and others who assumed that the information came from Mr. Ford and thought it wrong for a Vice President to be talking that way. Vice President Rockefeller isn't making that mistake. The Rockefeller story is that he never thinks about succeeding to the presidency and what he'd do if he succeeded Mr. Ford. There are several stated reasons for this alleged and to me unbelievable neglect of any Vice President's plain duty and obligation to be prepared for that eventuality. One of the stated reasons is that the Vice President is convinced that nothing is going to happen to Mr. Ford that would place Nelson Rockefeller in the presidency. Another reason is said to be that the Vice President finds his job immensely satisfying, a claim which if true makes him unique among recent holders of the office. The authoritative retort to that observation is that the Vice President thinks that his vice presidency *is* unique. For one thing, he is the first Vice President appointed to the office under the 25th amendment by the first President who succeeded to the presidency under that amendment. For another thing, Nelson Rockefeller will be the first and presumably the only Vice President to hold the office in the nation's bicentennial year.

When the suspicion is voiced that Rockefeller welcomed the appointment to the vice presidency and continues to value it principally because it is his only conceivable way to the presidency, after three unsuccessful runs for the Republican nomination in 1960, 1964 and 1968, the following reply is heard. That is simply not true. He welcomed the appointment and values the office now for several reasons that are sufficient in themselves. At his stage in life—he was 67 last July and will be 68 when the Republican candidates for President and Vice President are nominated next year—he is pleased and lucky to be where the action is. If he weren't Vice President, it's said with an audible sniff, he'd be conducting studies (which is what he was doing, with his Commission on Critical Choices, between his resignation from the New York governorship in December 1973 and his accession to the vice presidency in December 1974). He's the chairman of five presidential commissions, any one of which he'd be honored to head. He's the chosen partner—a junior partner, granted, but still the partner—of a President whom he professes to admire and genuinely seems to admire. He assumes and hopes that the Republican presidential nominee in 1976 will be Gerald Ford.

A question that comes up at every Rockefeller press conference and in every interview and conversation with journalists is whether he either expects or has been promised that he'll be Mr. Ford's choice for the vice presidential nomination next year. His invariable answer is that Mr. Ford should and will defer that choice until after he is nominated for election to the presidency. Rockefeller appears to be wholly sincere when he says this. But there is an element of cold and protective calculation in his stated view. He wants to be in a position to withdraw on his own initiative from consideration for the vice presidential nomination rather than appear to have been discarded by Mr. Ford or to face rejection by the Republican convention. Pride and self-protection aside, he is also prepared to withdraw if he becomes convinced, as he definitely is not convinced now, that conservative Republican opposition or any other factor would make him a liability rather than an asset to the nominee for the presidency.

LURIE'S OPINION

9-5-75

"YOU'LL HAVE TO MOVE A LITTLE TO THE RIGHT!"

The Vice President told a television interviewer in Milwaukee that he thinks Ronald Reagan's support and strength are greatly exaggerated and that, in any case, he isn't concerned about the outcome of a race for preference between President Ford and Reagan in next year's New Hampshire primary. He said he isn't concerned because he doesn't think that primary, the year's first, is as significant as most commentators and politicians think it is. He explained that he bases this view upon his experience in 1964 when Henry Cabot Lodge, then ambassador to South Vietnam, led both Rockefeller and Sen. Barry Goldwater in the New Hampshire primary and got nowhere at all after that. Behind this stated view, however, there is real apprehension that Mr. Ford will lose to Reagan in the primary. Rockefeller's purpose in saying what he did in Milwaukee and will be saying elsewhere is to minimize any harm that may be done to President Ford not only in the New Hampshire primary but in any or all of the 36 others to be held in 1976. Rockefeller considers all of them to be insignificant nuisances that ought not to have the effect they surely will have upon the Republican convention and its choices.

The Vice President's professed and seemingly genuine admiration for President Ford does not extend to a large portion of the President's White House staff and to the management of Mr. Ford's campaign instrument, the President Ford Committee. Excepting Henry Kissinger's NSC staff and the Domestic Council staff, which is headed and dominated by Rockefeller people, the Vice President considers that the President is largely and badly served by a bunch of amateurs and upstarts who are short on experience in national affairs and long on interest in themselves. When the chairman of the President Ford Committee, former Congressman and Secretary of the Army Howard ("Bo") Callaway, said at the start of the committee's work that conservative Republican opposition to Rockefeller made him a liability and that the committee was solely concerned with the candidacy of Gerald Ford, the Vice President told the President that he wasn't worried and that Mr. Ford shouldn't be worried by Callaway's remarks. Whether or not that was wholly and literally true, what undoubtedly did worry and vex the Vice President were news leaks from the White House staff to the effect that the President was sending a message to Rockefeller through

Callaway, the message being to be prepared for Mr. Ford's choice of somebody else for the vice presidential nomination next year.

Rockefeller first assumed that the leaks were coming from Press Secretary Ronald Nessen's staff. When he said as much to Nessen, Nessen denied it and convinced Rockefeller that the leaks were coming from somewhere else. Rockefeller has the impression that Nessen was pleased and flattered by being approached directly by the Vice President and given a chance to refute the suspicion. Rockefeller then went to the President's staff chief, Donald Rumsfeld, and asked him pointblank whether he had put Callaway up to his derogatory remarks and had been telling journalists that Callaway was saying what the President wanted him to say. Rumsfeld swore that he had nothing to do with Callaway's remarks and with the news leaks and was not, as some of the gossip alleged, trying to sew up the vice presidential nomination for himself. Rockefeller said rather coldly that he had no choice but to take Rumsfeld's denials and assurances at face value and would let the matter drop. He didn't, quite. He did not complain to the President. But he told the President about his conversations with Nessen and Rumsfeld. Very soon afterward, Rumsfeld told Callaway to knock it off and Callaway has not renewed his derogation of the Vice President.

Rumsfeld, who hoped in 1974 that he would be Mr. Ford's choice for appointment to the vice presidency, professes to hold Nelson Rockefeller in the highest esteem and to have no designs upon the 1976 nomination. Rockefeller and his principal assistants are aware that Rumsfeld and his deputy, Richard Cheney, are actually running the President's pre-nomination campaign and that Callaway gets most of his orders from them. The Vice President and his people have not been heard accusing Rumsfeld directly of using his position to do Rockefeller in. But I have yet to hear any expression of admiration and affection for Donald Rumsfeld in Nelson Rockfeller's vicinity. I suspect that some of the recent attacks upon the President's staff chief, in print and on the air, originated or were at least encouraged in that vicinity. The most authoritative account, however, is to the contrary. The Vice President's view is said to be that the reports of Rumsfeld chicanery, Callaway's recently stilled criticisms, and the like are no skin off Nelson Rockefeller's back. They bother him only because they give an impression of disorder in the President's shop.

November 8, 1975

———

Rereading the above in late 1976, I boggle only at the last sentence. No doubt the impression of disorder in the President's shop bothered the Vice President. But I sensed then and later believed that what burned him was the belief that Mr. Ford was letting his people cut the Vice President into disposable fragments.

XXXVIII

Jerry's Guys

Sen. Barry Goldwater regaled a group of colleagues and staff assistants in the Senate cloakroom on Monday morning, November 3, with an account of the telephone call from Florida the previous afternoon in which President Ford disclosed that he had fired Secretary of Defense James R. Schlesinger and CIA Director William E. Colby and intended to replace them with, respectively, Donald Rumsfeld and George Bush. The president also told Goldwater, as he did other influential members of Congress in calls from Florida that Sunday afternoon, about the pending announcements that Nelson Rockefeller had withdrawn from consideration for the 1976 vice presidential nomination and that Secretary of State Henry Kissinger had been asked and had agreed to give up his prized status, the basis of his power since 1969, as assistant to the President for national security affairs. It was evident to Goldwater's audience in the Senate cloakroom that he was thoroughly enraged by both the fact and the manner of the abrupt dismissal of Secretary Schlesinger, a moderate liberal who was esteemed by conservative Republicans because he advocated high defense expenditures and believed that Henry Kissinger had caused two Presidents, Richard Nixon and Gerald

Ford, to concede more to the Soviet Union that they should have in their quests for strategic arms agreements and for the broad accommodation that is generally called détente. According to one of Goldwater's listeners, he said that he asked the President what qualified Don Rumsfeld to be Secretary of Defense and that the entire reply to the question was: "He was a fighter pilot in the Korean war."

Rumsfeld was a student at Princeton University during the Korean war and a peacetime Navy pilot and flight instructor for two years after his graduation in 1954. At the Monday night press conference that he had called to announce the cabinet changes, the President said in a prepared statement that "Don has served with distinction as a congressman from Illinois, director of the Office of Economic Opportunity, director of the Cost of Living Council, and as ambassador to NATO." In answer to a question, he noted that Rumsfeld had "served in the Department of Defense as a naval aviator." In other answers, however, the President made it clear that the backgrounds and qualifications of the officials whom he was dismissing and of their replacements were secondary considerations with him. His primary consideration was that after replacing the inherited heads of the domestic departments with his own choices, he was determined in the 15th month of his presidency to accomplish the same thing in the fields of foreign policy and national security. His answers to this effect were widely disbelieved by reporters and commentators who suspected or were convinced that Mr. Ford was trying to conceal other and more fundamental reasons. There were other reasons, of course. But the relevant portions of his answers seem to me to be both believable and revealing. They and the events they concern show Gerald Ford to be intensely egoistic behind that humble facade of his, capable of an inhuman cruelty stupidly evinced, and desperately anxious to establish and prove himself as a national leader in his own right. Consider the following remarks, quoted in the sequence in which they were made: "I think any President has to have . . . his own team"; "They are my choices"; "These are my guys and the ones that I wanted"; "I wanted my own team"; "The President . . . ought to have the team with him that he wants." At the end of the press conference I asked Mr. Ford why it had taken him 15 months to form his own team and he answered in part: "I felt it was very important at the outset, because of the unusual circumstances in which I became President, to have continuity, to have stability in the area of national security and foreign policy . . . As time went on I felt that I could select, without any rupture of [foreign] relations, the kind of people, the individuals that I wanted to work with very, very intimately, and I have so selected them."

The President's inclusion of Henry Kissinger and his White House deputy, Lt. Gen. Brent Scowcroft, who becomes the assistant for national security affairs, among "my guys" seemed to many journalists to be inconsistent with Mr. Ford's basic explanation. It's completely consistent. The evidence that the President likes Kissinger as a person and admires him as an adviser is overwhelming. Mr. Ford's characterization of Scowcroft as a man who "speaks an independent mind," in reply to the sneer implicit in the factual but misleading statement that he has been "a Kissinger man," accurately reflected the President's justified estimate of his new national security assistant. Kissinger made it plain when Richard Nixon appointed him Secretary of State in 1973 that he wouldn't have accepted the appointment if he had not been allowed to keep his initial and much more important job as the President's security assistant. Twice this year, in interviews in April and July, President Ford defended Kissinger's retention of the dual role on the ground that he is "unique" and fitted to handle both jobs in a sense that nobody else may be. The decision to relieve Kissinger of the assistant's role was a sop to senatorial and other critics who variously distrust Kissinger, deplore his dominance in foreign affairs, and believe in principle that the two jobs should not be held by one person. Kissinger accepted the demotion—it amounts to that, despite Mr. Ford's assertion at the Monday press conference that the Secretary of State will continue to "have the dominant role in . . . foreign policy"—only a week before it was announced. He accepted it with great reluctance and with warnings to the President and others that it could substantially reduce his standing with and influence upon other governments. He must also know, though in a sort of psychological self-defense he may be slow to acknowledge even to himself, that the change is bound to diminish and finally eliminate his power over the other departments, principally Treasury and Defense, that are involved with his own department and with the National Security Council in the formulation and execution of foreign policy. It was as assistant to the President, not as Secretary of State, that Kissinger chaired and controlled the several interdepartmental groups and committees that prepare policy concepts and recommendations for the President. That function and that power now fall to Scowcroft, who may be expected to seize them gradually but also firmly and as the President's man, not Henry Kissinger's.

The dismissal of William Colby is (to me) the least surprising and least interesting of the changes. It was done cruelly and awkwardly, without notice to a loyal public servant, at eight o'clock on Sunday morning November 2. The President's replacement of Colby at the head of the intelligence community—the operative title is Director of Intelligence, not merely director of CIA—at a time of intense and potentially destructive congressional inquiry with a professional politician and known aspirant to the vice presidency and the presidency was incredibly ill-timed and inept. George Bush, a sometime Texas congressman, candidate for the Senate, chairman of the Republican National Committee and US ambassador to the UN who heads the American diplomatic mission in Peking, may have the abilities necessary to bring off a monumentally difficult assignment. If he does, they have escaped the notice of acquaintances who admire him for his amiability and his competence in handling less demanding tasks.

The most interesting change is the dismissal of James Schlesinger and his replacement at Defense with Donald Rumsfeld, who since October of last year has been the chief of Mr. Ford's White House staff. Like Colby's, Schlesinger's dismissal was announced to him in an unnecessarily abrupt, cruel and stupid fashion at 8:30 on that same Sunday morning. But the firing in itself is more understandable and, in a perverse sort of way, more justifiable than some of the other changes are. The simple and determining fact, first indicated to me in a talk with Vice President Ford on March 30, 1974, is that James Schlesinger rubs Mr. Ford the wrong way. On solely personal grounds, the President could not abide his Secretary of Defense. He found him pompous, professorial in the pejorative meaning of that term, self-righteous, overly convinced of the automatic rightness of his views and the wrongness of all opposing views. Mr. Ford didn't put it that way. He spoke only, and I later wrote on my authority without attribution to the Vice President, of what he considered to be Secretary Schlesinger's inability to understand and deal with Congress. In retrospect, however, the personal antipathy behind this view of Schlesinger was plain. After the events and press conference of November 3, it is plain—period. The President said at the press conference: "I wanted a change in the Defense Department because I wanted, in that case, a person that I have known and worked with intimately for a long period of time, a person who is experienced in the field of foreign policy and who served in the Department of Defense as a naval aviator." A person, in short, with whom he would be at ease. A sequel to a question that I asked at the very end of the press conference nailed down the point. My question reflected a skepticism that I didn't wholly share and the common wisdom in political and journalistic Washington that personal rivalry and policy differences between Secretaries Kissinger and Schlesinger persuaded the President that he had to get rid of one of them. The question was: "Are you saying and intending to be understood to say that neither personal nor policy differences between Dr. Kissinger and Mr. Schlesinger contributed to this change?" Mr. Ford answered: "That is correct." The President had asked me to repeat a question that preceded this one and he later worried that he may have misunderstood the second question. I was asked whether I had actually referred to "personal and policy differences" between the President and Schlesinger. I was told that if Mr. Ford had understood that to be the question, which of course it wasn't, his answer would have been: "There were no *policy* differences that contributed to the change." He had said in response to an earlier question at the press conference that "there are no basic differences" of policy between him and Kissinger on the one hand and Schlesinger on the other.

That answer was marginally correct, at best. There were important though not necessarily irreconcilable differences between Kissinger and Schlesinger over the degree of essential and wise concession to the Soviet Union and the necessary level of defense expenditure, among other things. The gravity of the difference between Schlesinger and Kissinger over the most recent US position in the second phase of strategic arms negotiations was exaggerated in many accounts of Schlesinger's dismissal. He had in fact assented, though reluctantly, to concessions offered to the Soviets at Kissinger's insistence last September in the hope of getting a final agreement on strategic arms levels and limitations in time for it to be signed by President Ford and Leonid Brezhnev at a meeting in Washington in 1975. Soviet objections, not Schlesinger's, obstructed agreement.

The critical policy difference, if there was one, was between Schlesinger and the President. It had to do partly with fiscal 1976 defense budget levels that were acceptable to the President and unacceptable to Schlesinger. A more important factor, however, was what Schlesinger viewed as a trend toward dangerously low defense levels in fiscal 1977 and afterward. In particular, the President's proposal to hold the fiscal 1977 national budget to $395 billion, $28 billion below what it might be at present spending levels, portended to Schlesinger a lower defense budget than he was willing to live with and administer. Two weeks before he was fired, he told Gen. Scowcroft to tell President Ford that this was his view and that he felt very strongly about it. The issue presumably figured in a long meeting on budget matters that Schlesinger had with the President the Saturday before he was fired. Schlesinger told his chief spokesman, Assistant Secretary Joseph Laitin, later in the day that the meeting went well and that, contrary to rumors already afloat in Washington, there was no intimation and no possibility that he was about to be fired. Two senior defense department officials were told by White House friends the same afternoon that the meeting was bitter, quarrelsome, "a disaster" for Schlesinger. Late that night, when he was asked to be at the White House at 8:30 am Sunday for a meeting with the President, Schlesinger was warned by Laitin but still found it almost impossible to believe that he was going to be dismissed. William Colby, fired and leaving the Oval Office at 8:30 Sunday morning, saw Schlesinger waiting in the West Wing lobby and left without telling the Secretary what had happened. Colby visited Schlesinger at his home that afternoon and they passed two hours together, sharing their sense of hurt.

Mr. Ford also announced at the Monday press conference that Secretary of Commerce Rogers C.B. Morton wanted out for personal reasons by the end of the year and that Elliot Richardson, the US ambassador in London, would be the next commerce secretary. The job is inferior in importance and prestige to Richardson's previous federal positions (Under Secretary of State, Secretary of HEW, Secretary of Defense and Attorney General). He agreed to take it a few hours before it was announced. With due respect for a mutual and biased friend's explanation that Richardson would take any job that a President urged him to take and that he thought would be in the national interest, I suspect that his primary reason for accepting the commerce appointment was also the President's primary reason for asking him to accept it. It brings Richardson home from an essentially empty ambassadorship and back on the domestic political scene, in position to seek or accept the Republican vice presidential nomination in 1976 if that turns out to be in the cards. Assuming Senate confirmation, Mr. Ford will have on his 1976 team three respectable prospects for the vice presidency in the persons of Rumsfeld, Bush and Richardson.

Vice President Rockefeller's written notice to the President that "I do not wish my name to enter into your consideration for the upcoming Republican vice presidential nominee" remains to be discussed. In my preceeding report, mainly on the basis of a conversation at the end of a trip to the Midwest with the Vice President on October 23 and 24, I reported two things that are relevant to the withdrawal. I wrote that the Vice President was putting himself in position to do what he did publicly on November 3 and privately in a long talk with the President on the afternoon of October 28, and also that Rockefeller thought it all too possible that Ronald Reagan, his principal conservative rival, might defeat Gerald Ford in major Republican primaries next year. These things were said to me, however, in a context that was very different from the one in which several of Rockefeller's associates put his withdrawal after it was announced. The chief impression left with me on October 24 was that Rockefeller was delighted with his job and with President Ford. The impression conveyed by others after the withdrawal was that he was frustrated, disappointed, seriously at odds with the President over important issues (aid to New York City and the punitive stinginess of a recently announced food-stamp proposal, for instance). In hindsight, I suspect that the Vice President's concern over the possibility that Reagan may lead Mr. Ford in the primaries is closer to the heart of the matter than the reported frustrations.

After the withdrawal and the simultaneous cabinet upheaval, I was authoritatively advised to consider the possibility that Ronald Reagan might deprive Gerald Ford of the presidential nomination and to think about what Nelson Rockefeller would certainly do in that event. He would go to any legitimate lengths to resist the nomination of Reagan and to bring about the nomination of an acceptable alternative, perhaps himself but more probably someone else. Could President Ford, playing now for the support of Reagan conservatives and Rockefeller moderates, be thinking along the same lines? He could be.

November 15, 1975

———

The last two sentences of the above report made no sense when they were written and make no sense now. Rockefeller associates' accounts of his frustrations and bitterness were more accurate than he led me to believe at that time.

XXXIX

Backing and Filling

In the 10 days following the demotion of Secretary of State Henry Kissinger and the dismissals of Secretary of Defense James Schlesinger and CIA director William Colby, the President and his people went to considerable lengths to make the upheaval look better than it did when Mr. Ford announced it. They made it look worse.

When the President was asked on November 3 whether he meant to say that "neither personal nor policy differences between Dr. Kissinger and Mr. Schlesinger" contributed to his dismissal of Schlesinger, he answered: "That is correct." His spokesmen and chief assistants stuck to that contention through the following week. When Mr. Ford was asked essentially the same question on *Meet the Press* on November 9, he answered in part: "I found in the last month or so that there was not as comfortable a feeling in the situation that I desired and that it was creating some problems. This doesn't mean that either of those individuals was not performing his job in a very effective way, but . . . I need a feeling of comfort within an organization— no tension, complete cohesion." Deputy Press Secretary William Greener told the President the next morning that there were sure to be questions about this obvious contradiction at the daily White House news briefing. Mr. Ford instructed Greener to reply that there was no contradiction, no difference between what he'd said on the two occasions. Told by a reporter before the briefing that the President surely couldn't mean this, Greener went back to Mr. Ford and got the same reply and instruction. At the briefing a reporter said to Greener: "Then he [the President] is saying that any interpretation of his answer that he was referring to tensions between Schlesinger and Kissinger, this is wrong?" Greener answered in part: "That is correct." He said privately that the President intended in his answer on *Meet the Press* to refer to tension between himself and Schlesinger, not between Kissinger and Schlesinger. Many accounts had the President denying that there were differences between Kissinger and Schlesinger. This he didn't do. He denied and later indicated that he intended to deny only that the differences contributed to his decision to fire Schlesinger. At a press conference on November 10, Kissinger readily acknowledged that "there were differences between Secretary Schlesinger and myself, as you would expect between individuals of strong minds . . . And no question, there were some personality disputes which neither of us handled with the elegance and wisdom that perhaps was necessary." The saddening conclusion is that the President's personal dislike of James Schlesinger caused him to fire a Secretary of Defense who was described by Henry Kissinger as "a man of outstanding ability and one of the best analysts of defense matters with whom I have dealt."

The widespread view that the dismissals of Schlesinger and Colby were accomplished and announced with unnecessary brutality elicited excuses and explanations that tell a good deal about how Gerald Ford works and about the atmosphere in which he works. It appears, for instance, that some of the President's unofficial cronies and advisers may have had more to do with the changes than either Henry Kissinger or Donald Rumsfeld, the Ford assistant who replaces Schlesinger, had to do with them. One of the advisers, former White House assistant Bryce Harlow, told Mr. Ford several weeks before he announced the changes that he ought to get rid of either Kissinger or Schlesinger and do it soon if it were true, as Harlow understood the President to believe, that the Secretaries of State and Defense were headed toward a serious personal and policy confrontation. The impact of a sudden dismissal would be bad at any time, Harlow reasoned, but either a dismissal or a resignation because of policy differences would be politically disastrous if it were postponed until the coming election year and the season of party primaries. Given Kissinger's preeminence and the President's known liking for him and dislike of Schlesinger, this amounted to advising Mr. Ford to fire Schlesinger right away. Harlow also reasoned that the shock would be offset by a show of positive leadership. Others also offered this advice and I do not suggest that Harlow's advice was decisive.

It's also said by Mr. Ford's apologists that his decision to fire Schlesinger and Colby would have been imparted to them in much less abrupt and brutal fashion if two unexpected events had not upset the intended sequence. One of these events was Vice President Rockefeller's private notice to the President on October 28 of his wish to withdraw from consideration for the 1976 vice presidential nomination. The other was the premature leak to *Newsweek* of the President's intention to fire Schlesinger and to deprive Henry Kissinger of his status as assistant for national security affairs. The White House story is that Mr. Ford originally intended to tell Schlesinger and Colby that they were through sometime in the week of November 3, before their dismissals were announced and after the demotion of Kissinger had been announced. After Rockefeller gave notice of his withdrawal, the President timed the Rockefeller announcement for Monday, the Kissinger announcement for Tuesday and the announcement of the dismissals for Wednesday. When *Newsweek* began checking its Schlesinger leak late on Saturday, November 1, the President decided that he had no choice but to tell Colby and Schlesinger of his intention as soon as possible. He had one of his assistants, John Marsh, ask them late Saturday night to be at the White House at eight and 8:30 Sunday morning. Marsh was with each of them when they got the word. He presumably is the source of the story that the word was given courteously and received quietly. It's true enough, as the White House explainers say, that there is no kindly way to fire two distinguished men and high officials. But the President had told Kissinger and Rumsfeld of his intention to fire Schlesinger and Colby on October 25. It was clear to Kissinger that the decision had been reached quite a while before then. The President told Rockefeller about the impending changes on October 28. Leaks or no leaks, there was no good reason to withhold the news from Colby and Schlesinger until the following week and the intended sequence allowed little or no more notice than they received.

Neither Kissinger nor Rumsfeld argued with the President when he called them to the Oval Office and told them of his intentions on Saturday, October 25. I'm told that they did argue later, at least to the extent of letting Mr. Ford know that they thought firing James Schlesinger was a mistake. Kissinger instructed his State Department associates and spokesmen to say as much on his behalf and he tried to convey that impression without being explicit at his press conference. The loss of his

"I SHOWED THEM WHO'S BOSS AROUND HERE, HUH, HENRY?"

White House status, with the power and prerogatives that went with it, was a harder blow than he let on. Pride aside, his belief that it would inevitably impair his influence in the world and with other governments must have been clear to the President. Kissinger spoke to at least one person of resigning, as he has been prone to do in moments of pique and frustration ever since Richard Nixon brought him to the White House in 1969. More than once in the past six months, he has swung from momentary thoughts of quitting to readiness to remain with Mr. Ford in the dual role of assistant and Secretary of State into another term if the President is nominated and elected in 1976. It is inconceivable after the demotion that he would remain into another term and that he would do the President and the country the disservice of quitting before this term ends.

The case of Schlesinger's successor, Donald Rumsfeld, is fascinating and I don't pretend to know what to make of it. The proffered story is that he thought firing Schlesinger was a mistake, told the President so during the week that followed October 25, and agreed to accept the nomination to succeed Schlesinger only on the Sunday that the Secretary of Defense and William Colby were dismissed. It is a fact that Rumsfeld formally accepted only after his 34-year-old deputy and White House successor, Richard Cheney, telephoned him from Florida that Sunday afternoon and said the President insisted that he take the job. It also is a fact that Rumsfeld has been preparing Cheney to succeed him as the White House chief of staff for the past eight months. Last March or thereabouts, Rumsfeld began seeing to it that Cheney had more and more contact with the President and that others on the staff knew he did. Junior assistants started saying in August that Dick Cheney and Don Rumsfeld were virtually indistinguishable and that Cheney's orders were obeyed as unquestioningly as Rumsfeld's were. The consensus in the White House press room is that anybody who'd believe that Rumsfeld didn't plot Schlesinger's ruin and his accession to the job would believe that Gerald Ford doesn't really want to be elected President. Sadly, the Ford White House begins to remind me of the Nixon White House. It's a place where a fellow doesn't know what to believe.

November 22, 1975

XL

Small Expectations

Paris

A lot of pressure from France and West Germany, a lot of bargaining with their governments and a lot of argument in Washington preceded President Ford's reluctant decision to join French President Valery Giscard d'Estaing and the heads of the British, West German, Italian and Japanese governments in a conference called and organized by Giscard d'Estaing "to discuss economic issues of mutual interest" at the Chateau de Rambouillet, a massive, ancient and ugly edifice set among lovely lakes, grasslands and forests some 30 miles southwest of Paris. After one full day, parts of two other days and two evenings with his peers and their foreign and finance ministers at the chateau, President Ford said in a formal statement that it had been "a highly successful meeting in all respects." A change in the text that had been prepared for him indicated that the economic summit had been less than successful in one rather esoteric but important respect. The prepared text had him saying that he and the other leaders had emerged from the conference with a "conviction that we can master our futures." The President actually spoke at the closing ceremony of "our conviction that *our peoples* can master their futures." One of the arguments that persuaded him to attend the conference had been that if it went well it could bolster the confidence of the people of the six countries in their governments and, more to the point, strengthen the confidence of the leaders themselves in their capacity to define and resolve the enormous economic problems that afflict their countries and the world. It was interesting that amid the general euphoria at the close of the conference the President chose not to claim that the latter effect had been achieved.

For many months the President and his chief advisers doubted that anything worthwhile could be achieved at such a conference. Giscard d'Estaing originally asked the governments of the US and of what he regarded as the only four other industrial democracies that really mattered to join France in a meeting devoted solely to international monetary policies. He made it clear publicly and privately that his purpose would be to persuade the US and other governments to abandon the system of floated currencies that the US more or less forced upon the Western economic community in 1971 and return to a system in which the exchange rates of the principal currencies would be fixed by government decision rather than left to the play of the world money markets. Administration doctrine, Mr. Ford's personal doctrine, Republican doctrine and the doctrine of the Federal Reserve Board and its chairman, Arthur Burns, forbade US agreement to the change demanded by Giscard d'Estaing. Mr. Ford, Secretary of State Henry Kissinger and Secretary of the Treasury William Simon therefore agreed among themselves that it would be foolish for the US to attend such a conference and put itself in the predictable and unpleasant position of opposing and frustrating the will of other governments. When the President and Secretary Kissinger stopped in Bonn on their way to the Helsinki conference in July, German Chancellor Helmut Schmidt argued strongly for a general economic conference to be attended by the chiefs of state or government of the principal non-Communist industrial powers. Schmidt nominally supported Giscard d'Estaing's proposal for a monetary conference, but it was clear to Messrs. Ford and Kissinger that Schmidt's actual purpose was as unpalatable to them as Giscard d'Estaing's was. The chancellor's overriding purpose was to use the conference as a means of bringing international pressure upon the Ford administration to go much further than it was willing to go in stimulating the US economy with enlarged budget deficits and expansion of the money supply. All of the prospective participants except the US wanted this because of the enormous importance to them of the US market for their exports. Chancellor Schmidt, faced with a worsening economic situation in Germany, wanted it more intensely than the others because German industry depends to a greater extent than the others upon its exports to the US. Here again, the President and Kissinger resisted rather than submit themselves to international pressures to take a course that they were determined not to take. At private meetings between sessions of the Helsinki conference, Giscard d'Estaing and Schmidt renewed their urgings. Prime Minister Harold Wilson of Great Britain supported them to some extent, though more from prideful desire that Britain be represented at the proposed conference than from a real and burning wish for it.

Subsequent developments led President Ford and Kissinger to agree to a conference from which neither of them expected much. President Giscard d'Estaing indicated privately that he was prepared to back away from his demand for totally and rigidly fixed exchange rates and settle for an understanding that at forthcoming meetings of the International Monetary Fund the conferees would advocate a modified float of the principal currencies, with value in terms of the dollar and the dollar's value in relation to other currencies allowed to fluctuate within narrow and agreed limits. Mr. Ford, Kissinger and the President's chief economic advisers concluded that the US could go that far toward Giscard d'Estaing's objective without abandoning the basic principle that market forces rather than government fiat should determine the rates. The other development was that key domestic indicators showed enough improvement in the US economy and enough progress toward recovery from the recession to enable the President to argue that no further stimulus was needed and indeed that the kind and degree of added stimulus wanted by Schmidt might defeat its purpose by reviving the waning inflation. Some recent changes in the indicators, among them rises in the wholesale price index and the rate of unemployment, made the counter-argument harder to sustain than it had seemed to be when the President decided to go along with a broadened economic summit, but he was stuck with it at Rambouillet and stoutly insisted that the adverse indicators did not mean that the US recovery was either slowing or illusory.

Mr. Ford decided to accept Giscard d'Estaing's invitation only after exposure to some fierce debate within and at the top of his administration. The debate in the main was between advisers and assistants whose principal concern was the President's political prospect of nomination and election in 1976 and those who were chiefly concerned with foreign policy and international relationships in general. The politicians opposed his going to the conference and the policy advisers favored his going. The opponents argued that there simply were no problem areas that could produce hard decisions and impressive declarations and that the President would be thought to be grandstanding, wasting time and effort that ought to be devoted to business at home. The chief arguments for going to the conference were that even though no major decisions and announcements could be expected the exercise would be worthwhile if the leaders and their ministers recognized the fact and analyzed the nature of "inter-dependence" in a time of worldwide economic distress. Publicized recognition by the US President that his country's economic condition and economic policies gravely affected the economies of other major "industrial democracies" and that their governments therefore had a legitimate interest and stake in the American government's economic decisions would be useful in itself. At the least it would assuage their resentment at what appeared to them to be arrogant exclusion from policy determinations that vitally affected them. In domestic terms it would provide the President with support for his efforts to discourage and defeat the more extreme American protectionists who were making increasing trouble for him.

After the President agreed with advocates of the conference, small working groups representing the six participating governments met in New York and finally in London to set an agenda and to determine in advance the issues on which defensible degrees of agreement or at least agreement not to disagree in public could be expected. Instead of putting a senior official from the State or Treasury Departments at the head of the American group Mr. Ford reached outside of government for former Labor and Treasury Secretary George P. Schultz. Only the media's profound lack of interest in the subject and George Shultz's reputation for complete integrity saved him and the President from an embarrassing row over what could have been made to seem a serious conflict of interest. Shultz is president of the Bechtel Corporation, a conglomerate with multinational construction and other interests that inevitably would be affected by international economic discussions. Although no effort was made to keep his role and the group's work secret, the preparations and Shultz's part in them were seldom reported.

In a speech in Pittsburgh on November 11, four days before the conference opened, Henry Kissinger undertook to define the American interest in the meeting, the positions the President would take and the objectives he would try to get agreement on. An interesting passage in the speech stopped short of acknowledging the feeling that the most useful thing the conference could accomplish would be to restore the leader's confidence in themselves and in their capacity to deal with their grievous problems. Kissinger came pretty close to it, however, when he cited the unemployment, inflation, losses of production, and arbitrary increases in oil prices that plague the Western industrial world, and concluded: "the deepest consequence is not economic, but the erosion of people's confidence in their society's future and a resulting loss of faith in democratic means [and] in governmental institutions and leaders." At the start of what soon would become a flood of conference rhetoric to the effect that the Western industrial world is in one hell of a shape and will be in worse shape unless something effective is done about it, Kissinger also set forth specific American aims at the conference. They provide the best available measure of what, from the US standpoint, the conference did and did not accomplish. Kissinger said the President would propose that ministers "responsible for economic policy meet periodically to follow up on policy directions set at the summit." He said the US would ask the conferees to pledge their governments to complete pending renegotiation of international trade terms along free trade lines by 1977. He said the President would "propose that we reaffirm our common determination to avoid new barriers to trade as well as actions which provoke countries to erect them." And: "The United States will urge the summit to recommit the industrial democracies to an even more forceful pursuit of the fundamental long-term goal of depriving the oil cartel of the power to set the oil price unilaterally." Finally the President would argue that under any revised international monetary system "Each country should be free to choose the exchange rate regime that best suits it, provided it respects international obligations to avoid trade and capital restrictions and competitive devaluations."

The grandiloquent "Declaration of Rambouillet" that followed the conference was mostly a rhetorical assertion of agreement upon goals rather than upon measures to accomplish the goals. Even so, it provided some indication of how far the US got with its specific proposals. The conferees agreed to support completion of international renegotiation of trade terms by 1977. They deplored protectionist measures by which countries "try to solve their problems at the expense of others" and simultaneously accepted Prime Minister Wilson's notice to the other five governments that Britain soon will impose import quotas in order to protect industries that cannot compete in their home markets. President Ford and his delegation, confronting strong pressures to take equivalent protective measures, were in no position to object very strenuously to the British course. Far from committing themselves to a joint attack upon the arbitrary pricing powers of the OPEC oil cartel, the other five conferees forced the US to settle for the feeble advocacy of "a harmonious and steady development in the world energy market." The announced agreement upon a controlled currency float rather than the fixed rates first advocated by France and the totally free float preferred by the US is subject to IMF approval and in any case was concluded before the Rambouillet conference opened. The other conferees merely affirmed what the US and France had already agreed upon. The majority rejected the Kissinger-Ford proposal that the conference be institutionalized and made a permanent instrument of cooperation by having the member governments' economic ministers meet periodically to review the steps recommended at Rambouillet and to consider what other measures should be adopted to forward recovery in the sick industrial world. It all added up to a poor score for the US but the outcome was no worse and perhaps a bit better than the President expected.

November 29, 1975

XLI

Hope in Britain

London

A White House reporter on a brief visit to London is asked many questions about Gerald Ford and his presidency. The obvious and expected questions—is it true, as some say, that Mr. Ford can't chew gum and walk a straight line at the same time?; is he likely to be nominated and elected in 1976?—tend to fuse into a central question that is especially interesting because it is asked by officials who occasionally visit Washington and who have access to the guidance given the British government by its Washington embassy. The central question is whether it's true that the President is served by an unusually competent White House staff, a staff so competent that it may be counted upon to save him from really disastrous error in either domestic or foreign affairs. One part of the visitor's two-part answer seems to surprise and please the questioners; the other part to surprise and sadden them. The part that seems to please them is that this President isn't nearly as dumb as the question assumes. The part of the answer that seems to sadden them is that with some individual exceptions President Ford is served by the weakest staff in recent White House history. If he has to be saved from disastrous error, the salvation won't come from his staff.

Enough of that. The reporter didn't come to London to hear and talk about President Ford. After three days on the fringe of the economic summit conference at Rambouillet in France, he came here to renew acquaintance and refresh impression in a city that he has known and loved since 1938. An immediate reward is a bit of information that escaped the reporter in Washington and Paris. The notion that Prime Minister Harold Wilson of Great Britain and Chancellor Helmut Schmidt of West Germany joined at and before the Rambouillet conference in urging President Ford to increase artificial stimulation of the US economy in order to expand the American market for British and German exports turns out to be a little off the mark. Wilson urged both Schmidt and Mr. Ford to step up the stimulation of their economies, arguing that the US and Germany were in better shape than any of the other "industrial democracies" represented at Rambouillet and therefore ought to heat up their recoveries for the benefit of Britain, France, Italy and Japan. One gathers that Mr. Ford and Schmidt in effect told Wilson to go stuff it while the Chancellor continued to urge the President to what he, Schmidt, was unwilling to do.

The big news in Britain is a surge of hope. It is hope of a most peculiar kind, arising from and resting largely upon the efforts of Britons to convince themselves that there is sound basis for it. The hope is not that Britain has hit the bottom of its long slide into economic ruin and is headed upward. It is rather that Britons of all classes at all levels—government, labor, management—have at last realized that the country is headed for ruin and have agreed to accept the sacrifices that are deemed necessary to avert national and personal catastrophe. Britons incessantly tell each other that this has happened and cite several events in proof that it has happened.

Last July the Wilson government imposed and the major unions, individually and through their Trades Union Congress, accepted an absolute limit of six pounds ($12.48 at current rates) per week in increases of all earned incomes, whether wages or salaries, until July 1976. Twenty years ago that would have been regarded as a prodigious level of general increase. Now it is considered to be sacrificially low, a guarantee that Britain's horrific wage and price inflation can be halted or at least held within practicable bounds if the limitation is observed through mid-1976 and retained for another year or so. The memberships of big unions, most recently the mighty Amalgamated Union of Engineering Workers, are ousting the extreme leftist leaderships that have long dominated them and turning to what pass for moderate leaders in Labour Britain. On November 5, announcing "an approach to industrial strategy," Chancellor of the Exchequer Denis Healey said that Britain must "reverse the relative decline of British industry which has been continuous for many years" and that in order to do so "the government emphasizes the importance of sustaining a private sector of industry which is vigorous, alert, responsible and profitable." The idea is to select some 30 industries that now or potentially contribute substantially to British exports and, when necessary, assist them either with direct subsidies or by buying a government equity in them. In all cases the government proposes to intervene in planning for and management of the aided industries to a degree that would be abhorred in the US but is welcomed by Britain's slap-happy managers.

At the opening of a new session of Parliament the Conservative party's first female leader, Mrs. Margaret Thatcher, applauded both the incomes limitation and the industrial policy while expressing acrid doubt that the Labour government is capable of administering either of them. Remarkably for a Labour Prime Minister, Harold Wilson attributed Britain's economic woes in part to "our own failure over a quarter of a century under successive governments to increase industrial investment" and to improve productivity "in any way comparable with that achieved by our leading competitors." Even more remarkably, he didn't pretend that the country is through the worst. Instead he said that because of previously agreed price increases that have yet to take full effect "the nation must expect to face a period in which there is absolute temporary reduction in living standards measured by the relationship between earnings and prices."

Here was recognition by the Labour leadership that profit is not necessarily sinful and indeed is necessary for a wide sector of British industry if Britain is to regain economic health. Here too, many thought, was admission that nationalization of key sectors of British industry had failed and that the country must look to privately owned industry rather than to nationalized industry for the exports essential to its recovery. *But*—have Britons generally and the Labour leadership in particular really recognized and agreed to cut out the cankers that eat at Britain's economic heart? There is reason to doubt it. The government jarred management representatives who collaborated in and applauded Chancellor Healey's "approach to industrial strategy" by announcing proposals to nationalize the aircraft manufacturing and shipbuilding industries, extend and tighten the destructive grip of the longshoremen's (dockers') union upon the country's ports and adjacent import storage areas, and hasten the application of a previously enacted law that will make the closed shop practically universal and greatly enhance the power of restrictive unions to control everything from productivity to publication. Union workers and leaders who accepted temporary pay limits balked at the barest beginning of efforts to modernize processes and improve productivity. Suicidal strikes in the ailing newspaper and automobile industries, among others, occurred while the Prime Minister and many others were proclaiming the dawn of a new rationality. Anthony Wedgwood Benn, the Secretary of State for Energy and a leader of the Parliamentary Labour party's restive left wing, denounced pending cuts in public spending on social services and signalled a determined fight within the party and the Wilson government to frustrate many of the measures that were widely deemed to be as necessary as they would be painful. The opposition to the government course was in keeping with good Socialist and liberal theology. But Britain's postwar economic record says beyond dispute that the country provides the world's outstanding example of good theology gone wrong.

Much else, including a move to grant partial autonomy to Scotland and Wales that could but probably doesn't presage the breakup of the United Kingdom, agitates and enlivens the British scene. One of its lighter aspects is the squawling over the rapid and legally required equalization of male and female rights and status. Some of the loudest squallers are female commentators in national newspapers, protesting that women don't want all the equalization and that it's an insult to British housewives. A male

visitor is entitled to laugh when he spots the following item in the
official roster of Her Majesty's Household: "Captain of the
Honourable Corps of Gentlemen at Arms—Rt. Hon. the
Baroness Llewellyn-Davies of Hastoe."

December 6, 1975

XLII

Ford in China

Whatever else may have happened to the government of the People's Republic of China since Richard Nixon's visit in 1972 signaled and formalized the eagerness of the US government to come to terms with it, the Peking regime has surrendered to the insistence of American Presidents that they be allowed to take absurdly and outrageously large entourages with them whenever and wherever they travel abroad. The wishes of host governments, their plaintive reminders that no other chief of state or head of government is trailed by so many people and demands such extensive accommodations, and the limits upon available accommodations in the visited countries are permitted to matter very little if at all. American Presidents, including the incumbent, are served by a corps of security agents and general advance arrangers who are taught to be restrained and courteous but on needful occasion can be savage and ruthless in pressing their demands. In 1972, for instance, information officials at the Chinese foreign office told Timothy Elbourne, the White House assistant making arrangements for the Nixon media party, that no more than 12 reporters, cameramen and television and radio technicians could possibly be admitted. Elbourne produced a list of 280 persons and got about half of them including the pathetic total of 20 writers admitted. The strains upon Chinese facilities caused tension but both the media and official aspects of the Nixon visit went off well.

This time, as if resigned to the inevitable, the Chinese hosts did not argue much. One hundred and sixty-three American journalists, technicians and executive freeloaders plus some 30 members of the White House press and transportation office staffs were lodged at the Minzu Hotel, a recently redecorated and quite comfortable hostelry normally reserved for low-level visitors from African, Asian and other countries that the People's Republic is cultivating. President Ford's deceptively small "official party" of eight, his wife and daughter, a listed supporting staff of 19 and a much larger unlisted support and security staff brought the total media and official party to well over 300. After the President's Air Force One and a second presidential jet with supporting staff arrived, a reporter who noticed an enormous pile of luggage in the Minzu lobby was told by a White House official that the pile would have been much larger if a baggage master at Andrews Air Force Base, the departure point near Washington, had not refused to load scores of empty suitcases in which members of various staffs hoped to bring home, at government expense and without customs duty, goods bought at Peking's hard currency "friendship stores." The journalists and technicians traveling on two chartered press planes were told as usual that they could pack "limited numbers of personal packages" into the cargo holds.

God knows what the enormous media party would have done for a story sufficient to justify its presence and the expense to its employers of arranging the same if Chinese Vice Premier Teng Hsiao-ping, the tiny and nut-hard successor to ailing Premier Chou En-lai, and the increasingly characteristic ineptitude of the Ford White House, whether on the road or in Washington, had not combined to provide what many reporters regarded as a whizzer of a story. Vice Premier Teng initiated it at a banquet for President Ford in the immense Great Hall of the People by saying in clearly implied effect to the President's face that he and his government were fools for failing and refusing to perceive that "the factors for both revolution and war are clearly increasing";

that the Soviet Union is "the most dangerous source of war"; that the US is suffering from "illusions of peace" and stupidly enhancing the chances of another world war with its policy of accommodation with the Soviet Union; and, in sum, that "rhetoric about détente cannot cover up the stark reality of the growing danger of war."

It was a shocker, to me and to other reporters in that magnificent hall, drinking with our Chinese hosts to American and Communist Chinese friendship. As one knew then in general, and as hasty research confirmed, the essence of it had been said before—in public toasts in Peking to Secretary of State Henry Kissinger and to West German Chancellor Helmut Schmidt in October, by Chinese Ambassador Huang Hua at the UN in New York on November 11, and by Teng Hsiao-ping in Peking on November 15. In a brilliant speech in Detroit on November 24, a review of what American foreign policy had been since the Second World War and is becoming now, Kissinger had said of the impending Peking visit that "Disagreements in national ideology exist, there will be no attempt to hide them." At a pre-China briefing in Washington on November 28, first talking in the guise of a "senior American official" who was disclosed by Press Secretary Ron Nessen on the public record to be Henry Kissinger, the Secretary of State recalled the lecture on the perils and illusions of US-Soviet détente that he got in Peking in October and said:"I consider it possible that either publicly or privately we hear substantially the same Chinese analysis that was made then."

That was all very well when it was said, but it didn't have much relevance at my table in the Great Hall when Vice Premier Teng said it straight to President Ford. When a young Chinese foreign office information official at the table was told by an American columnist that most Americans simply would not understand what Vice Premier Teng was talking about, the Chinese official said with evident sadness and seeming sincerity, "I am amazed, I am really amazed, that you do not understand." When I said I did not understand what the Chinese government did or did not want the US government to do, a freeze settled. President Ford had said in his reply to Vice Premier Teng that the US would puruse its policy of accommodation with the Soviet Union "without illusion." The young Chinese fastened on this remark and said that all his government asked was that détente be pursued without illusion that it would remove the danger of war—by implication, though he did not say, war instigated by the Soviet Union.

Two points, one minor and one major, strike me. The minor point is that the official Ford party in Peking, beginning at the top with the President and Kissinger, knew in advance of the Great Hall banquet that Teng was going to say what he said and should have anticipated the American press corps' reaction to it. They did not anticipate it, or if they did, dismissed it before the fact as the negligible reaction of what Kissinger later called "masochistic maniacs."

The texts of the respective toasts, Teng's to the President and the President's to Teng, were submitted to each party in advance. There was serious and prolonged American debate over whether to write a direct answer to Teng into the President's text. The decision was not to do so. It was a wise decision, but the serious discussion preceding it made nonsense of the subsequent official sneer that only news-hungry maniacs in the traveling press corps would take the affair seriously.

The major point is buried in Chinese rhetoric concerning the alleged follies and illusions of détente with the Soviet Union. Henry Kissinger made the point in secret briefings for White House and department officials before President Nixon visited Peking and Moscow in 1972. Kissinger said then, as I reported then, that Communist China's leaders lived in fear of nuclear attack by the Soviet Union and counted each day that it did not happen a gain and a salvation for them. The fear persists and in my judgment it suggests that nothing short of outright and egregious American insult to the People's Republic and its leaders could drive the Communist Chinese leadership to reject American cooperation and protection. Vice Premier Teng said in the seeming challenge to President Ford: ". . .The consistent policy of the Chinese government and people is: dig tunnels deep, store grain everywhere, and never seek hegemony." Hegemony in Chinese parlance means military domination of regional areas and the Soviet Union and the US are impartially accused of seeking it. That is by the way. Ponder the "dig tunnels deep" passage. Allowing for the historic Chinese reliance upon the notion of safety in tunnels and in the vast expanse of their land, the reference in a modern context is paranoiac. Communist China is a weak and frightened country and its leadership looks to the United States to protect and save it from the Soviet Union. Remember that, never forget it, and much else falls into place.

December 13, 1975

XLIII

After the Trip

Honolulu

Here in the sun and gentle warmth of Hawaii, after this reporter had left the aircraft that in seven days had hauled him from Washington to Alaska to Tokyo to Peking to Jakarta to Manila and that on the final legs from Manila and Honolulu back to Washington had come to be more like a hospital plane than a press plane, the weariness and mental fog that resulted from so jammed and insanely scheduled a presidential trip began to fade. A clearer understanding of President Ford's purposes and a fairer measure of accomplishment than was possible at the crux of the journey in Peking seemed to emerge. There follows in hindsight summary, some of it trivial and some of it of substantial import, what appears to be most worth noting about the expedition.

Gerald Ford ought to rid himself of the illusion, presumably imparted or at least encouraged by members of a White House staff that has previously been said in this space to be the poorest in a fairly long memory, that he has to justify trips out of the country by complicating them with irrelevant and tiring stops along the way. Traveling in mid-November to an economic summit conference near Paris that the President and the other participants wanted the world to take more seriously than it probably deserved to be taken, Mr. Ford addressed a black university crowd in Durham, North Carolina, and two Republican fundraising affairs in Durham and Atlanta. On the way to Peking, for what was intended to be and should have been the preeminent foreign affairs event of his brief administration to date, he added to the drain and rigors of the journey for himself and for everyone else in his huge official and media entourage with a side trip in snow and freezing weather to a welding shop and a pumping station along the route of that ecological atrocity, the Alaska oil pipeline. An otherwise unnecessary flight from Fairbanks to Anchorage for a couple of Republican shindigs and an overnight stay completed the initial charade. "Is he tired, Ron?" a reporter asked Press Secretary Ron Nessen in Honolulu. "Probably less so than everybody else on the trip," Nessen answered. "He has the only bed on the plane." Nessen referred to the bed in the President's quarters on Air Force One. In Peking and afterwards, the President and his wife, Betty Ford, looked very tired on several occasions. Mrs. Ford stayed over in Honolulu for some 30 hours after her husband flew on to Washington, keeping for her use the four-jet Boeing 707 that was Richard Nixon's Air Force One before he got the newer and even more sumptuous 707 that Mr. Ford inherited by appointment. Security agents and staff assistants who had been following the President in the older plane debarked from it in Honolulu and found seats for the last jump to Washington in press planes and in the cargo plane that had brought the President's armored limousine and a Secret Service convertible to Jakarta (the Chinese Communists wouldn't let the presidential cars into China). Honolulu newspapers expected Mrs. Ford to attend a Republican fund-raiser after resting awhile and the Republican National Committee in Washington could be billed for the considerable expense of holding the No. 2 presidential plane for her.

Mr. Ford showed himself to be aware in a helpless sort of way of some of the absurdities of presidential travel including the overblown media corps' overblown habits of shopping and shipping the proceeds home in inspection-free press plane cargo holds. "I understand they are laying on a special plane to take back all the things you bought," the President said to a reporter in Jakarta. He was joking, but it wasn't a total joke. One reporter shipped two Chinese bicycles on a press plane. He said he'd declare them and pay any customs duty due. Knowing him, I believed he would. I'd be astounded if some of his journalistic brethren and some of the official freeloaders were as honest. On the flight from Peking to Jakarta White House transportation director Ray Zook begged his friends in the press corps not to dump any more stuff upon him for free and uninspected transport home. He said the cargo holds of two press planes were already crammed to the doors. A third jet was chartered by NBC, CBS and ABC to transport heavy equipment and extra crews to and from China and didn't make the whole circuit.

We continue with the trivia only in order to note a White House situation that concerns the status and effectiveness of Secretary of State Henry Kissinger. The situation also involves Press Secretary Nessen, who has been wished well in this space and whose defects of performance have been blamed here more than elsewhere upon the guidance he gets from some of his senior superiors, by implication including President Ford. Events and attitudes observed on this trip drive me to the conclusion that this explanation has been unduly kind to Nessen. It is intolerable that Ron Nessen should be kept by the President and—one is bound to assume—knowingly kept by the President in a position to bait, derogate and sneer at Henry Kissinger, in my opinion one of this country's great and creative Secretaries of State, in the way that Nessen has done and by definition has been permitted if not encouraged to do during this journey.

The foregoing observation is based upon two episodes. One of them involved Nessen's reaction to a *Newsweek* report concerning him, Kissinger and Richard Cheney, the young White House staff chief who succeeded Donald Rumsfeld when Rumsfeld became Secretary of Defense. The thrust of the *Newsweek* report was that on Kissinger's personal orders Nessen was denied access to the Asian trip briefing books and that Cheney, when told of this by Nessen, ordered the books given to Nessen and reminded the NSC staff at the White House that Kissinger no longer heads that staff as the President's assistant for national security affairs. Kissinger said the story was an outrageous fabrication and asked why he should give a good goddamn about Ron Nessen's briefing books. Lt. Gen. Brent Scowcroft,

Kissinger's former deputy and successor as the President's national security assistant, also denied the story. The point of interest here is not the truth or falsity of the report, but the gloating fashion in which Nessen verified it in Peking and used it to suggest that he is higher in Gerald Ford's estimation and is more secure in his service than Henry Kissinger is.

The other episode followed a briefing that Kissinger gave a small "pool" of reporters aboard Air Force One during a leg of the Asian trip. He knew as he always does that "the senior US official" who is quoted after such briefings would be assumed to be him. Kissinger decided when he saw the text prepared by the pool reporters that it contained some indiscreet language which even if attributed to him only by implication and assumption could harm him, the country and the President. He asked the "poolers" to delete the possibly harmful language and they did. Nessen helped one of the pool reporters revise the text. He then turned upon the pool reporters and denounced them, saying he was amazed that they should be so weak and should grant to Henry Kissinger a favor that they would never grant to Ron Nessen. The practice of the background briefing on presidential planes may be wrong, though I don't think it is. It's arguable that the reporters were wrong in giving in to Kissinger in this instance, although the understanding in such situations is that the official is entitled to choose the words that will be attributed to a government source. However that may be, it most certainly was not the function, the place, the duty of the President's press secretary to object to deletions that were in part intended to protect the President. According to reporters who were on the plane at the time, as I was not, it amounted to a display of venom that was shocking in itself and evidence that matters are in sad disarray at the top of the Ford White House.

Nessen apart, the episodes inspire a brief observation about the situation and possible future of Henry Kissinger. Flaws in the conduct of the public aspects of this trip, such as the failure to remind the American press corps in Peking of earlier warnings in Washington that there might not be a communique summarizing the visit, and the failure to provide any official American account whatsoever of President Ford's meeting with Mao Tse-tung, suggested to me that Kissinger might have been strangely absent from or indifferent to the discussions of how to handle these matters. The official story was that Kissinger concurred in both decisions. Maybe so, but one may suspect that he had come to a point where he didn't give a hoot and passively left the business to the President's staff claque. After Kissinger's White House title and status were removed, I wrote that it was inconceivable that he would either remain into another term if Gerald Ford were elected in 1976 or that he would do the country and Mr. Ford the disservice of quitting before the present term ends. When Kissinger was told later that this had been written about him, he replied that a man in public life has to keep his options open.

President Ford in Honolulu, on the 34th anniversary almost to the minute of the Japanese attack on Pearl Harbor, tried to define the purposes of his trip and the essence of what he five times called "a new Pacific doctrine" and "our new Pacific policy." It was too bad that he loaded his speech with the words "new" and "doctrine" when it was neither. But there was nothing wrong, there was some value in restating such familiar truisms as that "American strength is basic to any stable balance of power in the Pacific," that "the partnership of Japan is a pillar of our strategy," and that "the normalization of relations with the People's Republic of China" continues to be the eventual objective that it's been since Richard Nixon visited Peking in 1972. The assertion, repeated to the point of stridency, that the US is "a nation of the Pacific Basin" and continues to be "a Pacific power" reflected a very real anxiety in the wake of the collapse of the entire US position and policy in Indochina that the peoples and governments of Asia might conclude that the US was no longer a dependable power and partner there or anywhere else. The President's homeward stops in Jakarta and Manila and particularly in the Philippines, where US air and naval bases constitute not only our forward military position in the Pacific but a strategic approach to the Indian Ocean, were intended to signal and further a beginning effort to rebuild among the non-Communist countries of southeast Asia a modified and less abrasive substitute for the position lost in Vietnam, Cambodia and Laos.

The chief flaw of the Honolulu speech, apart from the

President's flat and weary delivery, was simply that it was an inferior rewrite and adaptation of a much better and more forceful address that Henry Kissinger had delivered in Detroit on November 24. Some of the President's language and all of the central points appeared in the Kissinger speech, to distinctly better effect than they did after the President's personal staff prettied them up. Quoting Kissinger: "The United States is a Pacific power. No region is of greater importance to us . . . The security interests of all the great world powers intersect in Asia. Japan, China, the Soviet Union and the United States have important stakes in the region; all would be affected by any major conflict there . . . Thus, *throughout the first half of this decade* (emphasis added) we have sought to fashion a new Asian policy— a policy that gradually reduced our military presence and aimed, instead, at augmenting the strength and vitality of our allies." Here was acknowledgment that Kissinger's "new Asian policy" and Mr. Ford's "new Pacific doctrine" dated back into the Nixon time, a point that the President didn't conceal but didn't emphasize, either. Kissinger also acknowledged, with a frankness never equalled by the President on the trip, the "widespread initial apprehension" that the Indo-China disaster "might signal—or, precipitate—a general American retreat from Asia and even from global responsibilities." A major purpose of the President's journey was to allay what remained of that apprehension in Asia.

Two other points that the President got at in his summary speech were made more clearly and more forcefully by Kissinger in his November 24 speech and at a Peking press conference. One of them is that the US is edging, not as fast as the Chinese Communists would like but still edging, toward severing its diplomatic relationship with and defense commitment to the Taiwan government while maintaining commercial and other sub-official ties with it. The other point is that the US government may be closer than most people are aware to rearrangement of its ties with and relationship to South Korea. Kissinger said: "We are ready to talk to any interested country— including North Korea—about the future of Korea, provided only that South Korea is present."

December 20, 1975

XLIV

On the Skids

At the start of 1976, after 17 months in the presidency, Gerald Ford was on the skids. Three respected national columnists—George Will, Tom Braden and Joseph Kraft—wrote variously that the nation's first appointed President had become "a caretaker," "a joke" and a man who had brought his decline and his troubles upon himself with his own stupidities. Right after praising him for two controversial actions, vetoing a construction picketing bill and signing a compromise energy bill, *The New York Times* said editorially that "the abdication of Gerald Ford . . . has now become a discernible possibility." The *Times* meant abdication from the race for nomination and election in 1976, not from the presidency before the inauguration of the next President on January 20, 1977.

The views of columnists and newspaper editorialists are not necessarily conclusive and determining, of course. But there could be no doubt that in this instance they combine with events to contribute powerfully to the creation of a fact. The fact was that Mr. Ford was increasingly perceived to be a loser, a bumbler, a misfit President who for some reason or other, a reason probably unflattering and possibly dangerous in itself, was prone to slip on airplane ramps, bump his head on helicopter entrances, entangle himself in the leashes of his family dogs, and fall from skis in front of televison cameras that showed him asprawl in snow. Insidiously and unmistakably, mostly in gossip but occasionally in print and in broadcast hints, an impression that originated months ago in that hive of mis-impression, the White House press room, began to spread and to be related to the perception. The impression is that Mr. Ford drinks too much.

A Gallup poll showing that in late November Ronald Reagan of California had jumped ahead of President Ford in Republican preferences for the Republican presidential nomination continued to overshadow in general effect a later Gallup poll, published on December 22, showing both that approval of the President's overall performance had just risen five points, from 41 to 46 percent of the responses, and that in a contest for the presidency Gerald Ford as of December would lead Democratic Sen. Hubert Humphrey by a considerably wider margin than Ronald Reagan would. Typically of the Ford White House operation, Press Secretary Ronald Nessen confused and diminished the positive effect of the December 22 poll by mistakenly saying on Christmas Day in Vail, Colorado, where the President was vacationing, that the five-point increase in approval was something new and about to be published instead of old news that had been mentioned by Nessen at a briefing in Washington the previous Monday. Typically of the White House press corps operation, a reporter whined to Nessen on December 26: "How could you have gone so wrong on the Gallup poll? All of us in the networks and I think the newspapers as well went pretty hard with that." If reporters in Vail blamed themselves for failing to recognize old news, there is no sign of it in the record.

The main purpose of this report is to summarize what the President and some of his principal assistants say about his troubles and prospects and what is being done about some of the staff problems connected with those troubles. First, however, a few personal opinions and observations are in order.

As to the impression of excessive drinking, in my very few contacts with Mr. Ford I've seen him enjoy whiskies and martinis. On the only two occasions when my observation could have meant anything, I never saw him over-drink. On one public occasion, a political rally in North Carolina before he became President, he seemed to me to be inexplicably voluble and disconnected. Reporters whom I respect are convinced that they've observed him during what they call "martini speeches." With the possible exception mentioned, I never have. I know of no evidence whatever that drinking affects or interferes with his presidential performance or has anything to do with his infrequent though invariably noted physical bumbles. After all, surgery for a college football knee injury had the man on crutches at the 1972 Republican convention and anybody with that history should be a bit self-conscious and nervous walking up and down steep airplane ramps. What I've seen of Mr. Ford on golf courses—they'll never get me near enough to a ski course to observe him on skis—causes me to agree with Ron Nessen that the President is a graceful and well coordinated person.

As to the skids that he is on at this writing, I believe that columnists and others who assume that he is permanently and irrecoverably on a downhill slide to political humiliation and defeat overlook the inherent power of incumbency, Mr. Ford's capacities for retrieval, and the transparent deficiencies of his principal rival for the Republican nomination, Ronald Reagan. It's fashionable to hold that incumbency in Gerald Ford's case is irrelevant; that because he was appointed rather than elected and has never had a national constituency he actually has none of the powers over either the Republican convention or the electorate that sitting Presidents are supposed to enjoy. I could be misled by the interest in and respect for the presidency as such that have never been concealed in these writings. But I don't think I am. I believe that Mr. Ford's incumbency, assuming that it's no worse used than it was in his first 17 months, will see him through quite possible party primary defeats that otherwise could be ruinous and, with some offsetting primary victories here and there, will preserve him as the unbeatable candidate for the presidential nomination at the Kansas City convention. And Reagan? Here I admit to a prejudice that could be blinding. Ronald Reagan to me is still the posturing, essentially mindless and totally unconvincing candy man that he's been in my opinion ever since I watched his try for the Republican nomination evaporate in 1968.

Mr. Ford is worried, as he should be. One of his intriguing

characteristics, however, is that he displays his worry only to the public and—according to senior assistants—never to his staff. After his signing of a compromise tax bill with only the most tenuous and slippery acknowledgment of his hitherto adamantly asserted principle that every dollar of tax reduction ought to be matched with a dollar of reduced federal expenditure was interpreted as an abject retreat, he suddenly arranged a personal appearance in the White House press room with the preposterous claim that "I won on that issue 100 percent." After his televised plump into the snow on a ski slope at Vail, he groaned to reporters: "I was never skiing better until that stupid fall. It was pure stupid carelessness." It was evident that he comprehended all too well the impression of inherent maladroitness that the spectacle was bound to further. So why did he risk it? Because the fellow likes to ski, on expert testimony usually does it well, and said to people who warned him of the peril—*the hell with it.* That I admire.

The most authoritative statement of Mr. Ford's estimate of his political prospects was offered by him at the press conference called to offset his retreat on the tax bill. Here is the statement, condensed but not distorted: "The way I judge it is, whether I think I am doing a good job as President. The American people in the final analysis will judge whether I should be nominated and/or elected on the basis of how I conduct myself in this office and that is where the concentration will be. I think the final answer comes in the ballot box and if I do the job that will be the test, not any interim polls."

Here, without quotation marks but in close paraphrase, is a composite of views encountered at the White House after the return from China. Jerry Ford—it was said—is not dead politically, or anywhere near it. The fact, much as some of the goddamn reporters out there in the press room hate to admit it, is that things are picking up. Whatever you may think of the tax bill, the fact is that Congress did move toward the President's position. A lot of things—the tax bill, the energy bill, the (vetoed) construction picketing bill—have come to a crux or are getting near the crux. Many of the uncertainties and the appearance of *his* uncertainties that have made so much trouble for him are ended or ending. Wait for his State of the Union message and the legislative proposals that will follow it. They are very important. That message either will or won't be up to the opportunities and the challenge of this Bicentennial year. It ought to be a great message. I (the assistant speaking) believe it will be. Anyhow it and the legislative proposals will have Congress and the public reacting to the President, instead of the President reacting to them. That should be a plus.

A question often asked in interviews was, does the President appear to be concerned? The clearest answer, one that was similar to several others, went as follows: "If he is concerned, he doesn't show it. You have to understand, this man is a stoic. He has learned in 25 years (actually 27 years now) in politics not to fret, not to display his anxieties. He MUST be concerned. But he doesn't discuss or show it in ways that would upset his staff or upset him."

Two gut questions also got similar answers from every assistant they were put to. The first one was whether the President and the assistant in each particular conversation perceived that Mr. Ford simply was not projecting himself to the public as the decisive, strong-minded person that his assistants generally found him to be. The invariable answer was that the assistant indeed perceived it and worried about it and assumed but didn't know that the President did. The other gut question was whether the President will present himself to the Republican convention in Kansas City, seeking and expecting the nomination, regardless of what happens in the Republican primaries. The most emphatic of several similar answers was: "You can bet your last dollar that he will be there, asking for the nomination and getting it."

There were some variations—but no total dissents—from the generally conveyed impression of confidence in Gerald Ford and in his 1976 prospects. The most interesting variation, expressed in rather surprising quarters, was that the public impression of indecision at the top of the White House is neither entirely the doing of the media nor entirely false. According to the mildly negative view, Mr. Ford really is at times indecisive or, after a decision is made, more prone than any President should be to listen to a dissenting view from someone he trusts and thereupon change his mind and the decison, to the consternation of all concerned and to his considerable harm. A related and similarly secondary view—though a view held at high levels—is that the President is entirely too tolerant of backbiting and self-interested leaking of confidential information to favored reporters among some of his senior staff. Two examples are the leaks about who advised what during and after the dismissals of CIA Director William Colby and Defense Secretary James Schlesinger and the simultaneous removal of Henry Kissinger's status as assistant to the President for security affairs, and the unconscionable spectacle—described by me in this journal's December 20 issue—of Press Secretary Ron Nessen being not only allowed but encouraged to harass Henry Kissinger. I learned after the Nessen-Kissinger account appeared that Richard Cheney, the President's new chief of staff, stood beside Nessen on Air Force One during the flight from Peking to Jakarta while Nessen denounced reporters for "giving in to Henry" and making some legitimate changes in quotations of "a senior official" that Kissinger had requested. Cheney never uttered a word of disapproval of Nessen's conduct, then or later.

Two explanations of the President's and Kissinger's attitudes toward this sort of White House backbiting were heard during these inquiries. Mr. Ford was said to tolerate the Nessen sniping at Kissinger because he, the President, was confident that Kissinger understood that it doesn't mean a thing. The President's view was said to be that Kissinger knows that he continues to enjoy Mr. Ford's total confidence and therefore isn't bothered by the darts that come his way from White House people whom he regards as negligible pipsqueaks. Both at the White House and the State Department, Kissinger is said to be much less tolerant of the White House sniping than the President assumes he is, but also to believe that he in fact does have the President's unimpaired confidence and all the access to Mr. Ford that Kissinger's situation and problems require. My own impression and conviction are that the President seriously underestimates Henry Kissinger's sensitivity and the general effect, particularly upon other governments, that the continuing toleration of the sniping is having. Kissinger does a good deal to keep alive the notion that he is quite capable of quitting before Mr. Ford's present term is out. But that doesn't make it any less possible that the Secretary of State will quit rather than put up through 1976 with the White House, congressional, media and private harassment that has become his lot.

There was more agreement than I expected with recent judgments that the quality of the Ford staff falls substantially short of what he needs. The usual response was that the President is well served in particular areas on particular matters but that somehow "we don't seem to work together very well." Several moves to improve the operation have been taken or are in prospect. Lt. Gen. Brent Scowcroft, Kissinger's successor as assistant for national security affairs, is beefing up the NSC staff section assigned to monitor intelligence agencies and activities for the President. Richard Cheney has added David Gergen, the last head of the Nixon writing staff, to the central White House staff, partly to assist Cheney in developing policy ideas and partly to do what he can, without invading the turf of Counselor Robert Hartmann, to sharpen up the President's major speeches. Informally and very discreetly, Counselor John Marsh—a former Virginia congressman with a standing on the Hill and in government that Cheney has yet to earn—is moving in as Cheney's coequal "backup" in staff administration. Serious re-thought is being given to whether it made sense for Mr. Ford to turn the direction of his key Domestic Council over to Vice President Rockefeller and Rockefeller men.

January 3 and 10, 1976

XLV

Ford's Balancing Act

Wait for the State of the Union address, Mr. Ford's White House
people said during the six weeks preceding the delivery of that
speech at the opening of the second session of the 94th Congress
and the subsequent submission of his fiscal 1977 budget. It's got
to be a great speech and it's going to be, they said. Their
implication and their hope were that it would begin to turn the
tide of the President's waning fortunes. Their further hope was
that the budget and the legislative proposals to follow over the
next few weeks would complete the recovery process and set
Gerald Ford back on the road to sure nomination and election. At
11 o'clock on the morning following delivery of the speech to
Congress and on the three national networks, in a performance
that was among the President's best to date, the public response
in the form of telephone calls and telegrams to the White House
was tabulated. There had been 264 calls and wires, with 204
citizens applauding and 60 citizens criticizing the speech. Not
long before that, the White House had received more than
700,000 wires, telephone calls and letters urging the President to
veto a bill that would have enlarged the power of construction
unions to shut down construction projects. He vetoed the bill,

breaking his earlier promise to sign it, and Secretary of Labor John Dunlop resigned.

The response to the State of the Union speech lent a certain pathos or humor, depending upon the observer's bias, to the enormous efforts that went into the preparation and promotion of the address and the budget. No President in memory has ever suffered from the accounts that associates give of his part in both endeavors, and Mr. Ford is no exception. After due discount, however, a good deal about a President may be learned from these post mortems.

Day after day in the period immediately preceding the delivery of the speech, Press Secretary Ron Nessen volunteered reports of the hours—two, three, five per day—that the President had spent on it. At a climactic briefing just before the address was given, Nessen said that "in the last week or 10 days" Mr. Ford had spent "at least 50 hours writing the State of the Union." James Cannon, the Nelson Rockefeller protegé who heads the President's Domestic Council, said at the same briefing that "this is President Ford's first true State of the Union in which he is totally in control." Cannon meant that many of the positions set forth or reflected in Mr. Ford's 1975 State of the Union address had been adopted or at least shaped by circumstance before Richard Nixon resigned and the nation's first appointed Vice President succeeded him in August 1974.

How anything better than the sad and disjointed mishmash—a sandwich of substance, some of it sharp and some of it muggy, placed between inspirational goo at the beginning and end of the speech—could have come out of the production process escapes me. The speech listened better than it read, and that presumably was intended. State of the Union and other major presidential addresses nowadays are designed to be heard, not read, and this observer awaits a President who will have the courage and sense to assign the preparation of an important speech to one writer and tell the host of willing advisers and co-writers, including himself, to get lost. That didn't happen in this instance. The complexity of issues and the pressures upon any President being what they are, it could not reasonably have been expected to happen. But it's as true in government as in other publishing areas that good stuff is not produced in committee.

The committee process in this affair goes back to last summer. Mr. Ford then instructed Cannon to begin collecting and synthesizing ideas for the 1976 State of the Union speech and the fiscal 1977 budget. Cannon arranged and the Vice President conducted a series of citizens' forums around the country. They produced two thick volumes of summarized ideas, aimed at the budget and at the State of the Union message. A vast accumulation of transcripts and summaries from a parallel series of forums, organized by presidential assistant William Baroody and usually attended by Mr. Ford, added to the material for anybody who had the time and inclination to plow through it. My impression is that Mr. Ford, a hater of excessive paper, settled for the personal vibes he got at these sessions. However vaguely and indirectly, all of it contributed.

Just before Mr. Ford and a few members of his senior staff went to the snowy hell of Vail, Colorado, for the Christmas holidays, James Cannon called in ranking White House assistants to discuss their notions of what should go into the 1976 State of the Union address. According to the notes of a participant, the discussion was more concerned with the tone and thrust than with the substance of the coming speech. This seems to have been true throughout the succeeding and prolonged discussion of what the President should say. In the preliminaries to the 1975 address, the serious argument was over policy. This time, it was over style. My participating friend's account of the talk at Cannon's pre-Christmas conference is not definitive but it's believable. He was there.

L. William Seidman, the President's economics counselor and hometown friend from Grand Rapids, argued that Americans should be told in the speech that the governmental process is too big, too remote and obscure from the citizen, and that people should be assured of a desire to give them more participation in the policy process. Philip Buchen, the chief White House counsel who is another old friend from Grand Rapids, said the President should strike a high note of liberty for the individual to determine his own future and do what he could to fulfill it, and not depend upon government to fulfill it for him. Paul MacAvoy, a member of the Council of Economic Advisers, argued on somewhat the same line that people should be promised the chance and challenged to make their decisions for themselves. Alan Greenspan, chairman of the economic council, said the President should show himself to be aware of peoples' sense that government is too big and that nothing done by government works for them. Richard Cheney, the new White House staff chief who had recently succeeded his friend and sponsor, Secretary of Defense Donald Rumsfeld, cautioned the others at the meeting that many long-term and as yet unannounced decisions—for example, a then secret decision to recommend a mild increase in the Social Security tax rate—were involved in the pre-speech discussions. He admonished all present to keep their mouths shut and cited a domestic policy leak, painful to him, that had surfaced that morning. Frank Zarb, federal energy administrator, said the President should incorporate some of Zarb's energy conservation ideas (Mr. Ford did). More than any other person at the meeting, Zarb went to the core of why people were wondering about the President and said he should use the State of the Union speech to argue that they should keep in office a competent man who cared about their individual and national security and had behind him a quarter century of experience in government.

A story going about the White House is that Mr. Ford in an outline hand-written on the same kind of yellow note-pads that Richard Nixon uses set down the main thrust and structure of the speech soon after he returned from China in early December. The President writes notes and casual communications on yellow pads. But the story appears to be a distortion of the fact that he began around last October to pepper Counselor Robert Hartmann, a veteran associate who heads up the Ford speech operation, with notes on ideas for the State of the Union message. The best recollection is that Mr. Ford did not really concentrate upon the message until early January, when he had returned from Vail and Hartmann had returned from a rest at a home that he and his wife have had for years in the Virgin Islands. From that point, beginning on January 6 after the President returned to Washington from a farm policy speech in St. Louis, the tale takes on a quality of nightmarish comedy.

Hartmann had taken with him to the Virgin Islands a ratpack of Ford and other notes that had been accumulating since late fall. According to a source who could be none other than Hartmann, though I'm not supposed to say so—I refuse to write in the currently corrupted mode that "sources said"—Hartmann had found when he returned to the White House on Monday, January 5, a note from the President to the effect that it was time to get started on the State of the Union speech and that Hartmann should drop everything else. The President's note also said it might be a good idea to take a small group of assistants to Camp David, the presidential retreat in the Maryland mountains near Washington, and in isolation there thrash out ideas that might go into the address. In the Virgin Islands, during infrequent lapses from total languor, Hartmann had groped for a theme that would tie the Bicentennial year into the President's purposes and had dimly formulated the notion, expressed in the speech, that each generation's sense of confidence that life in America would be better for the next generation was threatened for the first time in our history. In discussion on January 6, the President liked that approach and said he wanted also to talk about where the country was, how we'd got there and where we were going, and to be very specific about what the federal government could and couldn't do. At eight o'clock Wednesday morning, January 7, the President presided at the daily senior staff meeting, as he's been doing once or twice a week since Richard Cheney took over from Donald Rumsfeld, and repeated substantially what he'd said to Hartmann. Mr. Ford said that he and Hartmann had selected eight other assistants and three secretaries who would go into purdah (not the President's word) at Camp David until they had agreed upon the main thrusts that the speech should take. The President said with veiled sternness that he expected assistants who were not chosen for Camp David to cooperate and made it clear that Hartmann was to be in charge.

Hartmann and Milton Friedman, the White House staff writer who principally helped Hartmann on the speech, discovered that afternoon that Camp David was preempted by Secretary of Agriculture Earl Butz for the rest of the week. They'd have thrown Butz out if he had not been entertaining a haggle of foreign agricultural types. The upshot was that the White House group repaired by air force helicopter late Wednesday and by airplane early Thursday to guest houses that had been offered by

Colonial Williamsburg, Inc., the tax-free enterprise at Williamsburg, Virginia, that has preserved and restored a fragment of the colonial past with Rockefeller money. The Ford people got free lodging and paid only for food and drink. They included Hartmann, Friedman, Seidman, William Baroody (substituting for Counselor John Marsh), cultural adviser Robert Goldwin, budget director James Lynn, chief economist Alan Greenspan, James Cannon and—I should make more of a point of this, but the hell with it—Stewart Spencer, executive director of the President Ford Committee working for the President's nomination and election. Just what they accomplished except argue about what should go into the State of the Union address all day Thursday, late Thursday night and until about one pm Friday remains obscure. They got thoroughly tired of each other's company and arguments and were happy to break it up shortly after midday Friday. Hartmann, Friedman and two secretaries stayed at Williamsburg until Saturday afternoon, putting together a first draft. Mr. Ford worked over it off and on until the following Wednesday, when the serious fun began.

Dozens of pages suddenly turned up from Baroody, Goldwin and Seidman, who rewrote and rewrote his draft of a recommended economic section with maddening frequency. Mr. Ford looked the stuff over and told Hartmann to take it away, out of sight, and work it and the original draft into a coherent whole. Hartmann retired to his home where he could work alone, his wife being still in the Virgin Islands. It seemed to Hartmann that it was at this point that the President really focused on what he wanted to say. He kept sending out by chauffeured White House car little notes on yellow foolscap and one not-so-little note of three pages on a single subject. Others also sent notes. Hartmann's portable typewriter went bad, with sticking keys, and he took an hour's nap while another typewriter was delivered. Otherwise he worked all of Wednesday night. He dispatched about half of that draft to the White House early Thursday and brought the other half in around 10:30. He did more work on it and took it to Mr. Ford at 22 minutes to noon. He remembers the 22 minutes because he said to the President, "I promised it this morning and I've got 22 minutes to go."

Hartmann and the President had some unexpected hell to go

through. David Gergen, a talented young man who headed the last Nixon writing staff and had just been brought onto the Ford administration staff by Richard Cheney, had prepared a separate draft. It went directly to the President on the Thursday in question, certainly not through Hartmann and presumably through Cheney. Its submission resulted in one of the oddest sequences in recent White House history. Hartmann learned of it on Friday morning, January 16, when the President showed it to him along with a wholly new draft that Mr. Ford had derived from the Gergen draft and Hartmann's most recent draft and had dictated late Thursday night, after a swim and dinner, to his long-time secretary, Dorothy Downton. I'm told that the President referred to the last Hartmann draft as "ours" and to the Gergen draft as "theirs." He said he thought he'd taken the best from both drafts and told Hartmann to go over the Gergen draft and insert into the Ford draft anything good in the Gergen draft that the President had overlooked. After reading the Gergen draft, Hartmann thought he knew who was behind it. Cheney, Gergen's boss and sponsor, could hardly have been totally uninvolved. But he'd played it very coolly and carefully with Hartmann, among other things getting Hartmann's prior agreement to bring Gergen onto the inner White House staff. Hartmann was sure that Alan Greenspan and James Lynn had principally inspired the Gergen draft. They had already made it clear in the West Wing councils that they thought the Hartmann draft that had last gone to the President stank. Some of the regiment of advisers, including Greenspan and Lynn, thought the speech should be mainly an exposition of the President's and the nation's ideals, liberally laced with conservative economic doctrine but nevertheless aimed more at hearts than pocketbooks. Like working-level officials who dealt with Mr. Ford on the budget, Hartmann understood that the President is happier with facts and pragmatic options, lending themselves to clear decision, than he is with idealistic rhetoric. One gathers that neither the Hartmann nor Gergen drafts (Gergen submitted part of a second version) went entirely one way or the other. As already indicated, the delivered draft was a mushy mixture of both.

The climax to a series of meetings, clearances, and arguments over the Ford draft came between three and six pm on Saturday, January 17, at a meeting in the cabinet room. Hartmann, arriving a bit late, found at the table the Williamsburg group plus John Marsh, Cheney and Lt. Gen. Brent Scowcroft, the assistant for national security affairs. Hartmann remarked rather sourly that since the rest of the gang was present he might as well have his own troops in the persons of Friedman and Robert Orben, a sometime professional gagster who has recently been named executive editor (under Hartmann) of the President's thinly staffed speech factory. Mr. Ford said sure, bring 'em in. There then ensued a savage, three-hour attack upon the draft before the group. Only Hartmann, the President and possibly Cheney knew that the President himself had drafted the version that some of the others proceeded to cut up. Harsh criticism went to the passage saying that "1975 was not a year for summer soldiers and sunshine patriots." Twaddle, the critics said, unaware that Mr. Ford had personally lifted it from Tom Paine and was proud of it. Other criticism went to a passage, similar to a part of the separate budget message, in which the President called for "a new realism" and for "a new balance" between domestic and defense spending, between federal and local government, and between individuals and all government. Twaddle, the critics snarled, supposing that in this and other disputed sections they were dealing with Hartmann junk. The "new balance" section was one of a few that the President had overlooked in the first Gergen draft and that Hartmann had inserted in the Ford draft.

At around six pm, the President wearied. He struck the heavy Cabinet table so hard that it shook and said, *God damn it,* he'd heard enough and it was time to finish this thing. He ordered the others to stay until it was finished and told Hartmann to have a final draft ready by noon Sunday. He then left. Seidman called after him that he had to leave someone in charge. The President ignored the call. Hartmann suggested a five-minute toilet break and during it conferred with the President in the Oval Office. When Hartmann returned to the cabinet room, Seidman again asked who was in charge. Hartmann, who has been heard to say that "I arouse the animal in people," said with cold finality that the President had settled that question when he had Hartmann organize and lead the Williamsburg group. Hartmann also said in the same chill tone that anybody who wanted the President to mediate a point could call him at the mansion but would be well advised not to do so. On that note, the group finished its haggling and work about 9:30 pm. Hartmann, Friedman and Orben polished a near-final draft by midnight. Hartmann telephoned the President and offered to bring the latest draft to the residence. Mr. Ford said he was going to bed and would look over the "final" draft Sunday morning. He also advised Hartmann to stay home on Sunday and leave the last agonies to Bob Orben and Hartmann's administrative assistant, Douglas Smith. Distorted rumors about this suggestion and about the President's outburst at the end of the Saturday afternoon meeting led to erroneous reports that the whole operation had been taken from Hartmann. I have reason to know that he was very much in charge to the end. Beginning at five pm Sunday, cabinet members were invited to come to the cabinet room and read the draft. Some minor changes were suggested. The President, still irritated, ordered Monday that each author of each of these changes be identified on his copy. He adopted a few of the changes and, for better or for worse, delivered the State of the Union address that Congress and the portion of the television and radio public that wished to or could stay through it heard the night of January 19.

January 31, 1976

After this piece was read at the White House, I was accused of excessive reliance upon Bob Hartmann. Mr. Ford found the piece amusing and accurate. I erred in two respects: Gergen appeared as "Gergin" in the *New Republic* account, and Cheney did not attend the final drafting session with the President in the Cabinet room.

XLVI

Kissinger's Troubles

At eight o'clock on the morning before Secretary of State Henry Kissinger flew to Moscow for another try at negotiating an improved and extended agreement on strategic arms limitation with the Soviet Union, navy doctors examined him and found him in good health. It was one of the few bits of good news that the Secretary has had in quite a while. His wife Nancy was in the Bethesda Naval Hospital with a recurrence of ulcers that Kissinger blames largely upon the tensions arising from his multitude of troubles. "It's harder on her than it is on me," he said the other day. He returned from Moscow with less progress toward a satisfactory arms agreement than he's hoped for. His conduct of the entire SALT affair since the interim Nixon-Kissinger agreement was reached in Moscow in 1972 was under severe and authoritative attack from such critics as former Deputy Secretary of Defense and arms negotiator Paul Nitze and former Chief of Naval Operations Elmo Zumwalt, Jr. His Middle Eastern policy of promoting step-by-step negotiations between Israel and its Arab enemies was subjected to similarly authoritative criticism by former Under Secretary of State George Ball in the current *Atlantic*. The leaders of that policy's presumed and principal beneficiary, Israel, felt that Kissinger and

President Ford were pushing them too hard and too fast toward concessions that they thought excessive and dangerous. Overwhelming Senate and House votes to deny further funds for assistance to anti-Soviet factions in Angola constituted a crushing repudiation of Kissinger's and President Ford's view that "resistance to Soviet expansion by military means must be a fundamental element of US foreign policy" and justifies covert intervention in such places and situations as Angola. Recent and pending Senate and House committee reports on CIA and other intelligence operations, and a private suit in connection with wiretaps in the Nixon years, bring into question Kissinger's official competence and personal probity. These and other pressures, including differences with important figures at the Ford White House, stimulated speculation among some of Kissinger's closest and most devoted associates that he may quit or be driven from office before the year ends.

Something, in short, has happened and is happening to the Kissinger mystique. Without attempting judgment upon all the factors and issues that have entered into the erosion of Henry Kissinger's reputation and prestige, I offer here the best account of his situation, his state of mind and his prospects that I've been able to put together from recent interviews and conversations.

Henry Kissinger is in part a victim of what Bryce Harlow, a friend and servant of Republican Presidents since Eisenhower's time, calls "the McNamara syndrome," meaning the tendency in Washington and elsewhere to tear at and bring down public figures when and after they have been long and perhaps excessively admired, in the way that Secretary of Defense Robert McNamara was brought down and finally fired by President Johnson. Also and in part, Kissinger may be the victim of a changing world in which alliances lose their sanctity, national obligations once taken for granted come to be viewed and rejected as perils and burdens, and officials who have personified that sanctity and those obligations in the sense that Kissinger has personified them come to be distrusted and rejected, too. It is a world that Kissinger as historian would examine and explain with delight and brilliance but that he as statesman may be unable to comprehend and master with the skill for which he was so recently acclaimed.

A suggestion that Kissinger may perceive himself and the current world in some such fashion comes from an official who has worked for him in Washington since 1969. According to this official, Kissinger in conversation with the few subordinates to whom he is really close takes "almost a Spenglerian view" of the western world and its prospects. The reference of course is to the late Oswald Spengler, another German by birth, whose *Decline of the West* impressed and (as it turned out) unduly depressed millions of people in the postwar 1920s. Kissinger is said in this version to view "the West" in his gloomier moments as a community in disintegration and probably beyond salvation.

My impression of Kissinger's view of his situation and the world is somewhat different. He appears to be principally concerned with what he considers the terrible damage recently done to US foreign policy and to the capacity of any President and of any Secretary of State to conduct an effective policy. He holds that the damage has been done by the intelligence investigations and disclosures; by the claim of Congress to responsibility and authority in foreign affairs that until lately were reserved to the Executive; and by the general slippage of confidence in public figures and institutions that has followed Watergate and

LURIE'S OPINION

"JUST RUMORS, HENRY!"

Vietnam. The effect upon the non-Communist world—"the West"—of diminished American will and capacity to lead seems to worry Kissinger more than the present state and prospects of that world. My further impression is that Kissinger considers his own situation and prospects to be closely and importantly connected with the prospects for continued US effectiveness and leadership in the world. He seems neither to recognize nor to acknowledge the erosion of his prestige that has been cited here as a fact. He is said to believe that with his prestige at home and abroad he may be the only available person who can hold what's left of American policy and influence intact and functioning through 1976, during what he expects to be a period of continuing and possibly irreparable damage. He considers himself obligated to the country and to the world to hang on if he can at least until after the November election. After that, one gathers, he may feel free to quit an office that, as lately as April 1975, he was prepared and half hoping to keep through another presidential term.

A factor that I've yet to see or hear mentioned may enter. Elliot Richardson's recall from his ambassadorship in London to be Secretary of Commerce is usually interpreted as a way to place him in line for the Republican vice presidential or even presidential nomination this year. Richardson's first position in the Nixon administration was Under Secretary of State. His success in that job was due in part to his close relationship with Henry Kissinger when Kissinger was assistant to the President for national security affairs and William P. Rogers was Secretary of State. Richardson could be an acceptable successor to Kissinger as an interim appointee or a full-term Secretary of State in the next administration.

Kissinger's chances of remaining at the State Department turn upon his standing with President Ford. When that relationship was last discussed here, the evidence was that the President retained total confidence in Kissinger and Kissinger remained confident that he has the President's confidence. That is still the basic conclusion but it has to be modified a little. Kissinger shares this observer's and other's wonder that Mr. Ford could be so obtuse as not to realize that his tolerance of potshots at Kissinger from the White House is bound to impair the Secretary of State's effectiveness with other governments. These continuing potshots take forms that are much more substantial than Press Secretary Ron Nessen's tendency—one that he has recently tried to suppress—to run down the Secretary of State. A mid-level official whose job extends across the foreign policy spectrum, from the State Department to the National Security Council, is convinced that in recent weeks Kissinger has been excluded from presidential and White House decisions that in the past would never have been taken without his knowledge and assent. Kissinger asks journalists and others on the White House fringe whether to their knowledge the potshotting is continuing. White House Counselor John Marsh, one of Mr. Ford's ablest assistants, has been noticeably less protective of Kissinger than former Counsel Roderick Hills, now chairman of the Securities and Exchange Commission, was when he dealt for the President with the Senate and House intelligence committees. Since Marsh took over that responsibility, he has given Kissinger associates and some congressional staffers an impression that he doesn't care about what NSC and other documents provided to the committees do to Kissinger so long as Gerald Ford is not directly affected.

Kissinger encourages his immediate subordinates at the State Department and his former subordinates on the NSC staff in the view, common to most of them, that the loss of his White House title during the "Sunday massacre" last November, when the President demoted him and fired CIA Director William Colby and Secretary of Defense James Schlesinger, did not significantly diminish the Secretary of State's control over the foreign policy process. How intelligent people could believe this is beyond my understanding. Kissinger is not among those who believe it, though he pretends to in the interest of sustaining his peoples' morale. His former deputy and successor as assistant to the President for national security affairs, Lt. Gen. Brent Scowcroft, has assented to Kissinger's continuance as chairman of the powerful Verification Panel, a group that reviews strategic armament matters, and expects soon to affirm his continuance as chairman of the Washington Special Action Group (WASAG), the inter-departmental committee that advises the President on how to handle emergency foreign situations. Kissinger is said to have been glad to relinquish the chairmanship of the Forty Committee, the group that passes upon proposals for covert intelligence operations, to Gen. Scowcroft. The standard wisdom among departmental and NCS staffs is that the two chairmanships retained by Kissinger preserve his control of the foreign policy process. Kissinger knows better. It was as assistant to the President that he developed and exerted the central command and authority, subject to the President, that he considered and still considers necessary for the effective formulation and management of foreign policy. In his judgment, he still has some of it but it's diminishing and at the present rate of erosion will be gone before 1976 is out. From the NSC staff standpoint, with a full-time assistant and a widely respected deputy assistant for security affairs, William Hyland, on duty at the White House, the system works better than it did when Kissinger went to the State Department and became a part-time assistant. That's not Kissinger's view.

It's premature to speak of Secretary Kissinger in the past tense. Whatever happens to him, however, this observer is reminded of what William Ewart Gladstone wrote in his old age about a friend of his early manhood, James Hope: "He possessed that most rare gift, the power of fascination, and he fascinated me."

February 7, 1976

XLVII

Tapping for Henry

Some of Secretary of State Henry Kissinger's problems, prospects and attitudes were discussed in general terms in the previous article. Here the specifics of one of his problems are addressed, with emphasis upon it because it resembles many others in the ways in which it brings his competence and credibility into question.

Nothing has damaged Kissinger's personal reputation more than the charge that he has been lying since 1973 about his role in and responsibility for FBI wiretaps placed upon 13 government officials and four journalists between May 1969 and February 1971. Morton H. Halperin, a former Kissinger assistant whose home telephone was tapped for 21 months, has filed a civil suit in a federal district court in Washington, seeking damages from Kissinger, Richard Nixon, Gen. Alexander M. Haig, former Attorney General John N. Mitchell, former Nixon assistants H.R. Haldeman, John Ehrlichman and Robert Mardian, FBI Director Clarence Kelley (in his peripheral role as successor to the late J. Edgar Hoover) and the telephone company serving Washington. The damages payable to Halperin could total anywhere between $300,000 and three million dollars, under a federal law allowing plaintiffs in such suits $100 for every day of proven violation of their rights by each defendant. The Halperin suit, abetted in its effect by some of the worst reporting of this and other Kissinger matters I've observed in 49 years in journalism, has done more than anything else to keep alive and compound the published assertions and intimations that Kissinger has been and still is lying about the wiretaps. Among the wider effects, the staff of Sen. Frank Church's special investigating committee has largely skipped that aspect of Kissinger's involvement in intelligence-related operations and has relied upon the Halperin suit to elicit the facts. Given its importance, the way the suit is being prosecuted and defended deserves attention it seldom gets in news reports.

Three attorneys in the Department of Justice criminal division—Robert Keuch (pronounced keek), Elizabeth Gere Whitaker and Edward Christenberry—are representing all of the defendants except the telephone company. The justification for free representation that otherwise could cost the defendants hundreds of thousands of dollars is that all of the individuals are being sued for actions taken in their official capacites. Morton Halperin, who has made a career of privacy and the protection of same since his and the other wiretaps were divulged in early 1973, is also getting free representation. He works for an affliliate of the American Civil Liberties Union, and its staff attorneys represent him in his suit against Kissinger. Halperin resigned from Kissinger's National Security Council staff in September 1969, eight months after he transferred to it from the Department of Defense. My recollection is that Halperin told me in 1970 that he quit the staff after learning that he wasn't going to be appointed Kissinger's chief deputy. One of the defendants, Gen. Haig, eventually got that appointment. Halperin says that my recollection is in error; that he quit mainly "because of the working relationships on the staff." He says Kissinger discussed with him but, because of opposition from other members of the staff, never offered him a position with the responsibilities but not the title of deputy assistant for national security affairs. Halperin and Kissinger told me in 1970 that Kissinger had urged Halperin to remain on the staff. In May 1970, in protest against the US invasion of Cambodia, Halperin relinquished—"resigned" would be an overstatement—the NSC consultancy, never much exercised, that he had retained after he quit the staff.

Kissinger's wiretap problem typifies the many other problems—his conduct of strategic arms negotiations and policing, his involvement as chairman of the White House "40 Committee" in various covert foreign operations, the glossing of the 1973 Vietnam peace terms, his taking the US into the Angola snarl—in which his troubles were brought upon him by circumstance and by others and in part were brought upon him by himself. Kissinger's public wiretap statements, from the day in early 1973 when he said in the White House press room that on President Nixon's orders his office had supplied names for surveillance and that he as head of his office took full responsibility for doing it, have been consistent. It was in private communication with journalists that Kissinger got himself into trouble and generated a doubt, usually reflected rather than explicitly stated in print and in broadcasts, about his believability. In two examples drawn from my experience, he at one point came close to passing the whole buck to his faithful assistant, Gen. Haig, and in another instance suggested that he had tolerated— he never to my knowledge said he initiated—the tap on Morton Halperin in the hope that it might convince Bob Haldeman, John Ehrlichman and other White House doubters that Halperin wasn't the security risk they said they thought he was. In this sort of evasion and twisting, Kissinger was at his worst. It has done him incalculable harm with the Washington reporters and commentators who deal with him and are influenced, for or against him, by contacts and communications of this kind.

In contrast with this feature of the private record, the public record is refreshing. It is summarized here because so much of it has been lost to notice in the rush of current and occasionally slanted reporting. The disclosures of the wiretaps and the allegations of Kissinger's reponsibility for them were still in the news when President Nixon in 1973 nominated Kissinger to be his Secretary of State while continuing to be his assistant for national security affairs. Two of Mr. Nixon's White House assistants, Bryce Harlow and Thomas Korologos, and one of Kissinger's NSC assistants, John F. Lehman, Jr., spent most of an afternoon and the night before Kissinger's Senate confirmation hearing drilling him on questions he was likely to be asked by the Senate committee, with heavy emphasis upon the wiretap issue. Kissinger convinced all three of them then, and they tell me that they remain convinced, that he was telling the truth when he gave them the answers that he gave the Senate Committee on Foreign Relations. The condensed essence of his answers to the committee, in open session and in executive session, later published, was: "In early May 1969 the President consulted the then Director of the FBI [J. Edgar Hoover] and the Attorney General [John Mitchell] about this problem [leaks of classified security information]. He was told that the most effective method was to tap individuals. My office was required to submit the names of those officials who had had access to the information that had leaked. The information was then transmitted by General Haig to Inspector [William C.] Sullivan of the FBI. I never recommended the practice of wiretapping, I was aware of it, and I went along with it to the extent of supplying the names of the people who had access to the sensitive documents in question."

In June 1974, while traveling with President Nixon to the Middle East, Kissinger reacted at a famous press conference in Salzburg, Austria, to reports that he'd lied in his 1973 testimony. He demanded a reopened Senate inquiry, said he'd resign if it didn't clear him, and at the resultant hearing said that what he'd testified in 1973 "remains completely true" except that the decisive meeting with President Nixon, Hoover and Mitchell occurred in April rather than May 1969. From this 1974 Kissinger testimony (condensed): "There was a discussion of specific individuals and Mr. Hoover suggested that four persons be put under surveillance, three of them people on the staff. There has never been any dispute that when my office submitted names I knew that an investigation was certain and a wiretap probable." Former Senator and chairman J. William Fulbright put in the record a letter dated July 12, 1974, from Richard Nixon. Three days short of a month before he was to resign, Mr. Nixon said in this letter: "Where supporting evidence was available, I personally directed the surveillance, including wire-tapping, of certain individuals. I am familiar with the testimony given by Secretary Kissinger before your committee . . . This testimony is entirely correct; and I wish to affirm categorically that Secretary Kissinger and others involved in various aspects of this investigation [of leaks] were operating under my specific authority and carrying out my express orders."

In early January 1976, Kissinger delivered written answers to written interrogatories from Halperin's attorneys. Kissinger shrank as he had in the past from naming the wiretap targets and from telling how involved individuals figured in White House discussions of the leaks and taps. In one of many answers, however, he said: "At the Oval Office meeting in April 1969, President Nixon authorized an electronic surveillance . . . While his authorization was in general terms and not limited to specific individuals, my understanding was that he then directed surveillance of Morton Halperin and certain others." These answers became public when they were filed in federal court. On January 15 Halperin and two of his attorneys attended a session at which Richard Nixon was questioned in San Clemente. Nixon's depostion will become public, less deletions agreed to by attorneys for all parties, when it is filed in federal court. In the meantime, any party to the proceeding who divulges what was said is subject to contempt proceedings.

On the morning of the 15th, before the deposition was taken, Daniel Schorr of CBS attributed to "friends who have recently talked to the ex-President" the view that "Mr. Nixon is expected to contradict Secretary Kissinger and deny that he specifically authorized a 1969 wiretap of Morton Halperin." In a report datelined Los Angeles and published January 18, Nicholas Horrock of *The New York Times* attributed to "associates of the former President" statements that Mr. Nixon testified in the deposition that "he never personally selected the persons to be wiretapped" and that "he had left the selection of the targets up to Henry Kissinger." Kissinger said January 19 that it was inconceivable to him that Mr. Nixon could have said this. Jack Brennan, the head of the tiny Nixon staff in San Clemente, said by telephone January 27: "President Nixon has discussed his deposition with absolutely no one, his wife or me, and if he would have discussed it with anyone, he would have with me. It's absolutely impossible that there's been a source from here." Halperin's attorneys acknowledged that they and Halperin gave reporters atmospheric details of the deposition session, none of the tidbits reflecting favorably upon Mr. Nixon. The attorneys assured Mr. Nixon's personal lawyers and the Department of Justice that they and Halperin did not divulge the substance of the Nixon testimony. It was suggested to me in Halperin quarters that Dan Schorr's advance information could hardly have come from Halperin people and that Nicholas Horrock's aftermath information could have come from William Safire, a former Nixon assistant who writes for the *Times*. Safire said in a conversation February 2 that he'd been in touch with Nixon people in San Clemente before the deposition was taken and that his impression was "confirmed by the Horrock story." Safire said he wasn't Horrock's source: "He did his own work." Neither Halperin nor government attorneys suggested that the Schorr broadcast and the Horrock report conflicted with their memory of Nixon's testimony. Both reports mentioned only the supposed contradiction of Kissinger. Neither showed any awareness of Mr. Nixon's July 12, 1974 letter to Fulbright and noted that if Richard Nixon testified on January 15 as he is said to have done, he contradicted himself.

February 14, 1976

XLVIII

Laundering the Spies

Any judgment of the administration proposals to change and control the country's foreign intelligence system and procedures must turn upon agreement or disagreement with President Ford's view that it is "essential to have the best possible intelligence about the capabilities, intentions and activities of governments and other entities and individuals abroad." If you agree, as I do, the President's proposals must be held on the whole to be good and reasonable, probably the most and the best that can be done to prevent abuse while preserving a viable intelligence instrument. If the national necessity for such an instrument is doubted, or is granted a lower priority than is accorded the individual rights that an effective intelligence system must invade to some degree, the proposals may fairly be held—as they indeed are considered by many responsible critics—to cloak and validate activites that in today's climate have come to be regarded as illegal or at best unacceptable. That is not my view. But it or something close to it seems likely to be the view of Congress. If this turns out to be so and the President's proposals to deal mainly with the acknowledged problems of intelligence by executive action are displaced by punitive legislation, an enormous and largely unreported federal effort will have gone down the drain and Mr. Ford's endeavor to impose upon the foreign intelligence function a system of monitoring and accountability that would provide needed control will have been frustrated.

Aftermath accounts of the evolution of major presidential proposals never do the incumbent President any harm and, staff loyalties being what they usually are, may be somewhat self-serving. Nevertheless, the proffered history of Mr. Ford's intelligence actions and proposals believably credits him with a foresight, a steadiness of course, and a capacity for firm decision and strong assertion of his views in the final stages that he and his people seem unable to project to the public in a convincing way. His own efforts to convey these qualities in speeches and in other public performances tend to fall flat and, too often, make him look ridiculous. This failure of projection is one of the defects that could cost Gerald Ford the Republican nomination this summer and present the country with the spectacle, still incredible to me, of that California figurine, Ronald Reagan, actually running for election to the presidency.

Mr. Ford's home-town friend and chief counsel, Philip Buchen, and his staff of White House lawyers began work on the legal issues involved a full year before a temporary entity, the Intelligence Coordinating Group, focused last September on preparation of the proposals while trying to respond, in its first order of business, to the mounting demands for classified information and documents from the Senate and House intelligence investigating committees. Mason Cargill and Timothy Hardy, young lawyers from the staff of the Rockefeller commission that had investigated allegations of "massive and illegal" CIA domestic activity, joined Buchen's staff after the commission reported in June and did the early work on the formal restrictions upon intelligence agencies that constituted one of the most important and contentious sections of the executive order issued by the President on February 18. Those restrictions went through more than 100 drafts and were strongly opposed by the principal intelligence agencies. The many exceptions issued with them provided much of the basis for complaint that the executive order authorized and validated more civil abuses than it professed to prevent. Everybody concerned, from the President down, recognized that a simple list of "shalt nots" without exceptions and qualifications would be more popular and politically effective than the adopted version was. It was also recognized that such a list would be a dishonest sham, issued in concealed knowledge that the agencies chiefly affected—the CIA, the National Security Agency and the Defense Intelligence Agency—along with numerous military and civilian sub-agencies, some of them secret and unidentified to this day, would be compelled by their own necessities to modify the restrictions whether the exceptions were publicly announced and defined or not. Some thought was given at staff and departmental levels to announcing a set of restrictions and exceptions and leaving everything else to Congress. Buchen and Attorney General Edward Levi took the lead in persuading the President—he was said not to need much convincing—that the inherently negative restrictions should be accompanied by positive control.

Donald Rumsfeld, who in September was chief of the White House staff and had yet to replace Secretary of Defense James R. Schlesinger, more or less invented the Intelligence Coordinating Group as a means of broadening and rationalizing the responsibility for White House and agency response to the increasing congressional demands for secret information and documents. The President made Counselor John Marsh chairman of the group and appointed to it the Secretaries of State and Defense, the Attorney General, the director of Central Intelligence (whom he was about to fire along with Secretary Schlesinger and then retain for a while), and Phililp Buchen. Henry Kissinger's former deputy and successor as the President's assistant for national security affairs, Lt. Gen. Brent Scowcroft, joined the group after Kissinger was relieved of his White House title.

Michael Raoul-Duval (Mike Duval for short), aged 37, a lawyer and associate director of the Domestic Council staff, was shifted to the White House Office staff and appointed executive director of the ICG. He and Marsh had the help of scores of bureaucrats at the White House, the Office of Mangement and Budget, and the various departments and agencies concerned with intelligence. They relied upon three officials in particular: OMB Associate

Director Donald Ogilvie, who at Gen. Scowcroft's instance conducted a massive study of the entire intelligence community's organization and management; Kenneth Damm, who had preceded Ogilvie at OMB; and Ray Waldmann, a former State Department and Domestic Council official, who with Damm assisted Duval in putting together a monumental series of studies for the President. These included Damm's organization and management survey, assembled in a binder one and a half inches thick; a comparative summary of major reports on the intelligence community and its problems—among them the Rockefeller CIA report and its source documents, a broader report on foreign policy and intelligence organization master-minded by former ambassador and Under Secretary of State Robert Murphy, and a 1971 intelligence management study conducted by James Schlesinger when he was at OMB. What Duval calls "a narrative discussion" summarized intelligence issues that had recently been raised and should be raised (must there be covert operations?; what were the moral and ethical problems involved?; should the collection of foreign intelligence be consolidated in one agency or left among competing agencies?; similarly, should the several analytical staffs be consolidated or left to compete with each other?). The summary of the Rockefeller, Murphy and other reports, supplemented with super-secret supporting data, was flown to President Ford in Peking when he visited China last November so that he could study it on his way home. The essence of all these studies and much else was crammed into a thick volume, bound in gleaming white leather and called "The Decison Book," that President Ford took with him for study during his Christmas vacation at Vail. Gossip had it that the President didn't work on this or anything else at Vail. Duval has evidence to the contrary: a photograph of the President, Marsh and Duval aboard Air Force One during a side trip to St. Louis, discussing the contents of "Decision Book" and looking grim.

It was apparent to Marsh, Duval and others that the President concentrated on his intelligence changes after he returned to Washington. At a memorable meeting with Mr. Ford on Saturday, January 10, Vice President Rockefeller startled the ICG members and staff with the vigor of his insistence that the

30 recommendations for reform and change that his CIA commission had submitted covered the necessary ground and that all this other stuff was wasted effort. Two of his chief recommendations were that the President recommend and insist upon a single House-Senate intelligence oversight committee and that the President should vest the chief executive responsibility for CIA oversight in his hitherto ornamental Foreign Intelligence Advisory Board. Mr. Ford bought the first recommendation and rejected the second in favor of a new, three-man civilian intelligence oversight board to be headed by Ambassador Murphy.

The two most hotly argued issues were settled only at the very last, although it was clear a good deal earlier that Mr. Ford had made up his mind on how to resolve them and was getting increasingly impatient with the persisting arguments and resistance from the Defense Department, civilian and military, and from the principal intelligence agencies. These issues were whether to define the responsibilities of the agencies in publicly stated terms, a concept that outraged intelligence professionals used to the freedoms of secrecy since the National Security Act was passed in 1947; and whether to vest major though not total control of intelligence agency budgets and resources in a three-member Committee on Foreign Intelligence (CFI) under a director of Central Intelligence with greatly expanded line authority over not only his own CIA but all other agencies dealing in "national" as distinct from more limited "tactical" intelligence.

At a near-final meeting on January 30 the President listened with discernibly thinning patience to a repetition of arguments he'd heard in person and read in memos from his new Secretary of Defense, Donald Rumsfeld, and the chairman of the Joint Chiefs of Staff, Gen. George S. Brown, among others, to the effect that Defense and the military services controlled at least three quarters of all intelligence money and resources and therefore should keep line authority over it. At a final meeting on February 16, after many meetings with Marsh, Duval, Buchen and Attorney General Levi, the President was stern, tough, emphatic. He reminded those present that he'd gone over every point time and again, individually and in groups, with everybody concerned and indicated without quite saying that he'd had enough. Rumsfeld, Brown and Deputy Secretary of Defense Robert Ellsworth (who is to represent Defense on the CFI) expressed their last doubts about giving so much power to the new director of Central Intelligence, George Bush. Gen. Scowcroft, Buchen, Marsh and Attorney General Levi supported the President against Rumsfeld, Ellsworth and Brown (speaking for the intelligence community) in favor of public charter. Levi, with the President throughout on the major issues, had some reservations about secrecy and surveillance legislation that was being submitted and promised. But there were no hard dissents, no assertions that what the President had so clearly decided upon was unacceptable. Everybody, in short, had got the message. Congress hasn't but that for Mr. Ford is another and sadder story.

March 6, 1976

―――――

Mr. Ford's decison to vest control of and responsibility for the entire intelligence community in the Director of Central Intelligence (George Bush) prevailed and worked out very well. One of the final "hotly argued issues" was unclearly stated in this piece. It was whether to define the missions of intelligence agencies other than the CIA by congressional statute or by executive order. Mr. Ford favored executive order.

Two for the Road

Here are some notes on the campaign performances of President Ford and Ronald Reagan, with special attention to Reagan because his try for the Republican nomination deserves discussion that it has not previously been accorded in this space.

During three days on the road with Reagan in New Hampshire and New York City, before the New Hampshire primary, and three days with Gerald Ford in Florida, this reporter found the audiences and their reactions to the candidates at least as interesting as the candidates were. This was particularly true of Reagan and of his impact upon his audiences.

The Reagan observed in New Hampshire was the masterful communicator that he'd been touted to be. But there were some odd and generally unnoticed aspects of the communication during the New Hampshire-New York phase. Although Reagan appeared to be in remarkably good shape for a 65-year-old fellow, he was noticeably tired at the start of the two mornings that he was observed after a day and evening on the road. He seemed to gather vigor as the days proceeded. The days and evenings weren't really as hard as the schedules made them seem to be. It was evident that Reagan's tour managers guarded his energies as carefully as Bob Haldeman used to guard Richard Nixon's in the White House and on the road. There was no turning up at factory gates at 7 or even 6 am, as some of the Democratic contenders were doing. Reagan's days began at a civilized hour, never before 8 o'clock, and "staff time" was set aside in the late afternoons and early evenings. Reagan's hard-bitten and thoroughly professional press secretary, Lyn (for Franklyn) Nofziger, insisted that the candidate's managers had no need to conserve his strength and that they actually were "working him like hell." The sensitivity was more revealing than the assertion.

The pattern of the audiences arranged for Reagan was also interesting. With one exception during the period in discussion, they were small groups of evidently committed supporters and school audiences composed mostly of teenagers and teachers. The exception was a general-audience meeting at the state university in Durham for one of Reagan's question-and-answer dialogues with citizens. President Ford had drawn about three times as many people to the same auditorium two nights before Reagan appeared. A raucous gang of young scruffies, billing themselves as representatives of the People's Bicentennial Commission and similar in age and behavior to the anti-war demonstrators of the Johnson and Nixon years, did Mr. Ford the favor of arousing audience sympathy for him. They'd had several previous encounters with Reagan and on this occasion seemed to be weary of the game, listless and bored with themselves, and so in a negative way they contributed to a tepid affair.

One of the unkind things being said by Stuart Spencer and William Roberts, the California campaign specialists who managed Reagan's sensationally successful runs for governor in 1966 and 1970 and are working now for President Ford, is that the articulate and seemingly outgoing Reagan is actually an introverted loner who detests crowds and "crowd situations." He seemed to be at ease with his New Hampshire crowds and to enjoy the appearances. At Durham after a short speech and a lengthy question-answer session, he invited his hearers to file by him for a handshake, a little conversation, and autographs, and in several instances spent minutes in earnest talk with individuals. He never plunged into crowds and "pressed the flesh" in the frenetic fashions of Johnson, Nixon, Ford. Florida news accounts of his final appearances in that state, where victory in its March 9 primary had become vital to his survival after his marginal loss in New Hampshire, noted small crowds and half-filled halls. In New Hampshire, that facet of the Reagan tours was intended and contrived and never explained.

The reaction of the high and prep school audiences in New Hampshire was both interesting and depressing. Reagan chose Phillips Exeter Academy, of all institutions, for a fierce and carefully prepared attack upon the Ford administration's policies of accommodation with the Soviet Union and Communist China, its alleged propensity for giving away far more than it was even trying to get in strategic arms negotiations with the Soviet Union, and its readiness—inherited from the Nixon administration and set forth in the Shanghai Communiqué of 1972—to dump the nationalist Republic of China on Taiwan at some undefined future stage. Each of these points, along with implied attacks on Secretary of State Henry Kissinger and a strong suggestion that Gerald Ford had been lying to the American public about the real nature and consequences of his foreign policies, brought many of the students to their feet, screaming and applauding. Public school students, all white in every instance observed for this report, were sent into transports of applause, clapping and stomping, by Reagan's denunciations of "forced busing to achieve racial balance" and of proposals to control the sale and ownership of handguns. The adult audiences were aroused to peaks of approval by Reagan's promises to reduce the power of the federal courts to interfere with local preferences and practices and, in general, to get the federal government "off the backs" of state and local governments.

The foregoing brings us to Reagan's famous $90 billion goof and his effort to extract himself from the hole that he dug with it. At the risk of expulsion from the company of respectable journalists, I herewith gallop to Ronald Reagan's defense in one important matter. He was widely reported to have said in a speech in Chicago on September 26 that the transfer from federal to state governments of responsibility for "welfare, education, housing, food stamps, Medicaid, community and regional development, and revenue sharing, to name a few . . . would reduce the [annual] outlay of the federal government by more than $90 billion, using the spending levels of fiscal 1976." He did say it, but most of the subsequent reports and interpretations had him saying *only* that. When I first heard him say in New Hampshire that his critics "neglected to say" that he'd actually proposed transfer to state governments of the federal "resources" necessary to finance the programs, I assumed that he was faking. He wasn't. The text of his Chicago speech shows that he preceded the passage just quoted in part with the following sentence—with emphasis added: "What I propose is nothing less than a systematic transfer of authority *and resources* to the states— a program of creative federalism for America's third century." It was Reagan's fault that the reference to "resources" was so brief and casual that it went practically unnoticed. A "fact sheet" issued with the text was so full of budgetary absurdities that it's been withdrawn and suppressed by the Reagan people. Otherwise critical commentators have conceded, however, that the proportion of federal and state responsibility for social programs is a valid issue and that Reagan, despite the flaws in his original proposal, did a service in raising it. Martin Anderson, a conservative young urbanologist who was one of the Nixon staff's best members in its first, best years, joined the Reagan staff in November to help Reagan out of the $90-billion hole and to inject some needed sense and sophistication into related Reaganisms. When Anderson says that the transfer or relinquishment of some federal revenue sources to the states is possible and practicable and that the modified Reagan proposal is not sheer demagoguery, I listen with a respect that I do not automatically grant to anything said by Ronald Reagan.

This piece was written when President Ford and his people were struggling to contain and conceal their increasing belief that Ronald Reagan was about to become a past-tense candidate. They were trying to contain and conceal it because, as Ford campaign manager Howard ("Bo") Callaway kept saying, for President Ford Committee workers in Florida and Illinois, where he was scheduled to campaign next, to conclude that the race was as good as won "would be disastrous." Yet, as a reporter who has never had any faith in his perceptions of crowds and their attitudes, I must admit that there was something infectious and suggestive of growing Ford support in the crowds drawn by the

President in Florida on February 28-29. The trip provided a mixed display of repellent demagoguery and attractive folksiness—demagoguery in the President's foolishly un-qualified statement to 1078 newly naturalized Cubans that "this administration will have nothing to do with the Cuba of Fidel Castro"; folksiness in the "Gee, it's wonderful to be with you wonderful people" note that Mr. Ford sustained throughout a 14-stop motorcade from Palm Beach to Ft. Lauderdale, mostly in pouring rain. The rain kept down the crowds, to the initial dismay of the President's official party. But the hundreds who turned out despite it in the smaller places (Briney Breezes, for instance) and the thousands in larger towns may have been a bigger plus for the President than the large crowds that appeared to hear him, smile with and at him, and beg for a handshake or a baby-kiss during the sunny Sunday that followed. Soaked, rumpled, hair askew, Mr. Ford said at one point on the rainy Saturday, "I don't look very good but I think I'm a darned good President." One didn't have to agree with him to take pleasure in his pleasure with the crowds, himself, and his prospects.

March 13, 1976

L

The China Caper

Henry Kissinger's first visit to Richard Nixon in San Clemente after Nixon quit the presidency occurred in January 1975. The visit did not surprise Kissinger's associates at the White House and the State Department. His attitude toward Nixon was and is well known to them. It is a mixture of pity, disgust with Nixon as a person, respect for much of his performance as President, and gratitude to him for raising Henry Kissinger to power and eminence first as assistant to the President for national security affairs and then as Secretary of State. The attitude has hardened somewhat since 1975. Associates have heard Kissinger summarize it recently with the statement that he's never known another man who combined such great gifts with such a capacity for depravity and such a drive toward self-destruction.

Among the subjects discussed at the 1975 meeting were Nixon's chances of rehabilitation. Kissinger remarked that Nixon retained a degree of respect in the world at large that he had lost, at least for the time being, in his own country. Nixon appeared to agree that the wise course for him was to remain secluded and inactive at San Clemente through 1976. Late in that year or perhaps in 1977 he might fulfill his wish, which he expressed to Kissinger with poignant fervor, to revisit some of the scenes of his foreign triumphs. The capital that he most wanted to revisit was Peking, where he and Kissinger in 1972 opened a new relationship between the US and Communist China. Mao Tse-tung had telephoned Nixon when he was in a Long Beach, California, hospital with phlebitis in the fall of 1974, after the resignation. Mao had said through an interpreter that he considered Nixon one of the greatest statesmen in history and had invited him back to China whenever he chose to come. Kissinger left San Clemente in 1975 with the impression that Nixon hoped and expected to revisit China in 1977.

Kissinger was still under that impression when and after he dined with Nixon at San Clemente on February 2, 1976, a Monday. Kissinger knew of and had no reason to disbelieve reports that Mao and other Chinese leaders had renewed the invitation to Nixon when his daughter Julie and her husband, David Eisenhower, visited Peking in January and were lavishly received and entertained. But the Secretary was soon saying of the February 2 meeting: "When I saw President Nixon he did not tell me that a trip by him to the People's Republic of China was imminent. He talked in very general terms of his intentions eventually to take a trip, but not that it was as imminent as it turned out to be."

This statement was occasioned by the events of Thursday, February 5. On that morning an official at the Communist Chinese liaison office in Washington telephoned Lt. Gen. Brent Scowcroft, President Ford's assistant for national security affairs, and asked for an appointment at three pm. Scowcroft reported the request to Kissinger and Kissinger wondered aloud why the Chinese official would want to see Scowcroft rather than the Secretary of State. At the appointed hour the Chinese official handed Scowcroft the text of an announcement to be issued in Peking at eight o'clock the following morning, Washington time, stating that former President Nixon had accepted an invitation to begin a visit to Peking on February 22, the fourth anniversary of his 1972 visit. Scowcroft immediately notified Kissinger and Richard Cheney, the President's staff chief. While Scowcroft and Cheney were delivering the Chinese statement to Mr. Ford, Nixon telephoned Kissinger from San

Clemente and told him about the invitation and acceptance. Nixon tried to explain, in a tone of apology, that the visit had been agreed upon within the past 36 hours. Kissinger, already informed by Scowcroft that the visit was arranged and about to be announced in Peking, saw no point in objecting to Nixon and didn't. One is told at the State Department that Kissinger concluded, silently and to himself, that Nixon lied when he said the matter had been arranged within 36 hours. Kissinger thought he knew the Peking Chinese well enough to know that they never did anything of importance that quickly. He also realized in hindsight that at the February 2 meeting Nixon had hinted without saying that a visit to China was closer than Kissinger expected.

That evening in the White House office of Jerry Jones, one of Cheney's deputies and the President's chief scheduler, a group including Jones, Press Secretary Ron Nessen and Terry O'Donnell, who handles the President's appointments, discussed the pending visit for nearly two hours. The predominant notes were rage at Nixon and apprehension that his publicized presence in Peking at the time of the New Hampshire primary on February 24 would revive and intensify memories of the Nixon pardon and be politically disastrous. Cheney and Scowcroft, calmer types than some of those in the Jones office, had appeared to an assistant who saw them just before they took the Chinese announcement into the President's office to be "ashen." David Kennerly, the President's chief photographer, burst into the Jones meeting at around nine pm yelling "that bastard!. . .that fucker!" and predicting political ruin for Gerald Ford. Subsequent news stories indicated that some White House reporters were foolish enough to regard Kennerly as an authoritative reflector of the President's mood. The best evidence, including Mr. Ford's later statements, is that he was annoyed and apprehensive but never as angry as some of his White House and campaign assistants were.

The most interesting aspect of the official reaction was the contrast between Kissinger's, the President's, and Press Secretary Ron Nessen's handling of what all of them recognized to be a potentially serious problem for Mr. Ford. Kissinger struck a note of respect for Nixon and of serious desire to learn whatever might be learned about Peking attitudes as a result of the visit. He said on February 12: "President Nixon was responsible for the opening to China and I believe this to have been one of the major diplomatic initiatives of the recent period. The Chinese are undoubtedly attempting to underline the importance they attach to this relationship by their invitation." After it was reported from Peking that Nixon had spent an hour and 40 minutes with Chairman Mao and nearly eight hours with Acting Premier Hua Kuo-feng, Kissinger said and repeated that *of course* he and the State Department would want to be told whatever Nixon had been told by his hosts. When Mr. Ford was asked at a press conference on February 17 whether he was "unhappy" and whether he planned to ask Nixon to postpone the trip, he answered: "I have no such plans. Mr. Nixon is going to the People's Republic of China as a private citizen at the invitation of that government." Then and later, the President emphasized over and over that Nixon was "going as a private citizen," that the visit had no significance, and that he as President had no personal interest in hearing from Nixon after he returned. Nessen, following the President's daily and explicit instructions, suggested again and again that Nixon was just one of 10,000 private American visitors to China since 1972 and that whatever Nixon might learn would be of minimal interest to the President.

Kissinger discussed the substantial difference between his and the presidential posture with Mr. Ford and heard no objection to the proposition that the Secretary of State simply could not pretend to the disinterest in the visit and what might be learned from it that the President found it politically necessary to display. Before the Secretary flew from Washington to Palm Springs, California, to be with his wife Nancy, who was recuperating from a stomach operation, he told the President and Gen. Scowcroft that he realized that another visit to Nixon in San Clemente might embarrass Mr. Ford. Kissinger said he felt, however, that the least he could do was telephone Nixon and welcome him home. This he did on Monday, March 1. The pleasantries over, Kissinger used the same call to tell Nixon how the President's people planned to get his China story. The White House plan was to send Lt. Gen. Vernon A. Walters, deputy director of the CIA and an accomplished linguist who had been President Nixon's interpreter, to San Clemente to receive an oral report. Nixon refused to accept this arrangement. He insisted upon submitting a written report direct to the Secretary of State—not, he emphasized, "through the bureaucracy" to the State Department. Jack Brennan, Nixon's chief assistant, told me later that Nixon had decided upon this procedure during the flight home in the Chinese government plane that had taken him and Mrs. Nixon to China. Kissinger said he'd have Scowcroft telephone San Clemente and get the word direct from Nixon. Kissinger so instructed Scowcroft. Before Scowcroft could telephone he learned that Warren Gulley, a retired Air Force sergeant who handles White House liaison with the Nixon establishment, had received the word by telephone from San Clemente and had passed it, presumably through Richard Cheney, to Mr. Ford. Scowcroft and Kissinger understood that Nixon had telephoned Gulley. Brennan told me that he had telephoned Gulley. Scowcroft saw no need to tell Mr. Ford that Kissinger had telephoned Nixon, and didn't. Kissinger, wanting the call publicized before a mystery developed, had his executive assistant, Lawrence Eagleburger, tell columnist Jack Anderson about it when Anderson asked about something else. Anderson broadcast the news the next morning and an enormous rumpus ensued. The rumpus was as silly as practically everything else connected with the Nixon visit to China.

March 20, 1976

LI

Ford's Way

On the road to the Republican nomination in Kansas City, a nomination that this reporter still expects Mr. Ford to get despite Ronald Reagan's first primary victory in North Carolina, the President continues to reveal a great deal about himself, his White House and his way of trying to run and lead the country.

A common supposition, one that Reagan himself advanced as a reason for staying in the race when he along with many others was misreading his own strength in North Carolina and assuming that he was going to lose and Gerald Ford was going to win the fourth primary in a row, is that he is driving candidate Ford to the right, toward more conservative positions than the President would otherwise take. This is a distortion of what has actually been happening. Mr. Ford has not taken a single "conservative" position for campaign purposes that he didn't already hold or wouldn't have taken in the natural course of the conservatism that he has practiced and exemplified ever since he entered Congress in 1949. What he has been doing of late, in response to Reagan and in appeal to the conservative voters whom the President must attract if he is to be nominated and elected, is expressing his basic and natural conservative views more vigorously and more often than he might be doing if he were not campaigning.

A possible exception to the foregoing generalization is the President's recent dumping of the term "détente" and his simultaneous argument that he isn't dumping the policy with the term while toughening his verbal stance toward the Soviet Union. But it can be argued—I think, demonstrated—that the seeming exception is more apparent than real and that there's been no actual and meaningful change in US policy toward the Soviet Union since the campaign heated up. Long before Ronald Reagan declared his candidacy, at a time when some of the President's political advisers were under the illusion that he as the incumbent, appointed though he was, could have the nomination for the asking, he prepared and submitted to Congress the first of what he continues to call with pride the two biggest defense budgets in US history. So recently as March 22 in Dallas, Secretary of State Henry Kissinger set forth once more "compelling reasons" for pursuing the strategic arms limitation talks (SALT) with the Soviet Union that since 1972 have been at the core of the détente policy. This part of the speech was overshadowed in the news by the Secretary's insistence, matching the President's recent and occasionally exaggerated talk along the same line, that "we are not the world's policeman—but we cannot permit the Soviet Union or its surrogates to become the world's policeman, either"; and, in a reference to Angola, that "the United States will not accept further Cuban military interventions abroad." This sort of bellicose talk, unsupported by any believable indication of what the US would do if the Soviet Union and its Cuban surrogate persisted in Africa or elsewhere in what Kissinger called the "adventurism" and "military expansionism" that were successfully practiced in Angola, worried such friends and frequent apologists for the Secretary as James Reston of *The New York Times*. But the toughened talk indicated no substantive departure from the search for US-Soviet accommodation that the President first refused to label "détente" last August. One of the assumptions underlying the policy since its inception has been that the Soviet Union must and, given proper incentive by the US, will restrain its expansive tendencies. People who have trouble reconciling the policy with basic conservatism should remember that the father of the policy in its recent form was Richard Nixon.

A factor in the Ford campaign performance that's received very little attention in the media is what's been happening at the White House. The essence of what's been happening there is that the presidential operation in both its governmental and political dimensions has improved since Donald Rumsfeld replaced Secretary of Defense James Schlesinger and was replaced as White House staff chief by his former deputy, Richard Cheney. The President's White House people are reluctant to discuss the fact, much less acknowledge and explain it. It doesn't necessarily reflect upon Rumsfeld—practically all of the assistants who are functioning more smoothly and efficiently now than they did when he was there were assigned to their jobs by him. Rumsfeld is a professional politician who transferred from Congress to the executive at President Nixon's urging in 1969. He largely directed Gerald Ford's early campaign for the nomination. In the opinion of some of his former White House associates, he quietly encouraged the President's decision to fire James Schlesinger and welcomed his appointment as Defense Secretary in the belief that it would further his political ambitions. Yet the White House end of the Ford political operation under Cheney, a non-politician, is unquestionably functioning better than it did under Rumsfeld, the politician. Jerry Jones, a Nixon holdover who was brought into the center of the White House operation by Gen. Alexander Haig, Nixon's last staff chief, has risen steadily in position and influence under Rumsfeld and lately under Cheney. Jones heads a so-called "scheduling committee" that has expanded its role since Rumsfeld left and coordinates a wide range of presidential activities, both administrative and political. Mr. Ford's overt campaign instrument, the President Ford Committee, must clear all of its recommendations for campaign appearances and other endeavors through the Jones committee. The ultimate recommendations go to the President through Cheney, a quiet fellow whose air of calm restraint is in sharp contrast with Rumsfeld's rather uptight nature and demeanor. The only coherent explanation of the recent improvement that I've heard at the White House is that "the fear of Rumsfeld" left with Rumsfeld and that the working atmosphere around Cheney is friendlier, more relaxed and therefore more efficient than it was under his patron and predecessor. The judgment is probably unfair to Rumsfeld but circumstances suggest that it's not wholly off the mark.

The improvement hasn't been total and the responsibility for the two most glaring of recent blunders rests with the President. One of them was his insistence, against much inner-circle advice, upon retaining former congressman and Secretary of the Army Howard ("Bo") Callaway at the head of the President Ford Committee and trying to paper over Callaway's deficiencies with the appointment of a theoretically subordinate political director, Stuart Spencer, a political technician who had a lot to do with engineering Ronald Reagan's election and reelection as governor of California. Callaway is a thoroughly likable Georgia politician and millionaire. The kindest thing to be said of him is that he is possessed of more good humor than intelligence. He recalls in his engaging fashion that he told Mr. Ford last summer: "Look, Mr. President, I know that I'm a good Secretary of the Army, but I'm not at all sure that I'd make a good campaign manager." He didn't. The committee's Washington headquarters and some of its state extensions were in shambles before Spencer was brought in last September. The later appointment of Rogers C. B. Morton, a former Maryland congressman and Secretary of Interior and Commerce, as a White House counsellor and campaign adviser, also helped. But the President was not persuaded to rid himself of Callaway until his bumbling efforts to further the family interests—specifically a Colorado ski resort—through federal favors while he was Secretary of the Army, a Republican national committeeman and lately the President's campaign chairman were disclosed.

The other blunder was the handling of Richard Nixon's report upon his recent visit to China. The White House handling of the report was exceeded in stupidity only by the handling of the visit itself. The stupidity stemmed in both instances from the President's insistence that the visit and anything that might be learned from it be minimized in every possible way, lest the sudden reemergence of Richard Nixon remind voters of Watergate and the Nixon pardon and be politically harmful to Mr. Ford. According to Jack Brennan, the head of Nixon's small staff at San Clemente and his companion on the China trip, the former President was well aware of the effort to derogate the venture and determined during the flight home that he would report only to Henry Kissinger, who had treated the event with more respect than the President and his spokesmen had.

By prearrangement with Kissinger, and with the President's knowledge and assent, Nixon prepared a written report of his

LURIE'S OPINION

NORTH CAROLINA

1

2

LURIE

3-24-76

conversations with Mao Tse-tung, Acting Premier Hua Kuo-feng, and other Chinese leaders. Kissinger knew on Monday, March 8, that Nixon, then back in San Clemente, was at work on the report and expected to have it delivered to the Secretary of State the following weekend. Warren ("Bill") Gulley, the White House assistant assigned to liaison with San Clemente, flew there on the weekend, partly by military and partly by commercial aircraft, and delivered two copies of the report to Lt. Gen. Brent Scowcroft, the President's assistant for national security affairs, on Monday the 15th. Scowcroft gave Kissinger the copy marked for him that day. Scowcroft gave Mr. Ford the second copy the next day.

Press Secretary Ron Nessen and Robert Funseth, Kissinger's chief spokesman at the State Department, learned only on the following Monday, the 22nd, that the report had been received. They learned it from *Time*. Nessen, acutely embarrassed, said the second copy had been "addressed to the President." It was not addressed to the President. Scowcroft appears to have read it before he passed it to Mr. Ford. CIA Director George Bush read it in Scowcroft's office after the President read it. Nixon had stipulated that distribution of the report be tightly restricted, that no copies be made, and that the two originals be returned to him. Brennan agreed with Gulley by telephone that the originals might as well be returned by ordinary mail instead of sent back to San Clemente by courier. Nessen quoted the President as saying the report was "very interesting and useful." Funseth quoted Kissinger to the same effect. It is inconceivable that the report of some 60 pages would have been mailed back to Nixon if it contained anything of vital national security interest. Classified intelligence information that may interest the former President is reviewed by White House Counsellor John Marsh, encoded, and transmitted to Nixon over a secured electronic circuit every two weeks or so. His China report did not require such care.

The extraordinary secrecy and reticence connected with the report's receipt, reading and return raised great storms in the White House and State Department press rooms. The affair probably interested the public far less than it interested Washington journalists. But it renewed an old and recently repaired rift between Nessen and Gen. Scowcroft and caused the President to censure Scowcroft, one of the ablest men at the White House, for failing to inform Nessen. Mr. Ford should have censured himself. He didn't inform Nessen, either, and the whole absurdity was essentially his doing.

April 3, 1976

LII

Ups and Downs

Here we are again on the road with Gerald Ford, observing him at his best and at his worst as he campaigns for nomination and election.

Some of the reporters who travel with the President rate his appearance at Bradley University in Peoria, Illinois, for a short speech and a question-answer session with the students his best public performance since he succeeded Richard Nixon. The audience was friendly, alert, responsive. Mr. Ford dealt briskly and knowledgeably with questions on subjects ranging from anti-trust policy to civil rights for homosexuals, investment tax credits for business, and the Nixon pardon. He said he was agin monopolies and for stimulative tax credits. The President on "civil rights for gay people": "I recognize that this is a very new and serious problem in our society. I have always tried to be an understanding person as far as people are concerned who are different from myself. That doesn't mean that I agree with or would concur in what is done by them or their position in society. I think this is a problem we have to face up to, and I can't give you a pat answer tonight." On whether he would "state unequivocally that there was no deal . . . in regard to resignation and subsequent pardon of former President Nixon:" "There was no deal made in any way whatsoever. Categorically, no . . . It was a decision made by me alone. Nobody else had any responsibility and I'll take the full responsibility for the consequences, good or bad."

In Illinois and elsewhere, the President had his ups and downs and some of the downs were mighty low. A Bradley student told him that the Air Force was closing its ROTC program at the university in 1977 and asked him how he justified this after Bradley had "for the past 27 years, through thick and thin, supplied the Air Force with highly qualified personnel." Mr. Ford replied: "Based on what you told me, I'm disgusted with the action of the United States Air Force. Quite frankly, it's incomprehensible, and we will do our darndest to rectify the error." The hall erupted with cheers. It turned out that Bradley had fallen below the required minimum number of ROTC entrants for two straight years and under established standards had thereby disqualified itself. A month afterward, the Ford staff was still wrestling with the problem of whether the President or an underling should sign a letter to the university admitting his mistake. At Rantoul, Illinois, near the Air Force's Chanute Field, the President burbled at a political reception: "And speaking of Chanute Field, we've got an outstanding Secretary of Defense in Don Rumsfeld who comes from the great state of Illinois, and I think Don ought to come down here and take a look at it." The implication was that Chanute was among the military installations about to be closed for economy and that the President was telling his Secretary of Defense not to close it. Cheers again, and again a contrary fact. There was no thought of closing Chanute Field.

On the second of two Ford trips to North Carolina, just before the primary that Ronald Reagan won against all expectations including his own, Mr. Ford seemed to this reporter and to some White House and campaign assistants to be lax, smug, letting down. Reagan's victory and the President's loss shocked Gerald Ford and his advisers. They reconciled themselves to the prospect that Reagan on the strength of that first primary win for him will be contesting the Republican nomination right down to the Kansas City convention. But the event that caused the most discussion and the biggest flap at the White House was not the outcome of the primary. It was a speech that Mr. Ford made in Charlotte to the North Carolina convention of the Future Home Makers of America. I along with practically everybody else in the travelling press corps, male and female, laughed and wise-cracked when the President said: "I regret to say that some people in this country have disparaged and demeaned the role of the home maker. I say—and say it with emphasis and conviction—that home making is good for America. I say that home making is not out of date and I reject strongly such accusations. Every American who chooses to be a home maker can take pride in a fine, fine vocation. You should never be embarrassed to say anywhere on the face of the earth, 'I am an American home maker and I am proud of it'."

Robert Orben, a senior Ford speech writer and editor whose specialty is supposed to be writing for the ear rather than the eye, was dismayed and astounded when he was told later that the travelling vultures of the press corps translated home maker into baby-maker. White House critics of the President's speech operation—and they include such ranking officials as chief economist Alan Greenspan and budget director James Lynn—seized upon the Charlotte speech as evidence that Mr. Ford should dump his veteran assistant and chief speech editor, Robert Hartmann, and most of the Hartmann-Orben staff. Whether this sentiment was expressed directly to Mr. Ford is doubtful; he does not welcome confrontations of a kind that would force him to choose between keeping or discarding his old friend Bob Hartmann, who in any case was vacationing in Hawaii when the home maker speech was written. A newspaper story about the flap had more impact than the speech itself, suggesting as it did that a drastic reorganization of the speech operation was required and imminent. It may be required but it is not imminent. Richard Cheney, the White House staff chief who is automatical-ly presumed to be behind any move to move in upon Bob Hartmann, is too wise a bird to attempt such a thing. Cheney's resident idea man and philosopher, David Gergen, occasionally submits drafts of important speeches and reviews some of the Hartmann-Orben drafts before they go to Mr. Ford. Gergen plays it coolly, though. He understands as others in the

President's vicinity do that Mr. Ford is occasionally dissatisfied but—as the best authority next to the President said to me—"basically satisfied" with what he's getting and emitting.

What the President emits is not invariably and necessarily confined to what he gets. And of course it is he, not his speech writers and editors, who must bear the responsibility for what he says and for the way he says it. Consider, for example, the Betty bit that he twice played during the second of two days in California and Wisconsin. A story reprinted in the San Francisco *Examiner* had the forthcoming Woodward-Bernstein book, *The Final Days*, reporting that Richard and Pat Nixon had no sexual relations during the 14 years preceding Nixon's resignation. At Fresno, addressing the state Republican committee, Mr. Ford said he'd like to stay the night "but Betty wants me to get home tonight." At a La Crosse, Wisconsin rally that evening the President said that "when you get a welcome like this the temptation is to stay maybe overnight, but on the way from California to here [after leaving Fresno] I called Betty and she said—I hope she meant it—that she wanted me home tonight." The audience laughed. I didn't.

During a question-answer session following his rally speech, the President handled several tough questions with impressive dash and conviction. A slender young man who was trembling with rage and emotion put it to Mr. Ford that "Congress finally ended a slaughter in Vietnam and now you want to get us involved in a similar situation in Angola." After the President said the effort to supply anti-Soviet and anti-Cuban Angolan factions with weapons involved no American military commitment, the young man retorted: "Yes, Mr. Ford, but weapons kill people." The President, tense and obviously aroused, stared over the crowd at his questioner and replied, "What do you think the Cuban 12,000 mercenaries did to other Angolans?" Mr. Ford had the better of that exchange, I thought. He didn't come off so well in a protracted monologue derived from and expanding upon a draft that his writers had prepared. He first struck the note in San Francisco when he said "the United States by any standard is number one, and we are going to keep it there." He said and said and said it in La Crosse: "I am sick and tired of hearing people who are always running down America. I am proud of America and I am proud to be an American . . . I happen to believe, as we look at the total, America is number one. We are number one . . . We have the greatest science and technology capability in the history of mankind. Our military capability is second to none, but there is one thing that is even more important than all of that. America is morally and spiritually number one and that will be the force to keep us moving so that America, and all its people, its government, will be number one forever."

Stop scaring me that way, Mr. President.

April 10, 1976

He didn't stop.

LIII

The Woodstein Flap

The pitch that Bob Woodward and Carl Bernstein, the *Washington Post* reporters who did more than any other journalists and any officials did to expose the evil of Watergate and drive Richard Nixon from the presidency, used with some of the 394 sources that they boast of having drawn upon for *The Final Days* (Simon and Schuster; $10.95) was that they'd written some pretty rough and marginal stuff in their Watergate news stories and were going to make up for it in this book with a reasoned and balanced account of Nixon's twilight and departure from the White House. My reading of the book is that they tried and failed to do this. The book is fascinating. It is beautifully done (I'd like to know more than they tell about the contribution of "Alice Mayhew, our editor," who is thanked "for the hundreds of hours she spent with us and with this manuscript"). It tells much that I never learned during what I think it's fair to say was as close a watch as any reporter kept upon the Nixon presidency. And in my biased opinion it is on the whole the worst job of nationally noted reporting that I've observed during 49 years in the business.

In this opinion I differ with most of the Nixon people who

figure in the book and with whom I've had time and opportunity to check. Most of these people say four things. First, they don't want to be identified as Woodward and Bernstein—"Woodstein" in the current Washington argot—sources. Second, they don't want whatever they say about the accuracy or inaccuracy of the book and of the references to them to be attributed to them. Third, and with some exceptions, they consider the book to be "basically accurate." I must have heard that 20 times in the week or so preceding the writing of this piece. Fourth, and also with some exceptions, they hold that the book exaggerates, over-dramatizes and occasionally distorts what the people whose view is reflected here say they told Woodstein. That's where I part with these people. They are more tolerant than I am of exaggeration, over-dramatization and distortion.

Finally, and for a thoroughly selfish reason, I object to the abuse of a method of reporting that Woodstein brag about and practice throughout the book. I object because, damn it all, it's my method. Woodstein never once attribute a statement to the source or sources of the statement. They and their research assistants interviewed on what journalists call a background basis and they write from background, on their own authority. So do I, usually and by preference. But the effect of piling statement upon unattributed statement for 450 pages is to give a good method a bad name. Two examples of the absurd length to which the device is carried are a long conversation reported in direct quotation between Nixon and his press secretary, Ronald Ziegler, as if Woodstein were in the room with them, and the direct quotation of a remark that one of Nixon's lawyers, Leonard Garment, made in chambers to Judge John Sirica. The Nixon-Ziegler conversation is from the transcript of a Nixon tape published by the House Judiciary Committee. The Garment remark ("Just wait") is from a published court transcript. The Woodstein claim when they were writing their Watergate stories in *The Washington Post* and their earlier book, *All the President's Men,* that they reported only what at least three sources had told them greatly wearied me. In this book, they profess to report only what they've been told by "at least two people." That is crap. What second source could confirm that Henry Kissinger, Fred Buzhardt, David Gergen, Pat Buchanan, Leonard Garment,

Ronald Ziegler—naming a few of the many who are thus
depicted—"thought" this or that in an elevator, during a dinner
or during an office conversation? Some of the best stories I've
ever gotten were known to one person only, the person who told
me. Woodstein must know it's crap. The fact that they persist in
the fiction in this book is a sign of insecurity. It supports the
perhaps patronizing but in my opinion fair judgment that they
comprehended only the evil of Watergate and not the totality of
the situations, relationships and motivations of many people
who figure in the book.

Here are some examples of Woodstein reporting that I've
checked with one or more of the people involved. Philip Buchen,
President Ford's life-long friend and chief counsel, and Clay
Whitehead, a Nixon official who worked with Buchen and others
to prepare the transition from Nixon to Ford, appear as follows in
an account of one of the pre-resignation meetings: "Whitehead
walked Buchen out to his car to talk privately. What would
happen if Nixon were impeached and convicted and then refused
to leave office? Maybe the notion of the President resisting
removal was not so absurd. Suppose he went crazy and tried to
use the military to retain office. The two men wondered if
perhaps they should raise the question with the Secretary of
Defense, James Schlesinger"—and so on. Buchen said to me the
other day, in a gentle jibe at the many who were refusing to be
quoted, "I'm not one of those who won't admit they talked to
Woodward and Bernstein." He said that every reference to him in
the book, including the one just quoted, is accurate.

William Watts, one of several Kissinger assistants who quit the
National Security Council staff in 1970 at the time of the
Cambodia invasion, figures with Kissinger and General Alexander Haig, then Kissinger's White House deputy, in a vivid
description of Watts' departure: "Watts went to see Kissinger
alone to state his objections. 'Your view represents the cowardice
of the Eastern Establishment,' Kissinger told him. Furious, Watts
got up out of his chair and moved toward Kissinger. He was
going to punch him. Kissinger moved quickly behind his desk. He
was not serious, he said." Watts then had a show-down talk with
Haig. "'You've just had an order from your Commander in
Chief,' Haig said. Watts could not resign. 'Fuck you, Al,' Watts

said. 'I just did.'" I've been told that this passage, particularly the
bit about Watts being about to punch Kissinger, exaggerates
Watts' importance and belligerence. Watts says it's "pretty
accurate."

The book lists among the qualitites of Lawrence Eagleburger,
one of Kissinger's close associates, "the ability to say, 'Henry,
you're full of shit.'" Eagleburger has been heard to say that about
Kissinger to others, but it is unimaginable that he's ever said it
directly to Kissinger. In a reference to Eagleburger and to Lt.
Gen. Brent Scowcroft, Kissinger's former deputy and his
successor at the White House, Woodstein writes that Kissinger's
"frequent descriptions of Nixon as irrational, insecure and
maniacal could at times just as easily apply to Kissinger as to the
President, they believed." I state as fact known to me that
Eagleburger and Scowcroft never believed this of either Nixon or
Kissinger, except perhaps of Nixon in his time of final
disintegration. Kissinger bad-mouths practically everybody he
knows, Presidents included. But several of his NSC assistants—
among them John F. Lehman, Jr., now deputy director of the
Arms Control and Disarmament Agency—tell me they *never*
heard Kissinger describe Nixon "as irrational, insecure, and
maniacal." Lehman, who was one of Kissinger's closest and best
informed assistants in the Nixon years, says that Woodstein
never approached him or tried to check anything with him. Ben
Bradlee, the *Washington Post*'s executive editor, says he encountered Kissinger at a social affair after the book appeared and
challenged him to deny anything in it. He attaches great
importance to the fact that Kissinger didn't deny anything. The
fact is meaningless. Apart from the little he's said publicly,
Kissinger isn't talking about this book.

Very few of the central facts and assertions in the book are
wholly new. I reported in this journal in 1974, for instance, the
view of some of Nixon's assistants that the pressures upon him
before he resigned had unbalanced him and the further view, less
widely held, that he'd been fundamentally unstable for years
before the end. Three episodes reported in the book, however,
are new, interesting and real additions to our knowledge of the
Nixon tragedy.

The most widely noted of these additions is the account of the

hours Kissinger spent with Nixon the night before he announced
his intention to resign: "Between sobs, Nixon was plaintive . . .
How had it come to this? How had a simple burglary, a breaking
and entering, done all this? Nixon . . . . was hysterical. 'Henry,'
he said, 'you are not a very orthodox Jew, and I am not an
orthodox Quaker, but we need to pray.' Nixon got down on his
knees. Kissinger felt he had no alternative but to kneel down, too
. . . And then, still sobbing, Nixon leaned over and struck his fist
on the carpet, crying, 'What have I done? What has happened?'"
This was one of the many passages Kissinger had in mind when
he complained in a public statement that the book lacks decency
and compassion. But the odd thing about the prayer story is that
it had come, directly or indirectly, from Kissinger. I am told and
believe that he never described this scene to the two assistants,
Lawrence Eagleburger and Brent Scowcroft, whom he rejoined
in his White House office after he left Nixon that night. Only two
errors in the account have been cited to me, the line about Nixon
beating the carpet and a report that Eagleburger listened on a
telephone extension to Nixon begging Kissinger not to tell
anybody that he'd broken down. I'm told Eagleburger hung up
when he realized Nixon was calling and didn't hear whatever
Nixon said.

Two other pieces of genuine news in the book are the
intention, frustrated by Gen. Haig, of two Nixon lawyers,
Leonard Garment and Fred Buzhardt, to recommend to the
President that he resign in November, 1973, and Gen. Haig's
attempt to hire Hugh Morrow, Nelson Rockefeller's long-time
press spokesman, as Richard Nixon's chief spokesman in early
1974. Garment and Buzhardt told Woodstein the resignation
story. Carl Bernstein learned by accident of the attempt to
recruit Morrow soon after it occurred and saved it for this book.
Haig believed in late 1973 that Nixon would weather the
Watergate storm and therefore refused to pass the Garment-
Buzhardt recommendation to Nixon. The account errs slightly in
having Morrow flatly demand that Press Secretary Ziegler be
fired and that Nixon come clean about his Watergate role.
Morrow declined when Haig told him that neither of these things
was going to happen, but he didn't make them absolute

conditions. One gathers that he didn't want the White House job, anyhow.

The two most serious flaws in the book are in the accounts of Henry Kissinger's relationships with and attitudes toward Nixon and Haig. It is simply not true that Kissinger viewed Nixon with "loathing" from the beginning of their relationship and throughout it. "Loathing" is much too simple and strong a term for the attitude of Kissinger, a very complex man, toward Richard Nixon, who also was and is a very complex man. They did not entirely trust each other, they were somewhat jealous of each other, but they needed and served and basically respected each other. It also is not true, as the book asserts, that Brent Scowcroft and Lawrence Eagleburger considered one of their priority duties to be the concealment of Kissinger's "loathing" of Nixon. They didn't believe then and don't believe now that Kissinger "loathed" Richard Nixon. I was told recently and on excellent authority that I was close to the mark when I wrote in March 1976 that Kissinger's attitude toward Nixon was and is "a mixture of pity, disgust with Nixon as a person, respect for much of his performance as President, and gratitude to him for raising Henry Kissinger to power and eminence . . . "

Much the same may be said of the Woodstein thesis that the relationship between Kissinger and Haig was essentially one of hostility and distrust. They were indeed rather wary of each other. Haig, like practically everybody else who worked for Kissinger in the Nixon years and who works for him now, found him to be a brutal and at times nearly unbearable taskmaster. But I never heard Haig, with whom I spent hours over the years in discussion of Kissinger, speak of him with anything other than tolerance, respect and occasional humor. And I have never heard Kissinger, with whom I have had a contact and a reporter's relationship that Woodstein never had, speak of Haig with anything other than profound appreciation and respect. To have them secretly warring with each other, holding out on each other, distrusting each other during the last months of the Nixon presidency and of Nixon's disintegration, as this book does, is to be incredibly mistaken and wrong. Kissinger and Haig spent hours upon hours, day after day and night after night struggling together to maintain at least the facade of a viable presidency until their ruined President at last departed. This was the tragedy that Bob Woodward and Carl Bernstein sought to relate and, with prodigious effort and in prodigious detail, reduce to the level of a sordid barroom brawl.

April 24, 1976

More *New Republic* readers than usually react to my pieces denounced me for criticising *The Final Days*. Their charge was that I was jealous of Woodward and Bernstein: They'd uncovered Watergate and I, pompous Establishment ass, hadn't. True, they did and I didn't. I'm not proud of that. But I'm not ashamed of it, either. For reasons that I can't explain to myself, much less to readers, it wasn't in the cards for a White House reporter to be atop of what at the start was a police story. Looking and reading back, I think I did a fair job of detecting and reporting the character flaws that underlay Watergate.

Enough of apology. On September 24, 1976, during one of General Alexander Haig's returns to Washington from Brussels, where he was US and NATO commander, I drew him closer than any other reporter then had to a comment upon the Woodward-Bernstein account of his relationship with Henry Kissinger. In the following transcript of a portion of our discussion, he mentions a son, who in 1975 was a student at Georgetown University in Washington, and his former military aide, Major (later Lieut. Colonel) George Joulwan.

Osborne: My questions concern *The Final Days*. Is the account given in that book of the personal and working relationship between you and Henry Kissinger mainly correct or mainly incorrect? I assume you read the book?

Haig: Yes, I did. I don't want to be quoted on it because I've made it a policy not to be quoted on the book. I would rather just comment on my relationship with Henry. And it has never been anything but very close—totally admiring and respectful in every sense of the word. I don't think Henry would ever say otherwise. I don't suggest by that that we didn't have our differences on policy issues from time to time. Where we did, I bluntly and I think accurately brought the thing to his attention. But we *never* [Haig's emphasis] were in a confrontation, at least from my perspective, and Henry has told me himself, he never harbored any reservations on his side.

Osborne: The story's around, you might be surprised by the people who believe it, that you saw Woodward or Bernstein, or both of them, and that you actually are the source of a lot of their stuff.

Haig: Untrue—absolutely untrue. They tried and tried to get me to see them for the book. I refused. Bob Woodward finally called me from London and said he'd come all the way over, could he come on to Brussels and see me and I said, sure, if you want me to tell you over a cup of coffee what I've already told you on the phone, I can't help you and won't, come on over. He did, and we had coffee together, and that was all there was to it.

Osborne: A story around was that with your permission George Joulwan did see them and was sort of an indirect source.

Haig: Totally untrue. George has never spoken to them. He has assured me that he never has. Now, there's a story around that they talked to my son. Totally untrue. They called my son, my son called me, and I said, No. He walked out of a class at Georgetown [University] one day and they were standing there and they said, 'Alex, we know your position. We just want to talk about your father, nothing about Watergate,' and he said fine— he's a fine and courteous young man—and all they asked him was what sports I liked, what books I read, what my personal hobbies were, and he told them. He never discussed anything in any way about Watergate.

LIV

Kissinger's Future

A caller and Gerald Ford discussed Secretary of State Henry Kissinger and his standing and relationship with the President the other day.

The visitor said he just wanted to look the President in the eye and hear from him the truth about his attitude toward, relationship with and expectations regarding Kissinger. Mr. Ford answered that he'd meant every word, he'd been telling the absolute truth—straight from the shoulder—when he said publicly and often that he expects the Secretary to remain in office as long as he wishes and (at Green Bay, Wisconsin on April 3) that "I would like Secretary Kissinger to be Secretary of State as long as I am President." What about such associates and friends as Howard Callaway, Rogers Morton, Melvin Laird who'd said recently and variously that Kissinger should quit, was going to quit, intended to quit before the year is out or before another term begins? Was the President sending signals to Kissinger through them? Mr. Ford said he was not. Were they sending signals to the President? The President said rather cryptically that he has a fine relationship with Henry Kissinger and expects to keep it that way.

Mr. Ford was reminded that he'd said after his defeat of Ronald Reagan in the Wisconsin Republican primary that "I thought that the results in Wisconsin certainly fully justified my faith in Henry Kissinger" and that "my full support for Secretary Kissinger is fortified by the decision in Wisconsin"—the point being that Reagan had delivered a savage attack on Kissinger just before the Wisconsin primary. Would a serious loss to Reagan in Texas, where Reagan was pressing his attack on Kissinger as an appeaser and betrayer of American interests, lead the President to conclude that Kissinger was too much of a political liability to retain during the rest of this campaign year? Although the fact was not mentioned to the President, Kissinger was wondering about that and was prepared to quit if he were asked to. Mr. Ford said there was no such possibility, no such thought in his mind. The Wisconsin and Texas primaries were entirely different. Wisconsin was a head-to-head preferential contest. The Texas primary would be a contest for delegates and not a direct preferential confrontation. So the President wouldn't read the Texas result as a vote for or against Kissinger, however Ford and Reagan fared. Anyhow, the President said, the polls continued to show and he continued to regard Henry Kissinger as a political asset, not as a political liability.

Did all this mean that the President *wanted* Kissinger to remain in the office and *wanted* him to continue as Secretary of State in the next Ford term if there is one? The President said that he wanted Kissinger to stay and that all he'd been saying applies to the next term. Finally, to what extent had he and Kissinger gone into the subject of Kissinger's future? The President said he'd said to Kissinger in private what he'd been saying publicly and that Kissinger had said that he'd quit whenever the President concluded that he was a political liability or ineffective for any other reason. That, the President said, was about as far as their discussions had gone.

It's plain to Kissinger associates who deal regularly and intimately with him that, whatever assurances he may have from the President, the constant barrage of speculation and the attacks from the Reagan Right kept him on edge. Personal sensitivities apart, and Henry Kissinger is abundantly equipped with them, he considers with reason that the speculation and the attacks in combination diminish his effectiveness with other governments. Lesser worries gnaw at him: among others, the flawed word portrait of him in the widely read and quoted Woodward-Bernstein book, *The Final Days*, and the distinct possibility that he may eventually be held liable for huge civil damages as a result of the suit brought against him and others by Morton Halperin, a former assistant who was wiretapped in 1969-71. Yet Kissinger sustains at least a semblance of his old elan. At this writing he is about to be off on his first tour of Africa, and he soon will be revisiting Latin America. At home he is often on the road defining and defending Ford-Kissinger foreign policy in speeches, question-answer exchanges with his audiences, and private sessions with local leadership groups. These expeditions refresh him and, particularly at the leadership sessions, he impresses otherwise critical hearers. In Phoenix on April 16, for instance, an editor of the conservative *Arizona Republic* attended a leadership discussion and wrote afterward that Kissinger "apparently chooses to fill his public pronouncements with eloquent platitudes and his off-the-record private conversation with earthy, direct and unmistakably revealing grasps of the crises brewing around American shores." Kissinger's public pronouncements are neither all that eloquent nor all that different from his private points. But the editor was correct in his perception that Kissinger is "tormented . . . by the painful suspicion . . . that America's political institutions lack the resolve and will to face up to international power pressures." It is from distorted versions of Kissinger's private talk to this effect that Ronald Reagan, retired Adm. Elmo Zumwalt, Jr., and other critics derive their mistaken impression and charge that the Secretary of State has relegated the US to "second place" in the world.

At an earlier leadership session in Boston, Kissinger provided an interesting insight into his thinking about his own and the next administration's future. A guest asked whom he would recommend to the next President as the next Secretary of State. Kissinger answered—and here I write with understanding that second-hand accounts of this kind can be no better than approximately accurate—that it would depend on whether the next President is a Republican or a Democrat and on what the

President's priorities are. If the next President is a Republican and his first desire is for a Secretary of State who thinks conceptually about foreign policy and would be good at helping the President formulate it, Kissinger probably would recommend Elliot Richardson. If the first need were for a Secretary of State who could effectively explain and defend foreign policy to Congress, Kissinger would recommend Melvin Laird. If the first requirement were for a Secretary who could explain and defend policy to both Congress and the public, Kissinger's choice would be John Connally. If the demand were for a Secretary who would be reasonably good at all these things—thinking out, formulating, explaining and defending policy—he would recommend his friend and sometime patron, Vice President Nelson Rockefeller. Kissinger said that he'd be in more difficulty if the next President is a Democrat. To the extent that he had thought this contingency through, and he hadn't thought it through very far, he probably and rather reluctantly would recommend former Ambassador and Deputy Secretary of Defense Cyrus Vance.

It was interesting that Kissinger, who must assume that if the next President is a Republican he will be Gerald Ford, didn't so much as hint that in that event he'd recommend himself. Many of his friends and associates are convinced that he's made up his mind to decline reappointment in the next term if Mr. Ford is the President and offers it to him. The question remains (and I don't think it's a serious question) whether Kissinger at the crunch can bring himself to forego the delights and pomps of power. A friend who believes that he will forego all that if he has the choice, and devoutly hopes that he will have the sense to do it, is Melvin Laird. Laird figured in Kissinger's decision at the President's request to remain in the office after last January 1, when he had intended to quit, reasoning that it was the right time, both from his and Mr. Ford's standpoints, for him to go. He submitted a letter of resignation to the President. Like Richard Nixon in late 1970, Mr. Ford urged him to reconsider and stay on. Kissinger thought it over during a short vacation in the Caribbean and, when he returned, discussed the matter with Laird. Laird urged him to stay through this term but to make up his mind, and to tell the President, that it would be time for him to go at the end of the term. Laird had this history in mind when he said in answer to a question at a University of Wisconsin student session recently that he expects Kissinger to leave at the end of the term. Laird was signalling Kissinger, not the President. Mr. Ford knows that Laird has so advised Kissinger. I suspect but don't know that there is a connection between these facts and the President's generous indication that he'd like to have Kissinger remain into the next term.

May 1, 1976

LV

Ford at Bay

During the two days between his primary disasters in Texas and Indiana, the President considered and discussed the possibility that he was doing something wrong and decided that he hadn't been making any mistakes that were important enough to require major changes in his way of campaigning for the Republican nomination. The controlling assumption in his discussions of the problem—principally with two White House assistants, Richard Cheney and John Marsh, and with the chairman of the Ford campaign committee, Rogers Morton—was that the only substantial change open to the President was to get even tougher and more emphatic than he recently had been in asserting his conservative views on such issues as defense, federal spending and economic policy. The notion that he might do better in the long run by turning in the opposite direction, toward the moderated stance that he must eventually take if he is to have a chance of winning the November election, was not seriously considered. Mr. Ford's basic conclusion, urged upon him by Cheney among others, was that he should not put himself in the position of catering openly to the Wallace Democrats whose cross-over votes for Ronald Reagan made the crucial difference in Texas and Indiana and worsened the anticipated defeats in Georgia and Alabama. The President agreed with Morton that some cosmetic changes—shorter speeches, shorter answers at public quiz sessions, more rallies and fewer lectures and seminars on such numbing subjects as revenue sharing and farm policy—were indicated. Mr. Ford, looking grim and determined in a brief appearance at the White House, said he'd try to emphasize what he considers to be his positive successes in foreign affairs, economic recovery and the restoration of trust in government. In general, however, the decision was to plod along pretty much as he had been doing and, in essence, to rely upon the conviction that the Republican convention cannot and will not be suicidal enough to nominate Ronald Reagan.

Maybe it won't. This reporter is among those who assume and hope that the convention won't be that nutty. A Harris poll indicating that at this writing Jimmy Carter, the probable Democratic nominee, would defeat Ronald Reagan by 53 percent to 34 percent of the popular vote raises a valid question as to what Reagan thinks he's doing. A *Time* poll gives Ford only 38 percent to Carter's 48 percent, but there is a significant difference. Harris concludes, as *Time* does not about Ford, that Reagan appeals to such a narrow segment of the electorate that he would be a certain loser to Carter. Influential supporters of Ford, including some who counsel him occasionally, realized after the Texas and Indiana primaries that Reagan may deny Ford a first-ballot nomination and may even have a chance—incredible to these people before Texas and Indiana—to win the nomination. And to what end? There is only one sane answer: to the end of sure and cataclysmic defeat.

At the very least, Reagan, by pressing his contest and subjecting an incumbent President to humiliating pressure and peril, cripples a presidency that has been impaired from the start by the circumstance of appointment—and Nixon appointment at that—rather than election. A minor consequence of Reagan's emergence as a substantial threat was the death of the illusion that Gerald Ford had overcome the effects of appointment and established himself in the public mind as a viable President with the advantages and strengths of incumbency. Granting the power of Reagan's appeal, the appeal that George Wallace once projected and monopolized, to the biases of a minority that is measured with fair accuracy by Reagan's 34 percent in the Harris poll, Mr. Ford could not be in the danger that he clearly was in after Texas and Indiana if his presidency had won the clout and acceptance that he and his people thought it had. Granting, too, that Reagan now has reason to think he has a chance to win the nomination, can he possibly believe that he has a chance to be elected? A wise Republican whose service to Republican Presidents and candidates dates back to Eisenhower recalled in answer to this question that Barry Goldwater believed until the day of his abysmal defeat in 1964 that he was going to win.

"We're in a state of shock," one of the President's mid-level assistants remarked on the day after the Indiana, Alabama and Georgia losses. The talk at this White House level tended to be that judicious emphasis upon the Ford record in Congress and the presidency might—just might—enable Gerald Ford to defeat Jimmy Carter in a general election. But how, after five losses in Republican primaries, including three on one day, could Republicans be convinced that Ford was a more likely winner than Reagan? The degree of shock and the intensity of this line of talk decreased as the inquirer went higher in the White House hierarchy. The Indiana post mortem was in process when this was written and what follows has to do only with the Texas aftermath.

It was freely acknowledged that the President and all his advisers, including Cheney, Morton and Sen. John Tower of Texas, has drastically underestimated the extent of the Wallace cross-over. In Lubbock, one of the cities the President visited on his final three-day effort in Texas, the customary vote in Republican primaries had been around 1700. On May 1st, more than 10,000 votes were cast in Lubbock's Republican primary. Mr. Ford got some 3700 of them. Republican poll-watchers in Lubbock and Dallas said they didn't recognize thousands of people who turned up. White House inquirers were told that about 3000 of the Lubbock ballots were marked only for the presidential nominee; the voters didn't care about other Republican races and most of the 3000 voted for Reagan. The President and his people took comfort from the indications, before and after primary day, that he'd pretty well closed the early gap between him and Reagan among regular Republicans and possibly would have won by a small majority if only

Republicans had voted in the primary. Mr. Ford and his associates simply could not believe that Reagan would win all the delegates in any other state, as he did in Texas. He proceeded to do precisely that in Georgia and took 45 of 54 delegates in Indiana.

Finding comfort in the indications of retained or growing strength among regular Republicans required a lot of optimism. In Indiana, cross-over Democrats gave Reagan a popular majority of some 17,000 in more than 600,000 votes, with a national effect in his favor that was far out of proportion to the margin. In eight more states where Democrats and independents may vote in the Republican primaries, a total of 378 delegates and convention votes are at stake. If the Texas-Indiana pattern holds, Reagan will win most of those delegates and the momentum that only a series of popular majorities can generate.

The Ford optimists are probably correct, however, in their surviving belief that Reagan at his strongest can do no more and no better than deny the President a first-ballot nomination. With all 378 of the cross-over state delegates, the 366 sure convention votes that he appeared to have after his Indiana, Alabama and Georgia victories, and the maximum additional number that he seems likely to pick up in other primaries and in caucuses, he would still be short of the 1130 convention votes required to nominate. The hitch from Gerald Ford's standpoint is that he, too, is unlikely to go into the convention with an assured, first-ballot majority. What gives the President's White House and campaign committee associates and presumably Mr. Ford himself a severe case of the horrors is the prospect, rapidly developing into a near certainty, that the nominee will be chosen only after a lacerating contest, before and at the Kansas City convention, that will effectively destroy what's left of the Ford presidency and—as that veteran divider and destroyer, Sen. Goldwater, keeps saying—may complete the destruction of the Republican party.

There is a view, of course, that neither consequence would be a disaster for the country. As one who prefers Presidents and presidencies to do well, I'd hate to see such a nincompoop as Ronald Reagan bring about either result.

May 15, 1976

LVI

Pressure on Henry

Henry Kissinger was hardly back from his first tour of southern Africa when he went running to trusted friends, Vice President Nelson Rockefeller notably among them, asking them whether he had become a political liability to the President and therefore should resign. Kissinger, who years ago proved himself a past master at getting people to beg him to do what he wants to do, heard what he presumably wanted to hear. He was urged and begged to calm down, hang in there, and ignore the complaints that some Republican politicians were making to the President. The immediate complaint was that Kissinger's advocacy of black majority rule in Rhodesia and South Africa and his declaration of "unrelenting opposition" to the white minority government of Rhodesia, just three days before the Republican primary in Texas, had contributed materially to Ronald Reagan's triumph and Mr. Ford's disastrous defeat in that contest. A more general complaint was that Kissinger had come to personify all in Ford foreign policy that was most vulnerable to Reagan's distorted, disgraceful and politically effective charges that the administration was giving the Panama Canal back to Panama and, in a soft-headed pursuit of peaceful accommodation with the Soviet

Union, letting that Communist power achieve strategic superiority over the United States.

The Republican complaints to the President were not really as weighty as Kissinger seemed to think they were when he returned from Africa on May 7. Sen. Robert P. Griffin of Michigan, the assistant Republican leader in the Senate, told reporters that one person at a Republican leadership meeting with the President had "suggested that Secretary Kissinger ought to go." Griffin didn't identify the person and others at the meeting said they didn't recall anyone going quite that far. Griffin said he didn't think Kissinger's resignation "would help politically." John Rhodes of Arizona, the House Republican leader, complained through a spokesman and in person that Kissinger's Africa trip and declarations were poorly timed. He also said, rather elliptically, that "in my opinion Henry Kissinger has been and is a fine Secretary of State" and that "one of the real signs of his greatness is that he will know when he has gathered enough barnacles and scars so he can no longer be an effective Secretary of State." A spokesman said Rhodes didn't mean that last remark to be the nudge that it could be interpreted to be. Rep. Robert H. Michel of Illinois, the assistant House Republican leader, was quoted as saying the Africa trip had a "devastating effect" in southern states and that Kissinger ought to be "muzzled." Asked through his secretary if he'd been quoted correctly, Michel sent word that he'd said it all and meant it all "in spades."

The prelude to the Africa trip and its aftermath perfectly illustrate Kissinger's relationship with the President, Mr. Ford's part in a difficult, risky shift in foreign policy, and his handling of the problem that it made for him.

When reporters tried to pin upon the President explicit responsibility for Kissinger's most incendiary statement in Africa, the declaration of "unrelenting opposition" to continued white minority rule in Rhodesia, Press Secretary Ron Nessen said over and over (with slight variations): "I want you to know that the President makes foreign policy and Dr. Kissinger carries out and enunciates that foreign policy, and that is what he has done on his African trip." A reluctance to add to Gerald Ford's

5-20-76

FOREIGN POLICY

"WHY ARE YOU QUITTING ME, HENRY?!"

liabilities in a period of unexpected and possibly ruinous erosion in the Republican primaries was understandable. But it seemed to me that the President would have been better served if Nessen had been authorized, as he obviously had not been, to be explicit and detailed about Mr. Ford's role in formulating and approving the positions stated by Kissinger in Africa. It's true enough that the President and Kissinger declared the United States to be for black majority rule and against white minority rule in the black countries of southern Africa only after the Soviet-Cuban success in Angola thoroughly frightened an administration that, like all of its predecessors, had been indifferent to the blacks of southern Africa and indeed to black Africa as such. It also may be argued that "majority rule", meaning black rule in Rhodesia, South Africa and Southwest Africa ("Namibia"), would not automatically and necessarily be in the national interest of the United States as that interest is usually and narrowly defined. But, however ignoble its immediate origins and motivation, the revised African policy that Gerald Ford authorized and Henry Kissinger enunciated is *right*. It is right morally and, I believe, will in the long run prove to be right politically and in terms of national security.

Mr. Ford's responsibility for the policy is total. He, Kissinger and a few advisers, including both political and national security assistants, discussed every aspect of the policy and possible alternatives to it before Kissinger went to Africa. Kissinger and others reminded the President that the enunciation of the policy at this time — the key statement of it occurred at Lusaka, Zambia, on April 27 — would surely have unfavorable political effects. I am told at the White House — not at the State Department — that Mr. Ford's reaction to this warning was instant, emphatic, unmistakable. He said that if this was the right and necessary thing to do and say, and he had come to believe it was, he was not going to let election-year considerations interfere with either the doing, the saying or the timing of it.

At a press conference before he left for Africa, Kissinger outlined the policy and the American commitment to "majority rule." The politicians who were soon whining about the timing had nothing to say about it then. In a season of weekly primaries, there was no "good time" for such an announcement, anyhow, so

that part of the complaint never made much sense. The passages
in Kissinger's Lusaka speech that made most of the trouble for
him and the President were: ". . . the United States declares . . .
that independence must be preceded by majority rule which, in
turn, must be achieved no later than two years following the
expeditious conclusion of negotiations [between black
nationalists and the white Rhodesian government];" and "the
Salisbury regime must understand that . . . it will face our
unrelenting opposition until a negotiated settlement is
achieved." A renewed promise in the Lusaka speech to press for
repeal of a law that permits the US importation of Rhodesian
chrome in violation of UN economic sanctions probably had to be
made, though neither the Nixon nor Ford administrations ever
really worked for repeal and Kissinger and the President must
have known that Congress probably won't repeal the law.
Congressman Gerald Ford voted for the law.

A passage in the speech that Kissinger drafted with the utmost
care and that the President fouled up when he tried to paraphrase
it during the final days of his Texas campaign had to do with
white rights under black rule in "Zimbabwe," the name that the
blacks intend to give the country. Kissinger said: "Finally, we
state our conviction that whites as well as blacks should have a
secure future and civil rights . . . A constitutional structure
should protect minority rights together with establishing
majority rule." Mr. Ford said in Texas: ". . . our policy would
guarantee minority rights for any individuals in any of those
countries in Africa." A reporter asked Press Secretary Nessen
whether the President meant, as Kissinger had carefully avoided
even suggesting, that the US would guarantee white rights.
Nessen checked and reported that the President did not mean
this — "we won't do the guaranteeing," Nessen said. Mr. Ford
proceeded to say in his next reference to the matter: "This
country has traditionally believed that under any and all
circumstances we should protect minority rights or guarantee
minority rights" and added that "as long as we seek to guarantee
the minority rights of individuals in Rhodesia," a peaceful
settlement should be attainable. He confined himself to saying
once that the US would do its best "to make sure that minority
rights . . . will be guaranteed" and then went back to saying: "We

believe that in the process of self-determination we must absolutely guarantee the rights of the minorities . . ." The US can neither make nor enforce such a guarantee. Mr. Ford never meant to say, while saying repeatedly, that it could and would.

A sad feature of the aftermath was the shortage of praise from quarters that should have been generously praising the President and Henry Kissinger. The Congressional Black Caucus welcomed the trip as a first step toward a viable Africa policy but said the proof will be in what happens next. Hubert Humphrey in a statement and eight more or less liberal Republican senators in a draft resolution commended Kissinger for charting "a more moral foreign policy" and for signalling "a new realism in United States policy toward Africa." These and a few other commendations got less notice than the feckless argument over whether the amended policy was good or bad politics. One of the few heartening features was the assurance conveyed to me that the President is determined to stick with Kissinger. If our Henry would accept that as fact and quit fretting all over the place, he and the President and the country would be the better for it.

May 22, 1976

———

The "assurance" mentioned at the end of this report was conveyed by a White House assistant at the direction of Mr. Ford.

LVII

Keeping Jerry Alive

The President's victories in Michigan and Maryland, after losing five of the previous six primary elections, did not erase the memory of Gerald Ford pleading with the people of his home state to believe that in the 21 months of his appointive presidency he'd been as courageous, truthful and effective as he said he'd been, and to save him from a defeat that could have led to his final defeat by Ronald Reagan at the Republican convention in Kansas City in August. It was an unpleasant and unforgettable experience, watching an incumbent President beaten to his knees and begging for the reprieve that only a victory in Michigan could provide. The disgrace of Richard Nixon, the predecessor who put Mr. Ford in line for the presidency by appointing him Vice President, does not offer a parallel. Watergate was a public horror but, except at the very end, Nixon went through his agony in private. He was unopposed for renomination and was at the peak of his power and prestige, intimations of the debacle to come notwithstanding, when he won reelection in 1972. Gerald Ford's distress was of a lesser order and different nature, the humiliation of a sitting President who was in danger of being done out of his party's nomination and had to counter the peril in public while campaigning for preferential votes and convention delegates in Republican primaries.

Mr. Ford maintained after the final figures from Michigan were in (65 percent of the popular vote, 55 of 84 convention delegates and votes for Ford) that he'd never doubted he'd win and had never considered what he'd do if he lost. It's true that on the day before the primary, after a Saturday and Sunday campaigning in Michigan, he told White House assistants he was pleased with the show of support that he had detected and expected to win. According to White House and campaign committee assistants who were in regular touch with him before the Michigan primary and after his jarring losses in Texas, Indiana, Georgia, Alabama and Nebraska, it's also true that there was never any serious contingency thinking and planning about what to do if he lost to Reagan in Michigan. But the atmosphere around the President in this interim of doubt was not as sunny as he indicated after the Michigan victory improved it and his spirits. The dominant note was one of grim determination to slog ahead, regardless of the Michigan outcome, to and through the last and crucial Ohio, New Jersy and California primaries on June 8, and to brace in the meantime for the grueling contest with Reagan for the favor of several hundred uncommitted delegates that would follow the primaries and probably determine the nomination. Even after the last two days of campaigning in Michigan, the highest hope generally held around the President and presumably held out to him was for a marginal victory that would be so narrow as to do him little or no good.

Events and Mr. Ford's observed demeanor during the fortnight preceding the May 18 primaries indicated that the possiblity of defeat at the convention and the probability of a destructive contest for the nomination were taken seriously by him and his people. Changes in tactics became evident. Blunt, personalized retorts to Reagan's charges of domestic mis-management and international folly gave way to gentler, generalized claims of accomplishment that made the same points without naming Reagan and—as the President and his advisers belatedly realized—unnecessarily dignifying his allegations and magnifying their impact. References to "a crisis of confidence in our government, especially at the White House" when Gerald

Ford succeeded Richard Nixon in 1974 amounted to an attack upon and comparison with his predecessor and benefactor that the President had hitherto avoided. His announced intention to emphasize his own virtues and accomplishments instead of his opponent's deficiencies resulted in embarrassing braggadocio that was out of character with Gerald Ford but probably offended picky reporters more than it did the citizenry. It was the President's manner and appearance, however, that most plainly attested the apprehension that prevailed behind the rather transparent show of confidence. At most of his public appearances he was tense, grim, smiling much less than is his custom, straining for wisecracks—Betty Ford became "First Mama" painfully often—that don't suit him. He frequently seemed to be tired, and some of his assistants said he was.

Stops in Tennessee and Kentucky, two of the six states where primaries on May 25 presented the prospect of another bad day for Mr. Ford, preceded his two-day swing through central Michigan. The doings in Johnson City, Memphis and Louisville made this observer wonder whether the President could believe that he was accomplishing much. Senator Howard Baker of Tennessee, whose readiness to be either Mr. Ford's or Ronald Reagan's vice presidential choice or an alternative to Reagan for the presidential nomination is apparent, said in Johnson City and Memphis that his being for Mr. Ford didn't mean that he was against any other Republican. Reagan, who also was campaigning in Tennessee, stayed at Baker's home that night. The state's junior Republican senator, Bill Brock, was nowhere to be seen. The crowd in Memphis, celebrating the opening of a midtown shopping mall, was possibly the least reponsive and most apathetic that Mr. Ford has ever addressed, and that's saying a lot. The President's haste to get on to Louisville and then to Michigan that night prevented his attending the Tennessee Republican party's biggest annual event, a leadership dinner in Nashville. Reporters travelling with the President were told that many Republican leaders thought he'd have done better to stay out of the state entirely than skip the dinner. A speech to an Armed Forces Day dinner in Louisville, following two perfunctory appearances before groups of Ford campaign workers, provided a chance to refute Reagan's charges, without naming

Reagan, that the administration is neglecting the country's defenses and national interests. The unsurprising word after the visit was that it did not appear to have lessened Reagan's perceived lead in Kentucky.

The big act in Michigan was a six-hour ride on seven gleaming Amtrak railway cars including Amtrak's only observation car with an open rear platform, through the central part of the state. It began in Flint with the President standing on the rear platform and crying out the theme-line of these two days: "I ask you to help us on Tuesday. We must win in Michigan, and Flint is very important." All the way, to generally small but friendly crowds, the several chosen lines were repeated. Harking back to Nixon and Watergate: " . . . when I took the oath of office . . . this country was having many, many troubles. There was a loss of confidence in the White House itself. We were on the brink of an economic recession"—and so on. About Jerry Ford: "In the last 21 months I think Jerry Ford has done a good job and I want your help. Of course I have had a lot of help from First Mama, too (Mrs. Ford, standing beside him, simpers and waves and the transcript notes "laughter") . . . Because of my openness, my candor and my proven intergrity, the American people know that they had a reason to have the feeling of confidence in the White House and the President of the United States." On the slow rise in employment and drop in inflation: "Everything that is supposed to be going down is going down and everything that is supposed to be going up is going up." Mr. Ford said again and again that what he had accomplished and offered could be summed up in a slogan: "Peace, prosperity and trust."

It was hard to get him off the rear platform. As the train pulled out of town after town—Lansing, Battle Creek, Kalamazoo— and finally into Niles, the loudspeakers carried his shouts to knots of people and even individuals along the tracks: "Hello . . . Good to see you . . . I need your vote." At Battle Creek the President was seen to redden, glare at someone in the crowd on the station platform, and shout: "We blew it in the right direction, young man, and those of you who don't agree—and if you would go out and look for a job, you would get one!" Sound tapes showed that somebody who was never identified had broken into Mr. Ford's account of the "real tough jobs" he had to handle when he took office with the remark: "You blew it." Press

Secreatry Ron Nessen checked with the President and quoted him as explaining that a young man who had been taunting him mentioned "the economy" and Mr. Ford jumped to the conclusion that he was saying he didn't have a job. On reflection, the President realized that the young man hadn't mentioned a job. Michigan has a high unemployment rate and the President's taunt was hardly calculated to help him. The primary result indicated that neither this outburst nor anything else hurt him much.

The accepted wisdom was that the President "turned it around" with this Saturday and Sunday and a previous day in the Detroit area. I wonder. People questioned in the crowds were usually reticent, embarrassed, tongue-tied. A burly man in the crowd at Niles said with a grin, "If you live in Michigan, you'd *better* be for him." But he was the exception. In the spring of 1974, when his reputation was already in tatters, Richard Nixon drew large and responsive crowds in the same area of Michigan and his candidate for Congress lost. At Holland, a town that annually celebrates its Dutch origins with a "Tulip Festival," upwards of 200,000 people had gathered along a three-mile route to watch the tulip parade. Although thoroughly damp from rain that stopped just before the President arrived, they had stayed to watch the Ford motorcade as it wended its slow way over the parade route. Mr. Ford waved to his left from his White House car, Mrs. Ford waved to her right. There were a few signs, all friendly; a few shouts from the crowd, all friendly. It was, arithmetically speaking, the biggest reception Gerald Ford had got during his presidency. Yet there was a curious lack of communication. It seemed to me that the people staring at him as he passed were mostly stolid, silent, musing. During the hour's progress the President never once stopped his car and got out to shake hands, which for him was a sensational departure from custom. On primary day the President did extremely well in that section, as he did in the entire state. But a peripheral fact strengthened my doubt that all the labor, expense and running around involved in primary campaigning makes much difference for a President or does a President much good. Gerald Ford won in Maryland, too, and he never campaigned in that state.

May 29, 1976

LVIII

Reagan's Half-Truths

A week on the last of the 1976 primary campaign trails with President Ford in Oregon and California and with Ronald Reagan in California left three impressions. There is nothing to say about Mr. Ford as a campaigner — a very dull campaigner — that hasn't been noted in this space and elsewhere. Traveling with Reagan is more fun and harder work than traveling with the President, partly because Reagan is a livelier person and speaker and partly because he can't afford to provide the texts and other aids to reporting that the White House establishment spews forth in expensive abundance. A reporter with Reagan has to rely upon his own notes and tape recorder, with the rare exception of a prepared summary of what the candidate may or may not actually say. The third impression is that Ronald Reagan is a master, the greatest master in this reporter's experience, of distortion that generally (but not always) contains a core of truth that makes it impossible or at least chancy to call the man a liar.

This does not apply to all that Reagan says on the stump. His account of his eight years as governor of California, for instance, including his bulling of a hostile legislature into doing what he wanted done and of trimming welfare rolls and costs without demonstrated harm to legitimate beneficiaries, is conceded by California journalists who don't admire him to be about as accurate as anyone expects a politician in the heat of contest to be. In this respect his performance is similar to that of former Governor Jimmy Carter of Georgia, who like Reagan naturally does not understate his achievements in office. Reagan is said by his staff to squirrel away unchecked anecdotes from news clippings and conversations with which he spices the standard speech — many politicians have one, but he sticks to his more faithfully than most — that he delivers at rallies and similar occasions. Most of these stories are peopled by misty characters whose identities and adventures tend to go unverified even by newspapers in the areas concerned. There is "the man in New Jersey" who was told by Social Security that he was dead, proved he wasn't, and after prolonged haggling was given $700 to pay for his funeral. There are the police and prosecutors in San Bernardino, California, who convicted a couple of hiding heroin in their baby's diaper and lost the case on appeal because the baby had not consented to be searched. There is Chicago's "Welfare Mary" (an actual person, somewhat enlarged by Reagan) who according to him drew $150,000 a year from fraudulent welfare claims and sported two Lincoln Continentals. And there is Reagan himself as depicted by Reagan in a San Diego TV interview on May 27, keeping fit at age 65 by riding horses on his ranch, digging his own post-holes and building his own fences because, "I like to do those things." His press secretary, Jim Lake, assured guffawing reporters that Reagan really does such work and has never been seen or pictured doing it because he values his privacy at home more than he would value the publicity.

More serious distortion and falsifications than the foregoing — if such they be — date essentially back to a 30 minute, paid-time TV speech that Reagan delivered March 31 and to a shorter TV statement that he made, also on paid time, on April 28. Several assertions in these effusions date back further, to the early weeks of the New Hampshire primary campaign and in a few instances to his gubernatorial campaigns in 1966 and 1970. The examples dealt with here were heard and observed during three days with him in the week of May 24 — at a couple of press conferences, in set speeches, in two TV interviews and in a 25-

minute chat, recorded by his staff electrician during a ride in his
campaign limousine from Los Angeles to Pasadena.

Perhaps the most serious distortion has to do with the Panama
Canal and negotiations for gradual transfer of its operation and
of sovereignty over the Panama Canal Zone to Panama. It is an
idiotic issue. But anyone of my age (69) who recalls the pride with
which parents and neighbors greeted the completion and
opening of the canal in 1914 must acknowledge that it symbolizes
something of enormous importance in the American memory
and psyche. Reagan says he didn't initiate the issue; people began
raising it during his New Hampshire campaign and reacted "with
stunned surprise" when he said yes, their government was
negotiating to give away the canal. When I heard the subject
raised in New Hampshire, it seemed to me that Reagan was
primed to make the most of it and that his inquirers and hearers
were primed to help him do it. After referring in his March 31 TV
speech to "negotiations aimed at giving up our ownership of the
Panama Canal Zone," he said: "Apparently, everyone knows
about this except the rightful owners of the Canal Zone — you,
the people of the United States." At a San Diego rally on May 27,
he said: "For two years, without your knowledge, your
government has been negotiating to give away sovereignty over
the Panama Canal Zone."

Reagan had been told that I hoped to discuss some of what I
regarded as his distortions and I said during our ride to Pasadena
that his repeated indication that both the fact and the nature of
the Panama negotiations had been concealed was one of these
distortions. He was reminded that Secretary of State Henry
Kissinger and Panama Foreign Secretary Juan Antonio Tack
signed and made public a "statement of principles" to govern the
negotiations on February 7, 1974. The statement said: "The
treaty of 1903 [which granted to the US "in perpetuity" the
rights and authority over the Canal Zone that it would possess
"if it were sovereign"] and its amendments will be abrogated by
the conclusion of an entirely new interoceanic canal treaty. The
concept of perpetuity will be eliminated. . . . The Panamanian
territory in which the canal is situated [the Canal Zone] shall be
returned to the jurisdiction of the Republic of Panama. The
Republic of Panama, in its capacity as territorial sovereign, shall

grant to the United States of America . . . the right to use the lands, waters and airspace which may be necessary for the operation, maintenance, protection and defense of the canal and the transit ships . . . The Republic of Panama shall participate in the administration of the canal [and] in the protection and defense of the canal."

After reminding Reagan that he had mentioned without explaining the Kissinger-Tack statement the previous day, I said in part: "That statement has been on the public record since February 7, 1974. It was reincorporated in Current Policy Paper No. 9 at the State Department last September [actually last November]. The fact and nature of the negotiations have been very poorly and inadequately reported. But I would say it has *never* been concealed." Reagan answered in part: "Well, where we perhaps differ on that is in answering questions I may here and there get careless and use the word 'secret' that would not apply. I have generally, if I used the word 'secret' said 'almost secret' negotiations. Now, in a country such as ours, where everything is out there, I cannot accept that it is just sheer coincidence that those two years of negotiations have been going on and then have the fiasco that took place during the Texas primary with the President there on Texas soil refuting me to the point that Ron Nessen had to say, 'Well, maybe the President's words were ill-chosen.'" Reagan referred to the President's mistaken statement to a canal defender on April 9 in San Antonio that "The United States, as far as I'm concerned, will never give up its defense responsibilities and capability. It will never give up the rights of navigation and so forth." The guiding statement, as shown above, commits the US to give up its "jurisdiction" (read "sovereignty") when a new treaty is negotiated and effective control much later — Panama says, in 25 years; the US says, in 40 to 50 years. Press Secretary Nessen apologized for the mistake and Mr. Ford said he'd been "imprecise."

In view of the 1974 statement's clear provision that the Canal Zone "shall be returned to the jurisdiction of the Republic of Panama," Reagan's frequent assertion — repeated to me during our conversation — that a House subcommittee recently uncovered the hitherto concealed fact that US "sovereignty" over the Canal Zone is in negotiation is worse than imprecision.

When I said the 1974 statement specifically said the question of sovereignty was to be negotiated, Reagan replied, "Ah, now that I question." When he was asked at a California news conference if he proposed to terminate the present negotiations, he said no, he didn't — there were other things than sovereignty that could rightly be negotiated. He said in his March 31 speech: "We should end those negotiations and tell the General [Panamanian dictator Omar Torrijos]: We bought it, we paid for it, we built it, and we intend to keep it." Reagan said in California that the negotiations have been suspended until after the November election. I was told at the State Department that Ambassador Ellsworth Bunker met with the Panamanian negotiators in Panama on May 1 through May 7 and expects another meeting by late summer.

One of Reagan's major themes, expressed forcefully in his March 31 TV speech and reiterated ever since, is that the administration and "this totally irresponsible Congress" have let the US slide from "Number One" to "Number Two" in relative strength as compared with the Soviet Union. Discussing and justifying this claim in his conversation with me, he cited among other things "the statements of Sen. Clark, of Iowa, that he asked the military experts at the Library of Congress to give him a report and admitted that he wanted it because he believed that all this talk [of our still being Number One] and all of the administration requests for more money was because they were just simply building a scarecrow to get more money for defense. And so he thought he would get a report from the Library of Congress that would bear this out and he had to admit himself that he got a report from the Library that was probably more terrifying than any of the statements that I have made — the report that we were indeed in a very dangerous position."

It was Sen. John C. Culver of Iowa, not Sen. Dick Clark, who asked for the report. When I quoted the foregoing remarks about the report to the defense specialist on Sen. Culver's staff and asked if they were correct, "allowing for a little political rhetoric," the assistant answered: "No, that's totally false. Number one, we did not expect the report to say any particular thing. We asked for an objective analysis of where we were, how we got there, and what was significant, and we confined that report to military capabilities rather than overall national strength versus the Soviet Union. What we got did not surprise us. What surprised us was the way it was initially misinterpreted in the press, because they looked at the numbers rather than the text. Now of course if you look at the numbers the Russians have narrowed the gap in many areas in the past 10 years. Our superiority is less, but overall we are still superior. What we got was not terrifying. Culver has never said anything like that, nor has he ever disavowed the report. He has been a little upset at the way press reports took the numbers out of context." Reagan says he took the numbers he's been using out of the Culver report. Thus in his March 31 speech and later statements: "The Soviet Army outnumbers ours more than two-to-one and in reserves four-to-one. They out-spend us on weapons by 50 percent. Their Navy out-numbers ours in surface ships and submarines two-to-one. We are out-gunned in artillery three-to-one and their tanks outnumber ours four-to-one. Their strategic nuclear missiles are larger, more powerful and more numerous than ours. The evidence mounts that we are Number Two in a world where it is dangerous, if not fatal, to be second best."

Taxed by President Ford and others with arguing that the US must match the Soviet Union man-for-man, tank-for-tank etc., Reagan retorts that of course he isn't that silly; he knows that what counts is strategic and nuclear capability. When he took that line May 27 on San Diego TV station KFMB, during the best interview that I've seen him undergo, staffer Tom Lawrence said he'd just heard a Reagan radio commercial in which Reagan left "the listener with the definite impression that you are drawing strictly a man-to-man comparison." Reagan answered in part:

"Well, I think this has to be done. I've been making the charge that we are not Number One any more. Now to do that you have to point out the facts to substantiate this charge, particularly when there's been a reluctance to admit it. So I have pointed out the difference in naval vessels, in tanks, in artillery pieces, manpower, all that. But then, the obvious question comes, how do you counter this? You don't counter it by trying to enlist as many men as they do. But you do go ahead with the development of missile systems, things of this kind that our Congress has been reluctant to go forward with."

Lawrence: "So you are saying that qualitatively, not numerically but qualitatively, we are second?"

Reagan: "Yes. As a matter of fact, where this came from is the defense expert of the Library of Congress . . . He said for a time it was our qualitative advantage that kept us ahead in spite of their quantitative advantage. But he had to say that no longer is true. They have been coming up in quality, in addition to making their quantity so much superior."

Sen. Culver's defense specialist said the foregoing remark is a distortion of the Library of Congress report. The report said our qualitative advantage is less than it was, but we still have it.

The KFMB interviewers — Lawrence, Dick Carlson and Harold Keen — broke with their hard but fair questions through the bland geniality that Reagan generally displays. At times his mouth set in an ugly, venomous curve. A recent California President had that look.

June 12, 1976

LIX

Back to Reagan

The inquiries that resulted in the previous piece about "Reagan's half-truths" turned up some examples of what Ronald Reagan and his people consider to be President Ford's distortions and deceptions. They will be noted before returning to Reagan's greater talents and sins in this respect.

Possibly excepting the President's recent assertions that he can and Reagan can't win the general election, nothing infuriates the Reagan staff more than the impression that Ford and Reagan are equally and identically opposed to gun control. Both of them oppose registration of guns and gun owners; both make the absurd argument that guns don't kill people — people kill people; and both advocate mandatory additional prison sentences for felons who use guns in the commission of crimes. When asked about this by gun nuts, as he often is when he invites questions from citizens, Mr. Ford usually confines himself to the sort of reply he gave April 30 at Lubbock, Texas: "I am opposed to the registration of a gun owner. I am opposed to the registration of firearms, period." The Reagan complaint is that the President never voluntarily mentions an administration bill that the Department of Justice drafted and after much difficulty persuaded Sen. Hiram Fong of Hawaii and Rep. Robert McClory of Illinois to introduce. When somebody else mentions the bill, the President encourages the notion that it merely restricts the importation and assembly of the cheap, foreign-made pistols known as "Saturday night specials." As a Reagan staff study says, the bill "would ban the manufacture, importation, assembly, sale or transfer by *any* person of *any* model of handgun, new or used, unless the model has been approved by the Secretary of the Treasury" and would penalize violations with up to five years in prison and $5000 fines. It's actually a weak bill, far short of what real and adequate gun control would require. But it's enough to outrage hordes of voting gunnies and is the target of a direct-mail campaign that Ford workers suspect but haven't proved to be a Reagan operation. One of the marvels of this political season, incidentally, is that nobody has asked either Ford or Reagan to explain just how a federal requirement that gun owners and purchasers register themselves and their guns would violate anybody's civil and constitutional rights, including the con-stitutional "right to bear arms."

There is no doubt that the Ford forces went to the outer limits of propriety with their exaggeration, amounting to distortion, of a couple of Reagan remarks about the Tennessee Valley Authority and Rhodesia. In Knoxville, TVA's head-quarters city, a television interviewer recalled that Sen. Barry Goldwater lost many votes for himself in 1964 by proposing to sell TVA's electric power facilities to private industry, and then asked Reagan: "If elected President, would you go along with that kind of argument, Governor?" Reagan answered in part: "Well, you are asking a question involving a gigantic combine of gigantic interests . . . and to say that I know all of the facets and details in that, I don't think I could give you an answer. But it would be something to look at and first of all to make sure that the citizens were the beneficiaries of anything of that kind." It was a careless and silly statement, the kind that Reagan's assistants despair of teaching him to avoid. But it hardly justified the President, campaign chairman Rogers Morton, Sen. Howard Baker and Reps. James Quillen of Tennessee and Tim Lee Carter of Kentucky in joining in a blitz of suggestions that Reagan had as good as proposed on the eve of the Tennessee and Kentucky primaries "to sell TVA."

In the course of arguing that the US should try to mediate between the ruling white minority and the subject black majority in Rhodesia, instead of denouncing minority rule and calling for black majority rule as the President and Henry Kissinger recently did, Reagan remarked June 2 in Sacramento that the use of American troops to prevent racial conflict might be a possibility and added: "Whether you'd have to go in with occupation forces or not, I don't know." It was another foolish statement, and Reagan soon retracted it. The Ford campaign committee blanketed California with television and radio ads saying: "Governor Reagan could not start a war. President Reagan could." President Ford said in Ohio that "my Republican opponent did indicate that he would think about stationing American military forces in Rhodesia." The Ford campaign committee issued denunciations of Reagan's "frightening" statement in the names of Vice President Rockefeller, Secretary of Commerce Richardson, Gov. Milliken of Michigan, Rogers Morton, Sens. Griffin of Michigan and Baker of Tennessee, and the President's brother, Tom Ford. The California ad was hardly the "absolute fabrication and misstatement" that Reagan said it was. But it and the accompanying blasts made excessive ado about very little.

No fuss at all was raised about an infinitely more frightening and dangerous argument that Reagan made in an interview with the Associated Press and, a few days earlier, in a conversation with me. Supporting his familiar contention that the Ford administration and the Democratic Congress have let the US fall behind the Soviet Union in military and nuclear strength, Reagan told AP reporter Walter Mears that a Soviet invasion of Western Europe could leave the US with no recourse except "the one thing that none of us wants at all, the nuclear button. The day we push the nuclear button, we [will] know that we do not have the nuclear superiority we once had, we don't even have parity." That is arguable and, when put in over-simple terms of numbers, technically accurate. The frightening and dangerous factor is the thought in Reagan's mind behind the sort of language he used in the AP interview. I know it's in his mind because he came right out with it in his talk with me. After invoking the specter of Soviet invasion, much as he had with the AP, he said to me: "What would be left to us is only one thing, the nuclear button, which no one wants and [my emphasis] *which I doubt if any American President would use under those circumstances."* So far as I know, no American President and no serious candidate for the presidency has said anything like this since Harry Truman placed Western Europe under American nuclear protection with the North Atlantic Treaty in 1949. If Reagan doubts that he said it to me, he has only to have his sound technician play back his tape of the conversation.

Our study of Reagan's little ways concludes with a tale of taxes. Last April 20 President Ford issued a remarkably full statement of his income, taxes, assets and liabilities for the years 1966 through 1975. Reagan had issued a much less detailed statement in February, failing among other things to distinguish between the federal, state and local taxes he had paid. When he was asked during a San Diego television interview on May 27 why he didn't disclose more than he had, Reagan answered in part: "We have a law in California about disclosure. I complied with that law. I think it's all that's required of a public official to assure the people that there's no conflict of interest in any way connected with the office he has or the office he seeks. As a matter of fact the White House contacted the Treasury Department after my release and tried to get more information and Secretary of the Treasury Bill Simon informed the White House that I had complied fully with the law and [done] all that was required."

Well, I asked Secretary Simon about that and was told a story that's more interesting than the Reagan version. According to Simon, the White House had never asked him and would never have dared to ask him for tax information about Reagan or anyone else. What happened was that he discovered upon returning to Washington from a trip that Press Secretary Ron Nessen and the President himself were publicly suggesting that Reagan ought to make as full a disclosure as the President had made. Simon was outraged. He protested at a White House staff meeting that Ronald Reagan had the same rights of privacy that all citizens had and certainly had every right to disclose as little or as much as he pleased about his income and taxes. Simon insisted that the official needling of Reagan cease and he says it ceased. My impression is that Nessen and Mr. Ford, when asked about the matter, still manage to get over the idea that the President is more frank and open about his finances than Reagan is.

June 19, 1976

LX

Remodeling Ford

At press conferences and other appearances around the country, Vice President Rockefeller is saying what Gerald Ford and his people at the White House are saying to each other and will be saying in public with ever-increasing fervor if the President is nominated at Kansas City in August. Thus Rockefeller when he is asked about the President's prospects: "I believe President Ford will be nominated on the first ballot and elected in November, and I can tell you why—because his record is extraordinary. Two years ago this country was faced with tremendously difficult problems: loss of respect and confidence in the executive branch of government; the economic crisis with inflation, unemployment, recession; and problems in the world that almost looked insurmountable. Two years later, what has happened? The President has restored confidence and respect in government, in the White House. He has cut the inflation rate in half. There are 3,200,000 more people working today in the United States than there were a year ago—and absolutely phenomenal growth. The growth rate of the economy is 8.7 percent. Nobody thought that inflation could be controlled and jobs restored both at the same time. But he has done it. He has done it by his courage, by his belief in fundamental values. And on top of all that, we have peace in the world. So in my opinion the American people are not going to want to change that kind of leadership."

The point of quoting this homily at length is that, with some allowance for an advocate's rhetoric, it is really believed by most of the people around the President and they, like him, are truly troubled and puzzled by the obvious failure of a large portion of the public to perceive and believe it. The astonishing, totally unexpected success of Ronald Reagan in forcing an incumbent President to beg and scramble for the votes of a few score uncommitted Republican convention delegates in order to win nomination has done more than Mr. Ford's steady decline in public opinion polls to convince his principal assistants and associates that something has been dreadfully wrong with the way in which he presents himself and is presented by his spokesmen to the country. With belated recognition of Reagan's root appeal to the Republican minority that by definition determines the choice of the party's presidential nominee, the conclusion at the Ford White House is that the President could not have been brought as low as he has been if the general public perceived him as those who serve and work with him perceive him. They perceive him as a strong, decisive and intelligent man with a genuine capacity for leadership who in two years has overcome the handicaps inherent in the circumstances that he is President by appointment rather than election and that his party is the party of Richard Nixon and Watergate. His people have come to realize—they grant with bitter realism—that many Americans, perhaps a majority, perceive him as a weak bumbler, a likeable but laughable figure who should never have been plucked from Congress and installed first in the vice presidency and then in the presidency.

It is typical of the Ford White House that a feeling that all of the foregoing is so, accumulating and growing though it has been for months, brought a decision at least to try and do something about the general perception of the President only in mid-July and then only because of the realization that he could not possibly win the election in November unless that perception is turned around and corrected. It obviously being too late to do anything in this respect to improve his chances of nomination, a month before the Republican convention chooses between Ford and Reagan in mid-August, a sudden burst of action and reorganization was aimed at improving his chances of defeating Jimmy Carter. The steps taken were in themselves in-house stuff, rather petty, but their nature and purpose and the way in which they came about are worth noting in some detail because they tell a good deal about this President and his White House.

One of the revealing things was the conclusion, evidently shared by the President, that nothing much can be done about Gerald Ford. Perhaps the statements and speeches drafted for him could be sharpened up. Perhaps the choices of occasions for his public performances could be improved. But it had to be and was assumed that he would remain his usually dull and dulling self, often lively in private but seldom able to convey those qualities in public. That is why Nelson Rockefeller dwells more upon the President's record than upon the President as a person. The Vice President is known to hold that Mr. Ford is a good President and a terrible campaigner and that he'd have done better than he did in the Republican primaries if he'd spent more time in the White House, being President, and less on the road. It also is why the President at a Washington press conference on July 9—his first at the White House since February—similarly emphasized his record when he said: "Once we get the nomination, we can start pointing out the distinct differences between the prospective Democratic nominee and myself; we can talk about the record that we have. It is a record that I think will be applauded by 99 and nine tenths of the delegates to the Republican convention. I think it will appeal to many independents, and . . . there are some Democrats who think the record of the Ford administration is a good one." And, finally, it is why the coming effort to improve the projection of Mr. Ford to the country will rely more upon setting forth the record of his two years in the presidency in a favorable way than upon public relations gimmickry with him as a person. There will be some of the latter, but not as much as might be expected.

Another fact made clearer than it had been is that the White

Remodeling Ford

House of Gerald Ford, a gentle and forbearing type who abhors dissension among his people and personifies good fellowship, is a cockpit of jealousies, rivalries and downright hatreds without recent precedent. At its lowest point and at its times of greatest internal tension, the Nixon White House never suffered anything near the in-fighting and back-stabbing that characterize the Ford White House. In a newspaper column that shook official Washington, Evans-Novak on July 10 reported that "recriminations, back-stabbing and personal power plays" at the White House and at the headquarters of the President's campaign instrument, the President Ford Committee, had "brought the campaign to the brink of anarchy." Such reports miss the mark in two respects. There is nothing new about the condition and, perhaps because it is chronic rather than a matter of sudden eruption, it has oddly little effect upon the overall Ford performance. In the instance dealt with here, it actually furthered some useful changes.

Many of the animosities involve two senior assistants who detest each other, Press Secretary Ron Nessen and Counsellor Robert Hartmann, a long-time Ford associate who heads the President's writing staff. Don Penny, a diminutive ex-comedian and producer of television spots who caught the President's fancy when he did some work on contract at the White House early this year, has called Hartmann "prick" to his face and has baldly stated to the President his, Penny's, opinion that Hartmann is a ruinously stupid and inept assistant whose deficiencies and follies are enough to bring Mr. Ford to defeat. The President remains unswerving in his devotion to and support of Hartmann and insistent that Penny stick around as a $150-per-day consultant, providing ideas and language to brighten up Mr. Ford's public self. Penny's uninhibited criticism in private of practically every facet of the Ford pubic relations operation had a lot to do with the President authorizing changes in mid-July.

Two of the changes were made possible by the accomplished and impending departures from the staff of two assistants whom Nessen has been trying to ease out for months. The nomination of Margita White, aged 39, a competent and attractive woman who has been the director of communications under Nessen since February 1975, to a 7-year term on the Federal Communications Commission, opened the way to transferring to that job David Gergen, staff chief Richard Cheney's principle idea man and the last head of Richard Nixon's writing staff. Gergen's deputy at the head of a greatly expanded Office of Communications staff with expanded responsibilities is William Rhatican, a gutsy Nixon veteran who lately has been Treasury Secretary William Simon's chief spokesman.

Margita White during her tenure as communications director was in some part a victim of a deliberate policy decision, reached at the start of the Ford incumbency, to diminish and downgrade the Office of Communications, which Nixon had estabished as his public relations-propaganda arm. Under Herbert Klein, its first director, the communications office did a quietly effective job of promoting the best and obscuring the worst of the Nixon performance. Klein's deputy and successor, Ken W. Clawson, ran an aggressive operation dedicated to the reelection of Richard Nixon and the destruction of George McGovern in 1972 and, after the Watergate scandals broke, equally dedicated to Nixon's survival. When Nixon fell and was succeeded by Gerald Ford, the hitherto autonomous office was put under the press secretary and, over time, reduced in both staff and functions. The result was that White was neither as prominent nor as effective as her Nixon predecessors had been. Nessen fretted and, as a sense of need to reinvigorate the President's image machine spread and grew, others joined him in wishing that Margita White would go away. She turned down an offer of a departmental public affairs job and agreed to leave only when she was offered a full 7-year term on the Federal Communications Commission. The predictable reluctance of a Democratic Senate to let a Republican President with a doubtful future put a Republican—even a female Republican—in such a plummy spot caused some Ford assistants to wonder whether Margita White had been lured out with a phony nomination. The expanded communications office remains nominally under Nessen but really autonomous. A *Chicago Tribune* report that Nessen had lost authority with the change enraged him and he typically blamed Hartmann for inspiring that interpretation.

For once, Hartmann passed up a chance to get at Nessen and had nothing to do with the report.

The simultaneous resignation of the President's television adviser, former CBS producer Robert Mead, resulted from his refusal since 1974 to submit to Nessen's direction and Nessen's steady, finally successful effort to isolate and frustrate him. Senior assistants who did not share Nessen's dislike of Mead felt nevertheless that the President needed a more aggressive and innovative television adviser and welcomed the chance to seek one. A few assistants, Hartmann among them, and quite a few White House correspondents noted with sour interest that Nessen had survived. They wondered why.

July 24, 1976

———

Mrs. White settled for a two-year vacancy on the FCC.

LXI

Being Presidential

The President's second press conference at the White House in 11 days, after nearly five months with no press conferences in Washington, produced some wonderful pictures and in several other respects furthered his humiliating fight for his party's nomination in August. The pictures showed him standing, confident and laughing amid a gaggle of reporters, on the White House lawn with the north portico of the executive mansion in the background. His answers to questions played upon his incumbency, an asset that of late had not been as helpful to his candidacy as it is traditionally assumed to be. By inference, Mr. Ford compared his 27 years in national politics and government with Jimmy Carter's single term of four years as governor of Georgia. The whole affair reflected the conclusion, arrived at in recent weeks and forced upon the President and his advisers by his dim performance in the Republican primaries, that his best hope of nomination and election lies in his being as presidential as possible even when he's campaigning and, at this pre-convention stage, wheedling and bargaining for the absurdly few individual delegate votes that he needed in order to defeat Ronald Reagan for nomination on the first ballot in Kansas City.

A reporter's reference to the publicized and rather pretentious process of interviewing and pondering that preceded Carter's choice of Senator Walter Mondale to run with him for the vice presidency gave the President his shot at his opponent's relative inexperience. Mr. Ford said he'd been thinking about his own choice for some time and continued: "I know all of the individuals who are being considered very well. I have worked with them, known about them. . . . Therefore it won't be a last-minute analysis. It will be one based on a good many years of experience and opportunities to know how they performed in public office and otherwise."

Two other answers displayed the President in his first direct reaction to the Carter campaign and, as it turned out, having his first direct impact upon a Carter position. The indications in the Carter and Mondale acceptance speeches at the Democratic convention that the nominees planned to make issues of the Republicans' Watergate past and of Gerald Ford's pardon of Richard Nixon caused the President to abandon his hitherto flat opposition to legislation that would remove the main responsibility for investigating and prosecuting federal official wrongdoing from the Department of Justice and vest it in special prosecutors. Mr. Ford announced that he'd go along with the general approach if the President were authorized to appoint a single, permanent special prosecutor, subject to Senate confirmation, rather than the temporary prosecutors who under pending legislation might be chosen either by the Attorney General or, if he failed to act upon a complaint, by appellate courts. The change was a sign of awareness that any appearance of indifference to Watergate and its lessons could be fatal to a Ford candidacy.

When the President was reminded of Senator Mondale's explicit and Carter's implied criticism of the Nixon pardon and was asked whether he considered it a liability, Mr. Ford defended the pardon in the same stanch way he has ever since he granted it. "I decided to grant the pardon in the national interest," he said, and he finished his answer on a note of defiance: "I would do it again." At a press conference in Plains the next day, Jimmy Carter in effect swallowed his own implied criticism and repudiated Mondale's explicit criticism of the pardon. He said he still thought the pardon "ill-advised" and "improper" but wasn't going to make an issue of it in his election campaign. Comparing his view with the one asserted by Mondale at the New York convention, Carter said with a remarkably open touch of pragmatism: "I personally think my position on the pardon is preferable from a political viewpoint. The American people know who pardoned President Nixon. They know the circumstances involved in the pardon. They don't need it raised for political advantage and they would resent it if it was."

At the latest press conference and at the previous one, much probing for the President's thoughts about a vice presidential nominee produced no information whatever. The White House inquirer is told that private discussions of the subject with Mr. Ford are no more informative. Seven acquaintances of mine, five of them officials and two of them private citizens, who have talked about the matter with the President insisted in late July that they had no inkling of what he intended to do or even of whether he knew then, after the Democratic convention and nominations, what he was going to do. My impression was that if anybody around Mr. Ford really had some indication, it was staff chief Richard Cheney and he wasn't saying. A reporter's inquiries over the past several weeks did, however, elicit some interesting indications of what the President was hearing and of how he reacted to it.

The most interesting figure among those who talk with him about the President's own nomination problem and about his vice presidential problem is Vice President Rockefeller. The gist of his advice to the President and to all others who will listen is well known. It goes as follows: now that Jimmy Carter has been nominated, forget the South. Don't let Carter's choice of a prominent and committed liberal, Senator Mondale, for the vice presidency trap the Ford forces into alienating the moderate-to-liberal segment of the electorate by excessive damnation of Carter as a hidden liberal and of his ticket as a dangerously liberal one. Go for the North and Northeast, where most of the big blocs of electoral votes are. Go for the moderate-to-liberal majorities in those states (New York, Pennsylvania, New Jersey,

Massachusetts, etc.). That means — no Reagan, no Connally for
the vice presidency, despite enormous convention pressures for
such a nominee. It means the choice of a moderate middle-
roader, middle perhaps to the point of being innocuous. Senator
Howard Baker of Tennessee is cited as an example. Governor
Dan Evans of Washington State, an able man who gets much
less national notice than he deserves, is another acceptable
prospect by this measure. The possibility that pro-Reagan
delegates, whether declared for him or officially committed to
the President, may be so insistent that they deprive Gerald Ford
of his choice and force Reagan or Connally upon him is
recognized by Rockefeller and by others who take the
Rockefeller line. If this happens, they argue, let Mr. Ford be in a
posture that makes it clear that the convention and not he has
condemned the Republican party to electoral suicide.

How does Gerald Ford respond in such discussions, whether
to the foregoing or to opposite advice? The answer provided by
one participant in Oval Office talk about campaign problems is
that the President doesn't respond. "With this President," says
the acquaintance quoted here, "you don't *discuss* anything. You
speak your piece, he listens, and that's all. You learn later, if at
all, usually through somebody else or from what is done or
announced, how he reacts to what you've said to him." It's not
that Mr. Ford is rude or secretive, according to this account. It's
simply that, except on matters about which he's already made
up his mind when a point is broached, he is wary of instant
decision and commitment and prefers to take his time.

It's especially interesting that Nelson Rockefeller is defending
and supporting Gerald Ford as loyally and strongly as he is.
Among the tensions at the Ford White House that were
described in my last report, none is potentially more destructive
and actually under better control than the tension between
Rockefeller and the President. Rockefeller feels that his
withdrawal last November from consideration for the vice-
presidential nomination was deliberately devised and forced
upon him. He is convinced that Donald Rumsfeld, former White
House staff chief and now Secretary of Defense, principally
contrived the pressure in furtherance of his own ambition to be

the nominee. Does Rockefeller hold the President fundamentally responsible? The answer heard in Rockefeller quarters is, *he
allowed it to happen.* Yet the Vice President continues to do a better
job of articulating Gerald Ford's claims to nomination and
election than the President does.

July 31, 1976

LXII

Nixon's Devils

A wish to believe in and promote public belief in what may be called the devil theory of Richard Nixon's downfall is surfacing among a number of his former White House assistants. Two of them, H.R. Haldeman and John Ehrlichman, fell with him and are appealing convictions and prison sentences for Watergate offenses. The devil theory exists in several forms and degrees. It ranges from the flat assertion in a few instances that Nixon is the innocent victim of conspiratorial plotters or at the least of hostile journalists and politicians who hated him and all he stood for, to the assortment of lesser suspicions summed up in a remark that recurs again and again among his former associates. Most of these people don't deny that Richard Nixon deserved impeachment, escaped it only by resigning on August 9, 1974, and would have been brought to trial in a common court if Gerald Ford had not pardoned him of any crimes that he may have committed while he was President. The remark is, "There are some things that have never been explained," and those who utter it seem to take a curious comfort from it. It has no bearing upon guilt or innocence. But it does suggest—to them anyhow—that the disgrace of their leader would not have been as complete and abject as it was, and that the pressures which drove him from office would not have been so cruelly displayed and applied, if unexplained forces and factors had not been at work.

The extent to which Richard Nixon in retirement at San Clemente subscribes to the devil theory is unknown. He has never attributed his downfall to his own and his confederates' misdeeds. In his announcement of his decision to resign on August 8, 1974; in his farewell moan to his staff on August 9; and in his introduction to his collected 1973 and 1974 presidential papers, he admitted nothing more than "mistakes and misjudgments" and blamed the need to resign upon the loss of congressional support. He recently accepted disbarment in New York rather than include in a letter of resignation from the New York bar an admission of Watergate guilt. In *Born Again*, Charles Colson's account of his White House service with Nixon and of his subsequent conversion to Christ—a conversion that I neither doubt nor deride after reading the book— Colson describes a talk with Nixon in the Lincoln Sitting Room in the executive mansion. Colson says he asked, "Mr. President, is our conversation being recorded?," and describes Nixon's reaction: "'What do you mean, recorded? Who would do that to us?' He sat upright in his chair, the smile gone, a flash of fear in his face. 'Would *they* do that?' he demanded."

The preeminent devil of the theory in most of its forms is the Central Intelligence Agency. An associated devil is Alexander Butterfield, a former air force colonel and college friend of Bob Haldeman who served as Haldeman's deputy from the start of the Nixon presidency in 1969 until April 1973. He disclosed the existence of the Nixon taping system to the Senate Watergate committee staff on July 13, 1973 and in public testimony on July 16. The CIA has been suspected, accused and exonerated of everything from planning, staffing and executing the Watergate burglary of the Democratic National Committee headquarters on June 17, 1972, to using its knowledge of that stupidity and of such White House misbehavior as wiretapping officials and journalists to bully and betray President Nixon and his associates in Watergate sin. Some Nixon people have never forgiven Butterfield for disclosing the taping system and then, in subsequent congressional testimony, discussing with obvious avidity and hostility Nixon quirks that suggested mental instability. Haldeman, Butterfield and others in the Nixon White House told me in early 1969 that Haldeman had persuaded Butterfield to interrupt a promising air force career and join the Nixon staff. In June of 1975, months after Butterfield had been accused on extremely flimsy grounds of having been a CIA plant in the White House, and after Chairman Frank Church of the Senate's special intelligence committee had said the committee found no evidence that this was true, Haldeman dealt with the related suspicions of Butterfield and the CIA in a syndicated newspaper series. Haldeman said:

"Alex originally approached the White House on his own initiative—not because I recruited him. He was soon to become an air force general. I have never understood why he insisted, against my advice, in dropping his commission. Or why he suddenly wanted to be part of the Nixon team. Was Butterfield a CIA agent? Maybe. I just don't know. In retrospect, I'm ambivalent as to whether the agency was out to get Nixon. I don't dismiss it as an impossibility. I do believe that there are a number of unanswered questions about the break-in at the Watergate. The agency had the capacity and perhaps, unknown to me, the motivation."

Ken Clawson, a last-ditch loyalist who was Nixon's last director of communications, told *The Washington Star* in the first interview he has given since he suffered a severe stroke: "Why in the world would Butterfield mention something about the internal taping system? I can only conclude that he was a CIA agent." Why being a CIA agent should have made Butterfield want to disclose the system he had supervised and hidden since 1971 is never explained. Other comments upon the Haldeman-Clawson suggestion and accusation are in order. Butterfield disclosed the taping system only in answer to a direct question under oath, first at a staff interrogation and then in public. It was a matter of truth or perjury. Butterfield did not "approach the White House"; he approached his friend Haldeman in New York, before the 1969 inauguration. Butterfield says and I believe that Haldeman insisted that he retire from active duty—

not "drop his commission"— in order to qualify for the only White House job then open to him. Butterfield's story that the possiblity of being for awhile at the top and center of national power excited and attracted him seems believable to me; it was true of Nixon assistants who have never been accused of being CIA plants.

John Ehrlichman's recently published novel, *The Company*, deals with the CIA as devil in a restrained fashion. His fictional CIA director, a character whose resemblance to former CIA Director Richard Helms is not even thinly disguised, uses his knowledge of Watergate doings and particularly of the bugging of officials and journalists to blackmail the incumbent President into protecting the director and a former President who died in office. Ehrlichman's director wanted concealment of his and the deceased President's part in a CIA murder that in effect sabotaged a Caribbean operation similar to John F. Kennedy's Bay of Pigs invasion of Cuba. There is a suggestion that Helms and CIA in his day knew about Watergate and the illegal surveillance associated with it. But *The Company* does not imply, as Haldeman does, that the CIA may have incited and entrapped Nixon and his Watergate companions.

A leading expert on the CIA and its possible involvement in Watergate is Senator Howard Baker of Tennessee, the ranking Republican on the Senate Watergate committee and the second-ranking Republican on Frank Church's special intelligence investigating committee. The press tended during both investigations to dismiss Baker as a Republican apologist. The fact is that he refused to be the stooge of the Nixon and Ford people. With the help of Fred Thompson, the chief minority counsel on the Watergate committee, and a small minority staff, Baker dug and dug into indications—notably the preponderance of past and present CIA people in the original Watergate burglary operation—that the CIA may somehow have been involved. His unproven suspicions that it was were set forth in an individual supplement to the Senate Watergate report and in *At That Point in Time*, Fred Thompson's fascinating book about the minority staff's role, frustrations and unresolved doubts.

As a member of the Church committee Baker dug again, deeper and more thoroughly than has been generally reported.

His conclusion, stated in an individual supplement to the committee report, must stand until further notice as the last and best word on the subject: "I wish to state my belief that the sum total of the evidence does not substantiate a conclusion that the CIA per se was involved in the range of events and circumstances known as Watergate. However, there was considerable evidence that for much of the post-Watergate period the CIA itself was uncertain of the ramifications of the various involvements, witting or otherwise, between members of the Watergate burglarly team and members of components of the Agency. . . .The investigation. . .produced a panoply of puzzlement. . . .An impartial evaluation. . .compels the conclusion that the CIA, as an institution, was not involved in the Watergate break-in." Devotees of the devil theory will note that this labored statement mostly covers the break-in and does not exclude involvement of CIA individuals in other Watergate chicanery.

Perhaps the most interesting and certainly the least noticed of the Baker minority staff's investigations during the Watergate inquiry was into evidence of Democratic foreknowledge of the break-in. I remember the hoots with which I and other reporters greeted then Vice President Spiro Agnew's suggestion at a 1972 campaign press conference that there was such foreknowledge. The story told by Fred Thompson in *At That Point in Time* involves columnist Jack Anderson, former Democratic chairman Larry O'Brien, various officials of the Democratic committee in O'Brien's time, the Nixon advertising operation in New York known as the November Group, a former Kennedy administration official and Manhattan publisher named William Haddad, and one Arthur James Woolston-Smith, who is described as a New Zealander based in New York with British, Canadian and US intelligence connections. Woolston-Smith is said to have heard about planning for the Watergate break-in and passed the information to Haddad and, through him, to Jack Anderson and Democratic committee officials. Two of Thompson's minority staff, Howard Liebengood and Michael Madigan, and James McCord, the retired CIA operative who led and botched the Watergate burglarly, figure in Thompson's sad summation: "Our exploration had covered many months and many witnesses. . . .We looked into an aspect of Watergate that had not been explored before—or since. Liebengood, Madigan and I all came to one conclusion: several people, including some at the Democratic headquarters, had advance knowledge of the Watergate break-in. An obvious effort had been made to conceal facts. . . .But did we have proof—proof beyond a reasonable doubt? The answer, reluctantly, was no. Additionally, for our suspicions to amount to anything conclusive, we would have to tie this advance knowledge to McCord, or someone else on the inside of the Watergate team, or at least to the plainclothesmen on duty the night of the break-in [who made the Watergate arrest]. We had no such link."

Nixon survivors in the Ford White House pay less heed to the devil theory than former associates elsewhere do. A midlevel survivor says he's never discussed the subject with his colleagues and adds: "I admire a lot of things Richard Nixon did, but I think he just blew it."

August 7 & 14, 1976

Alex Butterfield was not under oath when he disclosed the taping system to the Senate Watergate committee staff, but he knew that he would have to repeat what he said at the staff interrogation when he testified under oath to the committee. After Senator Baker read the foregoing article, he urged me to read an official transcript of the staff interrogation and predicted that I would conclude from it that Butterfield was primed and eager to reveal the taping system. No transcript of the staff interrogation was taken and a staff summary, prepared from memory several days later, is sealed by committee order. Donald Sanders, the Republican minority attorney who questioned Butterfield and elicited the tapes disclosure, told me that Butterfield seemed to him to answer with great reluctance when he was asked whether Nixon had a means of taping office conversations.

LXIII

GOP Chums

Kansas City

The most interesting observation heard during the early preliminaries to the Republican convention was that the continuing proliferation of binding party primaries may soon make national nominating conventions obsolete by committing so many delegates to vote for designated candidiates that there will be no point in assembling them to formalize an already accomplished result. It was a passing thought, thrown out so casually that it went officially unnoticed during debate on two proposals for rules changes that simultaneously promised initial tests of Ford and Reagan strength and dramatized the weakness of both candidates at this, the first Republican Convention since 1952 that has had to resolve a really serious contest for the presidential nomination.

A Reaganite proposed that candidates for the presidency be required to declare their choices for the vice presidency before nominations are voted. A Ford supporter proposed to require delegates to vote in accordance with state laws that mandate their choices on early ballots. Both suggestions were somewhat counter to assurances that Ford and Reagan leaders had given each other at deceptively chummy meetings in Washington.

The assurances were to the effect that neither side would use procedural and substantive disputes during preconvention committee sessions and at the convention to embarrass the other side and to manufacture indications of relative strength and weakness.

The first partisan to strain these understandings was John P. Sears, Ronald Reagan's national campaign director. By his account, Sears is the genius who principally persuaded Ronald Reagan to choose hitherto liberal Republican Senator Richard Schweiker of Pennsylvania for his vice presidential nominee and thereby shook and shocked the conservative true-believers who form the core of Reagan's national following. As things turned out, the choice probably damaged Schweiker more than it either hurt or helped Reagan. The spectacle of Senator Schweiker proclaiming from Mississippi to New England and finally in Kansas City that in accepting Reagan's invitation he had "changed constituencies" and felt free to reverse his previous positions on issues ranging from restrictions on labor unions to defense expenditure saddened liberal and conservative ideologues and must have finished him with many of his Pennsylvania followers. But the effect on Schweiker was the least of John Sears' concerns. His central concern, expressed in public taunts since the Schweiker choice was announced, was to goad President Ford into disclosing his preference for Vice President before the convention chooses between him and Reagan. Sears had said in Washington with bald frankness that he was taking the line he did because the President's choice, whoever it might be, was bound to offend some delegates and lose some convention votes. With an ineptitude that has become all too typical of the Ford White House, the President delayed a response to the Sears-Reagan pressure so long that he let himself appear to be supinely reacting to events instead of guiding them as Presidents are expected to do. It was finally said for him, in a singularly weak and indirect fashion, that he was going to do what he'd intended to do all the while—that is, recommend a Vice President to the convention "in the traditional way" after he was nominated for the presidency. His spokesman should have said but of course didn't, *if* he was nominated.

Sears' way of maintaining the pressure was evidence that Reagan was weaker in delegate strength than he and his spokesmen claimed to be in the preconvention week. Sears asked the Republican National Committee rules committee to recommend that the convention require "all persons seeking to be nominated for President" to announce their choices for the vice presidency "by 9 am on the day on which the nomination is to be held." He argued that his proposal "would give the delegates a necessary and much needed chance to . . . analyze the whole ticket," but everyone understood what he was up to. He knew that the RNC rules committee is stacked with Ford supporters and he expected his proposal to get the short shrift it got the next day. The convention rules committee to which the RNC committee would be reporting later in the week much more nearly reflected the close balance between Ford and Reagan delegates and could be expected to give Sears a kindlier hearing. After that there was the convention floor, where a proposal so blatantly aimed at embarrassing Ford could cause the eruption from Reagan zealots that Sears and other Reagan managers had undertaken to avoid. It's only fair to note, however, that this probably was not the purpose. The likely purpose, one of many indications both of the narrow gap between the candidates and of Reagan's desperate need for the few score additional votes that could give him the nomination, was to remind delegates wavering toward Ford that his unstated choice for the vice presidency could, when disclosed, make them wish they'd voted for Reagan.

The Sears-Reagan maneuver demonstrated the extraordinary circumstances that give this convention a positively weird tinge. A sizable proportion of Reagan's delegates clung to a hope that, despite his many disclaimers, he would demand or at least accept the vice presidential nomination if he were defeated for the presidential nomination. John Sears' proposal would, if adopted, make that unlikely event just about impossible because it would require Reagan to admit defeat and withdraw from the presidential race before Mr. Ford could conceivably propose him for the vice presidency. The Sears proposal amounted, in short, to confirmation that Reagan had been meaning it when he said over and over that he didn't want and would not accept the number two nomination. The Ford people were counting upon a decisive number of Reaganites in the convention rules committee and on the convention floor to vote against the proposal for this reason. Ben J. Clayburgh, the Republican national committeeman from North Dakota and a dedicated Reagan supporter, marched to a microphone during the RNC rules committee debate, tore up the text of the Sears proposal and said he opposed it because it would destroy the last possibility of a Ford-Reagan ticket. The Clayburgh performance indicated that the most passionate Reagan followers had abandoned all hope of forcing their idol upon Mr. Ford by a floor vote.

The Ford advocate who stirred the animals was Representative John Rhodes of Arizona, who was to be the convention's permanent chairman and was assumed to be on the President's list of vice presidential possibilities. Rhodes proposed that the convention require him as chairman to make delegates from the states (variously estimated at 19 to 22) that by law command them to vote on early ballots in accordance with primary, caucus or state convention dictates act in strict accordance with those laws rather than follow individual or factional preferences. The RNC rules committee adopted Rhodes' proposal and rejected fervent Reagan objections with brutal speed. Here again, however, everyone understood that the serious battles would occur in the convention rules committee and possibly on the convention floor. The meaningful question was why Rhodes proposed and Ford advocates fiercely defended the new authority and why Reagan's spokesmen fiercely opposed it.

The reason was a Ford fear and a Reagan hope that a normally negligible few of 324 delegates legally committed to the President from 16 states would defy their often vague state laws and vote according to their personal preferences for Reagan or, more likely, simply abstain from voting on the first or second ballots. The race for first-ballot nomination was so close that the failure of a few such delegates to vote could deprive the President of the 1130 necessary for nomination and give Reagan a shot at it on a second ballot. Rhodes wanted a rule that would enable him as permanent chairman to void abstentions for technical violations of state laws by having

delegation votes recorded in strict compliance with the laws rather than as the votes were announced from the floor by recalcitrant individuals or leaders. His need for that authority and the Reagan forces' evident though denied intention to do Gerald Ford in by abstention if all other means failed were sorry measures of the depths to which an incumbent President and his rival had fallen.

Much of the national press, hungry as usual for discord, interpreted a flare-up in the convention platform committee as a sign of formidable Reagan strength. It was evidence that the Ford managers couldn't get by with the domination that Richard Nixon's people imposed upon the 1968 and 1972 conventions. But it was more a sign of the times, and of initially poor command and organization in the Ford camp, than of Reagan might. Committee members rebelled, 49 to 36, against automatic submission to the appointment of subcommittee chairmen and chairwomen by the platform chairman, Governor Robert D. Ray of Iowa. Ray, a Ford supporter, was among those who had been notified that they might be recommended for the vice presidency. The seven subcommittees, authorized after the rebellion to choose their own chairpersons (there is no escaping this horrid perversion), rejected a Ray appointee, Representative Silvio Conte of Massachusetts, and replaced him at the head of the human rights subcommittee with Charles Pickering of Mississippi, a Reagan supporter who is regarded by Ford people as a reasonable fellow. This change and the selection of another Reagan supporter, Dorothy Zumwalt of Oklahoma, for vice chairwoman increased the chances that abortion and rights for women planks more acceptable to Reagan than to Ford might be adopted. But the whole business was less significant than the restive suspicion, and the manifest refusal to bow to the prospect, that the platform was actually being written by hidden Ford and Reagan manipulators. Governor Ray assured the members that it wasn't true and the Ford managers of the platform operation were anxious to have it believed that there was no draft at all.

There was a draft, in two parts. The Ford and Reagan managers between them succeeded for a remarkably long time in concealing the mechanics of the preliminary platform production. Two of the brighter members of the Ford and Reagan entourages, Michael Raoul-Duval at the White House and a former Nixon assistant, Martin Anderson, for Reagan, supervised the supply and coordination of Ford and Reagan views of what should go into the platform. Richard V. Allen, who was Richard Nixon's foreign policy adviser in the 1968 campaign and served briefly and unhappily on the NSC staff under Henry Kissinger, was recruited to draft the foreign policy and national security sections. It was a shrewd choice: Allen, now a consultant to Japanese and other foreign firms, is at once a capable writer and thinker and a hard-nosed anti-Communist who can't have many differences with Ronald Reagan. John P. Meagher (pronounced *may-harr*), chief minority counsel of the House Ways and Means Committee, drafted the basic domestic sections. Stephen Hess, a Brookings Institution fellow and author of political histories, who worked at the Nixon White House under Pat Moynihan, edited and melded the Allen and Meagher drafts. They were submitted to Governor Ray and to the relevant platform subcommittees, and as intended and expected, were revised to a modest extent in the final process.

What is to be remembered is the quiet collaboration between the Ford and Reagan forces. The common aim was to avoid conflict over issues that could fatally divide the party during the election campaign, and in the preliminary phase it was largely attained. Reagan assistant Peter Hannaford approved Allen's draft of a plank on the controversial Panama Canal issue, which said that the US must preserve and protect its "fundamental interest" in the Canal but stopped short of Ronald Reagan's prior insistence that US sovereignty over the Panama Canal Zone be preserved "in perpetuity." Such militants as Senator Jesse Helms of North Carolina and Representative Philip Crane of Illinois balked at this and similar compromises that seemed to them to be surrenders of conservative principle and forced through a good many changes, mostly minor. It was plain on the eve of the convention that Reagan's extremist followers were insisting that he not give in to his better nature. In their cutest maneuver, they appeared to have put Senator James Buckley of New York up to his at least temporary show of availability for the presidential nomination, thus threatening to throw it to a

second or later ballot and increase Reagan's chances of defeating
Ford. Jesse Helms expressed their mood when he described the
kind of hard-rock platform they wanted: "If we win with it,
great! If we lose with it, good!"

August 21 & 28, 1976

LXIV

Why Dole

Kansas City

Gerald Ford's choice of Senator Robert Dole of Kansas to be the Republican candidate for the vice presidency and the circumstances that led to the choice told a great deal about the President, about the Republican party as it was reflected at this convention, and about the nature and limits of the power that Ronald Reagan and Reagan Republicans exerted here.

None of the explanations of the choice that I have read and heard go to the central cause. The central cause was Mr. Ford's deeply personal need for success in Kansas City. His defeat of Ronald Reagan for the presidential nomination by 57 more votes than the necessary minimum of 1130 provided only the beginning, and a marred beginning at that, of the success that was so essential to him and to his confidence in himself. A rejection of his choice for the vice presidency or substantial opposition to it would have demolished the flimsy triumph of his own nomination with a nigh unbearable humiliation, not to mention the certainty that it would have eliminated whatever chance there was that the Ford ticket might prevail over the Carter ticket on November 2.

There is a factual basis for the foregoing analysis, which

amounts to an argument that personal victory and vindication in Kansas City were more important to Mr. Ford than Republican victory in the general election. At an airport campaign stop in Michigan, soon after the President won the New Hampshire Republican primary with a majority of less than one percent, White House Counsellor John Marsh, one of Mr. Ford's staff politicians, urged me to note and remember something Mr. Ford had said at a rally that morning. He had said in a tone of immense pride that the New Hampshire result proved for the first time that he could win an election somewhere other than in his home city and congressional district of Grand Rapids. Marsh said then, and others on the Ford staff said later, that the thin win in New Hampshire did wonders for the President's confidence. This was a way of saying, though none of his people put it so explicitly, that Gerald Ford was troubled, as many others were, by a nagging awareness that he had never proved himself as a candidate for national or even state-wide office. His need to do so was surely among the factors, along with the magic of the office to which he had risen by default, that drove him to renege on a promise he made when he was up for confirmation as the nation's first appointed Vice President. He promised never to seek election to the presidency. In the primary and pre-convention season, nomination was the goal and the test of success or failure, and Mr. Ford went after it with a single-minded concentration that bothered some of his advisers. Melvin Laird, for one, maintained to reporters and presumably to the President that Mr. Ford ought to campaign always as if he were running for the presidency and regard the nomination as an essential but nevertheless secondary way-stop. Instead, he let Ronald Reagan goad and frighten him into petty epithets and retorts that demeaned his office and did him no good. Mr. Ford took the advice eventually, but not before the departure from his normally even campaign style demonstrated the peculiarly personal importance that winning the nomination had for him and the panicky alarm that any threat to the winning of it aroused in him.

It of course was the presence and power of Ronald Reagan and his followers, who mustered close to half of the 2259 delegate votes that haunted and harassed the President. The Reagan forces lacked the votes to prevail on gut issues, including the nomination of their man. But their hard, unqualified ideological conservatism, going in many instances beyond the philosophy exemplified by Reagan, appealed to a sufficient proportion of delegates who were formally committed to Ford to make "the Reagan vote" a real and continuous threat. In this sense it may be said that at the final showdown over the vice presidential nomination Reagan was in a position to "veto" the President's choice of anyone other than himself or someone he approved. Questions put by reporters to White House staff chief Richard Cheney and other Ford spokesmen after the choice of Dole was announced indicated a suspicion that Reagan had done exactly this. The answer was that he had not and it was technically correct. The process that led to the choice and acceptance of Senator Dole involved much more than the vice presidential issue. It cut across the spectrum of convention concerns.

The most revealing part of the process was the disposal of the dispute over what to put in and exclude from the foreign policy and national security section of the Republican platform. Two interested parties, Ronald Reagan and Jimmy Carter, later exaggerated and distorted the outcome of these disputes. In a TV interview broadcast from his convention box on the night of Dole's nomination and of the Dole and Ford acceptance speeches, and then in a soupy appearance at the President's invitation with Ford and Dole on the rostrum, Reagan spoke of the platform as if it were his own and as if at his instance it constituted a clarion call to battle between the forces of freedom and the forces of tyranny. Carter said at a press conference in Plains that every dispute over the Republican platform resulted in a triumph for Reagan. The implication was that the finished document was a compendium of Reagan reaction. What happened was more subtle and more interesting than Reagan or Carter suggested.

The platform negotiations generally and the foreign policy negotiations in particular continued the quiet collaboration between the Ford and Reagan high commands that was described in my last report. Martin Anderson, acting for Reagan at the senior staff level, and Ford assistant Mike Raoul-Duval (Mike Duval for short) engineered a series of accommodations that enabled each faction to emerge with pride intact and with a prospect of at least minimal party unity in the election campaign.

Two examples will suffice. Reagan extremists proposed a plank that would have repudiated the Ford administration's efforts—efforts that were begun under Lyndon Johnson in 1964—to negotiate a decent relinquishment of sovereignty over the Panama Canal Zone to the Republic of Panama. The purpose is to remove a potential source of murderous friction between the US and all of Latin America while protecting fundamental US interests in the canal and preserving effective US control of it. Administration advocates in the foreign policy subcommittee and in the main platform committee proposed and the Reagan command persuaded Reagan kooks to accept a compromise that beefs up the assertion of American determination with half-a-dozen superfluous verbs and catered to Reaganite chauvinism without repudiating Gerald Ford and Henry Kissinger.

The second example concerns the opening to Communist China that Richard Nixon and Kissinger achieved in 1972 and that both Reagan and Jimmy Carter have praised. Since Kissinger disclosed the agreement to work toward "normalization" of relations between the US and mainland China, in the Shanghai Communique of February 1972, neither he nor any other responsible US spokesman has tried to minimize or conceal the certainty that the establishment of full diplomatic relations with the Peking government would require an end of formal diplomatic relations with the "Republic of China" on Taiwan. The initial hope at the State Department that it might be possible to retain the mutual defense treaty that Dwight D. Eisenhower and Chiang Kai-shek agreed upon in the 1950s and still normalize diplomatic relations with Peking has waned. But it remains a bare possibility and it was in this dimming hope that the Ford negotiators in Kansas City, necessarily with the assent of the President and Kissinger, accepted Reaganite platform language that seemed to commit a Republican President to retention at any cost of the pledge to defend Taiwan against

Communist Chinese attack. Two factors diminished the appearance of concession to the Reagan view. Language insisting upon retention of diplomatic relations with Taiwan—a condition that Peking would never accept—was dropped from the amended plank. It may also be argued, with some stretching of the adopted language, that the China passage promises only adherence to the mutual defense treaty while it is in effect and does not advocate indefinite maintenance of the treaty.

The collaboration was widely thought to have collapsed, but did not, with the submission of Reagan's "morality in foreign policy" amendment to the prologue—*not the substance*—of the foreign policy and national security section. Reagan asked the convention to adopt it as "a clear, forthright expression of principles America must live by" and used it mightily to further the impression that in the end the platform was more his than Gerald Ford's. Because it indeed shook up the Ford forces and also because it would be remembered as a diabolically clever example of Reaganist distortion, the plank's core lines are quoted here: "The goal of Republican foreign policy is the achievement of liberty under law and a just and lasting peace in the world . . . We recognize and commend that great beacon of human courage and morality, Alexander Solzhenitsyn, for his compelling message that we must face the world with no illusions about the nature of tyranny . . . In pursuing *détente* we must not grant unilateral favors with only the hope of getting future favors in return. Agreements that are negotiated, such as the one signed in Helsinki, must not take from those who do not have freedom the hope of one day getting it. Finally, we are firmly committed to a foreign policy in which secret agreements, hidden from our people, will have no part."

Commentators rightly interpreted the Reagan amendment as an attack upon key elements of Ford-Kissinger policy and the conduct of that policy. The targets ranged from the President's failure to invite Solzhenitsyn to the White House last year to the notion that agreements negotiated in secret are by definition "secret agreements." As Ronald Reagan has acknowledged, but usually neglects to say, secrecy during negotiations is essential for the development of useful agreements, and in any case they become public when they are

completed. How then could the Ford decision to accept inclusion
of the Reagan language without resistance be anything but an
outright surrender to Reagan? The answer was so simple that it
was all but universally overlooked. Senator Jesse Helms of
North Carolina, a fervent North Carolina professor named John
East, Congressman Philip Crane of Illinois and numerous other
Reagan kooks had concocted no less than 22 platform
amendments that would have explicitly and totally repudiated
every major aspect of Ford-Kissinger—which is to say
Republican administration—foreign policy. Although these
kookeries never got beyond furtive handouts to reporters,
many of the proposals would have been adopted if they had
been submitted to the convention. It must be concluded that
Helms, East, Crane and associated knuckleheads got orders to

LURIE'S OPINION

"WELCOME ABOARD, SENATOR DOLE!"

stop their dangerous nonsense and settle for the indictment by implication that was embodied in the morality plank.

Acceptance of the Reagan plank came hard to Mr. Ford and his advisers. The President, reacting initially on the basis of what he was told about it, rejected it out of hand. When he read the language he saw that it implied much, said very little, and specifically attacked nothing. Henry Kissinger and Brent Scowcroft, the President's assistant for national security affairs, sent word from Washington to Kansas City that the Reagan amendment was outrageous and must be rejected. In Kansas City Vice President Rockefeller took the same view until the President brought him around to a more relaxed position.

On the night that the Reagan proposal was submitted to the convention, the Ford forces narrowly defeated a procedural amendment—the primary test of Reagan's strength—that would have required Mr. Ford to name his choice for the vice presidency before the convention nominated its candidate for President. While this amendment was debated and voted upon, a group of Ford advisers met in the Skylight Lounge, a secluded eyrie atop the huge Kemper Auditorium where the convention did its business and perpetrated the traditional inanities. Mike Duval periodically reported the group's deliberations to Richard Cheney and through him to the President at the Crown Center Hotel. The President had agreed before the meeting that a decision about the Reagan plank should be deferred until the procedural amendment was voted up or down. Had the convention required the President to name his vice presidential choice before he wanted to, he and his advisers in the Skylight Lounge almost certainly would have decided to force the Reagan plank to a vote in the forlorn hope that the result would offset the humiliation of defeat on the procedural issue. The Skylight group included Senators John Tower of Texas, Hugh Scott of Pennsylvania, and the President's convention floor manager, Sen. Robert Griffin of Michigan. Two former White House assistants who were in Kansas City as unofficial advisers, Bryce Harlow and Dean Burch, and the President's chief delegate hunter and counter, James Baker, also participated.

What made this occasion worth recording were the tenor of

the deliberations and the role of Nelson Rockefeller. One of the problems with the Reagan amendment was the realization that speakers against it would have to say that its pious generalizations concealed denunciations of Kissinger's secrecy, of the Helsinki agreement, and of Ford-Kissinger dealings with the Soviet Union. Inasmuch as administration spokesmen were berating the press for interpreting the Reagan amendment in just this way, making the same argument as a reason for voting against it would have been embarrassing and probably futile.

A summons of Rockefeller to the meeting midway in the deliberations coincided with an imbroglio on the convention floor. Without getting into the details of that murky episode, it's enough to say that an angry Reagan delegate ripped out one of the New York delegation's floor telephones just as Duval was trying to get word to Rockefeller to come up to the lounge. When he was finally reached through an alternate line and departed in response to Duval's summons, he appeared to reporters and to millions watching on TV to have been ejected as a result of the telephone fracas. James M. Perry wrote in *The National Observer* that "people have been tossed out of saloons in downtown Utica, New York, with more style."

Soon after Rockefeller arrived in the Skylight Lounge, the procedural amendment was defeated. Duval reported to Cheney, and Cheney reported to the President, the consensus that there was no point in rubbing Reagan noses in the dirt and, furthermore, that the implied criticism in the Reagan morality plank was not worth another floor fight. Mr. Ford called Rockefeller to the phone and dictated a statement to him. The gist was that the Reagan plank merely stated the bases of administration policy and therefore was acceptable. Mr. Ford instructed Rockefeller to have Senator Roman Hruska, who was on the convention rostrum, read the statement to the delegates. Hruska did and the Reagan amendment was adopted by voice vote.

What did all that have to do with the selection of Robert Dole? The answer is that it had everything to do with the selection. Had the recommendation of the Skylight Lounge advisers and the decision of the President been to force the morality plank to a floor vote, it would have been an act of desperation. It would have been an act undertaken with the fear that Reagan's strength and the manifest hunger of many Ford delegates for the sort of bold and simplistic assertion of national purpose and pride that Reagan offered would have brought defeat that could affect the nomination vote.

The Ford performance throughout the platform and rules exercises was conditioned by fears of that sort, and the fears persisted after the President was nominated. After Mr. Ford announced his choice of Senator Dole, several reasons for it were advanced: Bob Dole is witty, he's a campaign slasher, he's from a cornbelt state and popular with farmers who still resent the temporary Ford embargo on grain sales to the Soviet Union. None of these reasons is good enough to explain the rejection of such possibilities as John Connally, Sen. Howard Baker of Tennessee, Elliot Richardson and William Ruckelshaus. A *New York Times* reporter who interviewed Reagan after it was all over wrote that Reagan had indicated a preference for Dole in a talk with the President. According to Richard Cheney, the President first indicated *his* preference for Dole after that talk. It was not, I'm sure, that the President let Ronald Reagan dictate the choice or veto some other choice in any explicit way. It was simply that there would be no risk of trouble at the convention from restive Reagan delegates, trouble that could impair or even wreck the impression of success in Kansas City, if Reagan had approved of the choice. It wasn't much of a reason for the choice. But then Robert Dole is not much of a candidate for the vice presidency.

September 4, 1976

———

After the foregoing was written, I was told variously that Rockefeller persuaded first Ford and then Kissinger to relax and accept the Reagan morality gunk, and that Duval and Cheney persuaded Ford to instruct Rockefeller to accept it and tell Kissinger that he had to accept it. The gut is that Ford, Rockefeller and Kissinger accepted a repellent and insulting platform passage.

LXV

Glimpses of Jimmy

When President Ford went to Colorado from Kansas City to savor his narrowly won nomination and to plan his leisurely campaign for election, I broke away for a fortnight's observation of the man who seems likely to be the next occupant of the White House. Here then are some impressions of Jimmy Carter, to be followed in my next report with excerpts from interviews with relatives and friends who may be assumed to know who Jimmy is and what makes Jimmy run.

The release of Carter's 1975 federal income tax return while I was in Plains interested me for a reason that had nothing to do with the fact that, largely because of a credit for investment in the family peanut shelling plant, he and his wife paid only $17,484.14 in tax on a gross joint income of $136,138.92. Carter caught practically none of the hell from the press that Ronald Reagan and Richard Nixon caught for comparably low taxes on comparable incomes. But the point of interest here goes back to a prejudice acquired during boyhood and early manhood in Mississippi and the South. The prejudice is against southern politicians who parade their nicknames and their religion. Inquiry establishes that Carter has been "Jimmy" since infancy and didn't adopt the nickname for political purposes. Inquiry also convinces me that he really is a devout "born again" Baptist Christian and does not play on the fact for political gain. Nevertheless, I was amused and pleased to see that Carter identified himself on his tax return as "James E. Carter" and on an accompanying financial statement as James E. Carter, Jr. He has been reported to get downright testy when other people drop the "Jimmy" and use his proper name. His father, who died in 1953, preferred to be known as "Earl." The James Earl Carter Memorial Library at Georgia Southwestern College in nearby Americus honors him and also encourages some of Carter's devoted but not wholly blinded friends in Americus to agree that he overdoes the Jimmy bit.

For a candidate who promises as his first order of presidential business to reform the federal bureaucracy, Carter relies upon and tolerates a strangely chaotic staff situation at his Atlanta headquarters. Reporters who have covered the Carter campaign for months attribute part of his success to the astute planning and management of a few young Georgians, notably among them campaign director Hamilton Jordan (pronounced jerden) and press secretary Jody Powell. Without presuming to quarrel with that judgment on the basis of a short look, I simply note the air of frantic rush that pervades the headquarters offices. During my visit, it caused two senior newcomers to wonder aloud whether there wasn't an awful lot of aimless wheel-spinning around them. That may be partly because since Carter's nomination the staff in Atlanta and elsewhere has expanded from some 250 to nearly 700 people. Today Powell's press staff is pretty much as it was during the leaner pre-convention time. Powell doubtless deserves his rating with most of the journalists who deal with him as one of the best in the business. The press operation under him, however, is among the worst I've encountered. This is partly because it's conducted by too few overworked amateurs. The main and obvious reason is that Carter confides only in Powell and Powell doesn't confide in anybody. He's too busy with other responsibilities to do an adequate informational job and his assistants, seldom or never knowing anything worth knowing, naturally can't do it for him.

The story behind Carter's "pardon-yes; amnesty-no" statement and the storm of boos it aroused during a speech to an American Legion convention in Seattle on August 24 indicates that Carter's communication with his staff and communication within the staff are less than perfect. Several assistants who participated in researching and preparing the speech said afterward that the pardon *vs* amnesty reference to Vietnam era draft dodgers and deserters was almost an afterthought and was never intended either to bring on the confrontation it did or to overshadow the substantive proposals for defense economies, military pension improvements and the like that took up more words and time than the pardon passage did. These assistants evidently didn't know that the passage in question was designed to bring on the confrontation that it caused. It put Carter on camera in the guise of a principled and courageous politician defying his detractors. A lot of Carter's personal care and thought went into these words: "I do not favor a blanket amnesty, but for those who violated selective service laws, (*e.g.*, draft evaders) I intend to grant a blanket pardon. To me, there is a difference. Amnesty means that what you did is right. A pardon means that what you did—right or wrong—is forgiven. So, pardon—yes; amnesty—no." Carter had been saying much the same thing for months. It was the hostile reaction, not the statement, that made the news as he must have known it would. At a press conference that immediately preceded the address, he said he expected many in his Legion audience to disapprove of the promise of a blanket pardon for evaders. Unknown to the assistants previously mentioned, he said to another assistant working on the speech: "I want a confrontation with that organization." He got it.

An unqualified promise to an Iowa farm audience that he as President would never embargo grain and other food exports illustrated a tendency to overstatement and got Carter into a revealing brush with reporters in Plains. The affair also dramatized the failure of both Carter and Ford propagandists to exploit mistakes of each candidate. Carter had said in his acceptance speech and on other occasions that one of his ways of deterring or punishing hostile foreign action would be a total suspension of trade with offending nations. This had to include embargoes on grain and other food exports of the kind for which Mr. Ford had been severely criticized in the midwestern grain belt. Carter's implied position could have been turned against him with important effect, but Ford spokesmen never had the wit to do it before Carter retreated. In the primary and pre-convention season, Mr. Ford never went beyond saying even in the sensitive Midwest that he did not foresee having to impose any more embargoes on exports. Only in his acceptance speech in Kansas City did he abandon caution and flatly promise "no more embargoes." After Carter committed the same indiscretion in Iowa, he and his people could have argued but didn't that at worst he'd been no sillier than Ford had been. At a press conference in Plains, he took a heavy and (I thought) excessive drubbing from reporters on this score and on his similarly overstated denunciations of Ford vetoes. He had to admit that he might have vetoed some of those bills. The interesting thing to me, standing in front of him on the Plains railway station platform, was the sight of his rather prissy mouth tightening and of the hard glint that came into his surprisingly small blue eyes. A long-time associate said later that a short while ago Carter probably would have blown his top and denounced the reporters for taking advantage of fair answers to unfair questions. Now he's learning to control that Carter smile and to suppress the anger that what he considers to be unjustified questioning of his wisdom and motives arouses in him.

On balance, being near but never with him (excepting a brief introductory conversation) for two weeks dispelled my anxieties about a Carter presidency. Those anxieties were rooted in the doubts that many southerners of my generation have about southern politicians on the national stage (I grew up in red-neck northern Mississippi before Carter was born). He came across as a man of grace, of great inner control, a man blessed with a loving family and with friends and associates who love him in the sense that John Kennedy was loved. Much else about Carter is remindful of Kennedy. Despite his years in Congress and careful preparation for the presidency, Kennedy came to the White House with much to learn about the demands of the presidency. So would Carter. Watching him learn on the job will be fascinating, if Jimmy gets there.

September 18, 1976

LXVI

Carter Talk

The people who talk about Jimmy Carter in the following excerpts from interviews conducted during the first week of September, in Plains and in nearby Americus, Georgia, have these claims to know something about him:

Billy Carter is Jimmy's younger brother. **Gloria Spann** is the older of two sisters. Her younger sister, Ruth Carter Stapleton, lives in Fayetteville, North Carolina, and practices what she calls "inner healing" throughout the world. **Alton Carter**, aged 88, is by seniority the head of the family and the brother of Jimmy Carter's late father, James Earl Carter. **Hugh Carter**, one of Alton's two sons, was elected to Jimmy's seat in the Georgia senate in 1966, has been Jimmy's friend since boyhood, and watches the home front in South Georgia for him now. Hugh breeds and sells worms and, with his father, runs an antiques store in Plains. **Mary Anne Thomas** is a friend who lives in the Sumter County seat, Americus. Her former husband, Russell, who is mentioned, is a peanut farmer and a friend of Jimmy Carter. **Bruce Edwards**, aged 29, has been the pastor of the Plains Baptist Church since January 1975.

"Jimmy's book" is his *Why Not the Best?*, a tract that his best friends wouldn't call an autobiography.

Billy Carter

Q: You've known your brother Jimmy all your life. What makes him tick?

Billy: I'm 13 years younger than Jimmy and I didn't really know Jimmy until I was about four years old. He came back to Plains *(from the Navy)* in the fall of 1953 and I left in the spring of '55 *(for the Marines, jobs in Atlanta, etc.)* and I didn't come back here to stay until the spring of '63. I went to Emory *(a Methodist college in Atlanta)* for two and a half years, flunked out, I was a career freshman, you might say. Never passed anything. Now about Jimmy. The family as a whole, I'd say we're all individuals. Me and Jimmy are extremely close but we're far apart, too. We all have a bad habit which I do, my Mother does, Jimmy does. We say what we damn please, regardless of whether anybody agrees with us or not. And Jimmy, I'm not saying this because he's my brother, but Jimmy's the smartest human being I've ever known. I say, from both learning and the ability to learn, and to change. He can take a subject he knows absolutely nothing about and by talking to people and by reading and by breaking down what he's heard, in a very short period he knows as much about it as anybody. I know more about peanuts than Jimmy does, but I won't let him know that because in a couple of days he'd know more than I do about peanuts.

Q. Was it the raising he got that makes him tick, or something born in him?

A: Partly raising, partly something born.

Q: I assume you got essentially the same raising?

A: No, mine was different. I was 13 years younger, like I say, and I was raised almost as the only child. It's kind of hard to be the first child in a family, I guess, and I know with my own kids it's a lot better to be the baby than to be the oldest. *(Note: Ruth Carter Stapleton, the younger sister, says somewhat the same thing in her book,* The Gift of Inner Healing: *"My father had loved me very deeply. . . .I had been raised to believe that I was God's gift to the world, the most beautiful child ever born." Discovering that she wasn't contributed to the agony that contributed to the spiritual experience that, according to Gloria Spann, led to Jimmy's being "born again." It's evident that Jimmy as the first born had a sterner upbringing than his brother and younger sister did, though not as stern a raising as he remembers now.)*

Q: Can he be hard to get along with? Some of the reporters who've covered him for months suspect that in private he can be a real mean son-of-a-bitch.

A: Not with me, no. I haven't seen him change. I went over there this morning *(to the Jimmy Carters' home in Plains)* and talked to him for an hour and a half, I guess.

Q: Does he discuss politics with you or, politics aside, what he's doing and whether you think he's doing well?

A: Believe it or not, I never discuss politics with Jimmy. The only thing we discussed this morning, actually, was our peanut program, which he's interested in. I keep up with it and it's my business to lean back and explain things to him. *(Note: "Our peanut program" was a euphemism for a terrific row between southwest Georgia peanut shellers, including the Carters, and Agriculture Secretary Earl Butz over government support levels for peanuts. A recent reversal of position by Butz could cost the Carters as shellers many thousands of dollars this year and benefit the Carters as growers by a few thousand dollars. Jimmy has said he'll divest himself of his peanut shelling interest if he's elected. He hopes to avoid total divorcement from his land.)*

Q: What do you think of your brother's book?

A: I never have read it. I read the rough draft. I don't know what I did with it, I gave it to somebody. My sister has written a couple of books and I've never read them, either. Ruth's a preacher of some kind I never have quite understood. I have never heard Ruth talk or preach and I'm not sure what her religion is. I think she's still a Baptist, but her personal religion is not an organized religion. As long as she believes in what she's doing, it suits her and it suits me.

Q: Your brother's religion and his definition of his religious faith—is it all genuine or is some of it put on for political reasons?

A: In my opinion, it's all genuine. I'm not religious at all, I don't go to church. Jimmy's religion, it's a private thing. You're from Mississippi, you know what I'm talking about. His religion first came out when some of these Yankee reporters came down here and went to a Baptist church. If you're a reporter in Plains on a weekend, you ain't got a damn thing to write about but going to church on Sunday. They didn't understand it. I think a lot of them writing the religious thing thought that southern Baptists were Holy Rollers.

Q: Were your father and your mother religious in the sense that Jimmy is?

A: No, sir. I was never made to go to church. I went to Sunday school until I was 14 or 15, usually by choice and when I didn't want to go was the only time I ever got spanked. But I was never made to go and Jimmy has never forced it on his children.

Q: What place do you think Jimmy's wife, Mrs. Rosalynn Carter, has had in his life and in his career and his ascent? Has she had a good deal to do with it?

A: I think she has. I think they have a perfect marriage. He discusses things with her. She works hard as hell, she campaigns full time, all the time. She gets paid for it, but not enough. She told me the other day, I forget the exact figure she asked for, but he cut her down to $75 a week, I think.

Q: People at his Atlanta headquarters tell me she has strong views on how to run the campaign and when she doesn't like what they are doing or what he's doing, she'll tell them so and tell him so. That check with your impression of her?

A: Yes, sir. She has strong views. She and me are in good situations. There are two of us left, me and her both, who can still tell Jimmy to go to hell and get by with it. Not in those words, of course, but you know what I mean. We can be loyal to Jimmy and still tell him when he's wrong.

Q: I hear that you ran for Mayor of Plains two years ago and lost by only four votes. That so?

A: Yes, sir, by something like that.

Q: How could you have lost in Plains? How could any Carter have lost in Plains, is what I'm trying to ask?

A: (laughing): Well, if you don't campaign and everybody else goes to church on Sunday morning and you ride around laughing and joking and drinking beer with your friends and everybody sees it and you don't try to hide it, you don't get elected mayor of Plains, Jawjuh.

Q: Seriously, was it a setback to you and the family for you to run and lose?

A: No sir, it was not. It really made no difference whatsoever. From what I hear, five people will probably be running this December—our local elections come every two years, you know—and I'll probably run again.

Gloria Spann

Q: What sort of family is the Carter family?

A: My sister Ruth has her own goals. I have my own goals. Jimmy has his. And Billy has his. My mother lives her own independent life. We don't try to follow each other. We don't compete with each other. What we really compete on is, who can be the most independent and who can go after their own goals. People ask me, do you ever get jealous? Your brother is going to the White House and don't you want to go? And I say, no, I don't want to go. Ruth knows what she wants. Billy knows what he wants. Jimmy knows what he wants. And my mother knows what she wants. And we all go after it.

Q. To what extent did your mother's influence or your father's influence shape Jimmy, make him what he is?

A: My father died in 1953, so he was with us through high school. The main thing is, he taught us to play.

Q. To play?

A: To play. He saw to it that we had every piece of athletic equipment we needed to be entertained in a little country house. Jimmy was taught to hunt with his father. There was a pond we could go swimming in. There was a tennis court—we played tennis. There was a pool table—we shot pool. There was always some form of recreation provided. We were never bored on the farm. I don't think Jimmy worked quite as hard as he says in the book *(giggling)*. And we weren't quite as poor as he says we were in the book. We always had plenty of clothing and food, as much as anybody and more than a lot of people had. We had ponies to ride. We had more than the most affluent have now. So how could we ever realize that we were poor? It really was a very good life. And then when we were teenagers my father built a house, the Pond House, for us to have a place to go. It was there with all the newest records, the pool table, the ping pong table, and it was open to us and our friends when we got to high school age so we had a place to go, to have our dances. It had two bedrooms, a bath, a kitchen. It could have been lived in, but we always used it for a playhouse. *(Note: The playhouse was built in the late 1930s and burned in 1960. It was replaced by the present Pond House where Miz Lillian Carter, the mother, usually lives in the summer and where Jimmy Carter put up visiting notables in 1976.)*

Q: When you were children, did you have to go to church?

A: My mother was a Methodist, but she joined the Baptist church when she married Daddy. When we were little, she didn't go to church. She stayed home on Sunday mornings. I think that was considered Mother's time to be to herself, away from us. Daddy took us to Sunday school.

We had to go to Sunday school, and we had to go to church during the revivals. But we didn't go very much to the regular services, the preaching. Daddy *loved* Sunday school and the Sunday school teaching. They always had very good teachers for the adult men and he really liked it. But he didn't care for the sermons. He went up town and met his friends at the drug store or at a filling station where they hung out and they had cokes and talked until after church. Sometimes he would let us go with him in the car and we would sit there in the car and watch them and that was fun, that was really fun *(giggling)*. And then we'd all go home after church was out and have Sunday dinner. That was a tradition. Daddy taught Sunday school when he was young, but when we were growing up he didn't take much part in church affairs. And he never cared to be a deacon. He never cared to hide the fact that he liked to take a drink. He didn't think a deacon should do those things and he wouldn't quit. And that's the truth. But don't misunderstand. He didn't get drunk, I never saw Daddy drunk.

Q: Was there something in the childhood years that set your brother Jimmy off from the rest of you; that made him as active in the church as he says he is and made his religion as important to him as he says it is?

A: Not in our childhood. That came later. There suddenly came a time in all of our lives when we needed something more than we had gotten from church or Sunday school or memorizing Bible verses, studying, all that. It was maturing. It was acceptance that, if there were a God, it was our God. If there is a God, it's got to be better than this and if there's not, why am I wasting all this time? And so we, each in our own individual way, have accepted and found out, there IS a God. There really is.

Q: Billy found that out?

A: (very softly): I don't know.

Q: He says he has no interest in religion, says he never goes to church. That right?

A: (giggling again, happy again): Beely's funny!

Q: What do you mean, funny? He's an amusing man, but he's also a very interesting man. You agree?

A: Yes, I do. Beely is just Beely!

Q: What do you think inculcated that belief in your brother Jimmy, that intensity of belief, that he says he has?

A: If you really want to know the truth, I can tell you in a minute.

Q: I want to know.

A: You see, Ruth had this experience in 1959. The best I can explain that experience is, it comes in awareness that God is with you. It changed her life, it changed my whole life. At different times Ruth discussed this with Jimmy. It took several years for him to realize how much it had changed her life, to have this freedom and certainty. In 1966, when Jimmy lost the election for governor, the bottom fell out of his life. He realized that he needed another foundation, a stronger foundation, for his life. He talked with me some, he talked with Ruth some. I believe it was at this time that he made his decision to go his way with God, and he did.

Q: After the defeat in 1966?

A: After the 1966 election. He's never said this, never declared it publicly. But there is no denying it. I think I'm right about it. I have never had any reason to doubt it. He was a good Christian man, a good Baptist before then, but I'm sure that that is when he was 'born again.'

Q: Now I'm going to ask you a question that I will ask your brother if I get the chance (Note: I didn't get the chance and never received an answer to a written version of the question that I submitted through Jimmy Carter's press secretary.)

A: All right.

Q: Your brother defines himself as a born-again Christian and Baptist. When I was growing up in a Baptist family in Mississippi, people who described themselves that way were assumed by everyone who knew them to believe—certainly my family believed—that there was a literal hell, a literal heaven, and a literal and eternal life after death that would be spent in one place or the other. Does Jimmy believe that?

A: I don't know. I really don't. But I'd say that's more fundamentalist than it is 'born again' in standard preaching. I never think about hell and I never think about heaven. I think about living abundantly— I do. And I've known other people who think and believe as I do, that the key to the whole thing is Christ in me. This is what I base my life on and I think it's what Jimmy bases his life on.

Alton Carter

Q: How did you Carters get here?

A: My daddy died in 1903. We lived down in Early County, about a hundred miles below here, right on the Alabama border. I was the oldest boy, I was 16, and I had to take hold of the family, you might say. My mother, she wasn't any businesswoman at all. I brought my mother and three sisters and this one brother, he was six years younger than I was, to Plains. My brother was James Earl Carter—everybody called him Earl. Nobody really knows who I am. I got three names, William Alton Carter, but they know me as Alton Carter and they all knew him as Earl Carter.

Q: Have you read Jimmy Carter's book?

A: Yes, sir.

Q: Was that family as poor and hard-pressed during his boyhood as he makes 'em out to be?

A: I don't think so. They never were hard up. You know yourself, you know folks who work hard as the devil all their lives and they never make a living. You know others, every time they lay their hand down on something and pick it up, there's two or three dollars under it. Well, that's the way Earl was. He'd make three times as much money as I could without any trouble. He was just a money-maker. He traded land and when he died he had about 4000 acres of land. He had made every bit of it his self and he kept it.

Q: The land that is now in what's called Carter Farms, was that Earl Carter's?

A: Some of it is. Jimmy's got every foot he ever had. He ain't sold a foot and he's bought some more. Now I'm not certain, but I think Jimmy's two sisters and his brother have sold their land. Jimmy, he ain't sold a foot, like I say.

Q: Is Jimmy a good businessman?

A: Well, I'll tell you what he done after he came back here from the Navy in 1953. He took that business and he's over doubled it, I think. He's not one of these extravagants, you know. He's very conservative. When he turns a dollar loose, he expects it to come back with fifty cents hanging on it. That's the kind of fellow he is.

Q: Which of the two, your brother Earl or Jimmy's mother—Miz Lillian, everybody seems to call her—had the most influence on Jimmy?

A: Well, I'll tell you. Miss Lillian's daddy, Jim Zack Gordy, was the biggest politician in this part of Georgia. You ever heard of Tom Watson? Well, Jim Zack was Tom Watson from A to Z. That's what Lillian's daddy was. The last job he had, he had it when he died, was doorkeeper of the state Senate. I just have an idea, I don't know whether I'm right or not, that Jimmy got his politics from his grandaddy Gordy. He didn't get it from the Carters. The Carters are not politicians like the Gordys were. The Gordys were politicians and, if you want to know the truth, that's all they were. Every one of them. Lillian now. She's got two sisters, they're the hottest politicians you ever saw.

Q: Miss Lillian, is she interested in politics?

A: She's right into it. She's been interested in every political race that I've ever known.

Q: You must know Mrs. Rosalynn Carter pretty well?

A: Rosalynn? Oh, yes, and I'm going to tell you something about her. If you ask me right now, who is the smartest woman in the United States, I'll tell you—her. She beats anything that you ever saw. She's a little country girl raised out here in the country, about six miles from Plains. She's smart as the devil, she's just wonderful the way she handles things. She's got Moedell *(he meant Mondale)* at their house today. She's had Muskie there. She cooks for them herself.

Q: You mean, she doesn't have a cook?

A: If she has, I never found it out. I was there the other night and I asked her, how do you handle all these big notables that come here and she says, I do the best I can and let the balance take care of itself. That's how she is.

Q: You ever been in politics?

A: Oh, yes sir, I was mayor of this town for 28 years between 1918 and 1954. A few terms in that time, I was out. When Jimmy told me in December 1974 that he was going for President and asked me what I thought, I told him he had a long way to go and some hard work ahead, and he realized it. I told him that the first year I was mayor of Plains, I tried to satisfy everybody and they like to run me crazy. I says, I learned that the only way you can get by is to do what you think is right and don't give a damn what other people think about it.

Q: What did Jimmy say to that?

A: He laughed.

Hugh Carter

Q: What distinguishes Jimmy, what makes him different?

A: Well, I'll tell you in a very few words. He and I grew up in this little town and the biggest thing in our lives has always been the church. This is not anything unusual for people living in a small town. We have always been Christians and we have always gone to church. The result is, we learned to love Christ early in life and when you speak of Christ, Christ of course represents many things. Jesus Christ was good and compassionate and loving, thought a lot of his fellow men, and was honest, and these traits have been instilled in the life of Jimmy. In addition to that, he's one of the sincerest people I've ever known. When you talk to Jimmy, he has an uncanny ability to let you talk. He's a good listener. Everybody likes to talk himself instead of listening to somebody else talk. And so when you go off and leave Jimmy Carter, even though you've seen him just that one time, there's something about him that you never forget, and it grabs you. It's because he's a good listener. But the most important reason is that he's compassionate, his Christian life is showing in everything that he says and he does. He's been going to church ever since he was this high *(gesturing from the waist)*. He made a public profession of faith and he was baptised when he was seven years old right here in the Plains Baptist Church. You know, we Baptists believe in waiting before we're baptised, so we know what we're doing.

Q: Were you surprised when he told you he was going for the presidency?

A: I was. He was still governor when he came out to my house here in Plains in October 1974, he was in blue jeans and sneakers, and knocked on my back door and said he wanted to come in and talk to me and my wife. He sat down in the den and said, I'm going to surprise you. And I said, all right what is it, and he said, I'm going to run for President of the United States, and I said *what?* Just like that. I said, Jimmy, what makes you think you can win? And he said, well, Hugh, I've had Teddy Kennedy and I've had Scoop Jackson and I've had all these big shots to Atlanta in the Governor's mansion, I've sat and talked with them, and I've decided, they're not any more qualified to be President than I am, I'm just as smart as they are and I believe I can make just as good a President as they can. He said, I believe I can make it if I can sell myself to the American people and they can realize that a southerner is just as intelligent and just as capable of being President as these other people are. So he convinced me right then.

Q: In Georgia terms, do you regard Jimmy as a liberal?

A: No, sir. I regard him as moderate to liberal. He ran for governor of Georgia as a moderate. You can't be conservative and be President of the United States. When you are President you have got to represent everybody—the conservatives, the moderates, the liberals. So I wouldn't call him a liberal, I'd call him moderate to liberal. Now this is Hugh Carter's opinion.

Q: You are known to be more conservative than Jimmy is. How would you describe yourself?

A: I'm conservative to moderate. Or moderate to conservative.

Mary Anne Thomas

Q: I gather that Jimmy Carter, after he came home from the Navy in 1953 after his father died, foregathered with you and some others over here from time to time to discuss what you all read and what to read.

A: Well, we did. Not just to discuss books, though. It would be to have supper and have a drink with your friends. Americus is not exactly an intellectual center, you know. There are just a few people you find who really want to talk about anything like that, so when you do find them you kind of leap on one another.

Q: You said you talked about other things. Such as?

A: Hell, I hate to say southern intellectuals, but—you said you're from Mississippi, you know—southerners in a small town that do read get together and talk about everything. We never talked about religion much, except in a very philosophical vein. So Jimmy's religious side is something that I just never knew much about. I'm not putting it into doubt, he's a southern Baptist and a pillar of the church. But also at that time in the early 1960s he was a school board member and he was going into the state Senate, and that is essential in Georgia politics. I mean, it's absolutely essential.

Q: I missed the connecting line there. What is essential?

A: Religion. Being a pillar of the church.

Q: Is Jimmy pretending, or is it real?

A: I don't know. Somewhere between Jimmy's gubernatorial campaigns in 1966 and 1970 we discussed religion. Russell and I were at Jimmy's house for supper one evening after Jimmy lost in 1966. Jimmy and a friend of his here in Americus were sponsoring a big Billy Graham thing—I forget exactly what it was, but I think it was a film of one of Billy Graham's revivals. I'd seen Billy Graham when I was living near Atlanta. There he was in a tent in Atlanta, no better than Oral Roberts, yelling Jesus Christ in one corner and yelling at the Devil in the other, and I thought it was terrible. If I wasn't religious prior to that, that finished me off. So here were Jimmy and this friend of his sponsoring this Billy Graham thing in Sumter County. That evening at Jimmy's house I got very aggressive. I'd believed in Jimmy, I still believe in him. But this was so political, it *was* political. I thought it was some sort of trick and I didn't like it. I thought, damn, here we go, the whole bit, and we got into it. Russell said to me afterward, Mary Anne, how would you feel if Jimmy had jumped on you in your house on one of your pet projects? It ended up with me calling Jimmy and saying, "Jimmy, I was disturbed and angry and I apologize," and Jimmy saying to me, "Lady, you know and I know you got a big mouth and you don't have to apologize to me."

Bruce Edwards

Q: Without asking you to speak for any member of your church, including Governor Carter, would you think that any member of this church who identified himself as a born-again Baptist Christian, as Governor Carter does, would be assumed by other members of the church to believe in a literal heaven, a literal hell and a literal eternal life after death?

A: I would say yes. I wouldn't speak for every individual but I would say, yes, most of our people do believe that.

September 25, 1976

———

To his discredit and my sorrow President Carter said nothing publicly when his friend, admirer, supporter and pastor, Bruce Edwards, was forced to resign from the Plains Baptist Church because he favored the admission of blacks.

LXVII

Rolling With Jerry

It was fun to be with the President and with some 400 of his supporters and guests on a sunny Saturday when they were riding high on a steam paddleboat down the river that Mark Twain in 1896 called "the great Mississippi, the majestic, the magnificent Mississippi." Because of upstream drought the Mississippi was at its lowest level in a hundred years but on the approaches to New Orleans it was still great, majestic, magnificent and lined with remnants of the willows and water oaks that in Mark Twain's time as a riverboat pilot were the borders of mighty forests. Being with the President and a smaller party the next afternoon was less fun but interesting. After a Sunday service in the Roman Catholic cathedral in New Orleans, in escort of the resident archbishop and providing a useful reminder that the President's somewhat equivocal stand on abortion pleases the Catholic hierarchy more than Jimmy Carter's position on the issue does, Mr. Ford motored through southern Louisiana and Mississippi into southern Alabama. He suggested to thousands of Southerners along the way that a reason to vote for him on November 2 is that he is if anything more conservative than they are assumed to be and a damn sight more conservative than their regional hero, Jimmy Carter of Georgia, really is.

A secondary but noteworthy aspect of Mr. Ford's three days in the depths of what until lately was generally thought to be certified Carter country—the trip ended with a day of crime-busting oratory and wooing of Cuban-Americans in Miami—was the fact that the whole expedition was well conceived and well executed. This is news because it has been possible to say as much of practically any Ford operation, governmental or political, only since the Republican convention in Kansas City. The defeat of Ronald Reagan for the presidential nomination and the saving of the Republican platform from total capture and mutilation by the Reaganites resulted from one of the few thoroughly efficient and effective jobs that Mr. Ford and his operatives have accomplished since he succeeded Richard Nixon. The many Nixon assistants and advisers who were recalled to duty for the Kansas City struggle and who largely won it for the President have faded back into the shadows of their law and public relations practices. Doing something as well as the Kansas City job was done cannot be said to have become a habit with the entire Ford establishment. But the direction and execution of the Ford election campaign have continued to improve since the President and his choice for the vice presidency, Senator Robert Dole, were nominated in Kansas City.

The direction comes from where it did during the poorly conducted primary and pre-convention phase—meaning from the White House and, specifically, from Gerald Ford and his White House staff chief, Richard Cheney. The only sense-making explanation of why the direction has improved is that the directors learned something, for once, from the depressing primary and pre-convention performance that enabled Ronald Reagan to come as close as he did to taking the nomination from the incumbent President. Cheney has transferred one of the ablest members of the White House Staff, James Cavanaugh, from the Domestic Council staff to be his administrative deputy, freeing Cheney for nearly full-time attention to the President's campaign problems and to the policy problems that necessarily affect and condition the campaign posture. The replacement first of Howard ("Bo") Callaway and then of former Congressman Rogers C.B. Morton with James Baker, III, originally a Nixon appointee at the Department of Commerce, at the head of the campaign adjunct of the White House, the President Ford Committee, and related personnel changes have improved the committee performance and smoothed the once rough relationships between Cheney's White House overseers and the working peons of the PFC. One of several ironies is that two of Ronald Reagan's best people— James Lake and Lyn Nofziger—have joined the President Ford Committee staff and are credited at the committee's Washington headquarters with substantial contributions to the performance. Washington lawyer John Sears, Reagan's campaign director, probably would be at the Ford committee, too, if anybody could figure how to bring him in without putting him either over or under James Baker and Stuart Spencer, who worked for Reagan in his California campaigns for governor and is Number Two at the PFC.

The history of the President's southern trip illustrates the workings of the Ford election machine. Ford advocates in the deep South, many of them recent supporters of Reagan, began to report in early and mid-September that Southern sentiment was turning against Carter to Ford. Just why, except that significant numbers of southerners were beginning to suspect that Carter was more liberal in the detested eastern establishment sense than he'd led them to believe, was unclear to the committee's southern scouts. The word, coming strongest from Louisiana and Mississippi, was that Carter was slipping and that the President had a chance to take parts of the South if he would grasp it. A suggestion from Louisiana that he spend a day on one of the increasingly popular sight-seeing steam sternwheelers that operate out of New Orleans, Memphis and other lower Mississippi ports was scorned at first because of the cost, a factor that is important this year because of the new federal election subsidy law's limits on expenditure. Then Byron M. (Red) Cavaney, the President's chief travel arranger, looked into the suggestion and became its decisive supporter. Here, it was clear to him and others, was a trigger for marvelous television pictures of the President being folksy afloat, addressing and mingling with rural (and Catholic) crowds along the levees, and providing journalists and invited politicians with a pleasant experience that could only benefit Candidate Ford. A two-day, overnight cruise from Memphis to New Orleans, instead of the eight-hour cruise in the vicinity of New Orleans that occurred, was foregone mainly because the tourist stern-wheelers are wide-deck craft built for standing and chair room and not for cabin accommodation. The day's charter of the New Orleans steamer *Natchez* cost the PFC $20,500 and the whole day's exercise took $42,000 of the $100,000 budgeted for the southern weekend. Upwards of 200 reporters, cameramen and radio-TV technicians paid many thousands of dollars of the committee costs, including for some of these gentry seven dollars for what was reliably reported to be a miserable lunch of soggy salad and shoe-leather beef. The *Natchez* martinis were excellent, at $1.50 a shot.

The southern trip was urged from the South and decided upon in Washington before Jimmy Carter's *Playboy* interview, with all that stuff about shacking up and screwing and Lyndon Johnson's talent for cheating and deception, was publicized. But the resultant publicity added enormously to the jollities that enlivened the boat trip and the next day's motorcade from New Orleans to Mobile. "In his heart he knows your wife" and "I'll see you in my dreams" were among the less scrofulous plays upon Carter's imbecilic remarks in *Playboy* that Ford assistants and supporters regaled each other with. Exaggerated accounts of the four-dash blanks that would shortly be seen in Norman Mailer's interview with Carter, in the *New York Times Sunday Magazine*, were avidly exchanged. When an advance photocopy of the interview disclosed a brief paraphrased indication that Carter had said he didn't care if people said fornicate in four letters, amidst an incredibly turgid and boring essay about Mailer with minimal attention to Carter, the letdown among the Ford folks was terrific. Apart from these comical manifestations, there were serious indications that serious southerners really believed all of a sudden that the President had a chance to win a half or more of the south's electoral votes. This reporter found it difficult then and still finds it difficult to accept this. But when such southern Republican professionals

as Harry Dent of South Carolina, Clarke Reed of Mississippi
and Ben Toledano of New Orleans said they believed it, their
conclusion had to be respected. Mr. Ford's personal pollster,
Robert Teeter of Michigan, was telling him the same thing and,
one gathered, was being believed at the White House.

Mr. Ford was in top campaign form—genial, sweaty and
seemingly happy as he mingled with crowds on levees, along
highways, at airports, at a shrimp wharf. But he overdid it at
times. He said in Biloxi, "All right-believing people who are law-
abiding ought to have the traditional right under the Constitution to retain firearms for their own national protection,
period"—a slip that could enable a questioner at the Ford-Carter
debate on defense and foreign policy to ask the President how a
simple federal requirement that buyers and owners of guns
register their weapons would impair anybody's legitimate
rights. In Mobile, where wounded and semi-paralyzed Governor George Wallace greeted him in a wheel chair, and again in
Miami, where many of the police chiefs whom he addressed
favored strict gun control, Mr. Ford skipped his standard pledge
of opposition to any form of control. He never mentioned the
administration bill, ostensibly aimed at   barring imports of
cheap foreign handguns, that would actually go much farther
than the President has ever acknowledged to regulate the gun
trade. He said that Senator Walter Mondale, the Democratic
vice presidential candidate, had voted to over-ride every one of
the President's 58—he kept saying 56—vetoes and had thereby
proved himself to be "the biggest spender in the Senate." Only
12 of the vetoes had come to a Senate vote when the President
spoke. Mondale voted to over-ride 11 of them and didn't vote on
one. The President's estimate of the amount saved by his
vetoes, which recently was $13 billion, jumped overnight in the
South from nine billion dollars to $10 billion. A frequent theme
was that "I won't be satisfied until we have a job for everybody
who wants a job and who will look for a job" and that "we also
want everybody who will work and save to have a home in a
decent neighborhood." When a reporter on the trip read the
housing passage to her black news editor in Washington, he said
he couldn't believe that the President had said it. It meant to
him, the black editor said, that the President by inference was

dismissing inner-city blacks. Extreme though this interpretation may have been, Mr. Ford invited it with his use of such
language in references to crime, gun control, jobs and housing.
Maybe the only safe procedure for candidates in this year of
pervasive cynicism and of blood-thirsty critics would be to
campaign in total silence.

October 9, 1976

———

The only Southern state that Ford carried was Virginia.

LXVIII

Ford, Ruff and Butz

San Francisco
Two episodes in late September and early October that involved
President Ford and must have diminished his chance, already
dim, for election to the office that he attained by appointment
and succession are dealt with in this report. They provide a
useful insight into the mind and character of the President and
into the workings of his White House, and one of them raised
troubling questions about the roles of the press and of official
investigative agencies in this season of endemic distrust.

The episodes were the disclosure that the Watergate Special
Prosecutor was investigating the use of campaign funds
contributed to Republican committees in Mr. Ford's home city
and county in Michigan, and the resignation of Secretary of
Agriculture Earl Butz after he admitted to the President that he
had indeed, as reported, remarked upon the sexual and anal
preferences of black people—"coloreds," he had called them—in
language so crude that it will not be quoted here. The remark
and the circumstances in which it was spoken justified Senators
Edward Brooke of Massachusetts and James Buckley of New
York, Congressman John Anderson of Illinois and Ambassador
William Scranton, among others, in saying that the President

should demand Butz's resignation rather than passively await it, which is what he chose to do for four days.

It was news to many people that a Watergate Special Prosecution Force still existed. Under the fourth and presumably last Special Prosecutor, 37-year-old attorney Charles Ruff, the staff had been reduced from some 200 lawyers and other employees to fewer than a dozen and had moved from mid-town Washington into a small, though formidably secured, office suite in a sleazy building near the Capitol. Ruff told a House subcommittee on August 26 that he expected to terminate the operation "probably within three or four months." The Michigan investigation had been secretly in progress for more than a month when he said this. It would have been extremely odd if he simultaneously expected in August to be out of business "within three or four months" and thought he was developing a case involving serious charges against the President.

The first anybody at the White House knew that something strange and surprising was going on in Grand Rapids and Kent

County was when acquaintances and friends of the President began telephoning White House Counsel Philip Buchen, who also is from Grand Rapids, and telling him that FBI agents were questioning them about the handling of local Republican campaign funds and seizing committee records dating as far back as 1964. Because FBI agents had gone over similar ground with the same local committees and people after Richard Nixon nominated Gerald Ford to be Vice President in 1973, Buchen and his Grand Rapids friends found this puzzling. Buchen, however, is a glacially calm type who doesn't puzzle easily and intensely, and he has said he didn't bother the President with the word from home at the time. In accordance with a strict rule against the slightest intrusion upon the Department of Justice and the FBI that was established in the first weeks of the Ford presidency, Buchen also didn't ask either of them what was going on. On Monday, September 20, a day or so after Buchen got the first calls from Grand Rapids, press secretary Ron Nessen received a telephone call from Jerry Landauer, an investigative reporter for *The Wall Street Journal*. Landauer said the *Journal* was about to go to press with a report that the FBI was conducting an investigation in Grand Rapids and Kent County that could involve the President. Landauer asked Nessen for comment. As Nessen recalls the conversation, he protested that nothing Landauer had told him about the story indicated that the President was involved. Therefore, said Nessen, no comment.

Still according to Nessen, Landauer said as innumerable news stories have maintained since then that local committees that had supported the President and had helped to finance his campaigns for reelection to Congress for 25 years were involved and, anyhow, that such an investigation of the use of Ford campaign funds in Mr. Ford's home city and county was bound to concern him in one way or another. Implicit in Landauer's first story and in many stories in other publications that followed was a suspicion that political contributions had been diverted to Gerald Ford's personal use or to political uses that the contributors had not intended. Charles Ruff's predecessor, Leon Jaworski, had said he investigated allegations of misuse of Ford political funds and found the charges baseless.

The House and Senate committees that confirmed Ford's nomination to the vice presidency considered similar charges and absolved him. Now, a few weeks from the 1976 presidential elections and just when Ford was overtaking Jimmy Carter in the polls, the suspicion was back in the news and, what was worse, back in it in a Watergate context that inevitably resulted from the reports that the Watergate Special Prosecutor was conducting the investigation. Reports and the ready admission at the White House that US Steel and several other corporations, all of them represented in Washington by lobbyists who are friends of the President, had paid Ford's travel and other expenses on several golfing weekends during his years in Congress added to the irritation and frustration. In terms of potential embarrassment and political harm, however, they were as nothing compared with the stories of the Michigan investigation.

In keeping with the policy adopted by the first Special Prosecutor, Archibald Cox, and followed by his successors, Charles Ruff and his young press spokesman, Dan Rosenblatt, refused to say whether such an investigation was in fact underway, what it concerned if it was, and specifically whether it involved or concerned the President. Nor would they give any indication whatever of who or what initiated the investigation if there was one. The Justice Department and the FBI were equally reticent. The first news stories, therefore, were derived from what Grand Rapids and Kent County politicians who had been interviewed by the FBI were saying in Michigan. The thrust of what they were saying was that the questions put to them by the FBI and the committee records subpoenaed by the Special Prosecutor seemed chiefly to concern contributions made to Ford campaigns over the years by two maritime unions, the Seafarers Union and the Marine Engineers Beneficial Association. Both unions for years were strong and generous supporters of Congressman Ford. He took pay from them and from other maritime unions for making speeches to them along lines that—he has said—"they thought would be appropriate." President Ford alienated them when he vetoed an outrageous bill that would have required *foreign* exporters of oil to the US to ship 20 percent of their cargoes in US tankers operated with

high-wage union crews. The MEBA in particular has turned to
lavish support—rhetorical, organizational and financial—of
Jimmy Carter this year and has been rewarded by him with
promises of support for some of its dearest and most selfish
aims, including a union monopoly of the training of commercial
maritime crews. A White House official was told when the
Michigan stories began to break that Jesse Calhoon, MEBA's
president and a vociferous Carter supporter, was feeding off-
record information to reporters working on the stories.
Whether Calhoon is the informant who set off the Special
Prosecutor's investigation has not been established at this
writing. Whoever that informant or misinformant may be, he
or she set in motion a faceless, chargeless process of indictment
by rumor that forced President Ford to say at a suddenly
summoned press conference on September 30 that he'd never
received Kent County political money for personal purposes. He
got to the heart of the issue raised by this affair when he said:
"There is a saying that is prevalent in the law that 'justice
delayed is justice denied.' I am certain that the people
responsible for any investigation will live up to . . . the Canon
of Ethics . . . which does require that . . . such investigations
. . . be full, complete and concluded as readily as possible."
While professing "full confidence in the integrity of Mr. Ruff"
and belief in "the Special Prosecutor concept," he was saying to
Charles Ruff: *Get this over and get off my back.*

He had every right to say it, with an aside to his own
Attorney General to the same effect. The current version of the
charters under which Special Prosecutors have worked since
the office was established on May 31, 1973 limits the Prosecutor
to investigating Watergate-connected behavior and allegations
of behavior within the three years of 1970, 1971 and 1972. The
Prosecutor may investigate allegations of non-Watergate
behavior of events that either preceded or followed those three
years, even when he is working on leads that arise from events
within those years, only with the permission of the Attorney
General. The Special Prosecutor may request this permission or
the Attorney General may expand the permitted period for
investigation by "Referral" of an allegation to the Special
Prosecutor. A remarkable thing about the early Michigan fund

stories was the slowness of the press to awake to the fact that Ruff could not have been going back to 1964 in his investigation, as he was reported to be doing, without Attorney General Edward Levi's permission. Ruff's spokesman, Dan Rosenblatt, and Robert Havel, the Justice Department's chief spokesman, told this reporter that this was true in late September, but neither of them would say that or whether Ruff was acting with the Attorney General's permission or by referral from the Attorney General. When the reporter said to Philip Buchen on September 28 that the seeming requirement of some authority from the Attorney General for what Ruff was reported to be doing "makes me wonder," Buchen replied: "Well, I'll leave you wondering. At the moment I won't be bothered by it."

Bob Woodward of *The Washington Post*'s Watergate team of Woodward and Bernstein finally extracted from Deputy Attorney General Harold A. Tyler, Jr. the fact that he, with Attorney General Levi's approval, had initiated the Ruff investigation last July by referral of an allegation of wrongdoing that somebody unknown to Tyler and Levi (Tyler said) had made to the FBI. The Woodward-Bernstein disclosure was followed by a tragi-comedy of press rivalry that did nobody, Woodward-Bernstein and Charles Ruff included, any credit. Tyler and the department spokesman, Robert Havel, complained convincingly that Woodward and *The Post*'s account had gone much farther than Tyler had gone to tie the President to the case. Nicholas Horrock of *The New York Times* wrote that "government sources" expected Ruff to say soon that he had investigated "allegations of campaign financing irregularities and found no basis to either continue the inquiry or bring criminal charges." The Associated Press had "a Justice Department source" saying that Ruff would soon clear the President in a public statement. Woodward and Bernstein thereupon quoted Ruff: "I will state that it has never been the policy of this office to keep the Justice Department informed of our day-to-day, minute-to-minute or month-to-month progress on any investigations . . . I have no plans to make any statement. If and when making a statement becomes appropriate, I will do so." After weeks of principled pap from the Special Prosecutor's office to the effect that he could not and would not comment upon any aspect of the matter, this gratuitous cooperation with Woodward and Bernstein to keep the story alive, facts or no facts, inclined me to vomit.

Space permits, thank God, the briefest possible summation of the Butz affair. Now that it's over and done with, apart from any effect it may have on the electorate's judgment of Mr. Ford, two questions about it are worth answering. One is how Earl Butz, who really is no fool despite the contrary appearance that he's often conveyed since he joined the Nixon cabinet in 1971, could have been stupid enough to say what he did in the presence of John W. Dean, III, the former White House lawyer who did more than any other individual to bring about the ruin of Richard Nixon, and who was known to Butz to be writing about the Republican National convention for *Rolling Stone* magazine. The other question is why the President didn't fire Butz out of hand instead of letting it appear that he could stay on if he wished and that, in any event, the basis for keeping him or allowing him to quit would be the discerned impact upon the Ford campaign for election rather than Butz's grievous offense against national and racial sensibilities.

The answer to the first question, I am told, is that it was just a matter of Butz being Butz. He is an inveterate teller of jokes, some of them funny and possibly half of them fit for rendition in polite company. There he was on an airliner bound from Kansas City to California, in the company of Dean and singers Pat Boone and Sonny Bono. It was a time for jokes and Butz told two, the second concerning a dog in intimate converse with a skunk. Butz explained in a public apology that the racial slur was really a joke told years before by some local politician, but he didn't say that this was what it was when he dumped it on Dean, Boone and Bono. The answer to the second question is rather similar, in that the President's handling of the affair was a matter of Ford being himself. It was said that he has long schooled himself to take hard decisions only after thought and delay, especially if they concern someone else. He was and remains fond of Butz. He sorely needed Butz's campaign help in the grain states. And, one is not told at the White House but is compelled to conclude, the President and the people around him simply were not repelled by the Butz language to the extent that they should have been, morally speaking. Richard Cheney, the President's staff chief, reported the matter to Mr. Ford almost 24 hours after Butz had warned Cheney that "a problem" was coming up with identification of him as the author of the remark and half a day after Cheney had told two press spokesmen, Ron Nessen and William Greener, about it. Let's face it, the Ford White House is not a place for outrage over this sort of thing.

October 16, 1976

———

Special Prosecutor Ruff announced after several more days of uncertainty that he'd found no evidence of the misuse of campaign funds for Mr. Ford's personal benefit.

LXIX

Ford's Boo-boos

In preparation for his second television encounter—I refuse to call it a debate—with Jimmy Carter in San Francisco on October 6, President Ford carefully prepared himself and was carefully prepared by various assistants and advisers for correct or at least defensible answers to anticipated questions about US relationships with the Communist Peking and anti-Communist Taipei governments, the cooperation of American firms with the Arab boycott of Israel, and the US attitude toward the Soviet presence in Eastern Europe. Mr. Ford answered questions on other subjects, for which he also had prepared and been prepared, with what I thought on the whole to be competence and knowledge superior to that displayed by Carter. But, with a degree of awkwardness and ineptitude that dismayed assistants and advisers who had helped him prepare for the occasion and other associates who were hoping and praying from a distance that he'd do at least as well as he did in the first encounter with Carter, the President blew his answers to questions on the subjects cited above. In doing so, he certainly diminished and possibly destroyed whatever chance he had for election on November 2.

Mr. Ford often fumbles his words. He often says more or less than he meant to say. He has often had to confess later that he didn't mean to say exactly what he'd actually said. Never during his presidency, however, had he so completely and disastrously misspoken. A week of inquiry among some of his closest associates as to how and why it happened produced a non-answer that is summarized in a dialogue with one of the associates.

Q. So there really isn't any explanation, is that what you are saying? It just happened? He just did it?

A. That's right, it just happened. I doubt that I'll ever know why and I doubt that he will. And I'm not sure that he really knew it was happening when it happened. Believe it or not, I'm not sure he heard himself saying what he was saying when he said it.

Several other assistants responded in approximately the same way to approximately the same inquiry. The following gist of what the reporter was told about the preparations for the October encounter is not intended to explain and does not explain the President's three boo-boos. It adds to the puzzlement and incidentally illuminates the workings of the Ford White House.

Mr. Ford got down to specific preparation for the San Francisco confrontation with Carter much later than he did for the first one in Philadelphia. Then a replica of the Philadelphia stage was put together in the seldom used White House theater. Bill Carruthers, the President's adviser on television techniques, and Don Penny, the speech coach and intermittent contributor of gags and sharpened language who had helped importantly with preparations for the acceptance speech at the Kansas City convention, drilled him for hours in tone, posture, response. The President spent many hours over many days studying massive volumes of position papers on economic and domestic issues. The San Francisco discussion was to be confined to foreign policy and defense. After dealing with these subjects for many years in Congress and over two years in the presidency, Mr. Ford felt that there wasn't much that anybody could tell him about them that he didn't know. The showing of polls and his own sense that he'd out-performed Carter in the first encounter added to his confidence that he'd do even better in the second round. There was no further drilling in camera and speech technique. Carruthers oversaw the little there was of that part of the preparation and Penny was largely excluded. The President paid cursory attention to position papers in Washington but concentrated on them in San Francisco on Tuesday and Wednesday before the Wednesday evening event (*damned* if I'll say debate!). Secretary of State Henry Kissinger and the White House assistant for national security affairs, Brent Scowcroft, spent 90 minutes with the President on the Sunday before he flew to San Francisco. Kissinger did not go to San Francisco with the President, presumably because neither of them wanted to assist Carter in promoting the notion that Kissinger conceives and runs Ford foreign policy.

Scowcroft did go. On Wednesday afternoon, a few hours before the President faced the cameras, Scowcroft pointed out to Mr. Ford that the Shanghai Communique of 1972, issued at the end of Richard Nixon's visit to China, included a unilateral US statement of hope that the dispute between the Peking and Taipei governments over the status and independence of the exiled "Republic of China" would be settled by peaceful means. It did not, Scowcroft reminded Mr. Ford, assert or constitute agreement between the US and Communist China that the dispute would be settled peacefully. That night Mr. Ford shook up Scowcroft and others familiar with the facts and with the President's actual knowledge of the facts when he said: "The Shanghai Communique does say that the differences between the People's Republic on the one hand and Taiwan on the other shall be settled by peaceful means. . .We will insist that the disputes be settled peacefully. . .as was agreed in the Shanghai Communique of 1972."

This was the least noticed of the President's mistakes. Another bumble that got less notice than it deserved was his misstatement of what he intended to do about American cooperation with the Arab economic boycott of Israel. The President had opposed legislation that would require disclosure and penalize past compliance with the boycott by US companies. He had indicated willingness to sign legislation that would require disclosure of future compliance. On Thursday

September 30, when it was apparent that Congress was not going to enact any boycott legislation before it adjourned, the President at a staff meeting in the Oval Office instructed deputy staff chief James Cavanaugh and other assistants to draft a directive ordering Secretary of Commerce Elliot Richardson to disclose future compliance. At this meeting he emphatically restated his opposition to the disclosure of past compliance. The memo to Richardson was duly drafted for issuance and announcement in San Francisco the Tuesday preceding the television tussle with Carter. Brent Scowcroft and other assistants argued that it would be perceived for what it would be, a shoddy presidential gimmick, and urged Mr. Ford either to skip it entirely or mention it in a vague way if a questioner raised the subject. The President dragged it in with this statement: "Because Congress failed to act I am going to announce tomorrow that the Department of Commerce will disclose those companies that have participated in the Arab boycott." Richardson and others had to explain forthwith that the directive applied only to future participation and Mr. Ford falsely and unnecessarily appeared to have retreated from his original intention.

The President had been drenched for two years in the subtleties of Henry Kissinger's view that the US had to recognize the Soviet presence in Eastern Europe as a fact without either condoning or condemning it. He got a renewed dose of it from Kissinger and Scowcroft in Washington and again from Scowcroft in San Francisco. He was urged to defend the controversial 1975 Helsinki agreement—attacked by Carter and Ronald Reagan, among others, as craven recognition by the US of Soviet mastery—on the ground that it actually forbade further Soviet military aggression in Europe. Some domestic advisers considered the Kissinger-Scowcroft line much too defensive and urged Mr. Ford to be tough and aggressive.

His absurd and immensely harmful assertion that "there is no Soviet domination of Eastern Europe and there never will be under a Ford administration" overshadowed everything else said in the discussion. The thought that anyone could possibly believe that this represented his real view, after many years of outspoken denunciation of Soviet dominance, so infuriated the

President that it took five days for his alarmed assistants to bring him around to a clear admission that he'd made a mistake. His personal poller, Robert Teeter, had small but representative samples of 125 to 130 people asked by telephone Wednesday night, Thursday morning, Thursday afternoon and Thursday night—"who do you think did the better job in the debate?" Ford led Carter by 11 points in the responses Wednesday night. Thursday and Thursday night, after the public had been saturated with news that the President had blundered, Carter led Ford first by 12 points, then by 27 points, and finally by 45 points. The fact that all sorts of people, not solely European-American "ethnics," shifted their approval from Ford to Carter caused Teeter to conclude: "The notion of ineptness, the impression that the President had made a mistake, was more important than the substance of the reference."

October 23, 1976

———

The recommended defense of the Helsinki agreement was not that it "forbade further Soviet military aggression in Europe," but that it discouraged further aggression by permitting changes of borders only by peaceful means.

LXX

Up for Grabs

At his second press conference in six days, in itself a notable event because it was only the third full-scale session of the kind at the White House since February, President Ford was asked whether and how he and his family were betting on the outcome of the November 2 election. He answered rather self-righteously that he and his family hadn't made any wagers but were confident that "when the votes are finally counted, the American people will want four years of the progress we've made in the last two"—meaning of course the two years since he succeeded Richard Nixon in the presidency. If White House assistants and outside advisers who were in touch with him reflected his mood, the President on the eve of a final, 10-day campaign swing around the country was almost but not quite as confident as his reply at the press conference indicated. The prevailing view around him was that the election could be won in the last two weeks, not that it was sure to be won by Mr. Ford and his choice for the vice presidency, Sen. Robert Dole. There was a genuine conviction, supported in the main by national polls and by the Ford campaign's state and national polls, that in the last fortnight of October the President was overtaking Jimmy Carter's previously commanding lead and that, in a phrase much in favor at the White House, the election really was "up for grabs."

There also was general agreement around the President that his third television encounter with Carter on October 22 could determine the outcome on November 2. It followed that Mr. Ford simply could not afford the sort of bloopers on Eastern Europe, the Arab boycott of Israel and US-China relations that had marred his otherwise superior performance on October 6. The resultant apprehension was sharpened by a realization that the "winner" of the third encounter—the candidate who was perceived by a majority of viewers to have put on the better performance—probably wouldn't attract much additional support to himself. For the "loser"—a candidate perceived to put on a distinctly poor performance—the last encounter could be disastrous if it turned enough potential supporters from him to his rival. Yet the President prepared more casually for the third meeting than he had for the second in San Francisco and with nothing like the intense study and drilling that had preceded the first encounter in Philadelphia. There were said to be two reasons. Questioning at the first meetings had been limited to specified subject areas—domestic and economic affairs, foreign policy and defense. Questioning at the third encounter was unlimited, on any subjects chosen by the questioners. Precise preparation was therefore difficult though not, in the judgment of the assistant principally responsible for it, impossible. They hoped, in fact, that with less overt effort the President would turn out to have been better schooled for the final meeting than he'd been for the first two. The second and probably controlling reason was that Mr. Ford, having been through two confrontations with Carter, had been taught or had learned from experience all that he'd ever learn about how to handle himself in such a situation.

Although the concluding swing was anticipated in the campaign scenario prepared before his nomination and adopted immediately afterward, a lot of discussion and some worry accompanied the final decision to go ahead with it. The consensus among the President's people is that, putting it kindly, he is not at his best on the stump. When he is his natural self, he's a touring soporific. When he makes a conscious effort to be sharp and aggressive in the guise of give-'em-hell Jerry, he tends to over-do it and make himself ridiculous as he did during a weekend journey, complete with a one-day train trip in Illinois, to that state and Iowa. Even when he's adjudged by his associates to be effective with the crowds that actually see and hear him, it's recognized that he gets spotty coverage on national television and reaches fewer citizens than he does with major set appearances in Washington and elsewhere. Then why do it? The common answer at the White House and among some of his official advisers was, "he had to do it." One of the concerned assistants called it "an Americana event—it's what the American people expect a President to do." Some of the people he consults, in and outside the White House, hoped that the President would moderate the jabs ("he wavers, he wanders, he wiggles and he waffles") that he had been throwing at Jimmy Carter and put more emphasis on the substantive differences, professed and real, between the two, with emphasis on the possible costs of Carter programs. Whatever the tone and tactics in the final 10 days, however, the object would be to draw Carter out of his shell of bland and pious generality. The hope was that this would attract from him to the President the many citizens who, according to various polls and surveys, were inclined toward Carter but uncertain that they really wanted to vote for him. It was to these "uncertains" rather than to the conventionally "undecided" that the President and his campaign planners chiefly looked for the additional support that he'd have to get in the final fortnight if he was to win election.

The rivals' open tactics aside, the weeks preceding the last stretch were a time of dirt, acerbity and, for Mr. Ford, aggravation. Columnist Jack Anderson, the *Los Angeles Times* and *The New York Times* reported that persons associated with the Ford campaign had tried to peddle rumors that Jimmy Carter had indulged in extra-marital affairs with three or more women. A Georgia volunteer at the President Ford Committee's Washington headquarters who had recommended in a memorandum that the committee investigate the rumors and exploit them if they proved true was summarily dismissed by PFC Chairman James Baker. Reporters who investigated found the rumors false. *The New York Times* reported that "sources interested in the election of Jimmy Carter" had leaked to it a government-sponsored survey of European opinion showing that the US had lost respect in Western Europe, as Carter was saying at a time when Ford was saying it had gained respect.

The goad that most disturbed and infuriated Mr. Ford came from John Dean, the former White House lawyer who blew the whistle on Richard Nixon and did more than any other individual to bring him down. Dean, promoting his Watergate book (*Blind Ambition*), appeared on three successive mornings on NBC's "Today" show in brief segments of a previously taped interview. In the interview and in his book he said that two Nixon assistants, William Timmons and Richard Cook, had persuaded then Minority Leader Gerald Ford to intervene in and help block a proposed House committee investigation in 1972, just before the year's presidential election, that could have begun uncovering the Watergate crimes. In his testimony before the Senate Watergate Committee in 1973, Dean asserted nearly everything of substance that he again alleged in the NBC interview and in his book. Timmons and Cook said Dean lied. At the 1973 hearings on his nomination to be Vice President, Mr. Ford acknowledged that he as Minority Leader had mobilized Republican votes on the committee to deny Chairman Wright Patman the subpoena power he needed to prosecute the inquiry. Mr. Ford denied only that he'd done it at the instance of the Nixon White House. The Dean interview reviving what amounted to a charge that he'd lied under oath enraged the President, occurring as it did just after Special Prosecutor Charles Ruff had announced that he found no basis for allegations that Mr. Ford had misspent political contributions.

At Mr. Ford's orders, Press Secretary Ron Nessen verified a report that NBC News paid Dean $7500 in 1975 for an option to buy the television rights to his book. Nessen and William Greener, the Ford campaign committee's chief spokesman, happily spread the word in Washington. The coincidence embarrassed NBC and enhanced the President's feeling that he was being victimized. First the Special Prosecutor and then Attorney General Edward Levi rejected the demands of two congressional Democrats, Elizabeth Holtzman of New York and

John Conyers of Michigan, for a criminal investigation of the suggestion that Mr. Ford had perjured himself at his confirmation hearings. That officially ended the matter but not the prospect that Democrats would continue to exploit the lingering impression that Mr. Ford had been less than frank in some of his responses.

October 30, 1976

LXXI

Ford at the Wire

Philadelphia

Six days before the end of this miserable presidential election campaign, Gerald Ford was half through a road trip that had turned out to be fundamentally phony. In glimpses caught on television screens at stops along the Ford route, Jimmy Carter appeared to be cautious to the point of fright and to be justifying the skepticism about him that reporters traveling with him reflected in published accounts and in conversations. A choice between this unimpressive pair being obligatory, I choose Carter. With that said, I move on to my proper business, which is to note some impressions of the President and of his performance during the 10 days before the election.

The road trip that was to take the President through Virginia, the Carolinas, California, Washington state and Oregon and back to the capital by way of New Jersey, Pennsylvania, Ohio, Texas and New York was phony because the conventional rallies and other events that occurred along the way were props for something else. The something else was a series of 30-minute television interviews for which the White House campaign adjunct, the President Ford Committee, had bought air time in states the Mr. Ford would have to carry if he was to have a chance of election. The interviews were supplemented with shorter TV and radio "spots" in a massive electronic blitz that would close the evening before the election with a half-hour on each of the three national networks. Taped shots of the President on the hustings, with his family and with accompanying dignitaries, padded out the first of the 30-minute interviews. They were conducted by Joe Garagiola, a retired baseball player turned sportscaster who traveled with the President. He would have done the work for free if his union had not required him to charge the PFC a minimum fee of $360 for each interview. Garagiola was regarded with considerable scorn by professional journalists, but they missed the point. The point was that, in the first Garagiola-Ford interviews the true Jerry Ford came across as he'd never come across from interviews with orthodox and certified journalists. The explanation begins with the fact that Joe Garagiola in his televised self proved to be a slightly modified Archie Bunker. He boasted of his ignorance of complex issues and invited the President to explain them in terms that ignoramuses like Joe could understand. Mr. Ford obliged, in terms that didn't explain anything but satisfied his pal Joe. Watching the President and Joe together on the screen, manifestly and perfectly at ease with each other, one realized that Gerald Ford really is Archie Bunker, slightly modified, and that he was depending for election upon the nation's Bunkers in their numerous variations.

A realization that this was a campaign trip only in the most nominal sense and was actually designed to provide taped scenes and other material for the television and radio scripts on which the Ford Campaign Committee was spending some four million dollars in the last 10 days was necessary if anyone on the road with the President was to retain sanity. It was also the occasion for bows and bids to interest groups that would have been roundly denounced if anyone interested in denouncing such behavior had bothered to notice. In Portland, at a regional convention of the National Association of Broadcasters, 13 of 14 questions addressed to the President during what was intended to be a news conference were crassly self-interested. Print reporters in the traveling press party were outraged and broadcast reporters were either embarrassed or moved to remind each other that nothing better was to be expected from the owners and managers in their industry. When NAB president Vincent Wasilewski tried to terminate the exhibition, Mr. Ford said "I am enjoying this" and invited more questions of the kind he had been getting. When press secretary Ron Nessen was asked whether questions of this sort had been anticipated, he said it was natural for broadcast executives to raise with the President matters of concern to them. In short, the meeting had been arranged to provide station owners and executives a chance to lobby the US President.

Some of the appearances were merely weird. In Chicago, during an afternoon chiefly devoted to preparing the second of his television sessions with Joe Garagiola, the President visited the home office of the Allstate Insurance Company, conferred with members of its executive committee, and addressed some of its employees in the headquarters cafeteria. Apart from a reiteration of his opposition to federalized health care, nothing in the President's remarks particularly concerned the insurance industry. He delivered essentially the speech that he had just delivered to a crowd in the central building of the Ford City Mall in Burbank, a Chicago suburb. The Ford City Mall is a huge shopping center, connected only by name with Gerald Ford. The acoustics in the closed space where the President spoke were terrible. A steady roar of indistinguishable chatter all but obliterated the President's remarks. "Listen very carefully," he said, thrusting his right forefinger at the noisy crowd. The tumult was unabated and Mr. Ford frowned, looking as if he'd just realized that nobody was listening very carefully. He grimly recited his central point—"my idea of tax reform is tax reduction"—and hastened through the similar profundities that comprised his standard rally speech.

A visit to a Jones & Laughlin steel plant near Pittsburgh puzzled the accompanying press. The visit occurred between shift changes, the workers present were working and had no time for handshakes, and Mr. Ford didn't appear to be any more interested in them than they were in him. He watched, and cameras watched him watching, 200 tons of molten iron being poured into a ladle. He didn't say a word in the hearing of reporters. That probably was just as well, considering that Jones & Laughlin was in the process of heavy layoffs and other plants in the Pittsburgh area were also furloughing or had furloughed thousands of workers. A camera crew under contract to the President Ford Committee had a preferred position during the visit. It was filming scenes for the Pennsylvania edition of the Ford-Garagiola interview to be broadcast in Pennsylvania. The President's major address in Pittsburgh was to the Pittsburgh Economic Club. The attending members had expected a discussion of economic problems and policy. They got a dissertation on Ford foreign policy. It was well conceived, well delivered, and singularly inappropriate. It caused one to wonder whether Mr. Ford and his people really cared at this stage about anything except the television interviews, the radio-television spots, and the pre-election shows in paid time on the three networks that were counted upon to snatch victory from Jimmy Carter.

November 6, 1976

LXXII

And So to Bed

Reporters who traveled with Gerald Ford on his last campaign trip began to suspect that he'd received some bad news about his chances of being elected President when he landed and spoke at Detroit's Metropolitan Airport on the afternoon before the election. With his wife Betty at his side, he marched straight from Air Force One to a microphone set up at the edge of the airport and read a brief statement. It was a plea to the people of Michigan to vote the next day for "the first son of Michigan to serve as President of the United States." It was not the plea itself, which was natural enough, but the sudden change from the strained and raucous style of the President's previous utterances that seemed strange. The President spoke in a low voice, in a tone of intense concern. At the end, he turned away from a cluster of reporters and cameramen and entered a White House limousine instead of pausing as he usually did at airports for a few questions and answers. His voice had cracked and fallen to a racking husk during the last two days at rallies in Pennsylvania, New York and Ohio, contributing to the growing impression of a troubled candidate. At an election-eve rally in Grand Rapids, "the home that we love so much," tears were in his eyes and he was discernibly close to sobbing as he lapsed into uncharacteristically incoherent recollections of his 25 years in Congress as the representative of the Grand Rapids district— "taking that trailer down through Ottawa County, Ionia County, Kent County, and sitting and listening to wonderful people who had a problem, who wanted to give me a little trouble, give me a hard time—and they did—but also we had a couple of friends that might come in and say nice things about us." On election morning at the Grand Rapids airport, accepting a mural depicting his and his family's history, he broke into sobs as he recalled his father and mother and said with watery sentiment that he owed everything he was to them. It was all a bit off key, considering that he was born of another father in Omaha, Nebraska, hadn't lived in Grand Rapids for years and, according to Mrs. Ford, intended to retire to their home in Alexandria, Virginia, a suburb of Washington, when he left the presidency. By the time he returned to Washington in the early afternoon of election day, I was among the reporters in his press party who supposed that we had attended the collapse of the hope and illusion that he was going to be elected to the office that he'd held by appointment and succession since August 9, 1974.

I am told at the White House that this supposition was totally wrong. According to the White House account, which I find believable and summarize without further qualification, Mr. Ford had known since last July that his election would require a miracle. The campaign plan drawn up for him in July and ratified after his nomination in August pinpointed with remarkable accuracy the critical, big-vote states where he was behind and where he could hope to come from behind only if there was a very late turn of support from Jimmy Carter to him. One of the doubtful states was Michigan. The news in late October that his lead in a state poll there had dropped from eight points to three points within the month couldn't have been much of a shock to him. His soppy behavior in Michigan just before the election was in part a calculated appeal for sentimental support, in part a natural peaking of emotion in a district and state that he really did love. Right up to election day and election night, he wanted to win and expected to win. But he'd understood all along and understood at the finish that he might very well lose and had braced himself for defeat. Senior assistants and close friends had often been told how he felt about the prospect. During a quarter century in competitive politics at the national level—Congress is national, though the contests are statewide and local—he was always prepared to accept defeat and that was as true now as it had ever been. *Now Jimmy Carter—Jimmy was different. This was his first experience in national competition. Everybody knew that he was a hard loser, he was simply not prepared to accept defeat.* (Mr. Ford obviously had heard stories, often exaggerated, of the crushing impact upon Carter of his defeat for the Georgia governorship in 1966. He was devastated, but he recovered quickly.) *Carter's friends had better stay close, watch him closely, if he lost this election. From all the President had heard, it could take Jimmy Carter two years to recover from defeat.*

Reporters at the White House and at the Sheraton Park Hotel in Washington, where thousands of supporters and the merely curious jammed a huge ballroom in the expectation that the President would appear either to hail victory or to acknowledge defeat, tended to think that the professions of continued hope in the early hours of Wednesday morning were artificial and silly. They were neither. Almost precisely as the President's July projection had predicted, the counted popular vote was running 51 percent to 48 percent when Mr. Ford went to bed at 3:15 am. The July projection had held forth the possibility but not a certainty that the higher percentage would be Ford's. Skeptical laughter greeted campaign chairman James Baker's pre-dawn assertion that a Ford victory was still "statistically feasible." It really was, though the hope of it occurring was very dim by then. Jack Germond, one of the country's best political reporters, calculated afterward in *The Washington Star* that shifts of 1500 votes in Ohio and 3500 votes in Hawaii, two of the six states that were undecided early Wednesday, would have given Mr. Ford a bare electoral vote majority of 270 to 268 for Carter. So it was that Mr. Ford was neither churlish nor foolish when he retired without acknowledging defeat and congratulating Jimmy Carter and also without appearing at the Sheraton Park, where the ballroom by three o'clock was a shambles of smashed plastic liquor glasses and weary hangers-on.

At 8:30 Wednesday morning the President's staff chief, Richard Cheney, met at the White House with the Ford campaign director, Stuart Spencer, and the chief Ford poller, Robert Teeter, among others. Upon the advice of Spencer and Teeter, the group agreed that there was no longer any chance of the electoral majority shifting from Carter to Ford. Mr. Ford was told and accepted this when he appeared in his office, somewhat refreshed but still haggard and barely able to speak, at 9:57 o'clock. The President, his wife and their daughter and three sons foregathered along with young Mike Ford's wife Gayle in the Oval Office and tearfully concluded that the time had come to admit defeat and congratulate President-elect James Earl Carter. A suitably warm and graceful telegram to "Dear Jimmy" was drafted, a telephone call was placed to Carter in his home in Plains, and the President husked out a few words of friendly congratulation to him. Richard Cheney read the telegram to Carter, with its promise of "my complete and wholehearted support as you take the oath of office this January." After what seemed to the assembled reporters to be an unconscionably long interval, the President and his family appeared in the White House press room. In a ghostly whisper, the President said a few words of greeting and asked Betty Ford to read a statement and the text of his telegram to Carter. This she did very softly. Her audience could see that she was close to weeping. She and the President pushed their way through the crowd of reporters, cameramen and TV-radio technicians, shaking hands and exchanging a few words with as many as they could reach. The Fords presumably took note of some journalists who were as near to tears as they were. When the family departed, Mrs. Ford led her daughter Susan by the hand. Susan, shoulders heaving, was quietly crying.

Throughout this episode, which could have been mawkish but was not, the President kept rigid control of himself. Once while Betty Ford was speaking he bit his lower lip. However much he had prepared himself for it, defeat had not come easily to him. Somewhere deep within himself, he must have been aware of the feeling among the tiny majority of voters who had preferred Carter to him that Jack Germond summarized as follows the day after the election: "Survey after survey showed that President Ford was the candidate they liked the most, trusted the most, considered the least political. But he was also the candidate whose capacity they doubted the most—and that was true from the first primary in New Hampshire last February 24 until yesterday." The outcome was a majority judgment, in short, that goodness and decency in the presidency are not enough. Let James Earl Carter, the psalm-singing sermonizer from Georgia, take heed.

November 13, 1976

———

"Psalm-singing sermonizer" was unjust to Carter and, I hope, unworthy of me.

LXXIII

Ford's Transition

Palm Springs

The defeated President golfed and swam and didn't pretend to do much else during the first of the eight days that he allotted himself for rest and recuperation at this desert resort. The few senior assistants who accompanied him instructed underlings to say without apology that they were playing golf or sunning themselves or doing nothing whatever except ducking the smallest presidential press party in recent history. The torpor among the journalists was such that they made unnaturally little of the disclosure that a courtesy telephone call that Gerald Ford placed to Richard Nixon the Thursday after the election had been unannounced for five days. The President's press secretary, Ron Nessen, learned about the call some 30 hours after it occurred and revealed it only when he was told to correct a report that there had been no communication between Messrs. Ford and Nixon. All in all, it was a good time for reflection and for putting together bits and pieces of the election story that had been overlooked during the last campaign weeks and the night and early morning when the result was in doubt.

One of the belated bits was that omens of defeat reached the

President and his principal assistants considerably earlier on
election evening than was known for quite a while afterward.
The managements of the television networks agreed in secret to
provide the President Ford Committee and White House
assistants with raw data from late polls and projections before
the information was evaluated and broadcast. Between six and
seven pm on election day, when committee and White House
spokesmen were expressing confidence of victory, it was
apparent to the President and to the very few officials who were
privy to the confidential material that the situation was even
shakier than they had expected it to be.

Jack Watson, the 37-year-old Atlanta lawyer who directed
Carter's pre-election planning for the transition from the Ford
administration, met in Washington with the President's staff
chief, Richard Cheney. Cheney called in three other Ford
assistants—Counsellor John Marsh, Staff Secretary James E.
Connor, and Special Assistant Michael Raoul-Duval (Mike
Duval for short)—who had previously been asigned by Cheney
to do preliminary planning for the transition that was not to be,
from Mr. Ford's appointive presidency to his elective presidency. Watson served notice that government office quarters in
Washington will be required for a Carter transition team that is
expected to grow from about 100 at the start to some 200.

Carter indicated at his first press conference after the election
that he hopes to be briefed soon by President Ford and "key
cabinet members" on foreign policy. Some of his remarks at the
press conference indicated that he also needs solid briefing on
other matters. In the first Carter-Ford television encounter,
Carter made it clear with a rambling non-answer to a question
about "incomes policy" that he didn't know what the term
means. At the post-election press conference, Carter said that if
the economy is stagnating next January "a tax reduction
primarily oriented toward the payroll tax level might be
necessary." When he was asked whether he referred to Social
Security payroll deductions, which "payroll tax" usually
connotes, or to income tax withholding from wages, he
answered with appropriate modesty: "I think the major thing
that I could say without being too specific, which I'm not
qualified to do yet, is that it would come in order to stimulate

purchasing power of consumer goods among those that might receive the tax benefits."

"It's a little academic now, I think," Jim Connor said in a tone of rueful humor when he was asked a day or so after the election about his work on what would have been the Ford transition if the President had won. It is indeed academic. It also reflects a side of Gerald Ford that might have increased the chances of election if the intended use of his transition had not been so thoroughly hidden. At his instruction, Cheney, Marsh, Connor and Duval lined out courses of action between election and inauguration that would have had him doing what he was widely criticized for not doing during the first two or three months after he succeeded Richard Nixon—that is, moving quickly and firmly to shape his immediate White House staff and key elements in the federal departments in his own image and after his own fashion. The last of the option papers prepared for the President were delivered to Cheney the Wednesday morning after the election. Mr. Ford was so preoccupied with the campaign before the election and so frustrated by the result that he hadn't seen the recommendations days afterward, much less made his choices among them. But it was plain from his initial instruction to Cheney to get the work done, about a month before the election, that he intended to seize the opportunity for change that Presidents normally have only in their first months in office or between reelection and their second inauguration.

The instructions that Cheney received from the President and passed first to Connor and later to Marsh and Duval were essentially as follows. First, prepare for study right after the election clear and actionable definitions of decisions that he would have to make, should make, or would have the opportunity to make, along with definitions of the options that would be open to him in making those decisions. Second, so far as White House and departmental staffing were concerned, deal only in generalities and structure—emphatically not in personalities. Mr. Ford wanted nothing said or done that would have people anxious and uncertain of their futures after the election and that would risk a repetition of the trauma that Nixon induced with his demand for resignations the day after his re-election in 1972. Third, the President wanted no recommendations for cabinet changes; he wanted total freedom to make those decisions without being burdened with staff recommendations. A list of perhaps 75 to 100 key subordinate offices in departments that might call for change would be welcomed—Connor prepared that list—but as for cabinet Secretaries, NO. Fourth, prepare a list of people whom he should consult about staff and other changes. And finally—*keep it very quiet,* again to avoid repeating the 1972 Nixon trauma.

Connor, a political scientist who as a White House Fellow working in the old budget bureau had observed the Johnson-Nixon transition in 1968-69, discovered that he and opposite numbers on the Carter side were getting identical advice from Richard Neustadt and associated students of the presidential process at the Kennedy School of Government at Harvard. The advice was to make maximum and vigorous use of the two months between election and inauguration if Ford won, and of Carter's first two months in the presidency if he won. That Ford should do so if he had the opportunity was Connor's only firm recommendation. Otherwise he confined himself to defining the likely requirements and opportunities for change and the options available to the President for accomplishing change. A typical Connor point was that Mr. Ford if elected would have to decide whether to retain, abolish or alter the cabinet-level Domestic Council and its staff. Different ways in which the functions of the Council staff might be enlarged or diminished and in which its place in the overall White House staff system might be changed were outlined in ways that left the President free to do any of several things—or nothing.

Mike Duval, a lawyer with a somewhat bolder approach than Connor's, offered several firm recommendations. He argued, among other things, that a President who was debarred by law from succeeding himself, as Ford would have been at the close of his elected term, could concentrate upon long-term policies and objectives and ride out the political risks involved in leaving to others—department heads, for example—the solutions of many day-to-day problems that a first-term President hoping to be reelected would have to struggle with. A corollary recommendation was that the President rely largely upon the

Office of Management and Budget rather than upon his
immediate staff for oversight and, to some extent, topside
management of federal departments and agencies. Heavy
reliance upon OMB and consequent reduction of the White
House staff figures importantly in the Carter approach to
reorganization. Duval, however, also recommended that OMB's
management and monitoring functions be strictly supervised
and controlled by the President's staff chief and a small
secretariat working under him. Drastic consolidations of
presidential functions now performed by several separate staffs
in areas of world affairs, national security, international
economic policy and domestic affairs were proposed by Duval.
This probably would have resulted in some reduction of the
overall White House staff. But that was not Duval's primary
objective. Staff reduction as such is not regarded at the Ford
White House as an absolute necessity and good in the way that
Jimmy Carter and his people regard and promise it. The Ford
view is that it is idle to talk about or aim at staff reduction or
expansion before the responsibilities to be met by the President
and his staff are redefined and determined. A contrary view
that presidential staffs since the Franklin Roosevelt days have
become increasingly overblown monstrosities and that reduction *is* an absolute necessity and good is set forth by Stephen
Hess, a political historian and assistant at the early Nixon White
House, in a new and magnificent study of the presidential
process. His *Organizing the Presidency* (Brookings; $3.95) is must
reading for President-elect Carter and his people. It would have
been must reading for Gerald Ford's aborted planners.

November 20, 1976

In response to a squawk from NBC, I rechecked at the White
House and was told that only NBC and CBS provided early
election indications. The arrangement was such that it could
have been made without the knowledge of NBC and CBS news
or corporate management.

LXXIV

Changing the Guard

In advance of Jimmy Carter's first meeting in Washington with Gerald Ford, here are some notes on the preliminaries to the changing of the guard at the peak and center of presidential power, the White House.

The President's mood a fortnight after his narrow defeat was described in different ways by different associates. In the last hours of the campaign, when he expected to win but knew that it was going to be close and he might lose, Mr. Ford predicted that if he were defeated he'd recover from disappointment and be his normal self within a couple of days. It was evident the day after the election and during an eight-day vacation in Palm Springs that the defeat had hit him and his family harder than they expected. But the common account of his assistants was that he recovered soon and well from his disappointment and buckled down to the business of being President in every sense of the word to the end on January 20. Robert Hartmann, the friend and assistant who has been longest in his service in Congress, in the vice presidency and the presidency, thought that he was puzzled by the defeat, finding it hard to understand why a small but decisive majority of voters failed to give him the credit he felt was his due for bringing the country out of the depths of Watergate and out of the 1974-75 recession. A reporter who asked for a retrospective interview in which Mr. Ford would be invited to review the highlights of his presidency and perhaps amplify his previous accounts of such episodes as the pardon of Richard Nixon and his decision to stand for election after saying he would never again run for public office, got another and more poignant insight. After discussing the request with the President, Press Secretary Ron Nessen told the reporter that Mr. Ford was reluctant to grant the interview and probably wouldn't. The President was still suffering, Nessen said, from a sense of hurt so deep and so profound that he didn't want to relive his presidency as yet and risk getting into a discussion of why he lost.

Weeks before the election Carter emissaries swarmed over Washington, asking former White House and agency officials what they thought Jimmy should do about reorganizing the government. One of the people who was asked this was Richard Cook, a former Nixon lobbyist with Congress and lately the Lockheed Corporation's chief Washington lobbyist. Cook told the Carter man the first thing that Carter should do if he was elected was chop the White House Office staff—the President's immediate and personal staff, as distinct from the much larger Executive Office of the President—from its recent total of about 500 bodies to no more than half that number. Cook believes with a passion, based upon service at the White House and with congressional committees, that big presidential staffs justify themselves by drawing into the White House powers and responsibilities that over-burden Presidents and should remain in departments and agencies. Inasmuch as Carter was saying again and again in speeches and interviews that reduction of the White House staff was one of his priority aims—"you can depend on it"—the Carter man might have been expected to agree with Cook. He didn't. He replied that any such cut would be impossible: Jimmy Carter if elected would have too many campaign workers, supporters and members of Congress to be rewarded or wooed with jobs at the White House and elsewhere.

Jack Watson, Carter's chief transition planner, indicated to

Ford assistants after the election that a major element of the White House establishment that was targeted for hard review and perhaps for abolition was the cabinet-level Domestic Council and its staff of some 20 professional assistants and 20 secretaries and other supporting help. As I reported last week, the Council and its staff had been marked for similar review by Mr. Ford's planners in case he won. James Cavanaugh, deputy to White House staff chief Richard Cheney and a former deputy director of the Domestic Council, told Watson that the Council staff was indeed a worthy candidate for abolition or at least relocation in the overall White House organization. Therein lies some interesting White House history. John D. Ehrlichman, a Nixon assistant who has just entered prison, created the Council as the base of his personal fiefdom and as a counter to the former Bureau of the Budget, now the Office of Management and Budget, which Ehrlichman regarded as a nest of bureaucrats who would do anything in their considerable power to defeat the aims of Richard Nixon. The Council itself never amounted to much; it's met only twice since it was founded in 1970. Its staff was what mattered; under Ehrlichman and to a lesser extent under his deputy and successor, Kenneth Cole, it oversaw the workings and often dictated the policies of the principal domestic federal departments. President Ford turned the Council and its staff over to Vice President Rockefeller, giving him general command of it and appointing Rockefeller men to the Council's executive directorship and three assistant directorships. Rockefeller hoped until late 1975 that the Council would be his vehicle for substantial participation in national policy making and particularly in the formulation of long-range policies. Soon after President Ford let his former staff chief, Donald Rumsfeld, and his first election campaign director, Howard Callaway, harass Rockefeller into withdrawing from consideration for the 1976 vice presidential nomination, the Vice President bitterly concluded that Rumsfeld, Cheney and others whom he regarded as his enemies on the Ford staff would never let him be effective in anything. Rockefeller thereupon relinquished his oversight role in the Domestic Council and said in effect, *the hell with it* to everything except campaigning and raising money for candidate Ford.

Carter's likeable and capable press secretary-designate, Jody Powell, spent most of November 16 with Ron Nessen. Powell declined Nessen's invitation to attend and participate in that day's briefing of the White House press corps and listened to the proceedings over a loudspeaker in Nessen's office. It was a typically sour briefing session, with Nessen misinformed about the subject of one announcement (the President's weekend with the Vice President at the Rockefeller estate) and several reporters grinding away as usual at pointless and useless questions. Powell, invited again by Nessen to go out and brave the grouchy beasts on his own, said with acrid humor that the reporters had been sufficiently fed for the day. But he didn't seem to be fazed. He left an impression that he is far from realizing that he can't be an effective spokesman for the new President while fulfilling the wide range of advisory and other reponsibilities that he already has and seemingly plans to expand. Nessen suggested that Powell might consider briefing only when he has something worth announcing instead of offering himself or a deputy to the reporters every day, just to give them an excuse for being. Powell said he didn't dare risk angering them and dissipating the good will he hoped they'd have for him at the start. Two days later, Nessen took his own advice and for the first time skipped a briefing because he had nothing to say.

Carter transitionists indicated they'd like to attend the President's almost daily conferences in preparation of the fiscal 1978 budget. That was more cooperation than the cooperative Mr. Ford was prepared to offer and he said no.

November 27, 1976

Skipping briefings when he had nothing to say became a habit with Nessen and an example to Powell.

Mr. Ford didn't have to say "no" to the suggested budget participation. Deputy OMB Director Paul O'Neill said it for the President. Dick Cook said later that the Carter transitionist's point was that sharp White House staff cuts would be difficult because of pressure for jobs, not "impossible."

LXXV

Jimmy and Jerry

When President Gerald R. Ford and President-elect James E. Carter—okay, he'll be Jimmy here from now on—emerged from their first meeting at the White House in the chilly dusk of November 22, it was as if the pain of defeat and of the impending departure from power would never end for Mr. Ford and his people. While Carter spoke of his "deep appreciation to President Ford for the gracious way in which he has welcomed me," the President stared straight ahead and was seen to swallow once and then again. Several members of the White House staff stood to the right of the vanquished and the victor: Richard Cheney with a caricature of a smile, John Marsh and Mike Duval with faces set as if frozen in grief. David Hume Kennerly, the President's photographer and a fellow never noted for humility, stood to the rear and let one of his assistants, Ricardo Thomas, take the big picture as Ford and Carter walked out of the Oval Office. Press Secretary Ron Nessen, winding up the long sad day in the White House press room, was visibly closer to breaking up than he'd been since the election as he dealt with the usual flow of idiotic questions (why hadn't the Fords invited the Carters to dinner, for instance; it had been announced that Mrs. Carter was flying back to Georgia that night and that the President-elect would go home the next afternoon after a round of meetings with congressmen and senators).

Why the sadness and disappointment should have persisted for so long—20 days had passed since the defeat, after all—was a mystery that the close result did not explain. Mr. Ford was said by associates to have pretty well pulled himself together during his eight days of golf and privacy in Palm Springs. Some of his assistants, particularly the ones at the top of his staff and therefore burdened with a heavy sense of responsibility for the defeat, went through days of traumatic self-questioning but were through that phase when the President returned to Washington. According to them, his inner hurt was obvious at such public moments as his farewell to Carter in a way that it wasn't in his dealings with them. With them, they said, he was notably cool, collected, assured. His instructions to them and through them—principally Cheney and John Marsh—to some 35 transition officers in departments and agencies who were assigned to deal with the Carter transition teams were to do all in their power to meet what the President called on the 22nd "my obligation and the obligation of those who work with me" to make the change of administrations as smooth and efficient as possible. Every major unit of the federal government was ordered to prepare transition books for the incomers, setting forth in clear terms the main problems and issues presently facing the incumbents and likely to face the new people. The first office to produce the required book was Vice President Rockefeller's; the second was the Civil Service Commission; and Secretary of the Treasury William Simon delivered his department's book to the President-elect in person.

There were relieving touches on the occasion of the Ford-Carter meeting. Midway of his campaign after his nomination, Jimmy Carter made much of ordering the agents guarding him to dispense with the big black limousines that come naturally with and to Secret Service details. He had himself hauled around for a while in modest sedans. The suggestion was that he'd do away with much of the accustomed grandeur at the White House when he got there. Maybe he will. But a line in the

November 22 schedule that his press staff handed out read "3:15 pm—enroute to White House (walking)." Walking, that is, the block down and across Pennsylvania Avenue from Blair House, the mansion where Presidents put up foreign and other honored guests. Jimmy and Rosalynn Carter arrived at the south portico of the White House in a tan Lincoln Continental limousine (District of Columbia license 344-900) that President Ford sometimes uses when he's away from Washington. A Secret Service agent drove the limousine, another agent sat beside the driver, and the customary station-wagon load of agents followed it, in addition to police cars fore and aft. Reporters who were allowed to observe the first minutes of the meeting in the Oval Office heard Carter say that a third conference of heads of the principal industrial nations might be a good idea and Ford answer that maybe a meeting first with the foreign ministers of the NATO alliance would be wise. Incredibly, the reporters also thought they heard Carter ask Ford, "Did you go to France?", referring to the economic summit conference at Ramboulliet, near Paris, in October 1975.

Most of the little said about Carter's meetings with budget director James Lynn, Secretary Simon, Secretary of Defense Donald Rumsfeld, HEW Secretary David Mathews and Federal Reserve Chairman Arthur Burns was routine banality. A few

LURIE'S OPINION   12-1-76

TRANSITION

interesting details came out, however. Secretary Simon did
practically all of the talking—about New York City's continuing
financial crisis and the International Monetary Fund loan that
Britain desperately needs to save it from disaster, among other
things—while Carter listened and gave no hint whatever of
what he'd do as President about these and other problems.
James Lynn expected to meet Carter alone and was surprised to
find Vice President-elect Mondale, transition director Jack
Watson and Bowden Cutter, the Carter man assigned to the
Office of Management and Budget for transition purposes, with
the President-elect. Lynn authorized his press spokesman, Alan
Wade, to say that Carter "asked all the right questions" and
appeared to be impressively knowledgeable during their two-
hour talk. It was evident that Carter understands that he can
amend some of the big items in the fiscal 1978 budget that
President Ford is required to submit before the January 20
inauguration but really cannot change it to the extent that his
recent statements suggest. The chances also are that Carter
understands in a way he didn't during his campaign that OMB
already does for Presidents much of the staff work that he's
spoken of having it do for him as if that were something new. It
may be further assumed that Lynn didn't hide his view that
Carter's cherished notion of "zero-base budgeting"—starting
literally from scratch every year with every department's
budget—is impractical nonsense in the form, probably oversimplified, that Carter usually decribes it.

The guiding rule at the White House and, the senior
assistants there hope, in the departments is to offer advice to
the Carter transitionists only when and if they ask for it. An
axiom of all transitions is that incomers suspect incumbents of
trying to con them into doing things the incumbents' way. The
incomers therefore tend to resist and discourage advice. Yet
there is a body of useful knowledge that comes only with
incumbency and probably cannot be effectively imparted to
incomers. This is especially true, as successive Presidents and
their assistants always have to learn for themselves, of the
White House system. The very core of White House knowledge
is that mistakes at the peak of federal power are terribly easy to
make, that once made they are almost always irretrievable, and

that—arguable judgment aside—they almost always result from bad information that has come to the White House from departments or agencies. The chief function of every White House staff, its highest and most necessary service to the President, is to distinguish sound from bad information and to extract sound information from the departments. That of course requires persons of quality in the principal staff positions, people who if they are new to government are willing to learn and able to learn very quickly from experienced people in or out of government. It doesn't necessarily require big staffs, it certainly doesn't require or justify huge staffs. But it requires substantial staffing, and the current total of 485 persons on the White House Office staff, roughly half "professional" and half secretarial, is really not the monstrous absurdity that it's often depicted to be. I'm inclined to agree with the Ford assistant who predicted the other day that Jimmy Carter probably will have realized before he takes office that the number is close to the necessary minimum and about right, however much in order some rearrangement and restructuring to suit the new President may be.

December 4, 1976

LXXVI

Carter in Transit

This account is derived from three weeks of hearing and watching some of the incoming Carter people and some of the outgoing Ford people instruct each other in the practice of government at the White House apex. The incumbents, mostly familiar only with the centralized Nixon and Ford White Houses, are being reminded that some past Presidents did some things in simpler ways with fewer assistants. The incomers are learning, and presumably telling their President-elect in what must be staggering stacks of memoranda, that much of the business of government at the White House level and below is not as simple as he thought or pretended to think it was during his campaign and after his election.

A President-elect who promises to consolidate and simplify the federal establishment is represented in Washington by the biggest and most elaborate transition staff in history. Its 200-plus members are ensconced in the major agencies and departments, studying their organizations and methods and boning up on present and pending issues and problems for incoming Cabinet secretaries and directors. Despite the promises of orderly governance, a good deal of confusion attends the exercise. On a recent day, for instance, when Carter spokesmen were saying the press was mistaken in its notion that lists of candidates for 75 or so presidential appointments were to be published before Carter made his choices, so that the public and interested parties could indicate their preferences, the names of 16 people from whom Carter will choose his principal economic officials were announced. Carter conferred with them at his home the next day and was very much in the act in other ways.

Stephen Hess, a former Nixon assistant and Brookings Institution Fellow whose new book, *Organizing the Presidency,* was favorably mentioned in this space, learned on Friday, November 19, how personally and directly Carter is involved. Hess is a member of the US delegation to the current session of the UN General Assembly. He was in his office at the US delegation headquarters in New York when a secretary told him that a Governor Carter was on the telephone. "Governor Carter?" Hess said. "What Governor Carter? I don't know any Governor Carter." The secretary said it was *the* Governor Carter. According to Hess, Jimmy Carter convinced him that he had read the book and was not relying on a staff summary. Carter said he was much impressed, asked Hess to send him some memoranda on White House staffing, and gave Hess his private telephone number and mail address—two items that at the moment are Washington's topmost totem symbols. Greg Schneiders, Carter's administrative assistant in Plains, telephoned again two days later and, after conveying Carter's apology for not calling himself, shook Hess with requests for detailed memos on White House staffing and functions ranging from the office of the President's military assistant to the First Lady's office. President Ford's staff chief, Richard Cheney, quietly passed the word that Hess was to be regarded and treated at the White House as one of Carter's principal transition representatives. In his capacity as an advocate of a reduced and minimal White House staff, Hess is a logical Carter choice. In two other respects, he isn't. He indicates in his book that he regards Carter's pledge to make Vice President-elect Walter Mondale a key and important member of the administration a silly piece of standard ritual that all Presidents go through and never fulfill. Hess' basic premise is that Presidents shouldn't try to manage the federal government from the White House. Instead, he argues, they should recognize that "the primary presidential role is to make choices—choices that are ultimately political in nature. *The President* (Hess' emphasis) *is the nation's chief political officer.*" It's a premise that sits oddly with a President-elect who puts the emphasis that Carter does upon what he calls "my commitment to a businesslike, tough, competent administration of the executive branch itself."

True enough, Carter proposes to hold his department and agency heads, particularly his Cabinet secretaries, responsible for accomplishing that "business-like, tough, competent administration." Whether Jimmy Carter or any other modern President can actually get by with doing that, and to all effects use and rely upon his Cabinet members as personal assistants and deputies to the extent that Carter intends, is a subject of fundamental difference between him and the chief incumbents, including the President, at the Ford White House. The proposition that it can be done is also fundamental to whether Jimmy Carter can install and implement the kind of presidency that he proposes to conduct.

The central question raised by the Carter proposition is whether a President's interests and the interests of the heads of the major departments will always or even usually be identical or at least close enough to be compatible. The controlling assumption now is that they will be only if the President has at his command a staff large enough and capable enough to police the departments, identify and sort out the many interests and factions that exist within big departments and usually involve two or more departments, and finally summarize situations for the President in actionable and understandable fashion. The argument from incumbents that a President must have this capability at his own command and within his own staff is of course self-serving. But it's worth attention when it comes from such a person as James Cannon, originally a journalist and Nelson Rockefeller assistant who directs the Domestic Council staff of some 25 "professionals" and 25 secretaries (including 10 people who are detailed from other agencies and are on their payrolls). Cannon speaking: "What I think is unique about the

Domestic Council staff—well, not unique but different from other coordinating bodies at the White House—is that we have one client, the President. However the next administration will want to structure its White House operation, it is imperative that there be some staff group in the White House that looks at all the myriad problems, ideas, opportunities that come to the White House—and everything in domestic affairs comes here now. That staff must be able to assess all of these things and present them to the President in such a fair and balanced way that he always has all sides of any issue and all the facts he needs to base a judgment on."

Would it be practical for Carter to take some or all of this oversight and coordinating responsibility out of the White House proper and pass it to the Office of Management and Budget? Cannon's answer is typical of the one generally heard around the present White House: "Anything will work if the President wants it to work—if he insists on it working. In my judgment, however, OMB has such a strong responsibility to control the spending of money that it's not in the best position to make a final presentation of a matter to the President. Its responsibility to keep spending down and income up is so dominant that there has to be somebody else, some other staff, to look at all the other aspects of programs and proposals that require money."

One of many related questions is whether any President nowadays can do without a chief of staff, regardless of whether he uses that name for the function. A Carter associate who thinks a President can is Matthew Coffey, one of the President-elect's chief talent hunters. Coffey, who was Lyndon Johnson's deputy personnel director, argued for a greatly reduced and simplified White House staff in a memorandum to Carter last June. He said the other day: "Running the place without a chief of staff is a terribly effective way to do it. It gives a President the opportunity to stand back, view things for himself, make up his own mind. The other way, everything comes to the President through a filter, and that filter by its very existence tends to control and screen the information that gets to the President." Gerald Ford, a simple man with a natural preference for simple procedures, refused for a while to call Donald

Rumsfeld a chief of staff and insisted on styling him a coordinator. Mr. Ford at length realized that he had to have somebody to track what his other assistants were doing and that Rumsfeld in fulfilling that function was in fact the President's staff chief, as Cheney is now. President Carter may be expected to come around to it, too.

December 11, 1976

———

In the week the foregoing was written, Carter's transition regulars put the freeze on Steve Hess and excluded him from the participation that the President-elect had wanted him to have. Cheney, getting the drift, said after my report appeared that he'd never told the Ford staff to treat Hess as I'd been told he had.

LXXVII

Closing In

While the press concentrated upon Jimmy Carter's Cabinet choices and the conflicts of interest and ideology that delayed some of them, the President-elect in Georgia and a few of his transition assistants in Washington closed in slowly and quietly in mid-December upon a problem that is central to the solution of a larger problem that he made for himself with his campaign promises to reorganize the federal government. The central problem is how to organize and use his White House staff, the instrument through which any President in these times must principally direct and control the vast federal establishment—to the limited extent, as some of the Carter people are learning and beginning to say, that it can be directed and controlled from the center.

The learning process, it develops, began much sooner than anyone would have realized from candidate Carter's frequently simplistic campaign references to the structure and business of government. Harrison Wellford, a 36-year-old Charlotte, NC, attorney who is overseeing the preliminary studies of federal organization and possible ways to improve it, and four associates spent last summer analyzing the structures and functions of nine councils and offices that exist alongside the White House Office and the Office of Management and Budget within the overall Executive Office of the President. Wellford and an expanded team of 12 associates got at serious study of the core White House operations, including some that had been looked at but not analyzed in depth during the summer, after the election and after Carter's transition coordinator, Atlanta attorney Jack Watson, set himself up in Washington at the head of the biggest entity in a preparatory force of some 200 people. The gist of what Watson, Wellford and their helpers appeared to have learned and to be learning in mid-December about the White House as it is and as in essence it's bound to be under any President comprises the remainder of this report.

It's agreed, has been informally reported to Carter and is soon to be formally reported to him in memoranda that he as President must have a White House staff large enough and of sufficient quality to serve him directly and personally in certain basic areas. Among them are the diverse and enormous range of interests and issues dubbed "domestic affairs;" national security and foreign policy; congressional relations; economics; and public relations, which depending upon the President's wishes may mean anything from the bare supply of minimal information to the elaborate propaganda apparatus that was created under Richard Nixon, cut back by Gerald Ford at the start of his presidency, and again enlarged for his campaign purposes. There is total recognition that the President must have in the persons of his chief assistant for domestic affairs, whatever the title, and in that individual's assistants, people who have only one client—the President—and only one body of interests—the President's interests. It is also recognized and is soon to be impressed upon the President-elect, if argument on the point be necessary, that the chief assistant and the staff charged with domestic affairs must be capable of discerning, sorting out and identifying for the President the many and often conflicting interests and factions within the major departments that will inevitably condition the proposals and recommendations that come to him from the departments.

An important question is whether recognition and acceptance of these realities can be reconciled with the President-elect's declared intention to let his Cabinet members, the heads of the major departments, run those departments without interference or bossing from the White House. And reconciled, too, with Jimmy Carter's declared intention to make the same department heads his principal advisers in their fields. The firm belief of the senior transitionists in Washington, beginning with Jack Watson, is that these seemingly contradictory requirements can be reconciled. The controlling proposition being put to Carter—not that he needs to be persuaded of its validity—is that White House monitors don't have to be White House intruders and overseers. A related proposition is that department heads and ranking department subordinates with interests that may not be identical with the President's interests are not thereby debarred from advising him. All that is needed, in this view, is a staff that has the knowledge, capacity and authority to identify the divergences of interest and make certain that the President is aware of them. Perhaps the most important point that incumbent assistants have effectively argued with Carter's emissaries is that the staff services that a President deems essential to his way of conducting his office must be retained within his own establishment and cannot be farmed outside the White House proper.

Both the areas of basic presidential need and the basic functions of the presidential staff as they are being described and reported to Jimmy Carter are to all effects identical with those prevailing at the Ford White House. It does not follow, however, that the Carter staff must be identical in either structure or numbers with the Ford staff. The belief of Jack Watson and presumably of his associates is that the necessary services to the new President can be provided by substantially fewer people than the 655, including 312 "professionals," who presently staff the key White House Office (485); Domestic Council (50); and National Security Council (125, including 47 "professionals"). Some of the reductions that Carter is pledged to accomplish may be imposed upon such White House units as the liaison staff maintaining contact with special-interest groups (blacks, Hispanics, Indians, trade associations, etc.) and the communications office that serves and cultivates publications and electronic media outside Washington.

Cutting back operations that are generally considered marginal may not be all that easy. The special groups, for instance, include constituencies that come to regard direct access to the White House as a matter of right once they get it, even if it's access to assistants who seldom or never see the President. Are publications, television and radio stations that are not represented in Washington to be deprived of services and special attention that many of them have similarly come to expect and value? This is the kind of hard question that the Carter transitionists are already up against and that the President-elect will have to deal with before he takes office. After the first of two press conferences in Atlanta during the week of December 13, Carter confided to reporters that he had just promised visiting mayors that two assistants on his personal staff will look after the legislative and other concerns of cities and counties. Four of the 25 "professionals" on the Ford Domestic Council staff do that now, full time. Carter's promise to the mayors may be read as an indication that he will be keeping others of that staff's functions, if not the structure as it's now constituted, within his personal establishment.

The organizational point that Carter publicly emphasizes nowadays is his repeated promise during his primary and general election campaigns to consolidate and simplify the federal government and bureaucracy. Inquiry as to what he has in mind, beyond the generalization, produces an interesting clarification. It is said that he does not intend, as the casual listener might suppose, to recommend the sort of massive consolidation of domestic departments that Richard Nixon proposed and Congress ignored. Carter is said to have in mind what Jack Watson calls "consolidation from below, a consolidation of functions" rather than "consolidation from the top" of departments and agencies as such. Such a consolidation of functions would have to entail some consolidation of agencies or at least of bureaus within agencies and departments. One example cited is the possible transfer of administration of the food-stamp program from the Department of Agriculture to wherever all public assistance programs are concentrated— presumably but not necessarily in the Department of Health, Education, and Welfare (HEW), a monster that must be targeted for dismantlement if the kind of consolidation of functions that Jack Watson talks about is to have meaning and reality.

December 25, 1976

LXXVIII

Goodbye to All That

Here are some notes on the scene and atmosphere at the White House in the twilight of the Ford administration.

It took the eight weeks after November 2 for people at the White House, from the President down, to get used to the fact of defeat. They were pretty well adjusted to it, through the stage of shock and sadness and preoccupied in most instances with the personal problem of what they do next, when Mr. Ford, his wife and daughter Susan flew to Vail, Colorado, for two weeks of rest and, if delayed snow falls in time on the mountain slopes, skiing for the President, Susan and the two Ford sons who joined them there. The trip from and back to Washington would be Ford's last as President aboard Air Force One. His very last flight on the great jet will be to Monterey, California, for a golf tournament after Jimmy Carter's inauguration.

The last flight, the last everything for him and for most of his people. There were goodbye parties almost every night. At a party for staff chief Richard Cheney, another White House assistant was heard to moan, "We're doing so many things for the last time." Excepting the few who were working on the President's last budget and his last State of the Union message, many of them were doing little or nothing and getting mighty tired of it. "This is awful, I can't take it much longer," a staff assistant in the press office yelled the other evening as he put on his coat and prepared to leave at the abnormally early hour of 5:30 pm. He said later that he was just kidding and came back to work for another hour, but his remark reflected a common feeling. Even earlier on another recent evening, Press Secretary Ron Nessen was told to get out a statement commending International Monetary Fund support for the ailing British pound and discovered that nobody was around to work on it. The statement was produced in the end and Deputy Press Secretary John Carlson cautioned the staff that there was such a thing as letting down too far.

Most people had their minds on getting jobs. Lawyers and law firms were looking each other over and some attorneys on the staff were planning to found their own firms. The prospects for individuals varied, of course, but on the whole the outlook was far better than it had been for those who left Richard Nixon's White House when or soon after he resigned. Association with Nixon and the Nixon White House was a liability. Association with Gerald Ford and the Ford White House, even for the many who were held over from the Nixon staff, is an asset in the private job market and in the very limited market among Republican senators, congressmen, and the minority staffs of congressional committees. Most of the assistants at "professional" levels have had offers or at least some indications of interest in hiring them.

Despite the repeated claims since 1969 that the practice of staffing the Whte House with detailees from career services and leaving them on their parent payrolls has been stopped, a surprising number of Ford assistants (27 of 45 "professionals" on the NSC staff, for instance) are in that situation and can return to the military, the Foreign Service and similar havens. The White House secretaries who do more than any other category of employees to keep the place ticking are in a peculiar difficulty. The salaries of all but the most junior of them range from $16,000 to $22,000 a year and a few get up to $25,000. It's a pay level that tends to price them out of the private job market and to a lesser extent out of the secretarial market in Congress. Six or so of the veterans among them have been asked to stay on at the

Carter White House, to give a little continuity, but they are the exceptions.

The retirement staff that federal law allows former Presidents will provide temporary jobs for some 25 employees at the Ford White House and long-term jobs for six or seven of them. President Ford's military aide, who was army Major Robert Barrett until he resigned from the service on December 16, is organizing and will head the Ford retirement staff. As "executive assistant to Gerald R. Ford," he will have a deputy and eight other people working directly for him. The initial transition staff also will include a press spokesman and two secretaries; a speech writer with a research assistant; three assistants and secretaries handling correspondence; and a staff lawyer with a secretary. Two employees are assigned to "scheduling," an indication that ex-President Ford intends to do a lot of traveling—"bouncing around the country," Barrett puts it—during the first retirement months. It seems munificent. But a staff on that scale is provided only for the first six months of retirement. The staff will be reduced at two-month intervals to about 13 persons by July 21 and finally to six or seven, including Barrett, by September 1. Most of the early staff will have offices in Washington, in two government-owned houses on Jackson Place, a block from the White House and opposite Lafayette Park. By September 1 at the latest, what's left of the retirement staff will have government office space near the Fords' home.

That home probably will be on the outskirts of Palm Springs, California. Barrett looked over a couple of houses that the Fords may choose from (they pay for their home) the week before the President flew to Vail. Barrett also found that there is no federal space, such as a post office or a military facility, in or near Palm Springs that could make room for the retirement offices. This means that if the Fords settle there the General Services Administration must rent offices, build something, or perhaps install the kind of prefabricated structure that Richard Nixon has and uses close by his San Clemente estate. At this writing one must say "if" the Fords settle in the Palm Springs area. Barrett said on December 16 that one of the luxury enclaves on the outskirts of Palm Springs is almost but not quite certain to be the Ford's retirement base. It was still possible, though, that they'd go somewhere else, possibly farther north in California, even—a remote possibility—in Florida, if "a really great deal" turned up. By that he evidently meant a suitable house and grounds for sale at a bargain price. It was evident that the Fords of Michigan were not about to go back to Michigan.

January 1 and 8, 1977

———

The Fords settled in Rancho Mirage, a separately incorporated suburb of Palm Springs.

LXXIX

Bleeding for Jimmy

A fellow who knows a lot about the agonies involved in organizing Jimmy Carter's White House staff said in reference to the West Wing, where Presidents' chief assistants have their offices, "I guarantee you, that place is going to be knee-deep in blood."

He was speaking in the first week of January, 16 days before President-elect James Earl Carter, Jr. was to be inaugurated, about the rivalries, uncertainties, procrastination and concerns without precedent in White House history that were complicating and delaying the announcement of most of the new President's choices for senior appointments to his staff, and his decisions on how that staff was to be organized. The mishmash of factors that contributed to the agonies and the delay provided indicative insights into the character and working ways of Jimmy Carter, and into the predictable atmosphere of his early presidency.

The unprecedented concerns had to do with the ethnic, racial and sexual mix of White House staff appointees that Carter insisted upon. Nothing like it had occurred in previous presidencies. Beginning with Harry Truman's presidency (1945-

53), and peaking in the presidency of Richard Nixon, the number of assistants appointed to the White House staff because they were blacks, women, or in rapport with such special-interest groups as union labor, had been increasing but remained small. To some extent under Nixon and to a larger but still minor extent under Gerald Ford, a few blacks and women had assignments that went beyond token representation. Anne Armstrong, the retiring US ambassador in London, dealt with general domestic affairs when she was on the Nixon and Ford staffs. Richard Parsons, a black lawyer and Nelson Rockefeller protegé who was put on the Domestic Council staff, was considered by colleagues to be among the best Ford assistants. He never regarded himself and was not regarded as a black speaking for and to blacks. But they were exceptions. Generally, women and blacks and Hispanics on the Nixon and Ford staffs were there because they were women, blacks and Hispanics. Carter insists that at the White House, as throughout the federal departments and agencies, women, blacks and ethnic Americans be appointed to functional staff jobs and that special representation of the sort that has prevailed in the past be abolished. His transitional talent hunters in Washington acknowledge that finding competent prospects who meet the Carter criteria proved to be unexpectedly difficult and delayed the process of selection.

This was not the sole reason for delay. Among other factors was Jimmy Carter's rule that nothing connected with the staffing and pattern of his administration and especially of his White House is final until he says it is. For a candidate and President-elect who has made as much as he has of delegating authority to others and away from the White House, he in the preliminary phase displayed a remarkable tendency to reserve final decisions to himself. As late as January 5, for instance, the important question of whether to keep an adequate domestic affairs staff within his White House establishment, or to farm that vital responsibility out to the principal domestic departments and agencies with minimal coordination from the White House, was undecided because Carter had not put his mind to it and would not let anybody else decide it for him. Stuart Eizenstat, the Atlanta lawyer who headed Carter's issues staff during the primary and election campaigns and has been on similar transition duty in Washington, was reduced to fighting for enough staff to enable him to do a good job as the President's assistant for domestic affairs. That the issue should arise was a depressing commentary upon the level of pre-inaugural understanding of the staff support that any President and any President's chief assistants must have if they are to be effective. A more flattering explanation of Carter's delay in deciding upon his initial staff pattern was advanced. This was that he doesn't want to begin his presidency with a rigidly structured staff system; he wants to have time to learn from experience, try alternative arrangements, and settle later in 1977 on the system that suits him. That makes sense and explains much that otherwise would suggest that no other incoming President in contemporary memory has been so ignorant of the basic necessities of the office.

There have been some basic decisions, though all of them in early January were tentative and dependent upon Carter's approval. One of the decisions was to implement, after six years of neglect, the topside management mission that Richard Nixon professed to launch in 1970 when he renamed the old Bureau of the Budget the Office of Management and Budget and made former Secretary of Labor George Shultz its first director. Under Nixon and then Ford, nothing much ever came of the "management" mission. Carter's OMB director-designate, Georgia banker Bert Lance, decided early in January—subject of course to the President-elect's okay—to split the office into two divisions commensurate with its name, one dealing with preparation of the federal budget and the other with management and nothing else. Harrison Wellford, a North Carolina attorney and former assistant to the late Senator Philip Hart of Michigan, who has directed the Carter transition study of governmental reorganization, has been asked to head the revised OMB's management division. Wellford wants it understood that the idea is not to manage the whole government from the OMB. It is to study present management systems, and departmental and bureau organizations, and to recommend the organizational changes and reforms that Carter promised.

No incoming appointee had a clearer charter than Columbia professor Zbigniew Brzezinski, Carter's chosen assistant for national security affairs. Yet even Brzezinski had to await Carter's formal approval before he could announce on the record his choice of a deputy—38-year-old David Aaron, a systems analyst who served on Henry Kissinger's NSC staff and is very highly regarded by people who worked with him then—and his plans to cut the staff by about one third, roughly from 45 to 30 professional assistants. The reduction is to be accomplished mainly by abolishing the staff's policy analysis section and consolidating some of the geographic sections. Rather oddly, considering the Carter administration's campaign commitment to greater concern with third-world countries, two area candidates for such consolidation and reduced (though not abandoned) NSC overview are Latin America and southern Africa. A point of major interest and much speculation, most of it gloomy, is how Brzezinski and Secretary of State-designate Cyrus Vance will get along. Brzezinski is known to believe that he, Vance and Secretary of Defense Harold Brown will work together more amicably than Henry Kissinger did with the comparable Secretaries when he was the national security assistant. Brzezinski, who seems to be well aware that his reputation for abrasive arrogance at least equals Kissinger's, has discussed with Carter the possibilities of friction. Brzezinski may be assumed to know that the new President will tolerate just so much and no more quarreling with Vance and Brown.

Another assistant with a strong charter is press secretary Jody Powell. His people and presumably Powell himself assumed that his plans for a press office operation expanded in functions though not in numbers were as good as approved in early January. The word in Washington was that this was not necessarily so. Powell proposes to operate with two deputies and four assistant press secretaries and to bring into his realm the Carter equivalent of the present Office of Communications, the production of the President's daily news summary, and presidential speech writing. The "communications" function, primarily the job of serving out-of-Washington media, will be handled by a greatly reduced staff under Pat Bario, one of two women chosen so far for the assistant press secretary spots. Powell plans to have 35 people doing what 44 do in the Ford administration. The transition planners hope to reduce staffing throughout the White House in about that proportion.

It's been reported as fact for weeks that Patrick Anderson, Carter's chief campaign speech writer, would be his chief White House writer, and that Greg Schneiders, a sometime Washington and New York restaurant operator who caught Carter's fancy in early 1976 and recently had been his executive assistant, would be President Carter's appointments secretary and trip scheduler. It was understood and believed at Carter's Washington headquarters in early January that Schneiders had been fired. According to Carter spokesmen in Georgia, Schneiders withdrew from consideration for the appointments job and it became increasingly doubtful that he would get any White House job after an FBI report on him revealed a history of bad debts and bounced checks resulting from business troubles. Patrick Anderson prefers, and is arranging with Carter's encouragement and with a promise of his cooperation, to write a book on the first year of the Carter presidency—instead of working in what seems to Anderson to be developing into a big and stifling White House bureaucracy. James Fallows, late of *The Washington Monthly,* will be Carter's chief White House writer. Like the fellow said, expect blood on the West Wing floor.

January 15, 1977

———

There was less blood on the floor than I expected during the first weeks at the Carter White House. Stuart Eizenstat won his fight for an in-house domestic affairs staff and wound up with a larger staff than he'd thought he'd need. Schneiders got a low-visibility White House job. Brzezinski got along better with Vance and Brown than Kissinger did with his Secretaries of State and Defense. Powell's press office empire developed as predicted.

LXXX

Farewell and Hail

The impending inauguration of Jimmy Carter and departure of Gerald Ford are occasion for another report on how the new President's White House establishment is shaping up and for a farewell to the outgoing President and his people. The farewell is kinder and, in my opinion, fairer than the editorial snarl of "good riddance" in *The New Republic's* January 15 issue. Much that was unkind was said over the years in this space about Richard Nixon, Gerald Ford, Henry Kissinger, Elliot Richardson, Alexander Haig and the rest of them. But they never were and never will be collectively dismissed by me as "clods, malefactors, narrow-minded reactionary zealots, egomaniacs, flunkies, lame-brains." To all of those departing, I say so long and thanks for what you told and taught me about the follies, burdens and rewards of presidential service.

Now to current business, in this instance the President-elect's notions of how to use his Vice President. Carter said in Georgia and in a televised interview that Vice President Mondale was to be "my top staff person" and that everybody on the Carter staff had been told by Carter to regard the Vice President as their boss. In view of the fact that Carter had not then and at this writing still had not named most of his senior White House staff, it was a silly statement and it invited distortions. So wise and experienced a commentator as James Reston of *The New York Times* understood that Mondale was to be chief of the White House staff. Carter's spokesman, Jody Powell, had to say that the President-elect didn't say or mean that; he'd repeatedly said and meant that he wasn't going to have a chief of staff. What Carter meant, Powell explained, was that Carter assistants were to regard any order coming to them from the Vice President as if it came from the President. Incumbents at the Ford White House, including some who thought that President Ford could and should have used Vice President Nelson Rockefeller more effectively than he did, concluded two weekends before the inauguration that Jimmy Carter was either extraordinarily naive or talking through his hat about the substantive responsibilities he intended to vest in his Vice President when he announced that in the very first week of the Carter administration he was sending Mondale to Western Europe and Japan to apprise our principal allies of the new President's foreign policy goals. The incumbents' reasoning, naturally not prejudiced in Carter's favor, was that anybody who was really intended to be the new President's "top staff person" would not have been detached from the White House scene and sent abroad during the first and formative days of the new administration.

Presidential and other staff assistants, outgoing or incoming, assume that the valid measure of standing with the boss is the location of the assistant's office. During the first months of the Nixon presidency, the measure was proximity: H. R. Haldeman occupied a small office next door to the President's Oval Office and Vice President Agnew had the biggest office in the West Wing, at a corner four doors down a corridor from the President's office. Everybody including Agnew understood that Haldeman mattered and Agnew didn't. After a few months of isolation and boredom in the corner office, Agnew had an elaborate suite, including a dining room and toilet, put together for him on the second floor of the Executive Office Building across West Executive Avenue from the West Wing. Haldeman moved into the corner office and successor staff chiefs— Alexander Haig, Donald Rumsfeld, Richard Cheney—have occupied it and identified it as the White House office second only to the Oval Office. It was understood at the Ford White House just before the Inaugural and departure that Hamilton Jordan, the Carter assistant who will not initially be acknowledged to be the new President's chief of staff, will have the corner office. Vice President Mondale was expected to have the EOB suite created for Agnew, and in addition, for token purposes, the West Wing office occupied recently by the departing President's friend and chief speech writer, Robert Hartmann. It's a nice office, with a splendid view of West Executive Avenue and the windows of the Vice President's working office in the EOB. But it ain't that corner office.

New Presidents never learn, or anyhow pretend not to learn, from past Presidents' experience with their Vice Presidents. This is not to say that President Carter cannot possibly break the pattern of history and use Vice President Mondale in ways that literally no President has ever proven able or willing to use his Vice President. I do suggest that it will be very difficult. Bromley K. Smith, a friend who was a national security assistant to Presidents Eisenhower, Kennedy and Johnson and was one of the few people on the Kennedy staff who tried to be courteous to Vice President Lyndon Johnson, defined the problem more succinctly than anybody else has to my knowledge, orally or in print. Smith said that Presidents simply don't have the time to spend with Vice Presidents that they'd have to spend if they kept their public pledges of total confidence and collaboration. Harry Truman, who was Franklin Roosevelt's Vice President for 82 days before he succeeded to the presidency, tried in his memoirs to explain the arms-length relationship that he had in his elected term with his dear and admired friend, former Senator Alben Barkley (the first Vice President to be called "the Veep"). Although Truman dealt with a broad problem in his usual sharp and narrow terms, his main point of fundamental and constitutional distance comes across from language that in the halcyon atmosphere of Carter's advent may seem parochial and out-dated:

> No Vice President is ever properly prepared to take over the presidency because of the nature of our presidential, or executive, office. The President is the man who decides every major domestic policy, and he is

the man who makes foreign policy and negotiates treaties. In doing these things it would be very difficult for him to take the second man in the government—the Vice President—completely into his confidence. The President, by necessity, builds his own staff, and the Vice President remains an outsider, no matter how friendly the two may be. There are many reasons for this, but an important one is the fact that both the President and the Vice President are, or should be, astute politicians, and neither can take the other completely into his confidence. The Vice President, as President of the Senate, associates continually with the shrewdest politicians in the country. . . The President cannot afford to have his confidential matters discussed in Senate cloakrooms. . . That is. . .one of the reasons why it is very difficult for a President to take the Vice President completely into his confidence.

Vice Presidents nowadays don't associate all that continually with senators, who anyhow tend to distrust Vice Presidents, whether or not they are former senators, even more than Truman thought Presidents must distrust them. But one assumes that Jimmy Carter would concede that Harry Truman in retirement knew more about the presidency and its complexities than Carter knows at the start of his and our great adventure.

January 22, 1977

———

Hamilton Jordan offered Mondale the corner office, and Mondale declined it. Mondale spent more of his time in the West Wing office assigned to him than he did in his larger EOB office. Well into the administration's second month, Carter's arrangement with him was working out better than I'd thought it could.

The editorial in the January 15 *New Republic* from which I disassociated myself ended as follows: "Nixon, Kissinger, Ford, Agnew, Mitchell, Butz, Connally, Haig, Rogers, Helms, Simon, Greenspan, Richardson, Rockefeller, Laird, Whitehead, Rumsfeld, Kleindienst, Finch, Gray. . .The list of clods, malefactors, narrow-minded reactionary zealots, egomaniacs, flunkies, lame-brains goes on and on. Good riddance to them all."

Index

174-175, 217, 243-244, 297; Ford trip, 29-31; military strength, 340-342; relations with China, 40, 243-245; *see also* Strategic arms limitation talks
United Nations ambassadorship, 125-129
U.S. News and World Report, 208
U.S. Steel, 55, 408

Vance, Cyrus, xiii, xiv, 319, 462, 463
Vanderhye, Margaret, 110
Veneman, John G., 132, 133
Vietnam, South, 120-124; history of U.S. involvement, 112-119

Wade, Alan, 444
Waldmann, Ray, 283
Walinsky, Adam, 156
Walker, William, 21, 45, 48-49, 73, 75, 84
Wall Street Journal, 205, 407
Wallace, George, 322, 323, 403
Wallison, Peter, 59
Walters, Barbara, xxi
Walters, Vernon A., 294
War Powers Act of 1973, 140
Ward, Fred, 89
Warren, Gerald, 87, 88
Washington Post, 147
Washington Star, 361
Wasilewski, Vincent, 425
Watergate, xii, 11, 80-81, 308-315, 359-364, 421;

tapes and documents, 16, 22-23, 81
Watergate Special Prosecution Force: Ford campaign fund investigation, 405, 406-410
Watson, Jack, 433, 438-439, 444, 452-454
Watts, William, 310-311
Weidenfeld, Sheila, 22, 87
Weinberger, Caspar, 132
Welles, Sumner, 115
Wellford, Harrison, 451-452, 461
Whitaker, Elizabeth Gere, 275
White, Margita, 351-352, 353
White House staff, 20-21, 41-46, 167, 213, 236, 351, 453; Carter transition, 433-436, 440, 440-456; chiefs, xxxii, 10-11, 47, 449-450, *see also* Rumsfeld, Donald; Nixon holdovers, 10-13, 14-18, 21-22, 44-46; organization, Ford, 47-51, Carter, 459-463; Press corps, 86-87, 185, 440; reduction, 436, 438, 453-454
Whitehead, Clay, 310
Whitman, Ann, 64-65
Why Not the Best (Carter), 385, 387
Wilderotter, James, 151
Will, George, 178, 252
Wilson, Harold, 172, 231, 232, 237, 238
Wilson, Malcolm, 63

Composed in Palatino by New Republic Books,
Washington, D. C.

Printed and bound by The Maple Press, York,
Pennsylvania

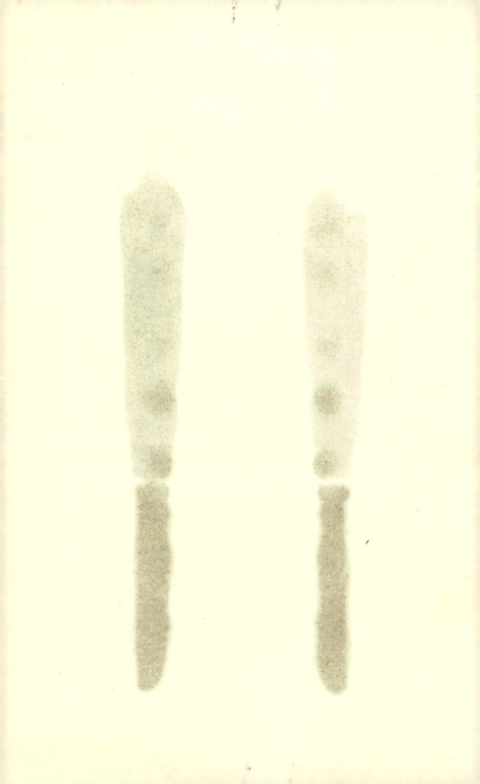